T5-BAG-633

Antoine Louis Claude Destutt de Tracy, Comte (1754–1836)

DESTUTT DE TRACY, PAR DAVID D'ANGERS

Antoine Louis Claude Destutt de Tracy, Comte

Book I

A TREATISE ON POLITICAL ECONOMY

Book I

A TREATISE ON POLITICAL ECONOMY

by

Destutt de Tracy

English translation by Thomas Jefferson

With a Foreword by

John M. Dorsey, M.D., LL.D.

Published by
Center for Health Education
4421 Woodward Avenue
Detroit, Michigan 48201

Printed by Edwards Brothers, Inc.

Cover symbol designed by Richard Kinney

CONTENTS

LIST OF ILLUSTRATIONS

Foreword

For he that hath, to him shall be given.

Mark iv, 25

I deem the content of a preface as most important for its reader. In it I put the bone and muscle of my insight. I am putting afresh here all of my reverence for my purely self-defining consciousness that I tried to refine in my previous writing. *Although all of my life's meaning occurs only in my mind, I tend to acknowledge my mind last in all of its functioning, even in my science of psychology. I count my insight into the nature of this disparity as my most life affirming self knowledge.* Since there is nothing so hard to observe as my acknowledgeable mental activity I naturally tend to overlook it instead of look it over. Yet from start to finish my observation is, and must be, occurring as my self consciousness.[1]

My fellowman who is interested essentially in his own *further* development of his conscious self identity, such a man of principle, is also apt to be a preface reader and often only a preface reader. He feels his freedom quickened by his author's declaration of independence. He renounces each so-called school of thought. Fact-finding for him means enlivening the romance of his own mental development. Confucius-like he seeks all that he wants in himself. He is his own desire, and works out his own salvation with diligence. Before I can discover that all of my enslavement is self enslavement I cannot fully know what I really mean by *slavery*.

By psychology of any theme I mean simply but specifically my systematic observation of that subject precisely where I find all of its meaning occurring, namely, always in my own mind. As my ever marvelous Emerson sensed his generic power, so do I, "Every known fact in natural science was divined

[1] See Borden P. Bowne, *Introduction to Psychological Theory* (New York: Harper and Brothers, 1886), pp. 4, 12.

by the presentiment of somebody before it was actually verified. . . . Our theism is the purification of the human mind," with self consciousness, I would like to add. It is in making conscious additions to my self identity as long as my life lasts, in the gradual expansion of my conscious power, in the continuous growth of my love of life, that my spirit finds its ideal fulfillment.

My *Psychology of Political Science* is a natural outgrowth of my *Psychology of Emotion* and my *Psychology of Language,* being the application on the dimension of my acknowledged fellowman of my mind's consciousness, as I had firmed it up for my self in each of the latter fully acknowledged self studies. The principal motivation and directive power of my conscious way of life derives from my mind's conscious consideration for the wholeness and allness of its natural constitution. I can live only by and in my wholeness alone and my consciousness for that psychic reality is essential for my well-being. It is the nature of my mind to make essential whatever I live. Advancing my life is my only possible advancement or progress or perfectibility.

I regard my greatest social issue to be that of my conscious control of my own American Government. While I have been considering its theoretical advantages it has been practically slipping away from me. The whole art of statesmanship is the rare art of each statesman's seeing nothing but his own individuality in the apparent plurality of it. As for wealth, I find my Emerson with the right view of conscious self development as usual:

> Man is born to be rich. He is thoroughly related, and is tempted out by his appetite and fancies to the conquest of this and that piece of Nature, until he finds his well-being in the use of the planet, and of more planets than his own.

With this ideal conception of self-possession my orientation to my political economy may be described as the glorious science of valuing my vital energy, a description as far as possible from deserving to be named "the dismal science."

My attention first grew itself in the direction of my individualistic political economist, Count Antoine Louis Claude Destutt de Tracy (1754–1836), in 1958 shortly after I began my research resulting in *The Jefferson-Dunglison Letters.* In working up my feeling my sense of identity with my Thomas Jefferson, I was greatly interested to discover what I could of each individual of his world for whom he seemed to feel the strongest feeling of his own conscious personal identity. Particularly in view of his skepticism regarding the medical profession of his era, I was specially pleased to discover Jefferson's notably laudatory allusions to Pierre Jean Georges Cabanis (1757–1808), M.D., member of the Senate and of the National Institute of France, Commander of the Legion of Honour, Professor in the School of Medicine of Paris, and member of the Philosophical Society of Philadelphia.

Fortunately, the Detroit Public Library, Medical Science Department, had a copy of Cabanis's *An Essay on the Certainty of Medicine.*[2] From reading this great essay, I could readily understand Jefferson's exceedingly complimentary remarks about Cabanis's *Relation of the Physical Constitution and Morality.* I soon learned that Tracy was the devoted pupil of Cabanis, and thus my interest quickened.

Joseph Dorfman describes Thomas Cooper, M.D., the "most dramatic of the Ricardians," a friend of Jefferson considered by the latter as "the greatest man in America in the powers of the mind and in acquired information. . . . The more dissatisfied he became with his personal state of affairs, the more gloomy he became about Democracy."[3] He denounced Tracy's *A Commentary and Review of Montesquieu* as "too theoretical and *too democratic.*"[4] I can find origins for Tracy's later liberal work in the valuable volume, *The Rise of French Liberal Thought: A Study of Political Ideas From Bayle to Condorcet.*[5]

[2] See Appendix.
[3] Joseph Dorfman, *The Economic Mind in American Civilization,* 5 vols. (New York: Viking Press, 1946–1959). A rich yield. In Vol. II, p. 527.
[4] Ibid., p. 532. My italics.
[5] Kingsley Martin, ed. J. P. Mayer (New York: New York University Press, 1954).

At the Alderman Library of the University of Virginia with John Cook Wyllie, I thoroughly enjoyed reading Tracy's manuscript in his own handwriting, his *Political Economy* he asked Jefferson to translate and publish. Then began a search for personal copies of Tracy's two books translated by Jefferson, the *Political Economy,* including an account of his Ideology,[6] and the conspicuously ignored *Criticism of Montesquieu's Spirit of the Laws.* To my extraordinary satisfaction, my excellent friend, Mr. William J. Norton, succeeded in finding each of these books for me, generously presenting them to me as gifts.

Already realizing very few copies of either book to be extant, I soon began to feel a responsibility for making the gist of their contents available, especially for my American reader, specifically on account of the fact that Tracy's writing indicates him to be most sensible regarding the oneness, wholeness and allness of his individual self. Over the years my intention to proceed immediately with this work was never put aside, but until now I have allowed priority to numerous other writings. The delay has been fortunate in that I have been able to secure richer and fuller accounts of Tracy.

Apart from my general acknowledgement I particularly wish to mention the tremendous helpfulness I have received from Iris Hartman. Ferris Hartman, a newspaper correspondent in Paris, has been most kind in helping Mrs. Hartman to secure access to public library materials in France. I have reflected gratefully over Iris Hartman's willing devotion to my exacting requests, including her arduously translating large passages of French into English, mainly for true scholarly satisfaction.

My writing about my Destutt de Tracy may lay claim to being biographical in the sense of being autobiographical, certainly in no sense of being an account of the life of Tracy. Only he could ever be able to write about his life experience.

[6] See W. Windelband's *A History of Philosophy,* authorized trans. James H. Tufts (New York: Macmillan and Co., 1896), p. 457: "The French government officials of the Revolution recognized as philosophy only Condillac's study of the empirical development of intelligence, and Destutt de Tracy gave it later the name 'Ideology'."

Regardless of the vast extent of my research in this direction I can never have a chance of discovering anything about Tracy's very self, or bring anything of his true nature before the living eye of my reader. In all of my study I can never feel anything but my own presence, quite as my reader can feel only *his* own presence in the pages of his author. All that my government can amount to is whatever I choose to make of it.

On May 31, 1936, my fondly esteemed self analyst, Sigmund Freud, affectionately wrote his friend Arnold Zweig about the latter's wish to become Freud's biographer, thus emphatically discouraging the attempt: "Anyone turning biographer commits himself to lies, to concealment, to hypocrisy, to flattery, and even to hiding his own lack of understanding, for biological truth is not to be had, and even if it were it couldn't be used."[7] Possibly my deep meaningfulness for this recorded attitude owes some of its depth to the fact, I much later discovered, that I was doing my self analysis with my Professor Freud at the time it was written.

As stated, the most my reader can ever really find in his author's book is a literary exercise of his own self activity, a word-picture of his own emotionality verbalized in his own creative reading. However, it can be only the rare reader whose conscious self identity can keep abreast of his mental growth, who can be aware of this real condition of his literary affairs.[8]

Working over the motivation of my writing about (my) Destutt de Tracy I conclude that it is the extraordinary help I have given my self by cultivating my sense of identity in my Tracy research. What I have always needed most for my further attaining biologically adequate conduct has been specifically a method for consciously feeling a true measure of the magnificent meaning of my being.

[7] *Letters of Sigmund Freud*, selected and edited by Ernst L. Freud, translated by Tania and James Stern (New York: Basic Books, Inc., 1960), Letter 285, p. 430.

[8] See my *Psychology of Language* (Detroit: Center for Health Education, 1971).

I found this ideal method as a result of awakening to 1) the enormous extent to which I was conducting my life on the principle of faultfinding and 2) the entire extent to which faultfinding is always merely denial of existing perfection. Then I was astounded by the profusion of pejorative and meliorative terms in my vocabulary, each one supporting my illusion of imperfection (unconscious perfection).[9] Certainly whenever I deny the truth of the perfection of my nature I thereby create my immediate need to live uncomfortably this distressing untruth. As Emerson clearly observed in his self, I too recognize that my constitution cannot tolerate a lie without protesting (creating a sign or symptom) against such exertion.

Thus Arthur O. Lovejoy traces the idea of improvement:

> The term "perfectibility" to which—though it was apparently invented by Turgot in 1750—Rousseau probably did more than anyone else to give currency, became the catchword of Condorcet and other subsequent believers in the reality, necessity, and desirability of human progress through a fixed sequence of stages, in both past and future.[10]

The prospect of human "progress" lends itself to the denial of the ubiquity of truth to the extent that it is not clearly recognizable as perfection succeeding perfection (instead of perfection emerging from imperfection). Denial of perfection and evil is one. My doctrine of evolution must mislead me as long as I reason it to be a process of changing what was not perfect in order for it to become perfect. Whatever is, perfectly is. An embryo is a perfect embryo; a fetus is a perfect fetus.

No achievement other than this kind of spiritual revival can duly honor the truly wonderful nature of my faultless individual human existence. Indeed as I begin to approximate

[9] Ibid., p. 51.

[10] *Essays in the History of Ideas* (Baltimore: Johns Hopkins Press, 1948), p. 25.

awareness for my real worth as a consciously whole person by giving heed to my self feeling, as such, my differentiation of human as opposed to divine becomes less and less tenable. Conversely, the less I take the trouble to account for my individuality as being wholly my own, the less worth I tend to attribute to my marvelous life. My scientist's coming to his universal doctrine of relativity of all reality may be helpful someday in his finally recognizing the absolute reality of his individuality.

Only as I grew in *conscious* stature could I recognize the greatest need of my fellowman to be his earnest and diligent cultivation of his appreciation for his true greatness that he has too rarely noted and cherished. When as a government offical I show some insight that all government is nothing but an abstraction in the mind of the individual considering it, then my Americanism is showing, not before.

Tracy regarded the ego as the feeling of effort associated with the activity of the will. He regarded happiness to consist of the free exercise of the faculties, in the feeling of force and ease with which one activates them. He described the faculties of man as a generalized statement of the operations produced by the functioning of his organs. He defines sensation insightfully as being active, not passive. Maine de Biran (1766–1824) developed this conception as the activity of the soul, the sensing of *spirit* rather than of mechanics. He upheld vigorously the value of full self consciousness. It is Tracy's appreciation that his only life is a self life, his only existence an individual existence, which gives him his extraordinary access to his mind's power.

André Marie Ampère (1775–1836), the physicist, observed that the consciousness of effort for *autopsia* (i.e., self consciousness) furnishes a new element absolutely different from all other sensations which is perceived in distinction from them but in combination with them. Even the fact of one's appreciation of his personal identity is most often lived as "taken for granted," so that imperceptible decrements of self consciousness result in a gradually waning of appreciation of life. Self consciousness is always lived as an active experience in the sense that thc activity is appreciated as a voluntary operation, a free movement.

Ideology as an analysis of sensation certainly led to the practice of self-study, mind scrutiny, mind consciousness,—the only psychological analysis being the viewing of one's own mind, acknowledging one's ecumenical ego. The radical individualist's view of his "nonmaterial world" is necessarily considered as mystic by his fellowman who has not practiced living consciously.

It is only my awakening specifically to *how* I entify my self identity only by my self consciousness that I can discover either my monstrous life discount in my poverty of self insight or my immeasurable wealth in my acknowledgeable self possession. Only my recognizable self appreciation can lay bare the extent of my life appreciation and thus spare my seeming self stultification through failure to exercise in full degree (that is, self consciously) my ineffable mental power. My source of helpfulness is all that I bring to my subject of political science. *My political living is most vital for my health.*

My principal desire is to provide all of the prominence I can to the absolute worth of (my) Tracy's timeless economic doctrime of *conscious* individualism. March 8, 1819, Jefferson wrote Lafayette of his friendship and respect for Tracy:

> Tell him his Political Economy has got into rapid and general circulation here, that it is already quoted in Congress and out of Congress *as our standard code;* and that the naming him in that as the author of the commentary on Montesquieu has excited a new demand for that work, and will call for a new edition, the former being exhausted.[11]

As I conduct what I can call my own affairs, e.g., those of my household, so do I tend to the business of all of my world that I can call my own, e.g., that of my community or nation. In my living of my own family I can observe

[11] *The Letters of Lafayette and Jefferson,* ed. Gilbert Chinard. (Baltimore, Maryland: The Johns Hopkins Press, 1929), p. 397. My italics.

my political psychology, to what extent it is authoritarian or even fitfully conscious self-government. Early in life I accustomed myself to being "taken care of," as if my absolutely inviolable individuality did not exist. My parent seemed to preach solidarity and yet propagate dissociation. At one moment I seemed to be allowed to appreciate my independent freedom to be my self; at another moment I seemed coerced to obey "somebody else." I was not able to feel my nature as sovereign of my own body experience much of the time. Such mental fission in my family living contributed to my cultivating indifference and ignorance about my whole political living while growing absorption in the price of tea in China. "The complicated politics of the day" is a fascinating illusion with which I can distract myself from my ever-present need to assume responsibility for being all of *my* ward politician or my president.

Therefore I may be mostly unconscious for the fact that my regard for all of the meaning I call my body is paradigmatic for my appreciation of the body of all of my mental functioning, including what I may call my body politic. This insight about the real reach of my mind is essential for my sane life orientation.

Only by trying every other possible political resort first have I been able at last to turn to conscious self government. Then for the first time I realize why I always shunned or shirked it, namely, on account of the *conscious responsibility* it entails. My difficult attainment of responsibility that is conscious is necessary in order for me to relieve my mind of responsibility that is unconscious in the form either of blame or guilt. My conscious responsibility for my welfare is a late bloomer, but until it arrives I seethe with rebellion against my own power that seems alien to me.

When I consciously become the "good man I put in office" it becomes understandable for me to liken my innumerable complaints about my local or federal government to any of my other life dissatisfactions such as pain (including unhappiness of any kind). It is also understandable if I find myself no longer mystified by my troubled existence once I become able to assume conscious responsibility for being the only possible source of my difficult experience.

I can now trace peaceful perspective upon my political troubles to my finally having learned how to acknowledge that all of my living is, and must be, entirely my own. Brief knowledge of the way I conduct my life may be sufficient to account for why I formerly seemed able to relegate responsibility for the care of my soul to my clergyman, my heart or head to my M.D., my education to my teacher, or my political psychology to my duly elected government official.

All political trouble is traceable only to each mind-insolvent citizen's inability to realize his own true greatness, hence goodness. He *is* all of his own politics. His money-getting or money value is mental only, uniquely variant for each individual. Worship derives from worthship. My living decides what worth I place upon money. My money cannot decide my life's worth. My only exchange for living is living itself. Money cannot buy it. I cannot afford to be without it.

In this volume I make as much as I can of individuality for it is all that can be real. When it is not heeded it is ignored. It is the only real seat of any government. The further a political scientist feels removed from his own individuality the more his political activity stands for warning that he is conducting his politics as if he could truly be out of his mind.

Thousands and thousands of more or less frantic books and articles are written, and shall be written, apologizing for the seemingly inept way my government official represents my political affairs, when only one explanation can be sufficient, namely, He can merely represent only his own political affairs. Endless political literature describes how my political representative is trying to do all that he can in his effort to please me, when only one statement is sufficient, namely, He can merely try to please his own resilient self. Excuse piled upon excuse tries to justify the disparity between the "American dream" of self sovereignty and the actual floundering of my political representative trying to enact more and more legislation to bring his American citizen under control, when only one sentence is sufficient, namely, All political control is, and must be, solely and entirely self-control, either conscious or unconscious.

My ever-growing freedom of will is as illimitable and as potentially unmannerly as is my life itself. Whatever I live of all of my world I will to live. With this most precious commodity there can be no such possibility as "going into the hands of a receiver." Inventing a duty is discovering a freedom. As all else of mine my duty must be grown by me. This realization spares me the awful expenditure of vainly trying to see to it that *my* fellowman does whatever it pleases me to conceive to be his duty. A man must do all of his finding of himself, and that life-task becomes easier as he starts realizing that there is nothing else that he can find. For the culture of his inherent righteousness he must not rely upon any so-called schoolmaster or political scientist who cannot sense keenly his own inalienable right to original creativity of wisdom of the love of life, ever individual. Upon every subject I find my introductory "I feel-" subsumes whatever sincerity I can summon by "I think-" or "I believe-."

My American dream becomes actualized as my mind grows strong enough to bear my responsibility consciously for 1) my being all that I mean by my political representative, and 2) my political representative's being all that he can mean by his constituent Dorsey (whether or not my statesman has independently grown this insight). How does my United States exist? It exists meaningfully in the spirited mind of each sovereign citizen, precisely where its existence can continue safely as long as each citizen consciously cherishes his self sovereignty as such.

I say to myself, "Suppose my political representative cannot feel his own identity in what he calls his constituency?"

I help my self most by living whatever I must live good-naturedly, rather than low spiritedly. I have found it essential for my sanity to learn to love difficultly so that I can live with love whatever seems unlovable (see my *Psychology of Emotion*). With this feeling I can work best with whatever requires my attention. Thus, I could not write this book without it.

Whatever I live with conscious pain or unhappiness of any kind (e.g., fear, hate, guilt, jealousy, shame) seems ego-alien to me. That is, it is minded involuntarily, so that it hardly enters into the unity I consider to be my self identity. Such distressing living thus detracts from my appreciation for my wholeness, functioning with life-negating rather than life-affirming power.

The following section provides a facsimile of the whole of my copy of Tracy's book, *Political Economy,* as translated from the French by Thomas Jefferson. It is with a sense of relieving my self of a heavy obligation that I make it available especially for my American reader. My persevering effort to secure what information I might about my Tracy has disclosed to me the inaccessibility of such vitally needed political insight and also the extent to which the very existence of this politically astute well-wisher of his United States of America merits widespreading appreciation in my countryman.

The book describes its author's conscious identification of the altruism of his adulthood with the egoism of his childhood, his recognition of the underlying sameness of his mind in all of his meanings for his world quite as in all of his sensations of his body, his discerning the truth of his own soul in every so-called commodity (property, money, or whatever article), his saving reduction of all of his political economy to its true worth as enabling his most helpful management of his whole personal individuality, his recognition of all that he calls his nation (particularly any reference to it as being a kind of living organism endowed with autonomous self helpfulness so mighty as to almost eclipse the power of its individual citizen) as really being the great production of his own creative mind, his heeding the demonstrable fact that his conscious individualism is his unfailing panacea for socialism or any other ism since each of the latter must owe all of its existence to his own unconscious individualism.

No matter how much I count, or count upon, my fellowman, —that all adds up only to me. I am my sole possible amount, of any possible meaning for me. In my science of politics, take my political economy for instance, my "wealth of nations" is no different from my wealth of notions insofar as its being wholly an abstraction of my mind is concerned. My so-called money, mined or minted, engraved or printed, can mean to me no more or less than what my mind makes out of it. I am my only possible treasury. For me to try to build my conception of the wealth of my nation out of any substance other than that of the immeasurable worth of my individual life is to pursue an economy of real want in the name of seeming wealth.

All that I can mean by "socialization" of any kind or degree must be entirely a product of my *individual* mind. To wit, "socialized" medicine can make no more sense than can socialized nutrition. Every science of man, as of all else, must base itself solidly upon its one reality: an individual scientist.

Recognition of this comprehensive organic integrity of the whole individual is respected by the physician whose medical examination always includes careful study of how his patient is living his fellowman or any existent of his world, quite as of how he is living his skin or any existence obviously beneath it. The insightful physician understands the complete localization of each patient's family, business, social, or environmental complaint as being organically integral to him. One's spouse, child, neighbor, stock market, politics or whatever is "worrying him to death" *cannot* be external to him. Fortunate is the citizen who can appreciate his own life's unity as all that can account for any of his health, family, religious, political or whatever interest.

Certainly I welcome any kind or degree of my reader's resistance as bearing nothing but unconscious witness to the value of this work. If it were not for mostly hidden rejection of the lifesaving importance of his self consciousness, the latter insight would have become the primary learning goal of my formal or informal educator from the beginning.

Therefore, I am prepared to welcome kindly any reader who can either consciously create whatever he reads or who must defend his mind's *status quo* in one way or another against seeing his identity in his author's radical self consciousness, even thus: "Political science, nothing! Political séance, you mean, do you not, conjuring up in your own mind whatever you mean by your congress or any other confusion!"

Again, a note about my psychology, about how my mind's growth (psychogenesis) explains the asssertion that "man is, by nature, a political animal" (Aristotle).

In its beginnings my mind experiences itself without making any issue of the fact that its experience is all and only its *being itself,* that "being itself" provides all of its functioning. Only later, probably in the second year of living, does my mind gradually start to create some notion of its self identity as constituting my life's sensibility enabling me ultimately to comprehend the intact integrity of my organic nature. Until then it merely senses, feels, perceives itself without burdening itself with much responsibility for its tremendous power. Thus it grows (creates) its seeing, hearing, touching or whatever self activity without even heeding itself as being the only source and course of all of its excitation.

Not until I develop some sense of being myself, as such, along with some sense of being whatever I cannot acknowledge as myself, can I even begin to consider that I am capable of any social (political) significance. However, once I begin to distinctify a unity in my mind that I name "I," then also I begin to distinctify other unities in my mind that I name not-I (e.g., you, he, she, we, they, it, etc.). Here my capacity for political self identity commences its development.

The title of this volume indicates literally that it is all and only about my mind's political individuality, that its words name political meanings that my mind creates. However, Why do I, and How can I ever, bring myself up as if I am not really all and only myself? Surely such personal irresponsibility of mine (including similar personal irresponsibility of my fellowman) must result in dire political consequence.

The Why of my early irresponsible mental functioning is readily understandable. Whatever mentality I hold myself responsible for, I must take the trouble to live with tender loving care. Every access of acknowledgeable self identity, every increment of my conscious living, no longer enjoys carefree functioning, but rather demands my sensitive devotion. Complete consciousness for whatever I live involves conscientiousness for it.

The How of my relieving my young and unprepared mind from excessive care is also clear. From the start I forfeit my feeling of the intact wholeness of my mind by seeming able to divide it into innumerable parts which then no longer *appear* to consist fully of my wholeness. All that my mind surveys is really its own, only, but is rarely appreciated as such. I even call my mind's creations mine, but only as an ineffectual manner of speaking, thus: my mother, my father, my sister or brother, my home, my town, my country, my opposite sex, my God. Hence it is my mind's diremptive power that enables me to deceive myself incredibly. Putting it politically, instead of my recognizing that I *am* whatever fellowman my mind's eye observes, I can claim to be taller or shorter, younger or older, blacker or whiter, richer or poorer, more feminine or masculine, stronger or weaker, more or less religious, etc., than he (she) is. Similarly I carry this self deception further to deceive myself that my fellowman is not his own all-that-he-lives, but instead can be different from, or resemble, his (her) very own fellowman.

Obviously such systematic disregard for the inviolably magnificent oneness of man easily explains the monstrous inadequacy of all that he ineffectually names "his" political interests. As long as I deceive myself to believe that I am merely but one among millions or billions of my fellowman I must remain incapable of true appreciation for the wholeness of my wonderful human nature that subsumes *all* that I name my fellowman. Then my majority rule approximates mob rule, rather than being recognizable as my own political device for honoring the majority of my own fellowman. Unable to sense that I am my only possible authority I long for "someone else" to take care of me. Unready to feel that all of my help is self help I naturally expect and look for assistance wherever I do not even expect to recognize myself, notably to my so-called society or government. However, I fully realize that my public or private educator is entirely within the proper limits of his imagination to dispose of his reading of this ultimatum of mine (to myself) as being far too far fetched.

I, an individual, cannot do any of my living *in* a home, or family, or neighborhood, etc. *All* of my living must be lived in me, only. Everyone speaking and writing of the urgent need for a vital culture *in* which the human individual might find it possible to grow to realize his potential, undoubtedly means well but defeats his intention in its very statement. I, an individual, cannot live *in* any environment whatsoever despite all appearance to the contrary. Such a possibility does not exist anywhere in my nature.

The profundity expressed in the above paragraph amounts to the one and only political doctrine that is indispensable to biologically fundamental appreciation for human individuality. It affirms every citizen's *uncommon* self-identity to be the first principle of his political freedom. It is an obvious interpretation of the validatory observation that so-called democracy must be a physical impossibility except insofar as it becomes recognizable to the individual citizen as a name for his own political process. His democracy enables him to discipline his mental power in the self-control essential for his declaring his own political independence, his own politically workable self sovereignty.

To be born politically free means to be born free to educate one's self purposefully in biologically adequate self appreciation; free to realize that one's gradually evolving immeasurable manpower requires most heedful discipline in the gradual cultivation of correspondingly great self control. My only real politics are my self politics. My only social order is my self order. A completely self contained individual, consciously or unconsciously, I am incapable of any so-called innate aggressive instinct except that which is needed for my (including my fellowman's) very own self preservation.

With rare exception, all unveeringly established formal and informal educational force of my world is directed towards my educator's inhibiting this comprehensive understanding of the marvel of his own (hence his fellowman's) individuality.

In his courageous book of essays daringly entitled *To Hell With Culture,* Sir Herbert Read introduces a most propitious one, "The Politics of the Unpolitical," by aptly quoting from Theirry Maulnier's *La Crise dans l'homme* (Paris, 1932),

> Whoever gazes into the future which is being forged for us, and can there perceive the monstrous and denatured brother whom one will necessarily resemble, cannot react except by a revolt into extreme egoism which must now be rehabilitated. Today the problem of the person effaces all others. The intelligence is placed in such circumstances that for it disinterestedness and resignation come to the same thing.[12]

My educational development, including my cultivating any knowledge of my political science, is entirely a process of my *growing it,* quite as I attain any extent of my body. Thus, whatever stage of growth of my self knowledge I have presently secured provides my only source for its further growing. In other words, the only possible unit and whole of my political science is my living (growing) of my individuality. Therefore, the all-important but routinely overlooked fact is that any new development in the libertarian direction of my conscious self sovereignty must be an outgrowth from whatever kind of political insight presently exists in me. Merely disowning or attacking my already existing government serves either to preserve it as it is or destroy it, thereby making way for a political system even more disregardful of citizen individuality.

Since *all* of my political science can be found only in the mind of each human individual minding it, it behooves me to reduce all so-called impersonal political science to what it really is, namely the political meaning in each politically minded individual citizen. Of whatever experience I create, it is helpful to strengthen my mind's conscious responsibility to be able to recognize, "It is I." Resistance to this process of extending my conscious self identity, my feeling of unhappiness (including pain), is motivated by my wish to sleep through such discomfort so that I can continue to dream,

[12]New York: Schocken Books, 1967, p. 38.

so to speak, that my distressful living is not-I.

My science of education bases itself firmly upon the absolute fact that whatever condition exists can be fully accounted for only by the force of the truth *constituting that existing condition.* Therefore it is only realistic to appreciate fully the whole right to exist of any actuality. In other words, my finding fault with any presenting condition merely indicates my limited ability to realize and appreciate the force of truth fully accounting for its presence.

If I wish any obtaining situation to become other than what it is, in any respect, I must first learn from studying the force of truth in it just exactly how it can alter itself into such a new development. In other words, my finding that the truthful accounting for any existing situation is always present, enables me to work most constructively with whatever it is. Otherwise I must work destructively with it, and end up with a less wished-for product than ever.

Applying this reality-orientation to political science, I can first recognize and then appreciate the desirability that I renounce all of my destructive faultfinding about it and devote myself to constructive fact-finding regarding it. Specifically, by depreciating my democracy as it is now able to be (instead of working with it caringly as being all that it *can* presently be) I may lose whatever political advantage I now enjoy, through substituting for my democracy any other seemingly workable government of mine, another form of my citizen coercion that must seem alien to my conscious self control. My study of the history of political science discloses alarming occurrence and extent of this kind of political regression offered in the name of political progress.

My properly taking an inventory of my assets begins with my discovering the only place where my ownership can have any existence for me, to wit, in the riches and reaches of my own mind. All of my real proprietorship, whatever can be "signed, sealed and delivered," must occur in me, and be created of me. To feel my identity in my fellowman is to take possession of that much of my own living. I pay full price for whatever I thus lay down my own life. Ideal feeling of ownership requires developed capacity for self consciousness. All of my sense of value is contained only in my own sensing it; and that includes so-called commercial value.

I can hardly begrudge my fellowman his factory, art gallery or whatever, who has purchased it at the quite reckless cost of that much appreciation for his own life. Conscious self education in the recognizable form of growing appreciation for the nature of my own natural power and glory is indispensable for uniting my capitalism with my idealism.

All of my poverty is a condition of self unconsciousness; all of my wealth is a condition of self consciousness. Even merely wishing for anything is a form of having (being) whatever is wished for. It is the clear recognition of such law of human nature that is absolutely indispensable for any so-called good government. Hence it is, my book describes where all of my potency is contained (where I too have always found my fellowman discovering all of his own potency), namely, in my own subjectivity.

There can be no going out of myself for what I may choose to call external politics, for all that I can understand by my universe is contained in my understanding, itself, and that is entirely a functioning of my subjectivity. Whatever is, subjectively is,—self-begetting, self-creating, self-empowering. My world is not merely for me or about me, it *is* I. My public educator aiming at this life orientation, reaching this enriching self consciousness, identifies his public with his private life. This conscious identification is all that can spare him the seeming conflict of his public and private living. Only my awareness for economic truth of self identity can resolve the painful illusion of any and every kind of costly conflict traceable to unacknowledgeable self identity.

It is only my fellow citizen's increasing depreciation of the value of his own life (of which increasing depreciation he is at best only vaguely aware) that forces him to require his government to seem essentially ochlocratic rather than to be his declared and cherished self-government. There being no other possibility, he has regularly prepared himself for self government only, but without being able to appreciate that necessity. However, his further trouble lies in his requiring similar unconscious self-government as the essential qualification of his government official. What is the consequence? *His unconscious politics.* That is, his own politics for which he cannot feel personally responsible and accountable, he must attribute to his own politician for whom he feels also quite as irresponsible and unaccountable.

I find the most significant understanding of myself traceable to my observation of what and how I *feel,* that is, whether or not I appreciate every kind of sensation (including emotion) as indicating my self-sprung vitality expressing what needs expressing. I enjoyed great enlightenment from realizing that my every negative attitude (disposition of feeling) towards life is merely inhibited positive feeling, after all.

I often stop to consider how very rarely even my politically trained reader has prepared and arranged his mind to be able to excite any of his own feeling of self identity while possibly turning or flipping the pages of this volume: a volume featuring my truth that each citizen's only hope for working up a sensible government for his precious living depends entirely upon how much he can independently work up adequate appreciation for the immeasurable worth of *all* of his life's wholeness. A politician can seldom afford this kind of sanity, blessed be his name. Therefore it is only understandable when he systematically decides that the social cost of systematic appreciation for human individuality is too great an expense to be borne by a democratic society. However, may *anybody* of my world just once find help in his (her) creative reading of this volume as his (her) author has found help in his creative writing of it,—but even if that optative prove too much to hope for, all well and good.

Everyone of my world is always *on his own entirely,* from the moment of his conception, doing all of his own living by himself, but this comprehensive view of human individuality must remain an open secret as long and as far as one must merely reason that he is an individual rather than (also) self-consciously own up to the allness-and-wholeness of his self-world (including the allness-and-wholeness of the self-world of his fellow creature).

Herewith some expert testimony to the difficulty in presenting the truth that only human individuality accounts for *all* of mankind. Truth loving political scientist Hannah Arendt observes,

> Truth and politics are on rather bad terms with each other. No one as far as I know, has ever counted truthfulness among the political virtues. . . . Seen from the viewpoint of politics, truth has a despotic character. It is therefore hated by tyrants, who rightly fear the competition of a coercive force they cannot monopolize. . . .

Jacques Barzun wrote of his Albert Jay Nock, "Nock's book on education in the United States could have saved us endless mistakes had we heeded it during the past half century." Now follow several of Nock's declarations of love from *Cogitations.*[13]

> The only thing that the psychically-human being can do to improve society is to present society with *one improved unit.* In a word, ages of experience testify that the only way society can be improved is by the individualist method. . . . (*The Memoirs of a Superfluous Man,* p. 307)

> The pressure of centralization has tended powerfully to convert every official and every political aspirant in the smaller units into a venal and complaisant agent of the federal bureaucracy. (*Our Enemy, The State,* p. 12)

> As far as spiritual activity is concerned, most of us who represent this present age are so dead while we live that it seems the most natural thing in the world to assume that we shall stay dead when we die. (*The Book of Journeyman,* p. 87)

> I know that if I were a rich man I would do precious little endowing institutions, and content myself with nosing out

[13] Selected and arranged by Robert M. Thornton (Irvington-on-Hudson, New York: The Nockian Society, 1970).

individuals of the right sort and endowing them. (*On Doing the Right Thing*, p. 238)

> I suppose that in the whole country today, one would have to go a long way to find a boy or girl of twenty who does not automatically take for granted that the citizen exists for the State, not the State for the citizen. . . . (*The Memoirs of a Superfluous Man*, p. 265)

> The sale of a book, at least in this country, is no guarantee of its good quality, but rather the opposite. (*A Journal of Forgotten Days*, p. 22)

On account of the greatly limited extent to which the wholeness-and-allness nature of human *individuality* is rarely even considered by (my) anyone, my Book Two concentrates upon 1) the description of political individuality, and 2) the political consequence of my being either conscious or unconscious for that due appreciation.

Harvey Wheeler asserts sensibly, "National interest politics is a false basis for the calculation of foreign policies."[14] Certainly that declaration holds when the politician cannot feel his own identity, only, underlying whatever he names either national interest politics or foreign policies. Speed the arrival of the all-powerful political insight: National or international politics is a false basis for the calculation of policy concerning the wished-for, systematic, sovereignization of conscious individual man.

Attempting to understand the evolution of my mental power (psychogenesis) is a collossal undertaking. Little wonder that it is seldom the subject of my study, and that not for long. I greatly appreciate the degree and extent to which I can use my mind's consciousness as if to dismember my mind itself for purpose of concentrated observation, without crediting the wholeness of my mind with being all of itself. For example, when I set out to study my body politic, or the body of any other interest of mine, how unheedfully I can seem to

[14] "The New Balance of Power Politics," *Center Report*, ed. Mary Kersey Harvey. Center for the Study of Democratic Institutions (June 1972), pp. 11–14.

remove myself from my body of my mind that is my only possible body. Soon when I call my attention to this impossible feat as if it were already an accomplished fact the stupendousness of my beloved folly may seem too startling for belief. Then my mental dissociation sets up as if to be able to do service for my mental unity.

Here is a literally classic instance of my thus being able to deceive myself with my mind's diremptive power.[15] My enlarging production of meaning for each use of my body is necessarily inseparable from my expanding creation of meaning that I do not consider to be my body. However, as an objective scientist I may proceed systematically to indulge my tempting illusion of two minds: 1) my body image and 2) my external-world image. With this illusional duality I can then presume my mind to be capable of losing itself entirely both in what I may term 1) my physical body and 2) my material externality.

The validatory truth is that neither the meaning of my body image nor external-world image has any reality whatsoever except that created by my whole mind's generative power. Disbelief in my own unlimited power is my only foundation for belief in any power other than my own. My dominion over my whole mindedness however may be acknowledged (conscious) or unacknowledgeable (unconscious) in my self. I am my only truth of my every moment but the consciousness I have systematically cultivated has to be thus systematically disciplined to reveal the truth of that truth. It is not truthful for me to claim to be impersonal. My mind has no dimension that can represent not-self. It is thoroughly understandable only to my insightful scientist, however, that mind is the ultimate substance of whatever may be negated (as being not-mind).

For getting along with my (including my Tracy's) so-called political affairs all of my indispensable help has come from my knowing something about *how to use my mind.* In my

[15] Also, my Christian's noting no complicated arithmetic in his belief in one God as including his equally firm belief in a Trinity.

Psychology of Emotion I recorded a systematic description of emotion in a form analogous to already established systematic description of sensation, thus enabling scientific consideration of the dynamics of emotion. Identifying sensation of the body ego (conventionally unappreciated as entirely mind) as its kind of emotionality and the emotionality of the extension of the body ego (conventionally referred to as the "mind") as its kind of sensorium—this synopsis accomplished a unity of the greatest indispensable helpfulness for arriving at a science of the whole mind. For example, conceiving all happiness or unhappiness as extended visceral satisfaction or pain, respectively, brings into focus the wholeness-and-allness meaning of mind.

For understanding my political science I have had to master certain following key truths of my mental functioning. Truth is all about itself, serving no purpose other than its own existence. It cannot be truly imparted; it must create itself.

1) Each of my mental powers gradually begins its particular functioning at a certain stage in the course of my developing my unique individuality, rightly asserting its developmental priority.

2) This evolution of my mental functioning is a lifelong process, rarely appreciated as such. It regularly occurs under the costly illusion that pain or unhappiness is not as lifeworthy as pleasure or happiness.

3) Consciousness is my mind's very own supreme power and glory, possibly activating itself indistinctly even before my birth.

4) Just how my consciousness evolves to its full functioning is of most decisive consequence for my appreciation for my life itself, including all that I call my political activity. I am my only proof of any kind or degree.

5) Lifesaving consciousness for the meaning of all of my awareness as being of necessity entirely and only in and about my own self, i.e., my full evolution of my consciousness, evolves most gradually and requires mental condition most favorable for its growth.

6) Such favorable mental condition consists essentially of

my growing only self experience that I can learn to live with sufficient liking to be able to want to sense it as uniting with my already acknowledgeable and recognizable self identity.

7) Mental condition unfavorable to my growing my lifesaving self consciousness consists essentially of my creating any of my experience that I cannot learn to live with sufficient liking to be able to want to sense my own self-identity in it. I learn to live only by living. (My present reader of this volume, with rare exception, may offer his mental condition as being a most apt illustration of such disfavor.)

8) Although all I can ever expect of my living is a furthering of its novel organic unity, I may have seemingly mechanised my mind with habits so that my illusion of familiarity can spare my awakening to the incessant novelty of my living. My self-unconscious living preserves my need to sleep.

9) Whenever I am not willingly exciting my self consciousness, I am subjecting myself to some of my own mentation without realizing it. For example, *all* that I name "external world" without feeling my (internal) self identity in it is traceable to my strongly established wish to "sleep through" my living that I cannot feel with sufficient love to acknowledge it as my own.

10) My living without my identity of my self in it suffers all of the risk and rack associated with irresponsibility. Without that most specific mental unity I call self identity I am incapable of caring what happens to my individuality.

11) On the other hand, the more my consciousness for my organic integrity augments, the stronger becomes my feeling of personal responsibility for my world. Little wonder the tremendous force of resistance I (including my reader) must resolve (by difficultly loving) in order to create even the slightest access of my conscious self identity.

12) I *sleep* to the extent that I cannot consciously sense my self identity in *any* of my living of my mind, e.g., in my sensing, feeling, perceiving, conceiving, or any other kind or degree of consciousness. All my avoidance of the helpfulness of pain or unhappiness is motivated by my wish to sleep.

13) Inhibition of the development of my (self) consciousness

results in signs and symptoms of most profound mental trouble of the nature of dreaming (accounting for illusion, delusion, crime, political corruption and every other unconscious self irresponsibility).

There is no alternative to my blaming my government official for not helping me, except my arduously disciplining my mind with awareness that all of my living must be entirely my own, that all of *my* government owes its existence to my creating its meaning in my mind, that there can be no help but self help.

Whether I can gradually make myself honor this specifically sanifying life affirmation or not, *my own psychic identity is the truth of the whole, and the whole of the truth, of all meaning that I can live,—politics or whatever.* My fully acknowledging any reality amounts to my fully appreciating my own identity in it.

My mental condition called IDENTITY is necessarily unitive, thus honoring the wholeness of my inviolable individuality; my mental condition so-called equality is necessarily divisive, implying illusional plurality instead of wholeness of oneness.

I can hear my Republican protest, "I cannot feel my identity in my Democratic fellowman," or the converse. I can hear my Black American protest, "I cannot feel my identity in my White American," or the converse. And so on, through the whole gamut of (illusional) pluralistic divisiveness such as man and woman, child and parent, poor and rich, *ad infinitum.* All well and good. However, the stubborn fact remains: What living of mine I refuse to feel is mine (without taking the trouble also to make sure that I can and do feel that it *is* mine) contributes to signs and symptoms of unwholesome nature revealing my rejected wholeness (poor health, corrupt politics, family or neighbor trouble, or whatever). Somewhat as my insightful Emerson worded his own conscious identity: Nothing is at last sacred but the integrity of my own mind; by absolving me to my self I secure the suffrage of my whole world.

A TREATISE

ON

POLITICAL ECONOMY;

TO WHICH IS PREFIXED

A SUPPLEMENT TO A PRECEDING WORK ON THE UNDERSTANDING,

OR ELEMENTS OF IDEOLOGY;

WITH AN

ANALYTICAL TABLE,

AND AN

INTRODUCTION ON THE FACULTY OF THE WILL.

BY THE COUNT DESTUTT TRACY,

MEMBER OF THE SENATE AND INSTITUTE OF FRANCE, AND OF THE AMERICAN PHILOSOPHICAL SOCIETY.

TRANSLATED FROM THE UNPUBLISHED FRENCH ORIGINAL.

GEORGETOWN, D. C.

PUBLISHED BY JOSEPH MILLIGAN.

1817.

W. A. Rind & Co. Printers.

MONTICELLO, October 25, 1818.

SIR,

I now return you, according to promise, the translation of M. Destutt Tracy's Treatise on Political Economy, which I have carefully revised and corrected. The numerous corrections of sense in the translation, have necessarily destroyed uniformity of style, so that all I may say on that subject is that the sense of the author is every where now faithfully expressed. It would be difficult to do justice, in any translation, to the style of the original, in which no word is unnecessary, no word can be changed for the better, and severity of logic results in that brevity, to which we wish all science reduced. The merit of this work will, I hope, place it in the hands of every reader in our country. By diffusing sound principles of Political Economy, it will protect the public industry from the parasite institutions now consuming it, and lead us to that just and regular distribution of the public burthens from which we have sometimes strayed. It goes forth therefore with my hearty prayers, that while the Review of Montesquieu, by the same author, is made with us the elementary book of instruction in the principles of civil government, so the present work may be in the particular branch of Political Economy.

THOMAS JEFFERSON.

MR. MILLIGAN.

PROSPECTUS.

Political Economy, in modern times, assumed the form of a regular science, first in the hands of the political sect in France, called the Economists. They made it a branch only of a comprehensive system, on the natural order of Societies. Quesnia first, Gournay, Le Trosne, Turgot, & Dupont de Nemours, the enlightened, philanthropic, and venerable citizen now of the United States, led the way in these developements, and gave to our enquiries the direction they have since observed. Many sound and valuable principles, established by them, have received the sanction of general approbation. Some, as in the infancy of a science, might be expected, have been brought into question, and have furnished occasion for much discussion; their opinions on production, and on the proper subjects of taxation, have been particularly controverted; and whatever may be the merit of their principles of taxation, it is not wonderful they have not prevailed, not on the questioned score of correctness, but because not acceptable to the people, whose will must be the supreme law. Taxation is, in fact, the most difficult function of government, and that against which, their citizens are most apt to be refractory. The general aim is, therefore, to adopt the mode most consonant with the circumstances and sentiments of the country.

Adam Smith, first in England, published a rational and systematic work on Political Economy; adopting generally the ground of the Economists, but differing on the subject before specified. The system being novel, much argument and detail seemed then necessary to establish principles which now are assented to as soon as proposed. Hence his book admitted to be able, and of the first degree of merit, has yet been considered as prolix and tedious.

In France, John Baptist Say has the merit of producing a very superior work on the subject of Political Economy. His arrangement is luminous, ideas clear, style perspicuous, and the whole subject brought within half the volume of Smith's work; add to this, considerable advances in correctness, and extension of principles.

The work of Senator Tracy, now announced, comes forward with all the lights of his predecessors in the science, and with the advantages of further experience, more discussion and greater maturity of subject. It is certainly distinguished by important traits; a cogency of logic which has never been exceeded in any work, a rigorous enchainment of ideas, and constant recurrence to it, to keep it in the reader's view, a fearless pursuit of truth, whithersoever it leads, and a diction so correct, that not a word can be changed but for the worse; and, as happens in other cases, that the more a subject is understood, the more briefly it may be explained, he has reduced, not indeed all the details, but all the elements and the system of principles, within the compass of an 8vo. of about 400 pages; indeed, we might say within two thirds of that space, the one third being taken up with preliminary pieces now to be noticed.

Mr. Tracy is the author of a Treatise on the elements of Ideology, justly considered as a production of the first order in the science of our thinking faculty, or of the understanding. Considering the present work but as a second section to those elements under the titles of Analytical Table, Supplement, and Introduction, he gives in these preliminary pieces a supplement to the Elements, shews how the present work stands on that as its basis, presents a summary view of it, and, before entering on the formation, distribution and employment of property, he investigates the question of the origin of the rights of property and personality, a question not new indeed, yet one which has not hitherto been satisfactorily settled. These investigations are very metaphysical, profound and demonstrative, and will give satisfaction to minds in the habit of abstract speculation. Readers, however, not disposed to enter into them, after reading the summary view, entitled "On our actions," will probably pass on at once to the commencement of the main subject of the work, which is treated of under the following heads:

Of Society.
Of Production, or the Formation of our Riches.
Of Value, or the Measure of Utility.
Of Change of Form, or Fabrication.
Of Change of Place, or Commerce.
Of Money.
Of the Distribution of our Riches.
Of Population.

Of the employment of our Riches or Consumption.

Of Public Revenue, Expenses and Debts.

Although the work now offered is but a translation, it may be considered in some degree, as the original, that having never been published in the country in which it was written; the author would there have been submitted to the unpleasant alternative either of mutilating his sentiments, where they were either free or doubtful, or of risking himself under the unsettled regimen of their press. A manuscript copy communicated to a friend here has enabled him to give it to a country which is afraid to read nothing, and which may be trusted with any thing, so long as its reason remains unfettered by law.

In the translation, fidelity has been chiefly consulted; a more correct style would sometimes have given a shade of sentiment which was not the author's, and which in a work standing in the place of the original, would have been unjust towards him. Some Gallicisms have therefore been admitted, where a single word gives an idea which would require a whole phrase of Dictionary English; indeed, the horrors of neologism, which startle the purist, have given no alarm to the translator; where brevity, perspicuity, and even euphony can be promoted by the introduction of a new word, it is an improvement of the language. It is thus the English language has been brought to what it is; one half of it having been innovations, made at different times, from the Greek, Latin, French, and other languages—and is it the worse for these? Had the preposterous idea of fixing the language been adopted in the time of our Saxon ancestors, Pierce, Plowman, of Chaucer, of Spencer, the progress of ideas must have stopped with that of the progress of the language. On the contrary, nothing is more evident than that, as we advance in the knowledge of new things, and of new combinations of old ones, we must have new words to express them. Were Van Helmont, Stahl, Scheele, to rise from the dead at this time, they would scarcely understand one word of their own science. Would it have been better, then, to have abandoned the science of Chemistry, rather than admit innovations in its terms? What a wonderful accession of copiousness and force has the French language attained by the innovations of the last thirty years? And what do we not owe to Shakespear for the enrichment of the language by his free and magical creation of words? In giving a loose to neologism, indeed uncouth words will sometimes be offered; but the public will judge them, and receive or reject, as sense or sound shall suggest, and authors will be approved or condemned, according to the use they make of this license, as they now are from their use of the present vocabulary. The claim of the present translation, however, is limited to its duties of fidelity and justice to the sense of its original; adopting the author's own word only where no term of our own language would convey his meaning.

ADVERTISEMENT.

At the end of my logic I have traced the plan of the elements of ideology, such as I conceived they ought to be, to give a complete knowledge of our intellectual faculties, and to deduce from that knowledge the first principles of all the other branches of our knowledge, which can never be founded on any other solid base. It has been seen that I divide these elements into three sections. The first is properly the history of *our means of knowledge*, or of what is commonly called our understanding. The second is the application of this study to *that of our will and its effects*, and it completes the history of our faculties. The third is the application of this knowledge of our faculties to the study of those beings which are not ourselves, that is to say of all the beings which surround us. If the second section is an introduction to the moral and political sciences, the third is that to the physical and mathematical; and both, preceded by a scrupulous examination into the nature of our certitude and the causes of our errors, appear to me to form a respectable whole, and to compose what we ought really to call the *first philosophy*. I even believe this to have been proved in my third volume, chapter the ninth.

If I cannot flatter myself with the hope of bringing so important a work to perfection, I wish at least to contribute to it as much as is in my power; and I hope to contribute to it, perhaps even by the faults from which I shall not have been able to guard myself. My three first volumes of *ideology, grammar* and *logic,* compose the first section, or the history of our means of knowledge.

I am now about to commence the second section or the treatise on the will and its effects; but before entering on this new subject I think it right to add yet something to that which I have said on the first. Here then will be found, under the name of a supplement to the first section, something further supporting by some new observations my manner of conceiving the artifice of judgment and reasoning.

I hope it will not be displeasing to the amateurs of this research; because in condensing and bringing more closely together the most important of my logical principles, I present them under a new aspect, and have moreover added some considerations on the theory of probabilities, which are not without interest, considering the little progress this science has hitherto made. Those too who are not curious as to the latter article, and who may be sufficiently satisfied with my theory of logic and convinced of its justice, may save themselves the trouble of reading this supplement, which is but a superabundance of proof.

Afterwards follows *the treatise on the will and its effects;* the first part of which I now submit to the public. It is to contain three. The first, which treats of our actions; the second, which treats of our sentiments; and the third, which treats of the manner of directing our actions and our sentiments. These three parts are very distinct in their foundation, although closely connected with one another; and I shall be very careful not to confound them, notwithstanding the numerous relations which unite them, and to avoid as much as possible all repetitions. But it will readily be perceived that there are general considerations which are common to them; and that before speaking of the effects and consequences of our *willing faculty*, and of the manner of directing it, we must speak of this faculty itself. This will be the subject of a preliminary discourse, composed of seven chapters or paragraphs. I fear it will appear too abstract; and that many readers will be impatient at being detained so long in generalities which seem to retard the moment of real entry on our subject. I can agree that I could have abridged them. If I have not done it, it is because I have been well persuaded that I should gain time under the appearance of losing it.

In effect I pray that it may be considered, that wishing really to place the moral and political sciences on their true basis, a knowledge of our intellectual faculties, it was necessary to begin by considering our faculty or will under all its aspects; and that this preliminary examination being once made, almost all the principles will find themselves established naturally, and we shall advance very rapidly afterwards, because we shall never be obliged to retrace our steps. If any one wishes to satisfy himself of the advantage of this course, he has only to commence reading the book after the preliminary discourse. He will see every instant that he has need of an incidental dissertation, to obviate the difficulties which will have been solved before: and so much the worsè for those who should not experience this necessity, for such are capable of being persuaded without sufficient reason. There are but too many readers endowed with this kind of indulgence; but it is not of their suffrages I am most ambitious. I consent then that they shall accuse me of having said too much; but I should be very sorry if those who are more difficult, should be able to accuse me of having passed over some links in the chain of ideas. It is especially in the commencement that this fault would be most unpardonable, for then it might lead to the most serious errors; and it is thence that arise all those erroneous systems which are the more deceiving, inasmuch as the defect is hidden in the foundation, and all that appears is consequent and well connected. Should the last reproach be urged, my only answer would be that I have made every effort not to deserve it; and I can at the same time protest, that I have not sought beforehand any of those results to which I have been conducted, and that I have only followed the thread which guided me, the series of ideas exerting all my attention not to break it. The judgment of the public will teach me whether I have succeeded, and I will not forestall it by any other preface than this simple advertisement.

My plan, my motives, and my manner of proceeding have been sufficiently explained in the preceding volumes.

ABSTRACT,

OR

ANALYTICAL TABLE.

ADVERTISEMENT.

Before commencing the second section of the elements of Ideology, which treats of the will and its effects, I am going to give a supplement to the first, which embraces the history of our means of knowledge. Then will come the introduction to the treatise on the will, which presents the general considerations common to the three parts of which this treatise is composed. The introduction will be followed by the first of these three parts, that which treats specially of our actions.

SUPPLEMENT

To ihe first section of the Elements of Ideology.

I have previously reduced the whole science of logic to two facts.

The first is that our perceptions being every thing for us, we are perfectly, completely, and necessarily sure of whatever we actually feel.

B

The second is that consequently none of our judgments, separately taken, can be erroneous: inasmuch as we see one idea in another it is actually there; but their falsity, when it takes place, is purely relative to anterior judgments, which we permit to subsist; and it consists in this, that we believe the idea in which we perceive a new element to be the same as that we have always had under the same sign, when it is really different, since the new element which we actually see there is incompatible with some of those which we have previously seen; so that to avoid contradiction we must either take away the former or not admit the latter. From these two facts or principles I deduce here fourteen aphorisms or maxims, which constitute in my opinion the whole art of logic, such as it proceeds from the true science of logic.

According to the last of these aphorisms, which enjoins us to abstain from judging while we have not sufficient data, I speak of the theory of probability.

The science of probability is not the same thing as the calculation of probability. It consists in the research of data and in their combination. The calculation consists only in the latter part: it may be very just, and yet lead to results very false. Of this the mathematicians have not been sufficiently aware. They have taken it for the whole science.

The science of probability is not then a particular science; as a research of data it makes a part of each of the sciences on which these data depend; as a calculation of data it is an employment of the science of quantity.

The science of probability is properly the conjectural part of each of the branches of our knowledge, in some of which calculation may be employed.

But it is necessary to see well what are those of which the ideas are, from their nature, susceptible of shades sufficiently precise and determinate to be referred to the exact divisions of the names of numbers and of cyphers, and in order that in the sequel we may apply to them the rigorous language of the science of quantities. To this again the mathematicians have not paid sufficient attention. They have believed that every thing consisted in calculation, and this has betrayed them into frightful errors.

In the state in which the science of probability is as yet, if it be one, I have thought I should confine myself to this small number of reflections, intended to determine well its nature, its means, and its object.

SECOND SECTION

OF THE

Elements of Ideology, or a treatise on the will and its effects.

INTRODUCTION.

SECTION 1.

The faculty of will is a mode and a consequence of the faculty of perception.

We have just finished the examination of our means of knowledge. We must employ them in the study of our faculty of will to complete the history of our intellectual faculties.

The faculty of willing produces in us the ideas of *wants* and *means*, of *riches* and *deprivation*, of *rights* and *duties*, of *justice* and *injustice*, which flow from the idea of *property*, which is itself derived from the idea of *personality*. It is necessary therefore first to examine this latter, and to explain beforehand with accuracy what the faculty of willing is.

The faculty of willing is that of finding some one thing preferable to another.

It is a mode and a consequence of the faculty of feeling,

SECTION 2.

From the faculty of will arise the ideas of personality and property.

The *self* of every one of us is for him his own sensibility.

Thus sensibility alone gives to a certain point, the idea of *personality*.

But the mode of sensibility, called the will or willing faculty, can alone render this idea of personality complete; it is then only that it can produce the idea of property as we have it. The idea of property arises then solely from the faculty of will; and moreover it arises necessarily from it, for we cannot have an idea of *self* without having that of the property in all the faculties of *self* and in their effects. If it was not thus, if there was not amongst us a natural and necessary property, there never would have been a conventional or artificial property.

This truth is the foundation of all economy, and of all morality; which are in their principles but one and the same science.

SECTION 3.

From the faculty of will arise all our wants and all our means.

The same intellectual acts emanating from our faculty of will, which cause us to acquire a distinct and complete idea of *self*, and of exclusive property in all its modes, are also those which render us susceptible of wants, and are the source of all our means of providing for those wants.

For 1st. Every desire is a want, and every want is never but the *need* of satisfying a desire. Desire is always in itself a pain.

2d. When our sensitive system re-acts on our muscular system these desires have the property of directing our actions, and thus of producing all our means.

Labour, the employment of our force, constitutes our only treasure and our only power.

Thus it is the faculty of will which renders us proprietors of *wants* and *means*, of *passion* and *action*, of *pain* and *power*.

Thence arise the ideas of *riches* and deprivation.

SECTION 4.

From the faculty of will arise also the ideas of riches and deprivation.

Whatsoever contributes, mediately or immediately, to the satisfaction of our wants is for us a *good;* that is to say, a thing the possession of which is a good.

To be rich is to possess these *goods;* to be poor is to be without them.

They arise all from the employment of our faculties, of which they are the effect and representation.

These goods have all two values amongst us; the one is that of the sacrifices they cost to him who produces them, the other that of the advantages which they procure for him who has acquired them.

The labour from which they emanate has then these two values.

Yes labour has these two values. The one is the sum of the objects necessary to the satisfaction of the wants that arise inevitably in an animated being during the operation of his labour. The other is the mass of utility resulting from this labour.

The latter value is eventual and variable.

The first is natural and necessary. It has not however an absolute fixity; and it is this which renders very delicate all economical and moral calculations.

We can scarcely employ in these matters but the considerations drawn from the theory of limits.

SECTION 5.

From the faculty of will arise also the ideas of *liberty* and *constraint.*

Liberty is the power of executing our will. It is our first good. It includes them all. A constraint includes all our evils, since it is a deprivation of the power to satisfy our wants and accomplish our *desires*.

All constraint is sufferance; all liberty is enjoyment. The total value of the liberty of an animated being is equal to that of all his faculties united.

It is absolutely infinite for him and without a possible equivalent, since its entire loss imports the impossibility of the possession of any good.

Our sole duty is to augment our liberty and its value.

The object of society is solely the fulfilment of this duty.

SECTION 6.

Finally, from the faculty of will arise our ideas of rights and duties.

Rights arise from wants, and duties from means.

Weakness in all its kinds is the source of all rights, and power the source of all duties; or in other words of the general duty to employ it well, which comprehends all the others.

These ideas of rights and duties are not so essentially correlative as is commonly said. That of rights is anterior and absolute.

An animated being by the laws of his nature has always the right to satisfy his wants, and he has no duties but according to circumstances.

A sentient and willing being, but incapable of action, would have all rights and no duties.

This being supposed capable of action, and insulated from every other sensible being, has still the same plenitude of rights, with the sole duty of properly directing his actions and well employing his means for the most complete satisfaction of his wants.

Place this same being in contact with other beings who develope to him their sensibility too imperfectly to enable him to form conventions with them; he has still the same rights, and his duties or rather his sole duty is only changed, so far as he must act on the will of these beings, and is under a necessity to sympathise more or less with them. Such are our relations with the brutes.

Suppose this same sensible being in relation with beings with whom he can completely communicate and form conventions, he has still the same rights unlimited in themselves, and the same sole duty.

These rights are not bounded, this duty is not modified by the conventions established; but because these conventions are so many means of exercising these rights, of fulfilling this duty better and more fully than before.

The possibility of explaining ourselves and not agriculture, grammar and not Ceres, is our first legislator.

It is at the establishment of conventions that the *just* and *unjust*, properly speaking, commence.

SECTION 7.

Conclusion.

The general considerations just read begin to diffuse some light over the subject with which we are occupied, but they are not sufficient. We must see more in detail what are the numerous results of our actions; what are the different sentiments which arise from our first desires, and what is the best possible manner of directing these actions and sentiments. Here will be found the division which I have announced. I shall begin by speaking of our actions.

FIRST PART

OF THE

TREATISE ON THE WILL AND ITS EFFECTS.

OF OUR ACTIONS.

CHAPTER I.

Of Society.

In the introduction to a treatise on the will it was proper to indicate the generation of some general ideas which are the necessary consequences of this faculty.

It was even incumbent on us to examine summarily,

1st. What are inanimate beings, that is to say beings neither *sentient* nor *willing*.

2d. What *sentient* beings would be with indifference without will.

3d. What are *sentient* and *willing* beings but insulated.

4th. Finally, what are *sentient* and *willing* beings like ourselves, but placed in contact with similar beings.

It is with the latter we are now exclusively to occupy ourselves, for man can exist only in society.

The necessity of reproduction and the propensity to sympathy necessarily lead him to this state, and his judgment makes him perceive its advantages.

I proceed then to speak of society.

I shall consider it only with respect to economy, because this first part concerns our *actions* only and not as yet our *sentiments*.

Under this relation society consists only in a continual succession of *EXCHANGES*, and exchange is a transaction of such a nature that both contracting parties always gain by it. (This observation will hereafter throw great light on the nature and effects of commerce.)

We cannot cast our eyes on a civilized country without seeing with astonishment how much this continual succession of small advantages, unperceived but incessantly repeated, adds to the primitive power of man.

It is because this succession of *changes*, which constitutes society, has three remarkable properties. It produces *concurrence* of *force*, *increase* and *preservation* of *intelligence* and *division* of *labour*.

The utility of these three effects is continually augmenting. It will be better perceived when we shall have seen how our riches are formed.

CHAPTER II.

Of Production, or the formation of our Riches.

In the first place what ought we to understand by the word production? We create nothing. We operate only changes of *form* and of *place*.

To *produce* is to give to things an utility which they had not before.

All labour from which utility results is *productive*.

That relative to agriculture has in this respect nothing particular.

A farm is truly a manufactory.

A field is a real tool, or in other words a stock of first materials.

All the laborious class is productive.

The truly *sterile* class is that of the *idle*.

Manufacturers fabricate, merchants transport. This is our industry. *It consists in the production of utility.*

CHAPTER III.

Of the measure of Utility, or of Value.

Whatever contributes to augment our enjoyments and to diminish our sufferings, is useful to us.

We are frequently very unjust appreciators of the real utility of things.

But the measure of utility which, right or wrong, we ascribe to a thing is the sum of the sacrifices we are disposed to make to procure its possession.

This is what is called the price of this thing, it is its real value in relation to riches.

The mean then of enriching ourselves is to devote ourselves to that species of labour which is most dearly paid for, whatever be its nature.

This is true as to a nation as well as to an individual.

Observe always that the conventional value, the market price of a thing, being determined by the balance of the resistance of sellers and buyers, a thing without being less desired becomes less dear, when it is more easily produced.

This is the great advantage of the progress of the arts. It causes us to be provided for on better terms, because we are so with less trouble.

CHAPTER IV.

Of the change of form, or of fabricating Industry, comprising Agriculture.

In every species of iudustry there are three things: theory, application and execution. Hence three kinds of labourers; the man of science, the undertaker, and the workman,

All are obliged to expend more or less before they can receive, and especially the undertaker.

These advances are furnished by anterior *economies*, and are called *capitals*.

The man of science and the workman are regularly compensated by the undertaker; but he has no benefit but in proportion to the success of his fabrication.

It is indispensable that the labors most necessary should be the most moderately recompensed.

This is true most especially of those relative to agricultural industry. This has moreover the inconvenience that the agricultural undertaker cannot make up for the mediocrity of his profits by the great extension of his business.

Accordingly this profession has no attractions for the rich.

The proprietors of land who do not cultivate it are strangers to agricultural industry. They are merely lenders of funds.

They dispose of them according to the convenience of those whom they can engage to labor them.

There are four sorts of undertakers; two with greater or smaller means, the lessees of great and small farms; and two almost without means, those who farm on shares and labourers.

Hence four species of cultivation essentially different.

The division into great and small culture is insufficient and subject to ambiguity.

Agriculture then is the first of arts in relation to necessity, but not in regard to riches.

It is because our means of subsistence and our means of existence are two very different things, and we are wrong to confound them.

CHAPTER V.

Of the change of place, or of Commercial Industry.

Insulated man might fabricate but could not trade.

For commerce and society are one and the same thing.

It alone animates industry.

It unites in the first place inhabitants of the same canton. Then the different cantons of the same country, and finally different nations.

The greatest advantage of external commerce, the only one meriting attention, is its giving a greater developement to that which is internal.

Merchants, properly so called, facilitate commerce, but it exists before them and without them.

They give a new value to things by effecting a change of place, as fabricators do by a change of form.

It is from this increase of value that they derive their profits.

Commercial industry presents the same phenomena as fabricating industry; in it are likewise theory, application and execution. Men of science, undertakers and workmen; these are compensated in like manner; they have analogous functions and interests, &c. &c.

CHAPTER VI.

Of Money.

Commerce can and does exist to a certain degree without money.

The values of all those things, which have any, serve as a reciprocal measure.

The precious metals, which are one of those things, become soon their common measure, because they have many advantages for this purpose.

However they are not yet money. It is the impression of the sovereign which gives this quality to a piece of metal, in establishing its weight and its fineness.

Silver money is the only true common measure.

The proportion of gold and silver vary according to times and places.

Copper money is a false money, useful only for small change.

It is to be desired that coins had never borne other names than those of their weight; and that the arbitrary denominations, called monies of account, such as livres, sous, deniers, &c. &c. had never been used.

But when these denominations are admitted and employed in transactions, to diminish the quantity of metal to which they answer, by an alteration of the real coins, is to *steal*.

And it is a theft which injures even him who commits it.

A theft of greater magnitude, and still more ruinous, is the making of paper money.

It is greater, because in this money there is absolutely no real value.

It is more ruinous, because by its gradual depreciation, during all the time of its existence, it produces the effect which would be produced by an infinity of successive deteriorations of the coins.

All these iniquities are founded on the false idea that money is but a sign, while it is value and a true equivalent of that for which it is given.

Silver being a value, as every other useful thing, we should be allowed to hire it as freely as any other thing.

Exchange, properly so called, is a simple barter of one money for another. Banking, or the proper office of a banker, consists in enabling you to receive in another city the money which you deliver him in that in which he is.

Bankers render also other services, such as discounting, lending, &c. &c.

All these bankers, exchangers, lenders, discounters, &c. &c. have a great tendency to form themselves into large companies under the pretext of rendering their services on more reasonable terms, but in fact to be paid more dearly for them.

All these privileged companies, after the emission of a great number of notes, end in obtaining authority to refuse payment at sight; and thus forcibly introduce a paper money.

CHAPTER VII.

Reflections on what precedes.

Thus far I believe myself to have followed the best course for the attainment of the object which I propose.

This not being a treatise expressly of political economy, but a treatise on the will, the sequel of one on the understanding, we are not here to expect numerous details, but a rigorous chain of principal propositions.

What we have seen already overturns many important errors.

We have a clear idea of the formation of our riches.

It remains for us to speak of their distribution amongst the members of society, and of their consumption.

CHAPTER VIII.

Of the distribution of our Riches amongst Individuals.

We must now consider man under the relation of the interests of individuals.

The species is strong and powerful, the individual is essentially miserable.

Property and inequality are insuperable conditions of our nature.

Labour, even the least skilful, is a considerable property as long as there are lands not occupied.

It is an error in some writers to have pretended there were *non-proprietors.*

Divided by many particular interests, we are all re-united by those of *proprietors* and of *consumers.*

After agriculture the other arts develope themselves.

Misery commences when they can no longer satisfy the calls for labour, which augment.

The state of great ease is necessarily transitory; the fecundity of the human species is the cause.

CHAPTER IX.

Of the multiplication of Individuals, or of Population.

Man multiplies rapidly wherever he has in abundance the means of existence.

Population never becomes retrograde, nor even stationary, but because these means fail.

Amongst savages it is soon checked, because their means are scanty.

Civilized people have more, they become more numerous in proportion as they have more or less of these means, and make better use of them. But the increase of their population is arrested also.

Then there exists always as many men as can exist.

Then it is also absurd to suppose they can be multiplied otherwise than by multiplying their means of existence.

Then finally it is barbarous to wish it, since they always attain the limits of possibility, beyond which they only extinguish one another.

CHAPTER X.

Consequences and developement of the two preceding Chapters.

Let us recollect first, that we all have separate interests, and unequal means.

Secondly. That nevertheless we are all united by the common interests of *proprietors* and *consumers*.

Thirdly. That, consequently, there are not in society classes which are constantly enemies to one another.

Society divides itself into two great classes, hirelings and employers.

This second class contains two species of men, namely the idle who live on their revenue.

Their means do not augment.

And the active who join their industry to the capitals they may possess. Having reached a certain term their means augment but little.

The funds on which the stipendiaries live become therefore with time nearly a constant quantity.

Moreover the class of hirelings receives the surplus of all the others.

Thus the extent which that surplus can attain determines that of the total population of which it explains all the variations.

It follows thence that whatever is really useful to the poor, is always really useful to society at large.

As *proprietors* the poor have an interest, first that property be respected. The preservation even of that which does not belong to them, but from which they are remunerated is important to them. It is just and useful also to leave them masters of their labour, and of their abode.

Secondly. That wages be sufficient. It is of importance also to society that the poor should not be too wretched.

Thirdly. That these wages be steady. Variations in the different branches of industry are an evil. Those in the price of grain are a still greater one. Agricultural people are greatly exposed to the latter. Commercial people are rarely exposed to the former, except through their own fault.

As consumers the poor have an interest that fabrication should be economical, the means of communication easy, and commercial relations numerous. The simplification of process in the arts, the perfection of method are to them a benefit and not an evil. In this their interest is also that of society in general.

After the opposition of our interests let us examine the inequality of our means.

All inequality is an evil, because it is a mean of injustice.

Let us distinguish the inequality of power from inequality of riches.

Inequality of power is the most grievous. It is that which exists among savages.

Society diminishes the inequality of power; but it augments that of riches, which carried to an extreme reproduces that of power.

This inconvenience is more or less difficult to avoid, according to different circumstances. Thence the difference in the destinies of nations.

It is this vicious circle which explains the connexion of many events which have been always spoken of in a manner very vague and very unexact.

CHAPTER XI.

Of the employment of our riches, or of Consumption.

After having explained how our riches are formed, and how they are distributed, it is easy to see how we use them.

Consumption is always the reverse of production.

It varies however according to the species of consumers, and the nature of the things consumed. First let us consider the consumers.

The consumption of the hired ought to be regarded as made by the capitalists who employ them.

These capitalists are either the idle who live on their revenue, or the active who live on their profits.

The first remunerate only sterile labour. Their entire consumption is a pure loss, accordingly they cannot expend annually more than their revenue.

The others expend annually all their funds, and all those which they hire of the idle capitalists; and sometimes they expend them several times in the year.

Their consumption is of two kinds.

That which they make for the satisfaction of their personal wants is definitive and sterile, as that of idle men.

That which they make in their quality of industrious men returns to them with profit.

It is with these profits they pay their personal expenses, and the interest due to idle capitalists.

Thus they find that they pay both the hirelings whom they immediately employ, and the idle proprietors and their hirelings; and all this returns to them by the purchases which all those people make of their productions.

It is this which constitutes circulation, of which productive consumption is the only fund.

In regard to the nature of things consumed, consumption the most gradual is the most economical the most prompt; is the most destructive.

We see that luxury, that is to say superfluous consumption, can neither accelerate circulation nor increase its funds. It only substitutes useless for useful expenses.

It is like inequality, an inconvenience attached to the increase of riches; but it can never be the cause of their augmentation.

History plainly shows what happens wherever useless expenses have been suppressed.

All theories contrary to this reduce themselves to this untenable proposition. That to destroy is to produce.

CHAPTER XII.

Of the revenues and expenses of government and its debts.

The history of the consumption of government is but a part of the history of general consumption.

Government is a very great consumer, living not on its profits but on its revenues.

It is good that the government should possess real property. Independently of other reasons it calls for so much the less of taxes.

A tax is always a sacrifice which the government demands of individuals. While it only lessens every one's personal enjoyments, it only shifts expenses from one to another.

But when it encroaches on productive consumption it diminishes public riches.

The difficulty is to see clearly when taxes produce the one or the other of these two effects.

To judge well of this we must divide them into six classes.

We show in the first place that the taxes of each of these six classes are injurious in ways peculiar to themselves.

We show afterwards who in particular are injured by each of them.

Is a conclusion asked? Here it is. The best taxes are, first, the most moderate, because they compel fewer sacrifices and occasion less violence. Secondly, The most varied, because they produce an equilibrium amongst themselves. Thirdly, The most ancient, because they have already mixed with all prices, and every thing is arranged in consequence.

As to the expenses of government they are necessary but they are sterile. It is desirable that they be the smallest possible.

It is still more desirable that government should contract no debts.

It is very unfortunate that it has the power of contracting them.

This power, which is called *public credit*, speedily conducts all the governments which use it to their ruin; has none of the advantages which are attributed to it; and rests on a false principle.

It is to be desired that it were universally acknowledged that the acts of any legislative power whatsoever cannot bind their successors, and that it should be solemnly declared that this principle is extended to the engagements which they make with the lenders.

CHAPTER XIII.

Conclusion.

This is not properly a treatise on political economy, but the first part of a treatise on the will; which will be followed by two other parts, and which is preceded by an introduction common to all the three.

Thus we ought not to have entered into many details, but to ascend carefully to principles founded in the observation of our faculties, and to indicate as clearly as possible the relations between our physical and moral wants.

This is what I have endeavoured to do. Incontestible truths result from it.

They will be contested however, less through interest than passion.

A new bond of union between economy and morality; a new reason for analizing well our different sentiments, and for enquiring with care whether they are founded on just or on false opinions.

Let us now consider our sentiments.

A TREATISE

ON

POLITICAL ECONOMY, &c.

SUPPLEMENT

TO THE

First Section of the Elements of Ideology.

In proportion as I advance in the digestion of these elements, I am incessantly obliged to return to objects, of which I have already treated. At the commencement of the grammar it was necessary to recall the attention of the reader to the analysis of the judgment, to render still more precise the idea of that intellectual operation, and of its results, and to repeat several of the effects already recognized in the signs, and several of their relations, with the nature of the ideas which they represent.

At the commencement of the volume which treats more especially of logic, I of necessity looked back on the ancient history of the science, to show, that true logic is absolutely the same science with that of the formation, the expression, and combination of our ideas; that is to say, that which has been since called Ideology, general grammar, or analysis of the understanding; and to show that my two first volumes are but the restoration, more or less fortunate, of the two first parts of the ancient logics, and the supplement of that which has always been wanting to these very important preliminaries. I have moreover been under the necessity of insisting also on the explication of the idea of existence, and on that of the reality of our preceptions, and of their necessary concordance with the reality of the beings which cause them, when they are all legitimately deduced from the first and direct impressions, which these beings make on us.

At present I find myself, in like manner, constrained to speak again of the conclusions of this logic, before advancing further, and not to apply my theory of the causes of certitude and error, to the study of the will and its effects, without having given it some new developements. The reader ought to pardon these frequent retrospects; for they arise almost necessarily from the nature of the subject, from the manner in which it has been treated hitherto, and from the necessity we are under, of anticipating a crowd of objections, when we wish to render a new opinion acceptable.

Let me be permitted then to mention here again, that I have reduced the whole science of logic to the observation of two facts, which result manifestly from the scrupulous examination of our intellectual operations. The first is, that our perceptions being every thing for us, we are perfectly, completely, and necessarily sure of all that we actually feel. The second, which is but a consequence of that, is that none of our judgments, taken separately, can be erroneous, since, for the very reason that we see one idea in another, it must be actually there; but that their falsity, when it takes place, is purely relative to all the anterior judgments, which we permit to subsist, and consists in this, that we believe the idea, in which we see a new element, to be the same we have always had under the same sign, while it is really different, since the new element we actually see there is incompatible with some of those which we have previously seen there. So that, to avoid contradiction, it would be necessary either to take away the former, or not to admit the latter.

After having established these two principles, or rather these two facts, I have given some elucidations, I have met in advance some objections, I have shown that these two objections are equally true, whatever be the nature of our ideas, and whatever the use we make of them; and hence I have concluded, that all the rules whatsoever which have been prescribed for the form of our reasonings, to assure us of their justice, are absolutely useless and illusory ; and that our sole and only means of preserving ourselves from error, is to assure ourselves well that we comprehend the idea of which we judge, and if it be doubtful, to make the most complete enumeration possible of the elements which compose it, and principally of those which may either implicitly contain or exclude that whose admission or exclusion is in question. It is here that, without more details, I have terminated my treatise on logic, which consequently finishes almost at the point at which all the others commence. This ought so to be, as I meant to speak only of the science; while other logicians, neglecting the science almost entirely, have occupied themselves only with the art. I confess my belief, that my labour is more useful than theirs; because, in every matter, it is always very difficult, from premature consequences, to remount to the principles which ought to have served as their foundation. Whereas, when we have well established the first truths, it is easy to deduce the consequences which flow from them. Yet this second operation is important also, and as a subject is not completely treated of, but when it is executed, I will present, before proceeding further, summarily, but methodically, the series of practical maxims, which result from my method of considering our means of knowledge. The use I shall afterwards make of these same means, in the study of the will and its effects, will be an example of the manner in which these rules are applied in all our researches.

APHORISM FIRST.*

We know our existence only by the impressions we experience, and that of beings other than ourselves, but by the impressions which they cause on us.

Observation.

In like manner, as all our propositions may be reduced to the form of enunciative propositions,

* I have employed the form of aphorisms, observations and corollaries, in order to say the most in the fewest words.

because at bottom they all express a judgment, so all our enunciative propositions may afterwards be always reduced to some one of these: *I think, I feel,* or *I perceive, that such a thing is in such a manner, or that such a being produces such an effect;* propositions of which we are ourselves the subject, because in fact we are always the subject of all our judgments, since they never express but the impression which we experience.

Corollary.

From hence it follows: 1st. That our perceptions are all of them always such as we feel them, and are not susceptible of any error, taken each separately, and in itself.

2dly. That if in the different combinations, we make of them, we add to them nothing which is not primitively comprised in them, implicitly or explicitly, they are always conformable to the existence of the beings which cause them, since that existence is not known to us but by them, and consists for us only in those perceptions.

3dly. That we know nothing but relatively to ourselves, and to our means of receiving perceptions.

4thly. That these perceptions are every thing for us; that we know nothing ever but our perceptions; that they are the only things truly real for us, and that the reality which we recognize in the beings that cause them is only secondary, and consists only in the permanent power of always causing the same impressions under the same circumstances, whether on ourselves, or on other sensible beings, who give us an account of them (also by the impressions which they cause in us) when we have become able to hold communication with them by signs.

APHORISM SECOND.

Since our perceptions are all of them always such as we feel them, when we perceive one idea in another, it is actually and really there, from the very circumstance of our perceiving it there: hence no one of our judgments taken separately and detached, is false. It has always and necessarily the certitude which belongs inevitably to each of our actual perceptions.

Corollary.

None of our judgments then can be false, but relatively to anterior judgments, and that suffices to render them false relatively to the existence of beings, the causes of our impressions, if these anterior judgments were just, relatively to that existence.

APHORISM THIRD.

When we see in an idea, or a perception, an element incompatible with those which it included before, this idea is different from what it was, for, such as it was, it excluded this new element which we see there; and, such as it is, it excludes those which are incompatible with it.

Corollary.

That it may then be the same idea which it was before, we must exclude from it the elemen which we see there at present, or if those which are repugnant to it, are misplaced in this idea, they must themselves be excluded from it; that is to say, it must be rendered such as it was, when they were erroneously admitted into it, which is to restore it again to the same state in which it was, before it was changed by a false judgment, without our perceiving it.

APHORISM FOURTH.

When we form a judgment of an idea, when we see in it a new element, one of these four things must necessarily happen: Either the judgment which we now form is consequent to a just idea, in which case it is just; and the idea without changing its nature has only developed and extended itself.

Or it is inconsequent to a just idea, in which case it is false; and the idea is changed, and is become false.

Or it is consequent to an idea already false, then it is false, but the idea is not changed; it is when it has become false previously, that it has changed in relation to what it was primitively.

Or it is inconsequent to a false idea, then it may be just or false; but never certain, for the idea is changed. But it may have become just, such as it was originally, or false, in a manner different from the preceding.

Observation.

Remark always, that an idea infected with false elements, and consequently meriting the name of false, taken in mass, may also contain many true elements. We may form then, in consequence of these true elements, just judgments, and then they will be completely true; as we may also form from them false judgments, which shall be completely false; but these judgments will not be formed from that idea, inasmuch as it is false, and in consequence of that which it has of falsity; they ought therefore to be considered as formed from a true idea, and enter into what we have said of these.

This is what most frequently happens to us, so few compound ideas have we which are perfectly pure, and without mixture of imperfection. Perhaps we have none. Perhaps it would suffice for us to have one alone, to render all our others the same, by the sole force of their relations and combinations, proximate or remote.

APHORISM FIFTH.

Thus all our perceptions are originally just and true, and error is only introduced to them at the moment when we admit an element which is opposed to them. That is to say, which denaturalises and changes them, without our perceiving it.

APHORISM SIXTH.

This would never happen to us, if we had always present to the mind, that which the idea comports, of which we judge. Thus all our errors really come from this: that we represent the idea imperfectly to ourselves.

APHORISM SEVENTH.

What precedes not appertaining to any circumstance peculiar to any one of our perceptions rather than to another, agrees generally with all.

Corollary.

Hence it follows, 1st. That our manner of proceeding is the same for our ideas of every kind.

2dly. That all our errors originate from the basis of our ideas, and not from the form of our reasonings.

3dly. That all the rules which can be prescribed for the forms of these reasonings, can contribute nothing to avoid error; or at least can contribute to it but accidentally.

APHORISM EIGHTH.

We have then no other effectual means of avoiding error, but to assure ourselves well of the comprehension of the idea of which we judge, that is to say, of the elements of which it is composed.

Observation.

That is not possible, unless we commence by well determining the extension of this idea, for it contains many elements in certain degrees of its extension, which it does not in others, that is to say, it is not exactly similar to itself, it is not rigorously the same idea in their different degrees of extension.

APHORISM NINTH.

This general and only method embraces several others, and first that of studying with care the object, or objects, from which the idea in question emanates, and afterwards that of guarding ourselves with the same care from the affections, passions, prejudices, dispositions, habits and manners of being, by which the idea could be altered.

Observation.

These two precautions are necessary, the first to assemble, as far as possible, all the elements which really appertain to the idea in question, the second to separate from it in like manner all those which are foreign to it, and which might mingle themselves with it, and alter it, without our perceiving it.

APHORISM TENTH.

After these two necessary preliminaries, if we are still in doubt as to the judgment we are to form, the most useful expedient of which we can avail ourselves, is to make an enumeration the most complete possible of the elements composing the idea, which is the subject of the judgment, and principally of those which have relation to the idea which we propose to attribute to it, that is to say, to the attribute of the contemplated judgment.

Observation.

The effect of this operation is to recal to ourselves, or to those whom we wish to convince of the truth or falsity of a proposition, the elements of the subject which implicitly comprehend the proposed attribute, or which on the contrary may exclude it.

It is the object which the logicians propose to attain by what they call *definitions;* but in my opinion they fall into several errors relatively to definitions, and they greatly mistake their effects and properties.

1st. They believe that there are definitions of words, and definitions of things, while in truth there are none but definitions of ideas. When I explain the sense of a word, I do nothing but explain the idea which I have when I pronounce that word, and when I explain what a being is, I still do nothing but explain the idea I have of that being, and which I express when I pronounce its name.

2d. They aver that definitions are principles, and that we cannot dispute about definitions. These two assertions are contraries, and yet both of them false.

In the first place they are contradictory, for if definitions are principles, we can and we ought frequently to question their truth, as we ought never to recognise any principle as true without a previous examination, and if we cannot contest definitions, they cannot be principles, since every principle should be proved before it is admitted.

Again, these two assertions are both false. Definitions are not principles; for facts are the only true principles; and definitions are not facts, but simple explanations founded on facts, as all our other propositions whatsoever. Now we may contest a definition, as every other proposition; for when I explain the idea that I have of a being, I do not pretend to say merely that I have this idea; I pretend also to affirm that this idea agrees with that being, and that we may so conceive it without error; now this is what may be false, and what may be contested. So also when I explain the idea which I have of the sense of a word, I do not solely pretend that I have this idea, I pretend further that it does not affect the real relations of this word with an infinity of others, that we may employ it in this sense without inconvenience and without inconsequence; now this is what again may be contested with reason. In fine, if I should pretend by a definition only to explain the complex and compound idea that I have actually in my head, yet it should always be allowed to show me that this idea is badly formed, that it is composed of judgments inconsequent the one to the other, and that it includes contradictory elements. Then definitions never are principles, and yet they always are contestible.

3dly. The logicians have believed that the definition is good, and that the idea defined is perfectly explained when they have determined it, *per genus proximum et differentiam specificam,* as they say; that is to say, when they have expressed that one of its elements which constitutes it of such a genus, and the one which in this genus distinguishes it from the ideas of the neighbouring species. Now this is still false, and is only founded on the fantastical doctrine, in virtue of which they believed they were able to distribute all our ideas into different arbitrary classes called categories.

That is false, first, because these arbitrary classifications never represent nature. Our ideas are connected the one to the other by a thousand different relations. Seen under one aspect they are of one genus, and under another they are of another genus; subsequently each of them depends on an innumerable multitude of proximate ideas, by an infinity of relations, of natures so different that we cannot compare them together, to decide which is the least remote. Thus we can never, or almost never find really *the proximate genus or specific difference* which deserves exclusively to characterise an idea.

Moreover, if we should have found in this idea the elements which in fact determine the genus and species in which it is reasonably permitted to class it, the idea would still be far from sufficiently explained, to be well known.

These two elements might even be absolutely foreign to the decision of the question which may have given place to the definition. Assuredly when I say that gold is a metal, and the heaviest of metals except platina, I have correctly ranged gold in the genus of beings to which it belongs, and I have distinguished it by a characteristic difference from those nearest to it in that genus. Yet this does not help me to know whether the use of gold, as money, is useful to commerce, or pernicious to morality, nor even whether it is the most ductile of metals. The two first questions depend on ideas too foreign to those which fix gold in a certain place amongst metals; and though the latter may be less distant, yet we do not know the direct and necessary relation between weight and ductility.

Logicians have been mistaken respecting the nature, the effects and properties of definitions. They are incapable of answering the end which they propose to attain by their means, that of presenting the idea of which we are to judge in such a manner that we cannot avoid forming a just judgment. The only mean of attaining this is to make the best description possible of the idea, and with the precautions which we have indicated.

Remark.

It is necessary to observe that all that we have advised in the 8th, 9th and 10th aphorisms, and also what we shall advise hereafter to be done, to know well the idea, the subject of the judgment in question is equally applicable to the idea which is the attribute of the same judgment, a knowledge of which is equally essential, and can only be acquired by the same mean.

APHORISM ELEVENTH.

The means indicated above of knowing well the idea of which we are to judge, are the only really efficacious ones in bringing us to the formation of just judgments; but they may very possibly be insufficient to give us a certitude of having succeeded. We must therefore add subsidiary means.

APHORISM TWELFTH.

The best and most useful of our secondary means is to see, on the one hand, if the judgment we are to form is not in opposition to anterior judgments, of the certitude of which we are assured; and on the other if it does not necessarily lead to consequences manifestly false.

Remark.

The first point is that which has so strongly accredited the usage of general propositions; for, as we can confront them with a number of particular propositions, we have frequently had recourse thereto, and we have habituated ourselves to remount no further, and to believe that they are the primitive source of truth. The second is the motive of all those reasonings which consist in a reduction to what is absurd.

Observation.

The process recommended in this aphorism is a species of proof to which we submit the projected operation. It is very useful to avoid error, for if the judgment we examine is found in opposition to anterior ones which are just, or necessarily connected with false consequences, it is evidently necessary to reject it; but this same process does not lead us directly and necessarily to truth, for it may be that no determining motive for the affirmative may result from the research.

APHORISM THIRTEENTH.

In a case in which we want decisive reasons to determine us, no other resource is left us but to endeavour to obtain new lights, that is to say, to introduce new elements into the idea which is the subject of the judgment we are to form. This can be done in two ways only, either by seeking to collect new facts, or by endeavouring to make of those already known combinations which had not previously occurred to us, and thence to draw consequences which we had not before remarked.

Observation.

The advice contained in this aphorism, is only the developement of the first part of aphorism 9th, and it can be nothing else; for when we are assured that we are not sufficiently acquainted with a subject to judge of it, there is no other resource but to study it more.

APHORISM FOURTEENTH.

Finally, when the motives of determination fail us invincibly, we should know how to remain in complete doubt, and to suspend absolutely our judgment, rather than rest it on vain and confused appearances, since in these we can never be sure that there are not some false elements.

Remark and conclusion.

This is the last and most essential of logical principles; for in following it we may possibly remain in ignorance, but we can never fall into error; all our errors arising always from admitting into that which we know elements which are not really there, and which lead us to consequences which ought not to follow from those that are there effectively.

In effect, if from our first impressions the most simple to our most general ideas, and their most complicated combinations, we have never recognized in our successive perceptions but what is there, our last combinations would be as irreproachable as the first act of our sensibility. Thus, in logical rigour, it is very certain that we ought never to form a judgment but when we see clearly that the subject includes the attributes : that is to say, that the judgment is just.

But at the same time it is also very certain that in the course of life we seldom arrive at certitude, and are frequently obliged, nevertheless, to form a resolution provisionally ; to form none being often to adopt one of the most decisive character, without renouncing the principle we have just laid down, or in any manner derogating from it. It is now proper to speak of the theory of probability. It is a subject I encounter with reluctance. First, because it is very difficult, and as yet very little elucidated; next, because one cannot hope to treat it profoundly when one is not perfectly familiar with the combinations of the science of quantities, and of the language proper to them. Finally, because even with these means the nature of the subject deprives us of the hope of arriving at almost any certain result, and leaves us only that of a good calculation of chances. Let us, however, endeavour to form to ourselves an accurate and just idea of it ; this will perhaps be already to contribute to its progress.

The science of probability is not a part of logic, and ought not even to be regarded as forming a supplement to it. Logic teaches us to form just judgments, and to make series of judgments: that is to say, of reasonings which are consequent. Now, properly speaking, there are no judgments or series of judgments which are probable. When we judge that an opinion or a fact is probable, we judge it positively; and this judgment is just, false, or presumptuous, according as we have perfectly or imperfectly observed the principles of the art of logic. But it will be said, that the science of probability in teaching us to estimate this probability of an opinion, teaches us to judge justly whether this opinion is or is not probable. I admit it: but it produces this effect as the science of the properties of bodies, physics, teaches us to form the judgment that such a property appertains to such a body; as the science of extension teaches us to form the judgment that such a theorem results from the properties of such a figure; as the science of quantity teaches us that such a number is the result of such a calculation; finally, as all the sciences teach us to form sound judgments of the objects, which belong to their province. Nevertheless we cannot say, and we do not say, that they are but parts of logic, nor even that they are supplements to it. They all on the contrary throw light on the subjects of which they treat only in consequence of the means and processes with which they are furnished by sound logic. This is useful to all the sciences; but none of them either aid it immediately, supply its place, make a part of it, or are supplements to it. The science of probability has in this respect no particular privileges under this aspect; it is a science similar to all the others.

But I go further; the science to which we have given the name of the science of probability, is not a science: or to explain myself more clearly, we comprehend erroneously under this collective and common name a multitude of sciences or of portions of sciences quite different among themselves, strangers to one another, and which it is impossible to unite without confounding them all. In effect, that which is called commonly the science of probability comprehends two very distinct parts, of which one is the research, and the valuation of data, the other is the calculation, or the combination of these same data.

Now the success of the research and valuation of data, if the question is on the probability of a narration, consists in a knowledge of the circumstances, proper to the fact in itself, and to all those who have spoken of it:—thus it depends on and forms a part of the science of history. If the question is on the probability of a physical event, this research of data consists in acquiring a knowledge of anterior facts and of their connection:—thus it appertains to physics. If the question is on the probable results of a social institution, or of the deliberations of an assembly of men, the anterior facts are the details of the social organization, or of the intellectual dispositions and operations of these men:—thus it depends on social and moral science, or on ideology. Finally, when it is only to foresee the chances of the play of cross and pile, the data would be the construction of the piece, the manner of resistance of the medium in which it moves, that of the bodies against which it may strike. the motion proper to the arm which casts it, and which are more or less easy to it. Thus these data would still depend on the physical constitution of animate and inanimate bodies. Then as to the research of data, and to the fixation of their importance, the pretended science of probability is composed of a multitude of different sciences, according to the subject on which it is employed; and consequently it is not a particular science.

As to the combination of the data once established, the science of probability is nothing, when we employ calculation therein, but the science of quantity or of calculation itself; for the difficulty does not consist in giving to abstract unity any concrete value whatever, and sometimes one and sometimes another, but in knowing all the resources which perfect calculation furnishes to make of this unity and of all its multiplied combinations the most complicated, and to connect them regularly without losing their clue.

We see then that neither in regard to the research and valuation of data, nor in regard to the combinations of these same data, the pretended science of probability is not a particular science distinct from every other.

We might rather consider it either as a branch of the science of quantities, and as an employment which we make of it in certain parts of several different sciences which are susceptible of this application, or as the reunion of scattered portions of many sciences, strangers the one to the other, which have only so much in common as to give place to such questions as can only be resolved by a very learned and very delicate employment of the admirable means of calculation furnished by the science of quantities in the state of perfection which it has at this time attained; but this is not seeing the theory of probability in its full extent, for we cannot always employ calculation in the estimation of probability. Nevertheless this manner of considering and decomposing what is called the science of probability explains to us already many of the things which concern it, and puts us in the way of forming to ourselves an accurate and complete idea of it.

We see first why it is the mathematicians who have had the idea of it, and who have, if we may so say, created andmade it entirely. It is because such as they have conceived it, it consists principally in the employment of a powerful agent which was at their disposal; they have been able to push to a great length speculations which other men have been obliged to abandon in consequence of a want of means to pursue them.

We also see why these mathematicians principally and almost entirely employed themselves on subjects of which the data are very simple, such as the chances of games of hazard, and of lotteries, or the effects of the interest of money lent; it is because their principal advantage consisting in their great skill in calculation, they have with reason preferred the objects where this art is almost every thing, and where the choice and valuation of data present scarcely any difficulty; and it is in fact in cases of this kind that they have obtained a success both curious and useful.

We moreover see why it is that all the efforts of these mathematicians, even the most skilful, when they have undertaken to treat in the same manner subjects of which the data were numerous, subtile and complicated, have produced little else than witty conceits which may be called *difficiles nugae*, learned trifles. It is because the farther they have pursued the consequences resulting from the small number of data which they have been able to obtain, the farther they have departed from the consequences which these same data would have produced, united with all those often more important, which they have been obliged to neglect from inability to unravel and appreciate them. This is the cause why we have seen great calculators, after the most learned combinations, give us forms of balloting the most defective, not having taken into account a thousand circumstances, inherent in the nature of men and of things, attending only to the circumstance of the number of the one and of the other. It is the reason why Condorcet himself, when he undertook to apply the theory of probabilities to the decisions of assemblies, and particularly to the judgments of tribunals, either has not ventured to decide any thing on actual institutions, and has confined himself to reasoning on imaginary hypothesis, or has often been led to expedients absolutely impracticable, or which would have inconveniencies more serious than those he wished to avoid.

Whatever respect I bear to the great intelligence and high capacity of this truly superior and ever to be regretted man, I do not fear to pass so bold a sentence on this part of his labors, for I am in some measure authorized to do it by himself. The title of Essay which he has given to his treatise, and the motto which he has prefixed to it, prove how much he doubted of the success of such an enterprise, and what confirms it is, that in his last work, composed on the eve of an unfortunate death, in which he has traced with so firm a hand the history of the progress of the human mind, and in which he has assigned to the theory of probabilities so great a part in the future success of the moral sciences, he uses with all the candour which characterises him these expressions, page 362—"This application, notwithstanding the happy efforts of some geometricians, is still, if I may so say, but in its first elements, and it must open to following generations a source of intelligence truly inexhaustible." Yet he had then made not only the learned essay of which we are speaking, but also a work greatly superior, the elements of the calculation of probabilities and of its application to games of hazard, to lotteries and to the judgments of men, which were not published till the year 1805.

I believe, then, that I have advanced nothing rash in observing that in subjects difficult by the number, subtility, complexity and intimate connexion of the circumstances to be considered, without the omission of any of them, the great talent of well combining those, not sufficiently numerous, which have been perceived, has not been sufficient to preserve the most skilful calculators from important errors and great misreckonings. We perceive that that was to be expected. But now I must go further, and all this leads me to a last reflection, which flows from the nature of things, like those which have just been read, which confirms several important principles established in the preceding volumes, which far from annihilating the great hopes of Condorcet tends to assure and realise them, by restraining them within certain limits; but which appear to me to show manifestly, how far the calculation of probabilities is from being the same thing with the theory of probability. Observe in what this observation consists.

The principal object of the theory of probability and its great utility, is in setting out from the reunion of a certain number of given causes, to determine the degree of the probability of the effects which ought to follow; and setting out from the reunion of a certain number of known effects, to determine the degree of the probability of the causes, which have been able to produce them. We may even say that all the results of this theory are but different branches of this general result, and may be traced to be nothing more than parts of it.

Now we have previously seen, and on different occasions, that for beings of any kind, to be successfully submitted to the action of calculation, it is necessary they should be susceptible of adaptation to the clear, precise and invariable divisions of the ideas of quantity, and to the series of the names of numbers and of cyphers, which express them. This is a condition necessary to the validity of every calculation from which that which has probability for its object, cannot be any more exempt, than that which conducts to absolute certainty.

Hence it rigorously follows, that there is a multitude of subjects of which it would be absolutely impossible to calculate the data, if even (which is not always the case) it should be possible to collect them all without overlooking any.

Assuredly the degrees of the capacity, of the probity of men, those of the energy and the power of their passions, prejudices and habits, cannot possibly be estimated in numbers. It is the same as to the degrees of influence of certain institutions, or of certain functions, of the degrees of importance of certain establishments, of the degrees of difficulty of certain discoveries, of the degrees of utility of certain inventions, or of certain processes. I know that of these quantities, truly inappreciable and innumerable in all the rigour of the word, we seek and even attain to a certain point, in determining the limits, by means of number, of the frequency and extent of their effects; but I also know that in these effects which we are obliged to sum and number together as things perfectly similar, in order to deduce results, it is almost always and I may say always impossible to unravel the alterations and variations of concurrent causes, of influencing circumstances, and of a thousand essential considerations, so that we are necessitated to arrange together as similar a multitude of things very different, to arrive only at those preparatory results which are afterwards to lead to others which cannot fail to become entirely fantastical.

Is an example desired, very striking, drawn from a subject which surely does not present as many difficulties of this kind as moral ideas? Here is one. Certainly none of those who have undertaken to estimate the effort of the muscles of the heart, have erred against the rules of calculation, nor, what is more, against the laws of animated mechanics, the certainty of which should still preserve them from many errors. Yet some have been led to estimate this effort at several thousands of pounds, and others only at some ounces; and nobody knows with certainty which are nearest to truth. What succour then can we derive from calculation, when even availing ourselves properly of it we are subject to such aberrations and to such prodigious incertitude?

It is then true, and I repeat it, that there is a multitude of things to which the calculation of probabilities like every other calculation is completely inapplicable. These things are much more numerous than is generally believed, and even by many very skilful men, and the first step to be taken in the science of probability is to know how to distinguish them. It is for the science of the formation of our ideas, for that of the operations of our intelligence, in a word for sound ideology, to teach us the number of these things, to enable us to know their nature, and to show us the reasons why they are so refractory. And it is a great service which it will render to the human mind, by preventing it in future from making a pernicious use of one of its most excellent instruments. It already shows us that the science of probability is a thing very distinct from the calculation of probability with which it has been confounded, since it extends to many objects to which the other cannot attain. This is what I principally proposed to elucidate.

Finally, as I have before announced, this observation does not destroy the great hopes which the pirecing genius of Condorcet had made him conceive from the employment of calculation in general, and from that of probability in particular, in the advancement of the moral sciences; for if the different shades of our moral ideas cannot be expressed in numbers, and if there are many other things relative to social science, which are equally incapable of being estimated and calculated directly, these things depend on others which often render them reducible to calculable quantities, if we may use the expression. Thus for example, the degrees of the value of all things useful and agreeable, that is to say, the degrees of interest we attach to their possession cannot be noted directly by figures, but all those which can be represented by quantities of weight or extension of a particular thing, become calculable and even comparable the one with the other; in like manner the energy and durability of the secret springs which cause and preserve the action of the organs constituting our life are not susceptible of direct appreciation, but we judge of them by their effects. Time and different kinds of resistance and waste are susceptible of very exact divisions. This is sufficient for us, and we derive thence a great multitude of results and of valuable combinations; now there is an infinity of things in the moral sciences which offer us similar resources; but there are also many which offer none, and once more it is of great importance to discriminate perfectly between them: For first, in respect to these latter, every employment of calculation is abusive;

and moreover there are often species of quantities presented which appear calculable, but which are inextricably complicated by mixture with those other species of quantities which I permit myself to call refractory, and then if calculation be applied thereto, the most skilful mathematicians are inevitably led into enormous errors; against this in my opinion they have not always been sufficiently on their guard. As to these two latter cases we may say of calculation what has been said of the syllogistic art as to all our reasonings whatsoever; that is, that it conducts our mind much less correctly than the simple light of good sense aided by sufficient attention.

This is all I had to observe on the science and calculation of probability, and I draw from it the following consequences: The theory of probability is neither a part of nor a supplement to logic. This theory moreover is not a science separate and distinct from all others. All sciences have a positive and a conjectural part. In all of them the positive part consists in distinguishing the effects which always and necessarily follow certain causes, and the causes which always and necessarily produce certain effects. In all of them also the conjectural part consists in proceeding from the reunion of a certain number of given causes to determine the degrees of probability of the effects which ought to follow from them, and in proceeding from the reunion of a certain number of known effects to determine the degree of probability of the causes which have been able to produce them. In these two parts, when the ideas compared are not of a nature to comport with the application of the names of numbers and of figures, we can only employ the ordinary instruments of reasoning, that is to say our vulgar languages, their forms, and the words which compose them. In these two parts equally when the ideas compared by the clearness, constancy, and precision of their subdivisions are susceptible of adaptation to the divisions of the series of the names of numbers, and of figures, we can employ with great advantage, instead of the ordinary instruments of reasoning, the instruments proper to the science of the ideas of quantity, that is to say, the language of calculation, its formulas, and its signs. It is this which constitutes in respect to the conjectural part the calculation of probability. It is necessary to distinguish it carefully from the science of probability; for the one is of use in all cases in which the object is a likelihood of any kind whatsoever; it is properly the conjectural part of all other sciences, whereas the other calculation has place only in those cases in which we can employ the language of calculation; it is but an instrument, of which unhappily the science of probability cannot always avail itself.

The science of probability consists in the talent and sagacity necessary to know the data, to chuse them, to perceive their degrees of importance, to arrange them in convenient order, a talent to which it is very difficult to prescribe precise rules, because it is often the product of a multitude of unperceived judgments. On the contrary, the calculation of probability, properly so called, consists only in following correctly the general rules of the language of calculation in those cases in which it can be employed.

This calculation is often extremely useful and extremely learned; but it is necessary carefully to distinguish the occasions on which we can avail ourselves of it, for however little the ideas which we attempt to calculate are mingled with those which I have named refractory, and which are truly incalculable, we are inevitably led into the most excessive misreckonings. It is what I think has happened but too frequently to skilful men, who by their knowledge, and even by their mistakes, have put us into the way of discovering their cause.

I will limit myself to this small number of results. I perceive that it is to diffuse but little direct light on a subject, which is so much the more important and the more extensive, as unfortunately certitude is for the most part far from us. But if I have contributed to the formation of a just and clear idea of it I shall not have been useless. I have much more reason than Condorcet for saying *"I have not "thought that I was giving a good work, but merely "a work calculated to give birth to better ones, "&c."**

* See page 183 of the preliminary discourse to the essay on the application of analysis to the probability of decisions, given by a plurality of votes, in 4to 1785, al'imprimerie royal.

This discourse, the elements of the same author which I have already cited, and the excellent lesson of M. Delaplace, which are to be found in the collection of the Normal schools, are, in my opinion, the three works in which we are best able to see the general spirit and process of the calculation of probabilities, and where we can the most easily discover the causes of its advantages and inconveniences, although they are not yet there completely developed.

Not wishing to occupy myself longer with the conjectural part of our knowledge, and not believing it necessary to add to the small number of principles which I have established before this long digression, and which embrace in my opinion every thing of importance in the logical art, such as it proceeds from true logical science; it only remains for me to endeavour to make a happy application of this art to the study of our *will and its effects.* It is this I am going to undertake, with a hope that my instruments being better, I may better succeed than perhaps men more skilful but not so well armed.

SECOND SECTION

OF THE

Elements of Ideology, or a treatise on the will and its effects.

INTRODUCTION.

SECTION FIRST.

The faculty of willing is a mode and a consequence of the faculty of feeling.

WHAT has been now read is the end of all that I had to say of human intelligence, considered under the relation of its means of knowing and understanding. This analysis of our understanding, and of that of every other animated being, such as we conceive and imagine it, is not perhaps either as perfect or as complete as might be desired; but I believe at least that it discovers clearly to us the origin and the source of all our knowledge, and the true intellectual operations which enter into its composition, and that it shows us plainly the nature and species of certitude of which this knowledge is susceptible, and the disturbing causes which render it uncertain or erroneous.

Strengthened with these data we can therefore endeavour to avail ourselves of them, and employ our means of knowledge either in the study of the will and its effects to complete the history of our intellectual faculties, or in the study of those beings which are not ourselves; in order to acquire a just idea of what we are able to know of this singular universe delivered to our eager curiosity.

I think for the reasons before adduced, that it is the first of these two researches which ought to occupy us in the first place. Consequently I shall go back to the point at which I endeavoured to trace the plan; and I shall permit myself to repeat here what I then said in my logic, chap. 9th, page 432. Obliged to be consequent, I must be pardoned for recalling the point from whence I set out.

"This second manner I have said of considering "our individuals, presents us a system of phenome-"na so different from the first, that we can scarcely "believe it appertains to the same beings, seen "merely under a different aspect. Doubtless we "could conceive man as only receiving impressions, "recollecting, comparing and combining them al-"ways with a perfect indifference. He would then "be only a being, *knowing and understanding* "without *passion*, properly so called (relatively to "himself) and without *action* relatively to other be-"ings, for he would have no motive to *will*, and "no reason and no means to *act;* and certainly "on this supposition whatever were his faculties "for judging and knowing they would rest in "great stagnation, for want of a stimulant and "agent to exercise them. But this is not man; he "is a being *willing* in consequence of his impres-"sions and of his knowledge, and *acting* in conse-

"quence of his will.* It is that which constitutes "him on the one part susceptible of sufferings and "enjoyments, of happiness and misery, ideas correla-"tive and inseparable, and on the other part capable "of influence and of power. It is that which causes "him to have *wants* and *means*, and consequently "*rights* and *duties*, either merely when he has re-"lation with inanimate beings only, or more still "when he is in contact with other beings, suscepti-"ble also of enjoying and suffering; for the rights "of a sensible being are all in its wants, and its "duties in its means; and it is to be remarked that "weakness in all its forms is always and essenti-"ally the principle of rights; and that power, in "whatsoever sense we take this word, is not and "can never be but the source of duties, that is to "say of rules for the manner of employing this pow-"er." Where there is nothing, the old proverb justly says the king loses his right: but a king as another person cannot lose his rights, but in as much as another individual loses his duties in regard to him; which is saying in an inverse sense, that he who can do nothing, has no more duties to fulfil, has no longer any rule to follow for the employment of his power, since it has become null. That is very true.

Wants and *means*, *rights* and *duties*, arise then from the faculty of will; if man willed nothing he would have nothing of all these. But to have wants and means, rights and duties, is to *have*, is to *possess*, something. These are so many species of property, taking this word in its most extensive

* We may say as much of all animated beings which we know, and even of all those we imagine.

signification: They are things which appertain to us. Our means are even a real property, and the first of all, in the most restrained sense of the term. Thus the ideas, *wants* and *means*, *rights* and *duties*, imply the idea of *property*; and the ideas of *riches* and *deprivation*, *justice* and *injustice*, which are derived from them, could not exist without that of *property*. We must begin then by explaining this latter; and this can only be done by remounting to its origin. Now this idea of *property* can only be founded on the idea of personality. For if an individual had not a consciousness of his own existence, distinct and separate from every other, he could possess nothing, he could have nothing peculiar to himself. We must first therefore examine and determine the idea of *personality*; but before proceeding on this examination, there is yet a necessary preliminary; it is to explain with clearness and precision what the willing faculty is, from which we maintain that all these ideas arise, and on account of which we wish to give its history. We have no other means of seeing clearly how this faculty produces these ideas, and how all the consequences which result from it may be regarded as its effects It is thus that always by remounting, or rather by descending step by step, we are inevitably led to the study and observation of our intellectual faculties, whenever we wish to penetrate to the bottom of whatever subject engages us. This truth is perhaps more precious in itself than all those we shall be able to collect in the course of our work. I will commence then by an exposition of that in which the willing faculty consists.

This faculty, or the *will*, is one of the four primordial faculties, which we have recognized in the human understanding, and even in that of all animated beings, and into which we have seen that the faculty of *thinking* or of *feeling* necessarily resolves itself when we decompose it into its true elements, and when we admit into it nothing factitious.

We have considered the faculty of willing as the fourth and last of these four primitive and necessary subdivisions of sensibility; because in every desire, in every act of willing or volition, in a word, in every propensity whatsoever, we can always conceive the act of experiencing an impression, that of judging it good either to seek or avoid, and even that of recollecting it to a certain point, since by the very nature of the act of judging we have seen that the idea, which is the subject of every judgment, can always be considered as a representation of the first impression which this idea has made. Thus more or less confusedly, more or less rapidly, an animated being has always felt, recollected and judged, previously to willing.

It must not be concluded from this analysis that I consider the willing faculty as only that of having definitive and studied sentiments which are specially called desires, and which may be called express and formal acts of the will. On the contrary I believe that to have a just idea of it, we must form one much more extensive; and nothing previously established prevents us from it: for since we have said that even in a desire the most mechanical, and the most sudden, and in a determination the most instinctive, the most purely organic, we ought always to conceive the acts of feeling, recollecting and judging, as therein implicitly and imperceptibly included, and as having necessarily preceded it, were it only for an inappreciable instant, we can without contradicting ourselves regard all these propensities, even the most sudden and unstudied, as appertaining to the faculty of willing; though we have made it the fourth and the last of the elementary faculties of our intelligence. I even think it is necessary to do so, and that the will is really and properly the general and universal faculty of finding one thing preferable to another, that of being so affected as to love better such an impression, such a sentiment, such an action, such a possession, such an object, than such another. *To love* and *to hate* are words solely relative to this faculty, which would have no signification if it did not exist; and its action takes place on every occasion on which our *sensibility experiences any attraction or repulsion whatsoever.* At least it is thus I conceive the will in all its generality; and it is by proceeding from this manenr of conceiving it that I will attempt to explain its effects and consequences.

Without doubt the will, thus conceived, is a part of sensibility. The faculty of being affected in a particular manner cannot but be a part of the faculty of being affected in general. But it is a distinct mode of it, and one which may be separated from it in thought. We cannot will without a cause, (this is a thing very necessary to be remarked, and never to be forgotten,) thus we cannot will without having felt, but we may always feel in such a manner as never to will. We have already said that we can imagine man, or any other animated and sensible being, as feeling in such a manner that every thing would be equal to him; that all his affections, although distinct, would be indifferent to him; and that consequently he could neither desire nor fear any thing; that is to say he could not will, for to desire and to fear is to will: and to will is never but to desire something and to fear the contrary, or reciprocally. On this supposition an animated and sensible being would yet be a feeling being. He could even be discerning and knowing, that is to say judging. It will be sufficient for this that he should feel the difference of his various perceptions, and the different circumstances of each, although incapable of a predilection for any of them, or for any of the combinations of them which he can make; only, and we have before made the remark, the knowledge of the animated being thus constituted would necessarily be very limited. Because his faculty of knowing would have no motive of action; and his faculty of acting, if even it existed, could not exercise itself with intention, since to have an intention he must have a desire, and every desire supposes a preference of some sort.

I will observe, by the way, that this supposition of a perfect indifference in sensibility shows very clearly, in my opinion, that it is erroneously that certain persons have wished to make of what they call our *sentiments* and *affections*, modifications of our being essentially different from those which they name *perceptions* or *ideas*, and refuse to comprehend them under those general denominations of *perceptions* or *ideas*: for the quality of being effective, which certain of our perceptions have, is but a particular circumstance, an accidental quality, with which all our modifications might be endowed; and of which, as we have just seen, all might likewise be deprived. But they would not be the less, as they are in effect *perceptions,* that is to say things perceived or felt. The proof is that some of these modifications, after having possessed the quality of being effective, lose it by the effect of habit, and others which acquire it through reflection, all without ceasing to be perceived, and consequently without ceasing to be perceptions. I think therefore that the word *perception* is truly the generic term.

As to the distinction established between the words *perception* and *idea,* I do not think it more legitimate if founded on the pretended property of an idea being an image. For the idea of a *peartree* is no more the image of a tree, than the perception of the relation of three to four is the image of the difference of these two figures, and no one of the modifications of our sensibility is the image of any thing which takes place around us. I think then, that we may regard the words *perception* and *idea* as synonimous in their most extensive signification, and for the same reasons the words *think* and *feel* as equivalent also when taken in all their generality: For all our thoughts are things felt; and if they were not felt they would be nothing; and sensibility is the general phenomenon which constitutes and comprehends the whole existence of an animated being, at least for himself; and inasmuch as he is an *animated* being, it is the only condition which can render him a *thinking being.*

However this may be, none of the animated beings which we know, nor even of those we can imagine, are indifferent to all their perceptions. It is always comprised in their sensibility, in their faculty of being affected, of their being so affected as that certain perceptions appear to them what we call agreeable, and certain others disagreeable. Now it is this which constitutes the faculty of willing. Now that we have formed to ourselves a perfectly clear idea of it we shall easily be able to see how this faculty produces the ideas of personality and property.

SECTION SECOND.

From the faculty of willing arise the ideas of *personality* and *property*.

Every man who pronounces the word *I* (*myself*) without being a metaphysician understands very well what he means to say, and yet being a metaphysician he often succeeds very badly in giving an account of it, or in explaining it. We will endeavour to accomplish this by the aid of some very simple reflections.

It is not our body such as it is to others, and such as it appears to them which we call our *self*. The proof is that we know very well to say how our body will be when we shall exist no more, that is to say when our *self* shall be no more. There are then two very distinct beings.

It is not moreover any of the particular faculties we possess, which is for us the same thing as *our self.* For we say I have the faculty of walking, of eating, sleeping, of breathing, &c. Thus *I* or my *self*, who possess, am a thing distinct from the thing possessed.

Is it the same with the general faculty of feeling? At the first glance it appears that the answer must be yes, since I say in the same manner I have the faculty of feeling. Notwithstanding, here we find a great difference if we penetrate further. For if I ask myself how I know that I have the faculty of walking? I answer I know it because I feel it, or because I experience it, because I see it, which is still to feel it. But if I ask myself how I know that I feel, I am obliged to answer I know it because I feel it. The faculty of feeling is then that which manifests to us all the others, without which none of them would exist for us, whilst it manifests itself that it is its own principle to itself; that it is that beyond which we are not able to remount, and which constitutes our existence; that it is every thing for *us;* that it is the same thing as *ourselves.* I feel because I feel: I feel because I exist; and I do not exist but because I feel. Then my existence and my sensibility are one and the same thing. Or in other words the existence of *myself* and the sensibility of *myself* are two identical beings.

If we pay attention that in discourse *I* or *myself* signifies always the moral being or person who speaks, we shall find that (to express ourselves with exactness) instead of saying *I have the faculty of walking* I ought to say the faculty of feeling, which constitutes the moral person who speaks to you has the property of reacting on his legs in such a manner that his body walks. And instead of saying *I have the faculty of feeling*, I ought to say the faculty of feeling which constitutes the moral person who speaks to you exists in the body by which he speaks to you. These modes of expression are odd and unusual I agree, but in my opinion they paint the fact with much truth; for in all our conversations, as in all our relations, it is always one faculty of feeling which addresses itself to another.

The *self* of each of us is therefore for him his proper *sensibility*, whatsoever be the nature of this sensibility; or what he calls his mind, if he has a decided opinion of the nature of the principle of this same sensibility. It is so true that it is this that we all understand by our *self*, that we all regard apparent death as the end of our being, or as a passage to another existence, according as we think that it extinguishes or does not extinguish all sentiment. It is then the sole fact of sensibility which gives us the idea of personality, that is to say which makes us perceive that we are a *being*, and which constitutes for us ourself, our being.

There is, however, and we have already remarked it,* another of our faculties with which we often identify our *self*, that is our will. We say indifferently it depends on me, or it depends on my will to do such or such a thing; but this observation very far from contradicting the preceding analysis confirms it, for the faculty of willing is but a mode of the faculty of feeling; it is our faculty of feeling so modified as to render it capable to enjoy

* See vol. 1st. chap. 13th, page 295, second edition.

and to suffer, and to react on our organs. Thus to take the will as the equivalent of *self*, is to take a part for the whole; it is to regard as the equivalent of this *self* the portion of sensibility which constitutes all its energy, that from which we can scarcely conceive it separated, and without which it would be almost null, if it would not even be entirely annihilated. There is then nothing there contrary to what we have just established. It remains then well understood and admitted that the *self* or the moral *person* of every animated being, conceived as distinct from the organs it causes to move, is either simply the abstract existence which we call the *sensibility* of this individual, which results from his organization or a *monade* without extension; which is supposed eminently to possess this sensibility, and which is also clearly an abstract being (if indeed we comprehend this supposition,) or a little body, subtile, etherial, imperceptible, impalpable, endowed with this sensibility and which is still very nearly an abstraction. These three suppositions are indifferent for all which is to follow. In all three *sensibility* is found; and in all three also it alone constitutes the *self*, or the moral person of the individual, whether it be but a phenomenon resulting from his organization, or a property of a spiritual or corporeal mind resident within him.

There remains then but one question, which is to know if this idea of *personality*, this consciousness of *self*, would arise in us from our sensibility in the case in which it would not be followed by *will*, in the case in which it would be deprived of this mode which causes it to enjoy and suffer, and to react on our organs, which in a word renders it capable of action and of passion. This question cannot be resolved by facts, for we know no sensibility of this kind, and if any such existed it could not manifest itself to our means of knowledge. For the same reason the question is more curious than useful; but whatever is curious has an indirect utility, above all in these matters which can never be viewed on too many different sides: we must not then neglect it.

On the point in question we certainly cannot pronounce with assurance that a being which should feel without affection, properly so called, and without reaction on its organs, would not have the idea of *personality*, and that of the existence of its *self*. It even appears to me probable that it would have the idea of the existence of this *self*: for in fact to feel any thing whatever, is to feel its *self* feeling, it is to know its *self* feeling: it is to have the possibility of distinguishing *self* from that which *self* feels; from the modifications of *self*. But at the same time it is beyond doubt that the being which should thus know its own *self* would not know it by opposition with other beings, from which it would be able to distinguish and separate it; since it would know only *itself* and its modes. It would be for itself the true infinite or indefinite, as I have elsewhere remarked,* without term or limit of any kind, not knowing any thing else. It would not then properly know itself in the sense we attach to the word to know, which always imports the idea of circumscription and of speciality; and conse-

* See vol. 3d, chap. 5, p. 27.

quently it would not have the idea of *individuality* and of *personality*, in opposition and distinction from other beings as we have it. We may already assure ourselves that this idea, such as it is in us and for us, is a creation and an effect of our faculty of willing; and this explains very clearly why, although the sole faculty of feeling simply constitutes and establishes our existence, yet we confound and identify by preference our *self* with our *will*. Here I think is a first point elucidated.

A thing still more certain, perhaps, and which will advance us a step further, is that if it is possible that the idea of individuality and personality should exist in the manner we have said, in a being conceived to be endowed with sensibility without will, at least it is impossible it should produce there the idea of property such as we have it. For our idea of property is privative and exclusive: it imports the idea that the thing possessed appertains to a sensible being, and appertains to none but him, to the exclusion of all others. Now it cannot be that it exists thus in the head of a being which knows nothing but itself, which does not know that any other beings besides itself exists. If then we should suppose that this being knows its *self* with sufficient accuracy to distinguish it from its modes, and to regard its different modifications as attributes of this *self*, as things which this *self* possesses, this being would still not have completely our idea of *property*. For this it is necessary to have the idea of *personality* very completely, and such as we have just seen that we form it when we are susceptible of *passion* and of *action*.

It is then proved that this idea of property is an effect, a production of our willing faculty.

But what is very necessary to be remarked, because it has many consequences, is, that if it be certain that the idea of property can arise only in a being endowed with will, it is equally certain that in such a being it arises necessarily and inevitably in all its plenitude; for as soon as this individual knows accurately itself, or its moral person, and its capacity to enjoy and to suffer, and to act necessarily, it sees clearly also that this self is the exclusive proprietor of the body which it animates, of the organs which it moves, of all their passions and their actions; for all this finishes and commences with this *self*, exists but by it, is not moved but by its acts, and no other moral person can employ the same instruments nor be affected in the same manner by their effects. The idea of property and of exclusive property arises then necessarily in a sensible being from this alone, that it is susceptible of passion and action; and it rises in such a being because nature has endowed it with an inevitable and inalienable property, that of its individuality.

It was necessary there should be a natural and necessary property, as there exists an artificial and conventional one; for there can never be any thing in art which has not its radical principle in nature;—we have already made the observation elsewhere.* If our gestures and our cries had not the natural and inevitable effect of denoting the ideas which affect us, they never would have become their artificial

* See on this subject, vol. 1st. chap. 16th, page 339, second edition, and different parts of the 2d and 3d volumes.

and conventional signs. If it were not in nature that every solid body sustained above our heads necessarily sheltered us we should never have had houses made expressly for shelter. In the same manner, if there never had been natural and inevitable *property* there never would have been any artificial or conventional. This is universally the case, and we cannot too frequently repeat, man creates nothing, he makes nothing absolutely new or extra-natural, (if we may be allowed the expression) he never does any thing but draw consequences and make combinations from that which already is. It is also as impossible for him to create an idea or a relation which has not its source in nature as to give himself a sense which has no relation with his natural senses. From this it also follows that in every research which concerns man it is necessary to arrive at this first type; for as long as we do not see the natural model of an artificial institution which we examine we may be sure we have not discovered its generation, and consequently we do not know it completely.

This observation will meet with many explications. It appears to me that we have not always paid sufficient attention to it, and that it is for this reason we have often discoursed on the subject which now occupies us in a very useless and vague manner. We have brought property to a solemn trial at bar and exhibited the reasons for and against it as if it depended on us, whether there should or should not be property in this world. But this is entirely to mistake our nature. It seems were we to listen to certain philosophers and legislators that at a precise instant people have taken into their heads spontaneously, and without cause, to say *thine* and *mine*, and that they could and even should have dispensed with it. But *the thine* and *the mine* were never invented. They were acknowledged the day on which we could say *thee* and *me;* and the idea of *me* and *thee* or rather of *me* and something *other than me*, has arisen, if not the very day on which a feeling being has experienced impressions, at least the one on which, in consequence of these impressions, he has experienced the sentiment of willing, the possibility of acting, which is a consequence thereof, and a resistance to this sentiment and to this act. When afterwards among these resisting beings, consequently other than *himself*, the feeling and willing being has known that there were some feeling like himself, it has been forced to accord to them a *personality* other than his own, a *self* other than his own and different from his own. And it always has been impossible, as it always will be, that that which is *his* should not for him be different from that which is *theirs*. It was not requisite therefore to discuss at first whether it is well or ill that there exists such or such species of property, the advantages and inconveniences of which we shall see by the sequel; but it was necessary first of all to recognize that there is a property, fundamental, anterior and superior to every institution, from which will always arise all the sentiments and dis-sentiments which are derived from all the others; for there is property, if not precisely every where that there is an individual sentient, at least every where that there is an individual willing in consequence of his sentiment, and acting in consequence of his will. These, or I am greatly mistaken, are eternal truths, against which will fail all the declamations that have nothing for their base but an ignorance of our true existence; and which are indebted to this ignorance for the great credit they have enjoyed at different times, and in different countries.

As no authority can impose on me when it is contrary to evidence, I will say frankly that the same forgetfulness of the true condition of our being is found in this famous precept, so much boasted: *Love thy neighbour as thyself.* It exhorts us to a sentiment which is very good and very useful to propagate, but which is certainly also very badly expressed; for to take this expression in all the rigour of the injunction it is inexecutable; it is as if they should tell us, *with your eyes, such as they are, see your own visage as you see that of others.* This cannot be. Without doubt we are able to love another as much and even more than ourselves, in the sense that we should rather die, bearing with us the hope of preserving his life, than to live and to suffer the grief of losing him. But to love him exactly as ourself, and otherwise than relatively to ourself, once more I say is impossible. It would be necessary for this, to live his life as we do our own.* This has no meaning for beings constituted as we are. It is contrary to the work of our creation, in what manner soever it has been operated.

* It is in consequence of a confused notion of this truth that people have never imagined expressions more tender, than to call one *my life, my heart, my soul;* it is as though one should call him *myself.* There is always something hyperbolical in these expressions.

I am very far from saying the same things of this other precept, which people regard as almost synonimous with the first. *Love ye one another, and the law is accomplished.* This is truly admirable, both for its form and substance. It is also as conformable to our nature as the other is repugnant to it; and it enounces perfectly a very profound truth. Effectively sentiments of benevolence being for us, under every imaginable relation, the source of all our good of every kind, and the universal means of diminishing and remedying all our evils as much as possible, as long as we maintain them amongst ourselves the great law of our happiness is accomplished, in as great a degree as possible.

I shall be accused perhaps of futility for the distinction which I establish between two maxims, to which nearly the same meaning has been commonly attributed; but it will be wrong. It is so different to present to men as a rule of their conduct a general principle, drawn from the recesses of their nature, or one repugnant to it, and it leads to consequences so distant among themselves, that one must never have reflected on it at all not to have perceived all its importance. To myself it appears such, that I cannot conceive that two maxims so dissimilar should have emanated from the same source;* †

* I conclude from hence that the expression of the one or the other of these precepts, and perhaps of both, has been altered by men, who did not really understand either. I shall often have occasion to make reflections of this kind, because they are applicable to many of these maxims which pass from age to age.

† The first is from Leviticus, chap. xix. The other is from the gospel of St. John, chap. xiii. See the remark in the questions on the miracles, Voltaire vol. 60, page 186. You will be astonished to see that Voltaire considered these two maxims as identical.

for the one manifests to me the most profound ignorance, and the other the most profound knowledge of human nature. One would lead us to compose the romance of man, and the other his history. The one consecrates the existence of natural property, resulting from individuality, and the other seems to disregard it, [la meconnaitre.] Perhaps it may be wondered that I should treat at the same time the question of the property of all our riches, and that of all our sentiments, and thus mingle economy and morality; but, when we penetrate to their fundamental basis, it does not appear to me possible to separate either these two orders of things or their study. In proportion as we advance, the objects separate and subdivide themselves, and it becomes necessary to examine them separately; but in their principles they are intimately united. We should not have the property of any of our goods whatsoever if we had not that of our wants, which is nothing but that of our sentiments; and all these properties are inevitably derived from the sentiment of personality, from the consciousness of our *self*.

It is then quite as useless to the purpose of morality or economy, to discuss whether it would not be better that nothing should appertain exclusively to each one of us, as it would be to the purpose of grammar to enquire whether it would not be more advantageous that our actions should not be the *signs* of the ideas and the sentiments which produce them. In every case it would be to ask whether it would not be desirable that we should be quite different from what we are; and indeed it would be to enquire, whether it would not be better that we did not exist at all; for these conditions being changed our existence would not be conceivable. It would not be altered, it would be annihilated.

It remains therefore certain that the *thine* and the *mine* are necessarily established amongst men; from this alone, that they are individuals feeling, willing, and acting distinctly the one from the other, that they have each one the inalienable, incommutable, and inevitable property, in their individuality and its faculties; and that consequently the idea of *property* is the necessary result, if not of the sole phenomenon of pure sensibility, at least of that of sensibility united to the will. Thus we have found how the sentiment of *personality* or the idea of *self*, and that of property which flows from it necessarily, are derived from our faculty of willing. Now we may enquire with success, how this same faculty produces all our *wants* and all our means.

SECTION THIRD.

From the faculty of willing arise all our *wants* and all our *means*.

If we had not the idea of *personality*, and that of *property*, that is to say the consciousness of our *self*, and that of the *possession* of its modifications, we should certainly never have either *wants* or *means*; for to whom would appertain this *suffering* and this *power*. We should not exist for ourselves; but as soon as we recognize ourselves as possessors of our existence, and of its modes, we are necessarily by this alone a compound of weakness and of strength, of wants and means, of suffering and power, of passion and action, and consequently of rights and duties. It is this we are now to explain.

I commence by noticing that, conformably to the idea I have before given of the willing faculty, I will give indifferently the name of *desire* or of *will* to all the acts of this faculty, from the propensity the most instinctive to the determination the most studied; and I request then that it may be recollected that it is solely because we perform such acts that we have the ideas of *personality* and of *property*. Now every desire is a want, and all our wants consist in a desire of some sort; thus the same intellectual acts, emanating from our willing faculty, which cause us to acquire the distinct and complete idea of our personality, our *self*, and of the exclusive property of all its modes, are also those which render us susceptible of *wants*, and which constitute all our wants. This will appear very clearly.

In the first place every desire is a want. This is not doubtful, since a sensible being, who desires any thing whatsoever, has from this circumstance alone a want to possess the thing desired, or rather, and more generally we may say, that he experiences the want of the cessation of his desire; for every desire is in itself a suffering as long as it continues. It does not become an enjoyment but when it is satisfied, that is to say when it ceases.

It is difficult at first to believe that every desire is a suffering; because there are certain desires, the birth of which in an animated being is always, or almost always, accompanied by a sentiment of well being. The desire of eating for example, that of the physical pleasures of love, are generally in an individual the results of a state of health, of which he has a consciousness that is agreeable to him. Many others are in the same case; but this circumstance must not deceive us. These are the simultaneous manners of being of which we have spoken in our logic,* which mingle themselves with the ideas, come at the same time with them and alter them; but which must not be confounded with them which consequently it is necessary well to distinguish from desire in itself. For first, they do not always co-exist with it. We have often the want of eating, and even a violent inclination to the act of reproduction, in consequence of sickly dispositions, and without any sentiment of well being; and it is the same of other examples which might be chosen. Secondly, were this not to happen, it would not be less true that the sentiment of well being is distinct and different from that of desire; and that that of desire is always in itself a torment, a painful sentiment as long as it continues. The proof is, that it is always the desire of being delivered from that state, whatsoever it is, in which we actually are; which consequently appears actually a state of uneasiness, more or less displeasing. Now in this sense a manner of being is always in effect what it appears to be, since it consists only in what it appears to be to him who experiences it: a desire then is always a suffering either light or profound, according to its force, and consequently a want of some kind. It is not

* See logic, vol. 3d, chap. 6th page 315, and following.

necessary for the truth of this that this desire should be founded on a real want, that is to say on a just sentiment of our true interest; for, whether well or ill founded, while it exists it is a manner of being felt and incommodious, and from which we have consequently a want of being delivered. Thus every desire is a want.

But moreover all our wants, from the most purely mechanical to the most spiritualized, are but the want of satisfying a desire. Hunger is but a desire of eating, or at least of relief from the state of langour which we experience; as the want, the thirst of riches, or that of glory, is but the desire of possessing these advantages, and of avoiding indigence or obscurity.

It is true, however, that if we experience desires without real wants, we have also often real wants without experiencing desires; in this sense that many things are often very necessary to our greater well being, and even to our preservation, without our perceiving it, and consequently without our desiring them. Thus for example, it is certain that I have the greatest interest, or if you please want, that certain combinations, of which I have no suspicion, should not take place within me, and from which it will result that I shall have a fever this evening; but to speak exactly I have not at present the effective want of counteracting these injurious combinations, since I am not aware of their existence; whereas I shall really have the actual want of being delivered from the fever, when I shall suffer the anguish of it, and because I shall suffer the anguish of it; for if the fever were not of a nature to produce in me, for some reason or other, the desire of its cessation, when I should be aware of its proximate or remote effects, I should not have in any manner the want of causing it to cease. We may absolutely say the same things of all the combinations, which take place in the physical or moral order, without our being aware of, or without our foreseeing, the consequences. If then it be true, as we have seen, that every desire is a want, it is not less so that every actual want is a desire. Thus we may lay it down as a general thesis, that *our desires are the source of all our wants*, none of which would exist without them. For we cannot too often repeat it, we should be really impassive if we had no desires; and if we were impassive we should have no wants. I must not be reproached with having taken time for this explication; we cannot proceed too slowly at first: and if I overleap no intermediate proofs, I omit nevertheless, many accessaries, at least all those which are not indispensable.

A first property then of our desires is now well explained; and it is the only one they have, so long as our sensitive system acts and re-acts only on itself. But so soon as it re-acts on our muscular system, the sentiment of willing acquires a second property very different from the first, and which is not less important. It is that of directing all our *actions*, and by this of being the source of all our *means*.

When I say that our desires direct all our actions; it is not that many movements are not operated within us, which the sentiment of willing does not in any manner precede, and which consequently are not the effect of any desire. Of this number are particularly all those which are necessary to the commencement, maintenance and continuation of our life. But first it is permitted to doubt whether at first, and in the origin, they have not taken place in virtue of certain determinations or tendencies really felt by the living molecules, which would make them still the effect of a will more or less obscure; unless it be by the all powerful effect of habit or by the preponderance of certain sentiments more general and predominant, that they become insensible to the animated individual, that is to say, to all results of the combinations which they operate, and finally if it is not for this reason, that they are entirely withdrawn from the empire of perceptible will, or from its sentiment of desiring and willing. These are things of which it is impossible for us to have complete certitude; besides these movements, vulgarly and with reason named involuntary, are certainly the cause and the basis of our living existence: but they furnish us no means of modifying, varying, succouring, defending, ameliorating it, &c. They cannot therefore properly be placed in the rank of our means, unless we mean to say that our existence itself is our first mean, which is very true but very insignificant; for it is the datum without which we should have nothing to say, and certainly should say nothing. Thus this first observation does not prevent its being true that our will directs all our actions, which can be regarded as the means of supplying our wants.

The movements of which we have just spoken are not the only ones in us which are involuntary. They are all continued or at least very frequent, and in general regular. But there are others involuntary also, which are more rare, less regular, and which depend more or less on a convulsive and sickly state. The involuntary movements of this second species cannot, any more than the others, be regarded as making part of our individual power. Generally they have no determinate object. Often even they have grievous and pernicious effects for us, and which take place although foreseen, and contrary to our desires. Their independence of our will then does not prevent our general observation from being just. Thus, putting aside these two species of involuntary movements, we may say with truth, that our desires have the effect eminently remarkable of directing all our actions, at least all those that really merit this name, and which are for us the means of procuring enjoyments or knowledge, which knowledge is also an enjoyment; since these are things desired and useful. And we must comprehend in the number of these *actions* our intellectual operations; for they also are for us *means*, and even the most important of all, since they direct the employment of all the others.

Now to complete the proof that the acts of our will are the source of all our means, without exception, it only remains to show that the actions submitted to our will are absolutely the only means we have of supplying our wants, or otherwise satisfying our desires; that is to say, that our physical and moral force, and the use we make of them, compose exactly all our riches.

To recognize this truth in all its details, it would be necessary that we should have already followed all the consequences of the different employments of our faculties, and to have seen their effect in the formation of all that we call our riches of every kind. Now it is this we have not yet been able to do, and which we will do in the sequel: it will even be a considerable part of our study. But from this moment we may clearly see that nature, in placing man in a corner of this vast universe, in which he appears but as an imperceptible and ephemeral insect, has given him nothing as his own but his individual and personal faculties, as well physical as intellectual. This is his sole endowment, his only original wealth, and the only source of all which he procures for himself. In effect, if even we should admit that all those beings, by which we are surrounded, have been created for us; (and assuredly it needs a great dose of vanity to imagine it, or even to believe it,) if, I say, this were so, it would not be less true that we could not appropriate one of those beings, nor convert the smallest parcel of them to our use, but by our action on them and by the employment of our faculties to this effect.

Not to take examples but in the physical line.—

A field is no means of subsistance but as we cultivate it. Game is not useful to us unless we pursue it. A lake, a river, furnish us no nourishment, but because we fish therein. Wood or any other spontaneous production of nature is of no use whatever, until we have fashioned it, or at least gathered it. To put an extreme case, were we to suppose an alimentary matter to have fallen into our mouths ready prepared, still it would be necessary, in order to assimilate it to our substance, that we should masticate, swallow and digest it. Now all these operations are so many employments of our individual force. Certainly if ever man has been doomed to labour, it was from the date of the day in which he was created a sensible being, and having members and organs; for it is not even possible to conceive that any being whatsoever could become useful to him without some action on his part, and we may well say, not only as the good and admirable La Fontaine, that *labour is a treasure;* but even that labour is our only treasure, and this treasure is very great because it surpasses all our wants. The proof is, that like the fortune of a rich man whose revenue surpasses his expenses, the funds of the enjoyment and power of the human species, taken in mass, are always sufficient although often and even always very badly husbanded.

We shall soon see all this with greater developements, and we shall see at the same time that the application of our force to different beings is the sole cause of the value of all those which have a value for us, and consequently is the source of all value; as the property of this same force which necessarily appertains to the individual who is endowed with it, and who directs it by his will, is the source of all property. But from this time I think we may safely conclude, that in the employment of our faculties, in our voluntary actions, consists all the power we have; and that consequently the acts of our will which direct these actions, are the source of all our *means*, as we have seen already that they constitute all our *wants*. Thus this fourth faculty, and last mode of our sensibility, to which we owe the complete ideas of *personality* and *property*, is that which renders us proprietors of *wants* and *means*, of *passion* and of *action*, of *suffering* and of *power*. From these ideas arise those of riches and poverty.

Before proceeding further let us see in what these last consist.

SECTION FOURTH.

From the faculty of willing arise also the ideas of *riches* and of *poverty*.

If we had not the distinct consciousness of our *self*, and consequently the ideas of *personality* and of property, we should have no *wants*. All these arise from our desires. And if we had not wants, we should not have the ideas of *riches* and of *poverty*; because to be rich is to possess the means of supplying our wants, and to be poor is to be deprived of these means. An useful or agreeable thing, that is to say a thing of which the possession is an article of riches, is never but a means proximate or remote, of satisfying a want or a desire of some kind; and if we had neither wants nor desires, which are the same things, we should have neither the possession nor the privation of the means of satisfying them.

To take these things in this generality, we perceive plainly that our riches are not composed solely of a precious stone, or of a mass of metal, of an estate in land, or of an utensil, or even of a store of eatables, or a habitation. The knowledge of a law of nature, the habit of a technical process, the use of a language by which to communicate with those of our kind, and to increase our force by theirs, or at least not to be disturbed by theirs in the exercise of our own, the enjoyment of conventions established, and of institutions created in this spirit, are so far the riches of the individual and of the species: for these are so many things useful towards increasing our means, or at least for the free use of them, that is to say, according to our will, and with the least possible obstacle, whether on the part of men or of nature, which is to augment their power, their energy, and their effect.

We call all these *goods*; for by contraction we give the name of *goods* to all those things that contribute to do us good, to augment our *well being*, to render our manner of being good or better; that is to say, to all those things, the possession of which is a good Now whence come all those goods? We have already summarily seen, and we shall see it more in detail in the sequel. It is from the just, that is to say from the legitimate, employment, according to the laws of nature, which we make of our faculties. We do not often find a diamond, but because we search for it with intelligence; we have not a mass of metal, but because we have studied the means of procuring it. We do not possess a good field or a good utensil, but because we have well recognised the properties of the first material, and rendered easy the manner of making it useful.

We have no provision whatsoever, or even a shelter, but because we have simplified the operations necessary for forming the one, or for constructing the other. It is then always from the employment of our faculties that all these goods arise.

Now all these goods have amongst us, to a certain point, a value determinate and fixed. They even have always two. The one is that of the sacrifices which their acquisition costs us; the other that of the advantages which their possession procures us. When I fabricate an utensil for my use, it has for me the double value of the labour which it costs me in the first place, and of that which it will save me in the sequel. I make a bad employment of my force, if its construction costs me more labour than its possesion will save me. It is the same, if instead of making this utensil, I buy it, if the things I give in return have cost me more labor than the utensil would have cost me in making it, or if they would have saved me more labour than this will, I make a bad bargain, I lose more than I gain, I relinquish more than I acquire. This is evident. In the acquisition of any other good than an instrument of labour, the thing is not so clear. However, since it is certain that our physical and moral faculties are our only original riches; that the employment of these faculties, labour of some kind, is our only primitive treasure; and that it is always from this employment that all those things which we call *goods* arise, from the most necessary to the most purely agreeable, it is certain, in like manner, that all these *goods* are but a representation of the labour which has produced them; and that if they have a value, or even two distinct ones, they can only derive these values from that of the labour from which they emanate. Labour itself then has a value; it has then *even* two different ones, for no being can communicate a property which it has not. Yes labour has these two values, the one natural and necessary, the other more or less conventional and eventual. This will be seen very clearly.

An animated being, that is to say sensible and willing, has wants unceasingly reproduced, to the satisfaction of which is attached the continuation of his existence. He cannot provide for them but by the employment of his faculties, of his means; and if this employment (his labour) should cease during a certain time to meet these wants, his existence would end. The mass of these wants, is then the natural and necessary measure of the mass of labour which he can perform whilst they cause themselves to be felt; for if he employs this mass of labour for his direct and immediate use it must suffice for his service. If he consecrates it to another, this other must at least do for him, during this time, what he would have done for himself. If he employs it on objects of an utility less immediate and more remote, this utility, when realised, must at least replace the objects of an urgent utility, which he will have consumed whilst he was occupied with those less necessary. Thus this sum of indispensable wants, or rather that of the value of the objects necessary to supply them, is the natural and necessary measure of the value of the labour performed in the same time. This value is that which the labour inevitably costs. This is the first of the two values, the existence of which we have announced; it is purely natural and necessary.

The second value of our labour, that of what it produces, is from its nature eventual: It is often conventional and always more variable than the first. It is eventual, for no man in commencing any labour whatever, even when it is for his own account, can entirely assure himself of its product; a thousand circumstances, which do not depend on him and which often he cannot foresee, augment or diminish this product. It is often conventional; for when this same man undertakes a labour for another, the quantity of its product, which will result to himself, depends on that which the other shall have agreed to give him in return for his pains, whether the convention were made before the execution of the labour, as with day labourers or hirelings, or does not take place until after the labour has been perfected, as with merchants and manufacturers. Finally this second value of labour is more variable than its natural and necessary value; because it is determined not by the wants of him who performs the labour, but by the wants and means of him who profits from it, and it is influenced by a thousand concurrent causes, which it is not yet time to develope.

But even the natural value of labour is not of an absolute fixture: for first the wants of a man in a given time, even those which may be regarded as the most urgent, are susceptible of a certain latitude; and the flexibility of our nature is such that these wants are restrained or extended considerably by the empire of will and the effect of habit. Secondly, by the influence of favourable circumstances, of a mild climate, of a fertile soil, these wants may be largely satisfied for a given time by the effect of very little labour, while in less happy circumstances, under an inclement sky, on a sterile soil, greater efforts will be requisite to provide for them. Thus, according to the case, the labour of the same man, during the same time, must procure him a greater or smaller number of objects, or of objects more or less difficult to be acquired, solely that he may continue to exist.

By this small number of general reflections we see then, that the ideas of riches and poverty arise from our wants, that is to say from our desires, for riches consist in the possession of means of satisfying our wants, and poverty in their non-possession. We call these means *goods*, because they do us good. They are all the product and the representation of a certain quantity of labour; and they give birth in us to the idea of value, which is but a comparative idea; because they have all two values, that of the goods which they cost and that of the goods which they produce. Since these goods are but the representation of the labour which has produced them, it is then from labour they derive these two values. It has them then itself. In effect labour has necessarily these two values. The second is eventual, most generally conventional, and always very variable. The first is natural and necessary; it is not however of an absolute fixture, but it is always comprehended within certain limits.

Such is the connexion of general ideas, which necessarily follow one another on the first inspection of this subject. It shows us the application and the proof of several great truths previously established. In the first place we see that we never create any thing absolutely new and *extra-natural.* Thus, since we have the idea of value, and since artificial and conventional values exist among us, it was necessary there should be somewhere a natural and necessary value. Thus the labour, from whence all our goods emanate, has a value of this kind, and communicates it to them. This value is that of the objects necessary to the satisfaction of the wants, which inevitably arise in an animated being during the continuance of his labour.

Secondly, we have seen further, that to measure any quantity whatsoever, is always to compare it with a quantity of the same species, and that it is absolutely necessary that this quantity should be of the same species, without which it could not serve as an unit and a term of comparison.* Thus, when we say that the natural and necessary value of the labor which an animated being performs during a given time is measured by the indispensable wants which arise in this being during the same time, we give really for the measure of this value the value of a certain quantity of labour; for the goods necessary to the satisfaction of these wants, do not themselves derive their natural and necessary value but from the labour which their acquisition has cost. Thus labour, our only original good, is only

* See vol. 1st, chap. 10th, page 187, and following 2d edition; and vol. 3d, chap. 9th, page 463.

valued by itself, and the unit is of the same kind as the quantities calculated.

Thirdly, in fine we have seen that, for a calculation to be just and certain, the unit must be determined in a manner the most rigorous, and absolutely invariable.† Here unhappily we are obliged to acknowledge that our unit of value is subject to variations, although comprehended within certain limits. It is an evil we cannot remedy, since it is derived from the very nature of an animated being, from his flexibility and his suppleness. We must never dissemble this evil. It was essential to recognize it. But it ought not to prevent us from making combinations of the effects of our faculties, in taking the necessary precautions; for since the variations of our sensible nature are comprehended within certain limits, we can always apply to them considerations drawn from the theory of the limits of numbers. But this observation ought to teach us how very delicate and scientific is the calculation of all moral and economical quantities, how much precaution it requires, and how imprudent it is to wish to apply to it indiscreetly the rigorous scale of numbers. However it be, as this rapid glance on the ideas of riches and poverty, derived from the sentiment of our wants, leads us to speak summarily of all our goods, we ought not to pass in silence the greatest of all, that which comprehends them all, without which none of them would exist, which we may call the only good, of a willing being, Liberty. It merits a separate article.

(†) See vol. 3d, chap. 9th, page 500, and following.

SECTION FIFTH.

From the faculty of willing arise likewise the ideas of *liberty* and *constraint*.

Nothing would be more easy than to inspire some interest in all generous souls, by commencing this chapter with a kind of hymn to this first of all the goods of sensible nature, Liberty. But these explosions of sentiment, have no object but to electrize one's self, or to excite the feelings of those whom we address. Now a man who sincerely devotes himself to the search of truth, is sufficiently animated by the end he proposes, and counts on the same disposition in all those by whom he wishes to be read. The love of what is good and true is a real passion. This passion is I believe sufficiently novel, at least it seems to me that it could not exist in all its force, but since it has been proved by reasonings, and by facts, that the happiness of man, is proportionate to the mass of his intelligence, and that the one and the other does and can increase indefinitely. But since these two truths have been demonstrated, this new passion which characterizes the epoch in which we live is not rare, whatever may be said of it, and it is as energetic and more constant than any other. Let us not then seek to excite but to satisfy it, and let us speak of liberty as coolly, as if this word itself did not put in motion all the powers of the soul.

I say that the idea of *liberty* arises from the faculty of willing; for, with Locke, I understand by liberty, the power of executing our will, of acting conformably with our desire. And I maintain, that it is impossible to attach any clear idea to this word when we give it another signification. Thus there would be no liberty were there no will; and liberty cannot exist before the birth of will. It is then real *nonsense*, to pretend that the will is free to exist or not.* And such were almost all the famous decisions, which subjugated the mind before the birth of the true study of the human understanding. Accordingly the consequences which were drawn from these pretended principles, and especially from this one, were for the most part completely absurd. But this is not the time to occupy ourselves with them.

Without doubt, we cannot too often repeat it, a sensible being cannot will without a motive, he cannot will but in virtue of the manner in which he is affected. Thus his will follows from his anterior impressions, quite as necessarily as every effect follows the cause which has the properties necessary for producing it. This necessity is neither a good nor an evil for a sensible being. It is the consequence of his nature; it is the condition of his existence; it is the datum which he cannot change, and from which he should always set out in all his speculations.

But when a will is produced in an animated being, when he has conceived any determination whatsoever, this sentiment of willing, which is always a suffering, as long as it is not satisfied, has in recompense the admirable property of reacting on the organs, of regulating the greater part of their movements, of directing the employment of almost

* See vol. 1st, chap. 13th, page 269, 2d edition.

all the faculties, and thereby of creating all the means of enjoyment and power of the sensible being, when no extraneous force restrains him, that is to say when the *willing* being is *free*.

Liberty, taken in this its most general sense, (and the only reasonable one) signifying the power of executing our will, is then the remedy of all our ills, the accomplishment of all our desires, the satisfaction of all our wants, and consequently the first of all our goods, that which produces and comprehends them all. It is the same thing as our *happiness*. It has the same limits, or rather our happiness cannot have either more or less extension than our liberty; that is to say than our power of satisfying our desires. Constraint on the contrary, whatsoever it be, is the opposite of liberty; it is the cause of all our sufferings, the source of all our ills. It is even rigorously our only evil, for every ill is always the contrariety of a desire. We should assuredly have none, if we were free to deliver ourselves from it whenever we should wish; it is truely the Oromazis and Orismanes, the good and the evil principle.

The constraint from which we suffer, or rather which we suffer, since it is itself which constitutes all suffering, may be of different natures, and is susceptible of different degrees. It is direct and immediate, or only mediate and indirect. It comes to us from animate or from inanimate beings, it is invincible or may be surmounted. That which is the effect of physical forces, which enchains the action of our faculties, is immediate, while that which is the result of different combinations of our understanding, or of certain moral considerations, is but indirect and mediate, although very real likewise. The one and the other, according to circumstances, may be insurmountable, or may be susceptible of yielding to our efforts.

In all of these different cases, we have different methods of conducting ourselves, to escape from the *suffering of constraint*, to effect the *accomplishment of our desires*, in a word to *arrive at satisfaction, at happiness*. For once again I say these three things are one and the same Of these different methods of arriving at the only end of all our efforts as of all our desires, of all our wants, as of all our means, we should always take those which are most capable of conducting us to it. This is likewise our only duty, that which comprehends all others. The mean of fulfilling this only duty, is in the first place, if our desires are susceptible of satisfaction, to study the nature of the obstacles opposed, and to do all that depends on us to surmount them; secondly, if our desires cannot be accomplished, but by submitting to other evils, that is to say by renouncing other things, which we desire, to balance the inconveniences, and decide for the least; thirdly, if the success of our desires is entirely impossible, we must renounce them, and withdraw without murmuring within the limits of our power. Thus all is reduced to the employment of our intellectual faculties: First, in properly estimating our wants, then in extending our means, as far as possible; finally in submitting to the necessity of our nature, to the invincible condition of our existence.

But I perceive that I have mentioned the word *duty*. The idea which this word expresses well merits a separate chapter. It is sufficient in this to have terminated the examination of all our goods, by showing that since all our means of happiness consist in the voluntary employment of our faculties, *Liberty*, the power of acting according to our will, includes all our goods, is our only good, and that our only duty is to encrease this power, and to use it well, that is to say so to use it as not ultimately to cramp and restrain it.

Would it be desired, before quitting this subject, to apply to this first of all goods, Liberty, the idea of value, which we have seen arise necessarily from the idea of good? And would it be asked, what is the value of liberty? It is evident that the sum of the liberty of a being feeling and willing, being the power of using his faculties according to his will, the entire value of this liberty is equal to the entire value of the employment of the faculties of this being: that if from this sum of liberty a portion only be detracted, the value of the portion detracted is equal to the value of the faculties, from the exercise of which he is debarred, and that the value of that which remains to him is the same with that of the faculties, the use of which he still preserves; and, finally, it is also manifest that, however feeble the faculties of an animated being, the absolute loss of his liberty is for him a loss truly infinite, and one to which he cannot set any price, since it is absolutely every thing for him, it is the extinction of every possibility of happiness; it is the loss of the sum total of his being; it can admit of no compensation, and deprives him of the disposal of what he might receive in return.

These general notions suffice for the moment. I will add but one reflection. It is commonly said that man, entering a state of society, sacrifices a portion of his liberty to secure the remainder. After what we have just said, this expression is not exact. It does not give a just idea either of the cause or of the effect, nor even of the origin of human societies. In the first place, man never lives completely insulated; he cannot exist thus, at least in his first infancy. Thus the state of society does not commence for him on a fixed day, or from premeditated design; it is established insensibly, and by degrees. Secondly, man in associating himself more and more, with his fellow beings, and in daily connecting himself more closely with them, by tacit or express conventions, does not calculate on diminishing his anterior liberty, or on weakening the total power of executing his will, which he previously had. He has always in view its increase. If he renounces certain modes of employing it, it is that he may be assisted, or at least not opposed, in other uses which he may wish to make of it, and which he judges more important to him. He consents that his will should be a little restrained, in certain cases, by that of his fellow beings: but it is that it may be much more powerful over all other beings, and even on these themselves on other occasions, so that the total mass of power, or of liberty, which he possesses should be thereby augmented. This I think is the idea which should be formed of the effect and the end of the gradual establishment of the social state. Whenever it does not produce this result, it does not attain its destination: but it attains it always in a greater or less degree, notwithstanding its universal and enormous imperfections. We will elsewhere develope the consequences of these observations. Now let us go on to the examination of the idea of duty.

SECTION SIXTH.

Finally, from the faculty of willing arise the ideas of *rights* and of *duties*.

The ideas of *rights* and of *duties* are, by some, said to be correspondent and correlative. I do not deny them to be so, in our social relations; but this truth, if it is one, requires many explanations. Let us examine different cases.

Let us make in the first place a supposition absolutely ideal. Let us imagine a being feeling and willing, but incapable of all action, a simple monad endowed with the faculty of willing, but deprived of a body, and of every organ on which its will can re-act, and by which it could produce any effect, or have influence on any other being. It is manifest that such a being would have no right, in the sense we often give to this word, that is to say none of those rights which comprehend the idea of a correspondent duty in another sensible being, since it is not in contact with any being whatsoever. But to the eyes of reason and of universal justice, such as the human understanding can conceive them, (for we can never speak of other things) this monad has clearly the right to satisfy his desires and to appease his wants; for this violates no law, natural or artificial. It is, on the contrary, to follow the laws of his nature and to obey the conditions of his existence.

At the same time this monad, having no power of action, no means of laboring for the satisfaction of his wants, has no duty: for it could not have the duty of employing in one way rather than another the means which it has not, of performing one action rather than another, since it cannot perform any action.

This supposition then shows us two things; first, as we have already said, that all our rights arise from wants, and all duties from means; secondly, that rights may exist, in the most general sense of this word, without correspondent duties on the part of other beings, nor even on the part of the being possessing these rights: Consequently these two ideas are not as essentially and necessarily correspondent, and correlative, as is commonly believed; for they are not so in their origin. Now let us state another hypothesis.

Let us suppose a being feeling and willing, constituted as we are, that is to say endowed with organs and faculties which his will puts in action, but completely separated from every other sensible being, and in contact only with inanimate beings, if there be such, or at least only with beings which should not manifest to him the phenomenon of sentiment, as there are many such for us. In this state this being still has not those rights, taken in the restrained sense of this word, which embrace the idea of a correspondent duty in another sensible being, since he is not in relation with any being of this kind; yet he has clearly the general right, like the monad of which we have just spoken, of procuring for himself the accomplishment of his desires, or, which is the same thing, of providing for his wants; because this is for him, as for it, to obey the laws of his nature, and to conform himself to the condition of his existence; and this being is such that it cannot be moved by any other impulsion, nor have any other principle of action. This willing being has then, in this case, all imaginable rights. We may even see that his rights are truly infinite, since they are bounded by nothing. At least they have no limits but those of his desires themselves, from which these emanate, and which are their only source.

But here there is something more than in the first hypothesis. This being, endowed like ourselves with organs and faculties which his will puts into motion, is not as the simple monad of which we spoke before. He has means, therefore he has duties; for he has the duty of well employing these means. But every duty supposes a punishment incurred by an infraction of it, a law which pronounces this punishment, a tribunal which applies this law; accordingly in the case in question the punishment of the being of which we speak, for not rightly employing his means, is to see them produce effects less favorable to his satisfaction, or even to see them produce such as are entirely destructive of it. The laws which pronounce this punishment, are those of the organization of this willing and acting being:

they are the conditions of his existence. The tribunal which applies these laws is that of necessity itself, against which he cannot guard himself. Thus the being which occupies us has, incontestably, the duty of well employing his means, since he has them; and of observing that this general duty comprehends that of well appreciating, in the first place, the desires or wants which these means are destined to satisfy, of well studying afterwards these means themselves, their extent and their limits, and, finally, of labouring in consequence to restrain the one and extend the other as much as possible: for his unhappiness will never proceed but from the inferiority of means relatively to wants, since if wants were always satisfied there would be no possibility of suffering. The insulated being in question, has then rights proceeding all from his wants, and duties arising all out of his means; and, in whatever position you place him, he will never have rights or duties of another nature: for all those of which he may become susceptible will arise from these, and will only be their consequences. We may even say that all proceed from his wants, for if he had not wants he would not need means to satisfy them; it would not even be possible he should have any means. Thus it would not be conceivable that he could have any duty whatsoever. If you wish to convince yourself of this, try to punish an impassive being. I have then had reason to say, that from the willing faculty arise the ideas of rights and of duties; and I can add, with assurance, that these ideas of rights and duties are not so exactly correspondent, and correlative, the one with the other, as they are commonly said to be: but that that of duties is subordinate to that of rights, as that of means is to that of wants, since we can conceive rights without duties, as in our first hypothesis; and in the second there are duties only because there are wants, and that they consist only in the general duty of satisfying these wants.

The better to convince ourselves of these two truths, let us make a third supposition: let us place this being, organised as we are in relation with other beings, feeling and willing like himself, and acting also in virtue of their will, but which are such that he cannot correspond fully with them, nor perfectly comprehend their ideas and their motives. These animated beings have their rights also, proceeding from their wants: but this operates no change in those of the being whose destiny we investigate. He has the same rights as before, since he has the same wants. He has, moreover, the same general duty of employing his means so as to procure the satisfaction of his wants. Thus he has the duty of conducting himself with those beings which show themselves to be feeling and willing, otherwise than with those, which appear to him inanimate; for as they act in consequence of their will it is his duty to conciliate or subjugate that will in order to bring them to contribute to the satisfaction of his desires, and as he is supposed incapable of communicating completely with them, and consequently of forming any convention with them, he has no other means of directing their will towards the accomplishment of his desires, and the satisfaction of his wants, than immediate persuasion or direct violence. And he employs, and ought to employ, the one and the other according to circumstances, without any other consideration than of producing the effects he desires.

In truth this being, organized as we are, is such, that a view of sensible nature inspires in him the desire to sympathize with it, that it should enjoy of his enjoyments and suffer of his sufferings. This is a new want which it produces in him, and we shall see in the sequel that it is not one of those of which he ought to endeavour to rid himself, for it is useful for him to be submitted to it. He ought then to satisfy it as the others, and consequently he is under the duty of sparing to himself the pain which the sufferings of sensible beings cause him, so far as his other wants do not oblige him to support this pain. This is still a consequence of the general duty of satisfying all his desires.

The picture which we have just drawn according to theory is the simple exposition of our relations with animals taken in general, which relations are afterwards modified in particular cases according to the degree of knowledge we have of their sentiments, and according to the relations of habit and reciprocal benevolence which take place between us and them, as between us and our fellow beings. I believe this picture to be a very faithful representation of these relations; for it is equally remote from that sentimental exaggeration which would make criminal in us any destruction whatever of these animals, and from the systematic barbarity which would make us consider as legitimate their most useless sufferings, or even persuade us that the pain which a sensible being manifests, is not pain when this sensible being is not made exactly like ourselves.

In fact these two systems are equally false. The first is untenable, because in practice it is absolutely impossible to follow it rigorously. It is evident that we should be violently destroyed, or slowly famished and eaten, by the other animated beings if we never destroyed them; and that even with the most minute attention it is impossible for us to avoid causing a great number of beings, more or less perceptible to our senses, to suffer and die. Now we have incontestably the right to act and to live, since we are born for the one as well as for the other.

The second system is not less erroneous, for in theory it rashly establishes between the different states of sensible nature a line of separation which no phenomenon authorizes us to admit. There is absolutely no one fact which gives us a right to affirm, nor even to suppose that the state of suffering in the animated beings with which we communicate imperfectly, is not exactly the same thing as it is in us or in our fellow beings;* and on this gratuitous supposition, this system condemns us to combat and destroy as a weakness the sentiment, the want the most general and imperious of human nature, that of sympathy and commiseration; a want which we shall soon see is the most happy result of our organization, and without which our existence would become very miserable, and even impossible. Moreover, in practice this system is opposed to the usage the most universal of all times and of all individuals; for there has never been, I believe, an animal in the human form, which has sincerely and originally felt

* Always perhaps with a degree of energy proportionate to the perfection of the organization.

that a sight of suffering, accurately expressed, was a thing of indifference. The indifference which is the fruit of habit, and the pleasure even of cruelty, for cruelty sake, a frightful pleasure, which may have been produced in some denaturalized beings by accidental causes, proves that it is the case of a natural inclination surmounted by time, or overcome by effort, and by the pleasure which arises in us from every effort followed by success. As to that cruelty which is the product of vengeance, it is a proof the more of the thesis I sustain; for it is because of the profound sentiment that the vindictive being has of suffering, that he wishes to produce it in the one that is odious to him, and he always partakes more or less involuntarily and forcibly of the evil which he causes.

These two opposite systems, but both fruits of a derangement of the imagination, are then equally absurd in theory and practice; this, of itself, is a great presumption in favour of the intermediate opinion which I establish, which moreover is found to be conformable to the usage of all times and all places, and to furnish reason from the conditions of our nature, well observed, for what our manner of being, in respect to the animals, has in it singular and contradictory at the first glance. But what is more forcible, and absolutely convincing, in my opinion, is that the same principle which I have established, *that our rights are always without limits, or at least equal to our wants; and that our duties are never but the genral duty of satisfying our wants*, will explain to us all our relations with our fellow beings, and establish them on immoveable bases, and such as will be the same everywhere, and always, in all countries, and in all times, in which our intimate nature shall not have changed.

Let us now make a fourth hypothesis which is that in which we are all placed. Let us suppose the animated being we are now considering in contact with other beings like himself. These beings have wants, and consequently rights, as he has, but this makes no change in his. He has always as many rights as wants, and the general duty of satisfying these wants. If he could not communicate completely with these beings like himself, and make conventions with them, he would be in respect to them in the state in which we all are, and in which as we have just seen we have reason to be in regard to the other animals.

Will any one say this is a state of war? He will be wrong. This would be an exaggeration. The state of war is that in which we incessantly seek the destruction of one another; because we cannot assure ourselves of our own preservation, but by the annihilation of our enemy. We are not in such a relation, but with those animals whose instinct constantly leads them to hurt us. It is not so as to the others; even those which we sacrifice to our wants, we attack only inasmuch as these wants, more or less pressing, force us. There are some of them which live with us in a state of peaceable subjection, others in perfect indifference. With all we wound their will only because it is contrary to ours, and not for the pleasure of wounding it. There is even in regard to all this general necessity of sympathising with sensible nature, which pains us at the sight of their suffering, and which unites us more or less with them.

This state then is not essentially a *state of hostility*. It frequently becomes such: but this is by accident. It is essentially the *state of alienage* (d'etrangete) if we may thus express ourselves. It is that of beings, willing and acting separately, each for his own satisfaction, without being able to explain themselves mutually, or to make conventions for the regulation of the cases in which their wills are opposed.

Such, as we have said, would be the relations of man with his fellow men, if his means of communicating with them were very imperfect. He would not be precisely for them an enemy, but an indifferent stranger. His relations would even then be softened by the necessity of sympathising, which is much stronger in him in the case of animals of his own species; and we must still add to this necessity that of love, which strengthens it extremely in many circumstances, for love has not perfect enjoyment without mutual consent, without a very lively sympathy; and when this sympathy, necessary to the full satisfaction of the desire, has existed, it frequently gives birth to habits of good will, from whence arises the sentiment of fraternity, which produces in its turn ties more durable and more tender.

Nevertheless, in this state quarrels are frequent; and, properly speaking, justice and injustice do not yet exist. The rights of the one do not affect the rights of the other. Every one has as many rights as wants, and the general duty of satisfying these wants without any foreign consideration. There does not begin to be any restrictions on these rights and this duty, or rather on the manner of fulfilling this duty, but at the moment in which means of mutual understanding are established; and consequently conventions tacit or formal. There solely is the birth of justice and injustice, that is to say of the balance between the rights of one and the rights of another, which necessarily were equal till this instant. The Greeks who called Ceres *Legislatrix* were wrong. It is to grammar, to language, they ought to have given this title. They had placed the origin of laws, and of justice, at the moment in which men have amongst them relations more stable, and conventions more numerous. But they ought to have remounted to the birth of the first conventions, informal or explicit. In every way the duty of moderns is to penetrate further and more profoundly than the ancients. Hobbes, then, was certainly right in establishing the foundation of all justice on conversations; but he was wrong in saying before, that the anterior state is rigorously and absolutely a state of war, and that this is our true instinct, and the wish of our nature. Were this the case we should never have withdrawn from it.* A false principle has led him to an excellent consequence. It has always appeared to me singularly remarkable, that this philosopher, who of all men who have ever written is perhaps the most recommendable for the rigorous con-

* We must however admit that nature, or the order of things, such as they are, in creating the rights of every animated individual, equal and opposed to those of another, has virtually and indirectly created the state of war; and that it is art which has caused it to cease, or at least has frequently suspended it amongst us, by conventions. This still agrees with our general principle, that we create nothing; were there not natural and necessary wars, there never would have been any conventional and artificial ones. The invincibly permanent state of the relations of man with animals of other species, is what disposes him most to treat his fellow beings in an hostile manner.

catenation and close connexion of his ideas, should not however have arrived at this fine conception of the necessity for conventions, the source of all justice, but, by starting from a false or at least an inexact principle, (a state of war the natural state); and that from the just and profound sentiment of the want of peace among men, he has been led to a false idea the necessity of servitude. When we see such examples, how ought we to tremble in enouncing an opinion?*

Yet I cannot help believing that which I have just explained to be true.

It seems to me proved, that from our faculty of willing proceed the ideas of *rights* and *duties;* that from our wants proceed all our *rights,* and from our means all our *duties;* that we have always as many *rights* as wants, and the single *duty* of providing for these wants; that the wants and the rights of other sensible beings, whether of our own or a different species, do not affect ours; that our rights do not begin to be restrained, but at the moment of the birth of conventions; that our general duty is not changed for this as to its foundation, but only to the manner of fulfilling it; and that it is at this moment alone, that justice and injustice properly so called commence.

It is not yet the time to develope all the consequences of these principles, but it is time to terminate this long preliminary, by the reflections to which it gives rise.

* This latter error of Hobbes has not, however, been produced in his excellent head, but by the too energetic impression made by the unhappiness of his country; which unhappiness was caused by efforts, the object of which in their origin was resistance to oppression.

SECTION SEVENTH.

Conclusion.

The general considerations on which we have just dwelt, are those which first present themselves to our understanding when we begin to observe our will. However little we reflect thereon, we see first that it is a mode of our sensibility, which arises from a judgment, clear or confused, formed on what we feel, that if our pure and simple sensibility begins to give us an obscure idea of our *self*, and of the possession of its affections, this admirable mode of our sensibility, which we call *will*, by the resistance it experiences, causes us to know beings different from us, and completes our idea of *individuality*, of *personality*, and *property*, exclusive of whatsoever affects us.* It is not less visible, that this faculty of willing is the source of all our wants, and of all our miseries; for an indifferent being would be impassive; and it is equally manifest that this same faculty, by the wonderful power it has of putting our organs into action, and of giving motion to our members, is also the source of all our means and of all our resources; for all our power consists in the employment of our physical and intellectual forces.

It follows from this, that every animated being, in virtue of the laws of his nature, has the right of satisfying all his desires, which are his wants, and the sole *duty* of employing his means in the best possible

* This truth has been developed vol. 1st. chapter of existence, and in different parts of the two other volumes.

manner for the attainment of this object; for endowed with *passion*, he cannot be condemned to suffer but as little as possible, and endowed with action, he ought to avail himself of it to this end. It follows thence, further, that *liberty*, the power of executing his will, is for a willing being the first good, and includes them all, for he would be always happy if he had always the power of satisfying all his desires; and all his ills consist always in *constraint*, that is to say in the inability to satisfy himself.

We see moreover that the employment of our force, labour of every kind, is our only primitive riches, the source of all others, the first cause of their value, and that labour itself has always two values. The one is natural and necessary: it is that of all those things which are indispensable to the satisfaction of the wants of the animated being which performs this labour during the time he is performing it. The other is eventual, and often conventional: it consists in the mass of utility that results from this same labour.

In fine we see, with equal clearness, that the manner of fulfilling our single duty, that of well employing our means, varies according to the circumstances in which we are placed; whether it be when we are in contact with those beings only which do not manifest any sensibility, or when we have to do with animated beings, but to which we can make ourselves but imperfectly understood, or when we are in relation with sensible beings like ourselves, with whom we can perfectly correspond and make conventions. At this point justice and injustice, properly so called, and true society, commence; the object and motive of which is always to augment the power of every one, by making that of others concur with it, and by preventing them from reciprocally hurting one another.

All these first ideas are good and sound, at least I think so, and begin already to throw some light on the subject with which we are occupied; but they are far from being sufficient. They do not sufficiently inform us what are the numerous results of the employment of our force, of our labour, in a word of our actions, and what new interests their combinations produce among us, nor what are the different sentiments which germinate from our first desires, or what they have useful or injurious to the happiness of all and every one: nor, finally, what is the best possible direction of these actions and sentiments. These are, however, so many subjects necessary to be treated of in order to give a complete history of the *will and its effects;* and it is there we find again the division we announced. It is requisite then to enter into further details, and I will now begin to speak of our actions.

OF OUR ACTIONS.

FIRST PART

OF THE

TREATISE ON THE WILL AND ITS EFFECTS;

OF OUR ACTIONS.

CHAPTER I.

Of Society.

The introduction which has been just read is consecrated entirely to an examination of the generation of some very general ideas; the casting of a first glance on the nature of that mode of our sensibility which we call the will, or the faculty of willing; and to the indication of some of its immediate and universal consequences.

We have therein seen summarily; first, what are inanimate or *insensible* beings, such as many appear to us, which may well exist for the sensible beings, which they affect, but which do not exist for themselves, since they do not percieve it; second, what would be the nature of beings feeling, but *feeling every thing with indifference,* so that from their sensibility no choice, no preference, no desire, in a word no will would result; third, what are those beings *sentient and willing,* such as all the animals with which we are acquainted, and especially as ourselves, but insulated; fourth, and in fine, what beings, *feeling and willing* in our way, become when they are in contact and *in relation with other ani-*

mals of their species similar to themselves, and with whom they can fully correspond.

These preliminaries were necessary, that the reader might readily follow the series of ideas, and clearly perceive the connexion, of this second section of the elements of ideology with that which precedes it. But it would be inconvenient, in a treatise on the will, to say more of beings not endowed with this intellectual faculty; and it would not be less superfluous, having the human species principally in view, to occupy ourselves longer with beings that should be sentient and willing, but living insulated.

Man cannot exist thus; this is proved by the fact, for we have never seen in any corner of the world an animal in the human form, however brutish he might be, which has no kind of relation with any other animal of his own species: that is not less demonstrated by reasoning. For such an individual, strictly speaking, may exist although very miserably, yet certainly he could not reproduce himself. That the species may be perpetuated, it is indispensable that the two sexes should unite; it is even necessary that the infant, produced by their union, should receive for a long time the cares of his parents, or at least those of his mother. Now we are so formed that we have all, more or less, a natural and innate inclination to sympathy; that is to say we all experience pleasure from sharing our impressions, our affections, our sentiments, and those of our fellow creatures. Perhaps this inclination exists amongst all animated beings; perhaps even it is in us from the origin a considerable part of that which so powerfully attracts the two sexes towards each other. What is certain, is that it afterwards augments it prodigiously. It is then impossible that approximations, which our organization renders inevitable, should not develope in us this natural disposition to sympathy, fortify it by exercise, and establish amongst us social and moral relations. Moreover, we are also so organized, that we form judgments of that which we experience, of that which we feel, of that which we see, in a word of all which affects us; we distinguish the parts, circumstances, causes and consequences thereof; and this is to judge of it. It is then impossible that we should not soon be aware of the utility we may derive from the succour of our fellow beings, from their assistance in our wants, from the concurrence of their will, and of their force with ours, a new reason why approximations, fortuitous at first, should become durable and permanent between us; this also is what takes place always, and every where. It is this also which always, and every where, produces the admirable and wise invention of a language more or less perfect, but always as appears, more circumstantial, and more capable of detailed explanations, than that of any other animal. It is then the social state, which is our natural state, and that with which we ought alone to occupy ourselves.

I will not however in this place consider society under a moral relation. I will not examine how it developes, multiplies, and complicates, all our passions and affections; nor what are the numerous duties it imposes on us, nor whence arises for us the fundamental obligation of respecting the conventions on which it rests, and without which it could not subsist. These are researches which will be the object of the second part of this treatise. In this I shall consider the social state only under its economical relation, that is to say relatively to our most direct wants, and to the means we have of satisfying them. It is that which may lead us surely to estimate the value and utility of all our actions, to judge of their merits by their consequences, and consequently of the merit of those sentiments which determine us to one action rather than another.

Now what is society viewed under this aspect? I do not fear to announce it. Society is purely and solely a continual series of exchanges. It is never any thing else, in any epoch of its duration, from its commencement the most unformed, to its greatest perfection. And this is the greatest eulogy we can give to it, for exchange is an admirable transaction, in which the two contracting parties always both gain; consequently society is an uninterrupted succession of advantages, unceasingly renewed for all its members. This demands an explanation.

First, society is nothing but a succession of exchanges. In effect, let us begin with the first conventions on which it is founded. Every man, before entering into the state of society, has as we have seen all rights and no duty, not even that of not hurting others; and others the same in respect to him. It is evident they could not live together, if by a convention formal or tacit they did not promise each other, reciprocally, surety. Well! this convention is a real exchange; every one renounces a certain manner of employing his force, and receives in return the same sacrifice on the part of all the others. Security once established by this mean, men have a multitude of mutual relations which all arrange themselves under one of the three following classes: they consist either in rendering a service to receive a salary, or in bartering some article of merchandize against another, or in executing some work in common. In the two first cases the exchange is manifest. In the third it is not less real; for when several men unite, to labour in common, each makes a sacrifice to the others of what he could have done during the same time for his own particular utility; and he receives, for an equivalent, his part of the common utility resulting from the common labour. He exchanges one manner of occupying himself against another, which becomes more advantageous to him than the other would have been. It is true then that society consists only in a continual succession of exchanges.

I do not pretend to say that men never render gratuitous services. Far from me be the idea of denying benevolence, or of banishing it from their hearts; but I say it is not on this that all the progress of society reposes, and even that the happy consequences of this amiable virtue are much more important under a moral relation,* of which we are not at this time speaking, than under the economical relation which now occupies us. I add that if we urge the sense of the word exchange, and if we wish, as we ought, to take it in all the extent of its signification, we may say with justice that a benefit is still an exchange, in which one sacrifices a portion of one's property, or of one's time, to procure a moral plea-

* In developing and exciting sympathy.

sure, very lively and very sweet, that of obliging, or to exempt oneself from a pain very afflicting, the sight of suffering; exactly as we employ a sum of money to procure an artificial fire work, which diverts, or to free ourselves from something which incommodes us.

It is equally true that an exchange is a transaction in which the two contracting parties both gain. Whenever I make an exchange freely, and without constraint, it is because I desire the thing I receive more than that I give; and, on the contrary, he with whom I bargain desires what I offer more than that which he renders me. When I give my labour for wages it is because I esteem the wages more than what I should have been able to produce by labouring for myself; and he who pays me prizes more the services I render him than what he gives me in return. When I give a measure of wheat for a measure of wine, it is because I have a superabundance of food and nothing to drink, and he with whom I treat is in the contrary case. When several of us agree to execute any labour whatsoever in common, whether to defend ourselves against an enemy, to destroy noxious animals, to preserve ourselves from the ravages of the sea, of an inundation, of a contagion, or even to make a bridge or a road, it is because each of us prefers the particular utility which will result to him from it, to what he would have been able to do for himself during the same time. We are all satisfied in all these species of exchanges, every one finds his advantage in the arrangement proposed.

In truth it is possible that, in an exchange, one of the contractors, or even both, may have been wrong to desire the bargain which they conclude.—It is possible they may give a thing, which they will soon regret, for a thing which they will soon cease to value. It is possible, also, that one of the two may not have obtained for that which he sacrifices as much as he might have asked, so that he will suffer a relative loss while the other makes an exaggerated gain. But these are particular cases which do not belong to the nature of the transaction. And it is not less true that it is the essence of free exchange to be advantageous to both parties; and that the true utility of society is to render possible amongst us a multitude of similar arrangements.

It is this innumerable crowd of small particular advantages, unceasingly arising, which composes the general good, and which produces at length the wonders of perfected society, and the immense difference we see between it and a society imperfect or almost null, such as exists amongst savages. It is not improper to direct our attention for some time to this picture, which does not sufficiently strike us because we are too much accustomed to it.

What is it in effect which a country anciently civilized offers to our contemplation? The fields are cleared and cleaned, freed from the large vegetables which originally covered them, rid of noxious plants and animals, and in every respect prepared to receive the annual cares of the cultivator. The marshes are drained. The stagnant waters which occupied it have ceased to fill the air with pestilential vapours. Issues have been opened for them, or their extent has been circumscribed; and the lands which they infected have become abundant pastures, or useful reservoirs. The asperities of the mountains have been levelled; their bases have been appropriated to the wants of culture; their parts least accessible, even to the regions of eternal snow, have been destined to the nourishment of numerous flocks. The forests which have been permitted to remain have not continued impenetrable: The wild beasts which retired to them have been pursued and almost destroyed; the wood which they produce has been withdrawn and preserved, the cutting them has even been subjected to periods the most favourable for their reproduction; and the care bestowed on them almost every where is equivalent to a species of culture, and has even been sometimes extended to a most diligent culture. The running waters which traverse all these lands have, likewise, not remained in their primitive state: The great rivers, have been cleared of all the obstacles which obstructed their course; they have been confined by dikes and quays, when this has been necessary; and their banks have been disposed in such a manner as to form commodious ports in convenient situations.—The course of streams less considerable has been restrained for working mills and other machines, or diverted to irrigate declivities which needed it, and to render them productive. On the whole surface of the land habitations have been constructed from distance to distance, in favourable positions, for the use of those who cultivate the ground and attend to its produce. These habitations have been surrounded with enclosures and plantations, that render them more agreeable and more useful. Roads have been made to go to them and to take away the produce of the earth. In points where several different interests have concentrated, and where other men have become sufficiently necessary to the service of the cultivators, to be able to subsist on the wages of their labour, habitations have been multiplied and made contiguous, and have formed villages and small towns. On the banks of large rivers, and on the shores of the sea, in points in which the interests of several of these towns have coincided, large cities have been built; which have themselves in time given birth to a still greater one, which has become their capital and their common centre, because it has been found the most favourably situated to unite all the others, and to be provisioned and defended by them. Finally, all these towns communicate with each other, with the neighbouring seas, and with foreign countries, by means of bridges, causeways, canals, in which the whole of human industry is displayed. Such are the objects which strike us at the first aspect of a country where men have exercised all their power, and have appropriated it to themselves for a long time.

If we penetrate the interior of their habitations we there find an immense number of useful animals, raised, nourished, made obsequious, by man,—multiplied by him to an inconceivable point; a prodigious quantity of necessaries of every species, commodities, furniture, utensils, instruments, clothing, articles, raw or manufactured, metals, necessary or precious; finally, whatever may sooner or later contribute to the satisfaction of our wants. We admire there above all things, a population really astonishing, all the individuals of which have the use of a perfected language, have a reason developed to a certain point, manners sufficiently softened, and an industry sufficiently intelligent, to live in such great numbers near to one another, and amongst whom in general the poorest are succoured, the weakest defended. We remark, with still more surprise, that many of these men have attained a degree of knowledge very difficult to be acquired, that they possess an infinity of agreeable or useful arts, that they are acquainted with many of the laws of nature, of which they know to calculate the effects, and turn them to their advantage, that they have even had a glimpse of the most difficult of all sciences, since they are able to distinguish, at least in part, the true interests of the species in general, and in particular those of their society, and its members; that in consequence they have conceived laws often just, institutions tolerably wise, and created a number of establishments proper for spreading and still increasing instruction and intelligence; and finally, that not content with having thus insured interior prosperity they have explored the rest of the earth, established relations with foreign nations, and provided for their security from without.

What an immense accumulation of means of well being! What prodigious results from that part of the labours of our predecessors, which has not been immediately necessary to the support of their existence, and which has not been annihilated with them! The imagination even is astonished; and the more so the more it reflects on it, for we should consider that many of these works are little durable, that the most solid have been many times renewed in the course of ages, and that there is scarcely one which does not require continual care and maintenance for its preservation. We must observe that of these wonders that which strikes our attention is not the most astonishing; it is, as we say, the material part. But the intellectual part, if we may so express ourselves, is still more surprising. It has always been much more difficult to learn, and to discover, than to act in consequence of what we know. The first steps, especially in the career of invention, are of extreme difficulty. The labour which man has been obliged to perform on his own intellectual faculties, the immensity of the researches to which he has been forced to have recourse, that of the observations he has been obliged to collect, have cost him much more time and pains than all the works he has been able to execute in consequence of the progress of his understanding. Finally, we must remark that the efforts of men, for the amelioration of their lot, have never been nearly as well directed as they might have been, that always a great portion of the human power has been employed in hindering the progress of the other, that this progress has been troubled and interrupted by all the great disorders of nature and of society; and that many times perhaps all has been lost and destroyed, even the knowledge acquired, even the capacity of re-commencing that which had been already done. These latter considerations might become discouraging. But we shall see elsewhere by how many reasons we ought to be assured against the fear of such misfortunes in future. We will also examine to what point the progress of the species, taken in mass, augments the happiness of individuals, a condition necessary to enable us to rejoice at it. But at this moment let it suffice to have shown the prodigious power which men acquire when united; while separated they can with difficulty sustain their miserable existence. Smith, if I am not mistaken, is the first who has remarked that man alone makes exchanges, properly speaking. See his admirable chapter, 4th of the 1st book of his treatise on the wealth of nations. I regret that in remarking this fact he has not sought its cause with more curiosity. It was not for the author of the theory of moral sentiments to regard as useless a scrutiny of the operations of our understanding. His success and his faults ought to have contributed equally to make him think the contrary. Notwithstanding this negligence his assertion is not the less true. We clearly see certain animals execute labours which concur to a common end, and which to a certain point appear to have been concerted; or fight for the possession of what they desire, or supplicate to obtain it; but nothing announces that they really make formal exchanges. The reason, I think, is that they have not a language sufficiently developed to enable them to make express conventions; and this, I think, proceeds (as I have explained in my second volume, article of interjections,—and in my first, on the subject of signs,) from their being incapable of sufficiently decomposing their ideas, to generalise, to abstract, and to express them separately in detail, and in the form of a proposition; whence it happens that those of which they are susceptible, are all particular, confused with their attributes, and manifest themselves in mass by interjections, which can explain nothing explicitly. Man, on the contrary, who has the intellectual means which are wanting to them is naturally led to avail himself of them, to make conventions with his fellow beings. They make no exchanges, and he does. Accordingly he alone has a real society; for *commerce is the whole of society*, as labour is the whole of riches.

We can scarcely conceive at first that the great effects, which we have just described, have no other cause than the sole reciprocity of services and the multiplicity of exchanges. However this continual succession of exchanges has three very remarkable advantages.

First, the labour of several men united is more productive, than that of the same men acting separately. Is there a question of defence? Ten men will easily resist an enemy, who would have destroyed them all in attacking one after another. Is a burden to be removed? That of which the weight would have opposed an invincible resistance to the efforts of a single individual, yields immediately to those of several acting together. Is some complicated work to be executed? Several things are to be done simultaneously. One does one while another does another, and all contribute to effect what a single man could not have produced. One rows while another steers, and a third casts the net or harpoons the fish; and thus they attain a success impossible without this concurrence.

Secondly, our knowledge is our most precious acquisition, since it is this that directs the employment of our force, and renders it more fruitful, in proportion to its greater soundness and extent.—Now no man is in a situation to see every thing, and it is much more easy to learn than to invent.—But when several men communicate together, that which one has observed is soon known to all the others, and it is sufficient amongst them that one is found who is very ingenious, in order that precious discoveries should promptly become the property of all. Intelligence then will increase much more rapidly, than in a state of insulation, without calculating that it may be preserved, and consequently accumulated from generation to generation; and still without counting, what is clearly proved by the study of our understanding, that the invention and employment of language and its signs, which would not take place without society, furnish our minds with many new means of combination and action.

Thirdly, and this still merits attention: when several men labour reciprocally for one another every one can devote himself exclusively to the occupation for which he is fittest, whether from his natural dispositions or from fortuitous circumstances; and thus he will succeed better. The hunter, the fisherman, the shepherd, the labourer, the artisan,—doing each a single thing—will become more skilful, will lose less time, and have more success. This is what is called the division of labour, which in civilised society is sometimes carried to an inconceivable point, and always with advantage.—The writers on economics have all attached an extreme importance to the division of labour; and they have made much noise with this observation, which is not ancient; they have been right. Yet this third advantage of society is far from having an interest equally eminent with the two former, the concurrence of force and the communication of knowledge. In all cases, that which is most difficult is to assign to things their true value; for this, we must know them perfectly.

Concurrence of force, increase and preservation of knowledge, and division of labour,—these are the three great benefits of society. They cause themselves to be felt from the first by men the most rude; but they augment in an incalculable ratio, in proportion as they are perfected,—and every degree of amelioration, in the social order, adds still to the possibility of increasing and better using them.—The energy of these three causes of prosperity will show itself still more evidently, when we shall have seen more in detail the manner in which our riches are formed.

CHAPTER II.

Of Production, or of the formation of our Riches.

It is so true that we cannot reason justly while the sense of words is not well determined, that it is very important in political economy, to know what we ought to understand by the word production, in the language of this science. This question, which in itself is not without difficulty, has been still much perplexed by the spirit of system and prejudice.—It has been treated of by many able men, at the head of whom we should place Turgot and Smith. But, in my opinion, no one has thrown so much light on it as Mr. Say, the author of the best book I know on these matters, although he leaves still something to be desired.

All the operations of nature and of art resolve into transmutations, into changes, of *form* and of *place*.

Not only we never create any thing, but it is even impossible for us to conceive what it is to create, if we understand by this word to make something of nothing; for we have never seen any being whatsoever arise from nothing, nor return to it. Hence this axiom, admitted by all antiquity, "*nothing comes from nothing, or returns to nothing.*"*—

* It is very just. I shall believe in the possibility of a creation, when any body shall show me one, or even an annihilation.

What then do we do by our labour, by our action on all the bodies which surround us? Never any thing, but operate in these beings changes of form or of place, which render them proper for our use, which make them useful to the satisfaction of our wants. This is what we should understand by—to produce: It is to give things an utility which they had not. Whatever be our labour, if no utility results from it it is unfruitful. If any results it is productive.

It seems at first, and many likewise believe it, that there is a more real production in that labour which has for its object the procurement of first materials, than in that which consists in fashioning and transporting them; but it is an illusion. When I put seed in contact with air, water, earth, and different manures, so that from the combinations of these elements results wheat, hemp, or tobacco, there is no more creation operated, than when I take the grain of this wheat to convert it into flour and bread, the filaments of this hemp to make successively thereof thread, cloth, and habiliments; and the leaves of this tobacco to prepare them so as to smoke, chew, or snuff them. In both cases there is a production of utility, for all these labours are equally necessary to accomplish the desired end, the satisfaction of some of our wants.

The man who draws fish from the depths of the sea is no more a creator than those who dry and salt them, who extract the oil, the eggs, &c. &c. or transport these products to me. It is the same with those who dig in mines, who convert the mineral into metal and the metal into utensils, or furniture, and who carry these instruments to those who want them. Each adds a new utility to the utility already produced, consequently each is equally a producer. All equally study the laws, which govern the different beings to turn them to their profit; all employ, to produce the desired effect, the chemical and mechanical forces of nature. What we call her vegetative force is not of another nature, it is but a series of elective attractions, of true chymical affinities with all the circumstances of which we are undoubtedly not acquainted, but yet know how to favor them by our labours, and to direct these in such a manner as to render them useful.

It is then erroneously that they have made agricultural industry a thing essentially different from all the other branches of human industry, and in which the action of nature intervenes in a particular manner; accordingly they have always been greatly embarrassed to know precisely what they should understand by agricultural industry, taken in this sense. They have comprised therein fishing and hunting. But why not likewise comprehend the industry of erratic shepherds? Is there so great a difference between raising animals to nourish ourselves, and killing or taking them ready raised to nourish ourselves in the same manner. If he who extracts salt from sea water, by exposing it to the action of the rays of the sun, is a producer, why should not he who extracts the same salt from the water of a fountain, by means of the action of fire, and that of the wind, in buildings of graduation, be a producer also? And yet what specific difference is there between his manufacture, and all those which yield other chymical products? If we rank in this productive class him who extracts minerals from the earth, why not also comprehend him who extracts metals from these minerals? If one produces the mineral the other produces the metal, and where shall we stop in the different transformations which this matter undergoes, 'till it becomes a piece of furniture or a jewel?—at what point of these successive labours can we say, here we cease to produce, and do nothing but fashion? We may say as much of those who seek wood in forests, or turf in bogs, or who collect on the shores of the sea or of rivers the useful things which the waters have deposited there. Are they agricolists, fabricators, or carriers? And if they are all these at the same time, why are they more producers under one of these denominations than under the two others?—Finally, to speak only of culture, properly so called, I demand that it be precisely determined who is the true producer, the agricolist by excellence, he who sows or he who reaps; he who ploughs, or he who fences; he who conveys manure into the fields, or he who leads the flocks to fold in them? For my part I declare that they all appear only as so many different workmen, who concur in the same fabrication. I stop here, because one might propose to the partisans of the opinion I combat a thousand questions, as insoluble as these, in their system. When we set out from a false principle difficulties arise in crowds: perhaps this is one of the great causes of the obscure, embarrassed, and almost mysterious, language which we remark in the writings of the ancient economists. When ideas are not precise it is impossible that expressions should be clear.

The truth is simply, that all our useful labours are productive, and that those relative to agriculture are so like the others, in the same manner as the others, for the same reason as the others; and have in this nothing particular. A farm is a real manufactory; every thing is operated there in the same way, by the same principles, and for the same causes. A field is a real utensil, or, if you please, a store of first materials, which any one may take if it yet belongs to nobody; and which must be bought, rented, or borrowed, if it has already an owner. It does not change its nature, whether I employ it in the raising of grain, in bleaching linen, or for any other purpose. In every case it is an instrument necessary to produce a desired effect, as a furnace, a hammer, or a vessel. The only difference between this instrument and every other, is that to use it, as it cannot be removed, we must go to it, instead of its coming to us.

Once again, agricultural industry is a branch of manufacturing industry, which has no specific character which separates it from all the others.—Would you so generalise this term as to extend it to all the labours which have for their object the procurement of first materials? it is then certain that agricultural industry is the first in date and the most necessary of all, because it is necessary that a thing should be procured before it can be applied to use; but it is not for that reason exclusively productive, for most of its productions must yet be further wrought before they become useful to us; and moreover we must then comprehend in agricultural industry, not only that of hunters, fishers, shepherds, miners, &c. but also that of the rudest savages, and even that of all those beasts which live on the spontaneous productions of the earth, since these are first matters which these creatures procure for themselves; in truth, they are immediately consumed, but this does not change the thesis. Certainly these are singular agricolists, and singular producers.

Will it be insisted that agricultural industry shall be restrained to agriculture, properly so called?—then it is not the first in chronological order, for men are fishers, hunters, shepherds, and mere vagabonds, in the manner of brutes, long before they are agricultors. It is not even the only industry productive of first materials, for we employ many for which we are not indebted to it. Doubtless it is always very important, and is the principal source of our subsistance, if not of our riches; but it cannot be regarded as exclusively productive.

Let us conclude that all useful labour is really productive, and that all the laborious class of society merits equally the name of productive. The truly sterile class is that of the idle, who do nothing but live, nobly as it is termed, on the products of labours executed before their time, whether these products are realised in landed estates which they lease, that is to say which they hire to a labourer, or that they consist in money or effects which they lend for a premium, which is still a hireing.—These are the true drones of the hive, (fruges consumere nati) unless they render themselves deserving by the functions which they discharge or the knowledge which they diffuse; for these are, also, useful and productive labours, although not of an immediate utility in relation to riches;—we will speak of them hereafter.

As to the laborious class and that immediately productive of our riches, as its action on all the beings of nature always reduces itself to the change *of form or of place*, it naturally divides itself into two, the manufacturers comprising agriculturists, who fabricate and fashion, and merchants who transport, for this is the real utility of the latter. If they did nothing but buy and sell,—without transporting, without retailing, without facilitating any thing,—they would be nothing more than incommodious parasites, gamesters, stock-jobbers; of the one and the other of whom we shall shortly speak; and we shall quickly see how much light our manner of considering things throws on the whole progress of society. We must now explain a little more fully in what this utility consists, our only production which results from all labour well understood; and to see how it is appreciated, and how it constitutes the value of whatsoever we call our riches.

CHAPTER III.

Of the Measure of Utility or of Values.

This word utility has a very extensive signification, for it is very abstract, or rather it is very abstract because it is abstracted from a multitude of different significations. In effect there exist utilities of many different kinds. There are some real, some illusory; if some are solid some are very futile, and we often stupidly deceive ourselves in respect to them. I could cite many examples, but they would not perhaps be to the taste of all readers. It is better that every one should choose those which please him. In general we may say that whatever is capable of procuring any advantage, even a frivolous pleasure, is *useful*. I think this is the real value of this word, for in the end all we desire is to multiply our enjoyments and to diminish our sufferings; and certainly the sentiment of pleasure and of satisfaction is a good. All goods are even nothing more than that differently modified. Whatever, then, procures it is useful.

If it is not easy to say clearly what this utility is of which we speak, it appears still much more difficult to determine its degrees; for the measure of the utility of a thing, real or supposed, is the vivacity with which it is generally desired. Now, how are we to fix the degrees of a thing so inappreciable as the vivacity of our desires? We have, however, a very sure manner of arriving at it. It is to observe the sacrifices to which these desires determine us. If, to obtain any thing whatsoever, I am disposed to give three measures of wheat which belong to me; and if, to obtain another, I am ready to part with twelve like measures,—it is evident that I desire the last four times more than the other. In like manner, if I give a man a salary triple of that which I offer another, it is clear that I value the services of the first three times more than those of the second; or, if I personally do not value them so much, it is however the value generally attached to them, so that I could not procure them at a smaller price; and, since, in fine, I make this sacrifice freely, it is a proof that its object is worth it even to me.

In the state of society which is nothing but a continual succession of exchanges, it is thus that the values of all the products of our industry are determined. This fixation, without doubt, is not always founded on very good reasons; we are often very dear appreciators of the real merit of things. But, in fine, in relation to riches, their value is not the less that which the general opinion assigns to them; whence we see, by the way, that the greatest producer is he who performs that kind of labour most dearly paid for. It imports little whether this labour should be a branch of agricultural, manufacturing, or commercial, industry; and, from hence, we also see that, of two nations, that which has most riches, or most enjoyments, is that whose workmen are the most laborious and the most skillful in every kind, or who devote themselves to the kinds of labour most fruitful; in a word, whose labourers produce the most value in the same time.

This brings us back to the subject of which we had already begun to treat in the introduction, (sections three and four): our only original property is our physical and intellectual force. The employment of our force, our labour, is our only primitive riches. All the beings existing in nature, susceptible of becoming useful to us, are not so actually as yet. They only become so by the action which we exercise on them; by the labour, small or great, simple or complicated, which we execute to convert them to our use. They have no value for us, and with us, but by this labour, and in proportion to its success. This is not saying that if they have already become the property of any one, we must not begin by making a sacrifice to him, in order to obtain them, before disposing of them. But they have not become the property of any one, but because he has previously applied to them a labour of some kind, the fruit of which the social conventions assure to him. Thus this sacrifice itself is the price of some labour; and, previous to any labour, these beings had no actual value, and that which they have is never derived but from some employment of our force, of which they are more the object.

This employment of our force, this labour, we have also seen has a natural and necessary value; without which it would never have had an artificial and conventional one. This necessary value is the sum of the indispensable wants, the satisfaction of which is necessary to the existence of him who executes this labour, during the time he is executing it. But here, where we speak of the value which results from the free transactions of society, it is clearly seen that we have in view the conventional and market value; that which general opinion attaches to things, erroneously or reasonably. If it is less than the wants of the labourer, he must devote himself to some other industry, or he must perish. If it is strictly equal to them he subsists with difficulty. If it is greater he grows rich, provided always that he is economical. In every case this conventional and market value is the real one, in relation to riches; it is the true measure of the utility of the production, since it fixes its price.

However, this conventional value, this market price, is not solely the expression of the estimation in which we generally hold a thing. It varies according to the wants and means of the producer and consumer, of the buyer and of the seller; for the product of my labour, even should it have cost me much time and pains, if I am pressed to dispose of it, if there are many similar to be sold, or if there are but small means of paying for it,—I must necessarily part with it for a low price. On the contrary, if the buyers are numerous, urgent, rich, I may sell very dear what I have procured very easily.* It is therefore on different circumstances, and on the equilibrium of the resistance between sellers and buyers, that the market price depends;

* Merchants know well that to prosper there is no other mean, but to render the merchandise agreeable, and to be within reach of the rich? Why do not nations think the same? They would rivalise industry only, and would never think of desiring the impoverishment of their neighbours;—they would be happy.

but it is not less true, that it is the measure of the value of things, and of the utility of the labour which produces them.

There is, however, another way of considering the utility of labour, but that is less relative to the individual than to the human species in general. I explain myself by an example. Before the invention of the stocking loom, a man, or a woman, by knitting could make a pair of stockings in a given time; and received wages proportionate to the degree of interest which was taken in the procurement of the product of that labour, and to the difficulty of this particular labour comparatively with all other kinds.—Things thus regulated the stocking loom is invented; and, I suppose that by means of this machine, the same person, without more trouble or more knowledge, can execute precisely three times as much work as before, and of the same quality. It is not doubtful but at first it would be paid three times higher for to those who wear stockings, the manner in which they have been made is indifferent. But this machine, and the small talents necessary for working it, will quickly multiply, since the industry of those who dedicate themselves to this labour is supposed neither to be more painful, nor more difficult, than the industry of those who knit; it is certain they will not have greater wages, although they do three times more work.* Their labour, then, will not be more productive for them; but it will be so for society, taken in mass,—for there will be three

* I abstract the price of the machine, and the interest it ought to yield.

times as many persons supplied with stockings for the same sum; or rather, to consider only the fabrication of the stockings, every one can have now as many as he could formerly for the third of the money it then required, and consequently will have two-thirds remaining to supply other wants. We may say as much of him who bruised corn between two stones before the invention of mills, with respect to the miller, who does not perhaps gain more; but who grinds an hundred times more, and better.—This is the great advantage of civilized and enlightened society: every one finds himself better provided in every way, with fewer sacrifices,—because the labourers produce a greater mass of utility in the same time.

It is this also, by the by, which shows the error of those who, to judge of the greater or less degree of ease of the poor classes of society in other times, compare only the price of a day's work with the price of grain; and who, if they find that the first has less increased than the second, conclude that the labourers are more straitened than they were. This is not exact, and probably not true; for, first, we do not eat grain in its natural state; and it may happen that it may have augmented in price, while bread has not, if we now grind and bake more economically. Moreover, although bread is the principal expense of the poor, he has also other wants. If the arts have made progress, he may be better lodged, better clothed, have better drink, for the same price. If the society is better regulated, he may find a more regular employment for his labour, and be more certain of not being troubled in the possession of that which he has gained. In fine, it may very well be, that for the same sum he enjoys more, or at least suffers less. The elements of this calculation are so numerous, that it is very difficult, and perhaps impossible, to make it directly. We shall see in the sequel other means of deciding this question, but at this moment it leads us from the object with which we are occupied. Let us return.

We have seen that the sole and only source of all our enjoyments, of all our riches, is the employment of our force, our labour, our industry, that the true production of this industry is utility; that the measure of this utility is the salary it obtains; and besides that the quantity of utility produced is what composes the sum of our means of existence and enjoyment. Now let us examine the two great branches of this industry, the change of form and the change of place, the fabrication and the transportation, or that which is called manufacturing and commercial industry.

CHAPTER IV.

Of the Change of Form, or of manufacturing Industry, comprising Agriculture.

Since the whole of society is but a continual succession of exchanges, we are all more or less commercial. In like manner, since the result of all our labours is never but the production of utility, and since the ultimate effect of all our manufactures is always to produce utility, we are all producers or manufacturers,—because there is no person so unfortunate as never to do any thing useful. But by the effect of social combinations, and by the separation of the different kinds of occupation which is its consequence, every one devotes himself to a particular kind of industry. That which has for its object the fashioning and modifying all the beings which surround us, to fit them for our use, we call specifically manufacturing or fabricating industry; and, for reasons before given, we comprehend in this that which consists in extracting the first materials from the elements which contain them, that is to say that which is called agricultural industry.—Let us examine the processes, and manner of operation, of fabricating industry in general.

M. Say has well remarked, that in every kind of industry there are three distinct things: First, to know the properties of the bodies which we employ, and the laws of nature which govern them; secondly, to avail ourselves of this knowledge to produce an useful effect; thirdly, to execute the labour necessary to attain this object. That is to say there is in every thing, as he expresses it, theory, application, and execution.

Before the existence of society, or during its infancy, every man is for himself the fabricator of whatever he wants; and, in every species of fabrication, he is obliged to fulfil alone the three functions of which we have just spoken. But in a more advanced state of society, by the effect of the happy possibility of exchanges, not only every one devotes himself exclusively to the particular industry for which he has the most advantages; but, also, in each kind of industry, the three functions of which we are speaking are separated. Theory is the part of the scientific, application that of the undertaker, and execution that of the workman.

These three species of labourers must derive a profit from the pains they take, for a man is born naked and destitute. He cannot amass 'till after he has gained; and before having amassed he has nothing, on which to subsist, but his physical and moral faculties;—if the use he makes of them produces nothing he must find a different method of employing them, or he will perish. Every one, then, of the labourers of whom we speak must find a salary in the profits resulting from the fabrication in which he co-operates.

But all have more or less need of advances, before they begin to receive this salary,—for it is not in an instant, and without preparation, that their service becomes sufficiently fruitful to merit a recompence.

The man of science, or he whom at this moment we consider as such, before he can have discovered or learned truths immediately useful and applicable, has had need of long studies. He has had to make researches and experiments; he has needed books and machines; in a word, he has been obliged to incur charges and expenses, before deriving any advantage from them.

The undertaker does not less experience the necessity of some preliminary knowledge, and of a preparatory education, more or less extensive.—Moreover, before he begins to fabricate, he must obtain a place, an establishment, magazines, machines, first materials, and also the means of paying workmen 'till the moment of the first returns. These are enormous advances.

Finally, the poor workman himself has not certainly great funds—yet there is scarcely a trade in which he is not obliged to have some tools of his own. He has always his clothes and his small collection of moveables. If he has but simply lived 'till the moment in which his labour begins to be worth his bare subsistence, this must always be the fruit of some former labour, that is to say of some riches already acquired,—which has provided for it. Whether it be the economy of his parents, or some public establishment, or even the product of alms, which has furnished the expenses,—there are always advances which have been made for him, if not by him; and they could not have been made if every one before him had lived from day to day exactly as brute animals, and had not absolutely any thing remaining from the produce of his labour.

What, then, are all these advances, great or small? They are what are commonly called *capitals,* and what I simply name *economies.* They are the surplus of the *production* of all those who have gone before us, beyond their *consumption,*—for if the one had always been exactly equal to the other there would be no remainder, not even wherewith to raise children. We have inherited from our ancestors but this surplus; and it is this surplus, long accumulated in every way, always increasing in accelerated progression, which makes all the difference between a civilized nation and a savage horde,—a difference, the picture of which we have before sketched.

The economists have entered into many details on the nature and employment of capitals. They have recognized many different kinds. They have distinguished capitals productive and unproductive; capitals fixed, and others circulating, moveable, and immoveable, permanent, and destructible. I see no great use in all these subdivisions. Some are very contestable, others founded on very variable circumstances, and others again entirely superfluous. It seems sufficient for the object we propose to remark, that prior economies are necessary to the commencement of every industrious enterprise, even of small extent; and it is for this reason that in every country the progress of industry is at first so slow,—for it is at the commencement above all that economies are difficult;—how can it but be difficult to make any accumulations, when a person has scarcely any thing beyond strict necessaries.

However, little by little, with the assistance of time and of some happy circumstances, capitals are formed. They are not all of the same kind; they are not all equal; and this gives birth to three classes of labourers, who co-operate in every fabrication, each raising himself to that to which he has been able to attain, or fixing himself at that which he has not been able to overpass. It is easy to perceive that this is the source of a great diversity in salaries. The man of science, he who can enlighten the labours of fabrication, and render them less expensive and more fruitful, will necessarily be sought after and well paid. It is true that if his knowledge is not of an immediate utility, or if being useful it begins to diffuse itself and to become common, he will run the risk of seeing himself neglected, and even without employment; but while he is wanted his salary will be large.

The poor workman, who has nothing but his arms to offer, has not this hope: he will always be reduced to the smallest price, which may rise a little if the demand for labour is much greater than that which is offered; but which will fall even below the necessaries of life, if more workmen offer themselves than can be employed. It is in these cases they perish through the effect of their distresses.

These two kinds of co-operators in fabrication, the man of science and the workman, will always be in the pay of the undertaker. Thus decrees the nature of things; for it is not sufficient to know how to aid an enterprize with the head or the hands: there must first be an enterprize; and he who undertakes it, is necessarily the person who chooses, employs, and pays those who co-operate. Now who is he who can undertake it? It is the man who has already funds, with which he can meet the first expenses of establishment and supplies, and pay wages till the moment of the first returns.

What will be the measure of the recompense of this man? It will be solely the quantity of utility which he will have produced and caused to be produced. He can have no other. If having purchased an hundred francs worth of articles, whatsoever, and having expended a hundred more in changing their form, it happens that what goes from his manufactory appears to have sufficient utility to induce a person to give four hundred to procure it, he has gained two hundred francs. If he is offered only two hundred for it, he has lost his time and his pains; if he is offered but one hundred, he has lost the half of his funds; all these chances are possible. He is subject to this incertitude; which cannot affect the hireling, who always receives the price agreed on, whatever happens.

It is commonly said that the profits of the undertaker (improperly called salaries, since no one has promised him any thing,) ought to represent the price of his labour, the interest of his funds, and indemnification for the risks he has run: it is necessary and just that it should be so. I agree if you please that this is just, although the word just is here misapplied; because no one having contracted an obligation with this undertaker, to furnish him with these profits, there is no injustice committed if he does not receive them. I agree further that this is necessary, for him to continue his enterprize, and not to become disgusted with his profession. But I say that these calculations are not at all the cause of his good or bad success. This depends solely on the quantity of utility he has been able to produce, on the necessity that others are under of procuring it, and finally on the means they have of paying him for it; for that a thing should be demanded it is necessary it should be desired; and to buy it, it is not sufficient to have the desire of possessing it, we must also have another article to give in return.

In this simple exposition, you already find all the mechanism, and the secret springs of that part of production, which consists in fabrication. You even discover the germ of the opposite interests, which are established between the undertaker and those on wages on the one part, and between the undertaker and the consumers on the other, amongst those on wages, between themselves, amongst undertakers of the same kind, even amongst undertakers of different kinds, since it is amongst all these that the means of the mass of consumers are more or less unequally divided; and finally amongst consumers themselves, since it is also amongst all of them, that the enjoyment of all the utility produced is divided. You perceive that the hirelings wish there should be few to be hired, and many undertakers, and the undertakers that there should be few undertakers, particularly in the same line as themselves, but many hirelings and also many consumers; and that the consumers, on the contrary, wish for many undertakers and hirelings, and if possible few consumers, for every one fears competition in his own way, and would wish to be alone in order to be master. If you pursue further the complication of these different interests, in the progress of society, and the action of the passions which they produce, you will soon see all these men implore the assistance of force in favour of the idea with which they are prepossessed; or, at least, under different pretexts, provoke prohibitive laws, to constrain those who obstruct them in this universal contention.

If there be a class which does not follow this direction, it will be that of the consumers; because all the world being consumers, all cannot unite to form a club, and to demand exceptions; for it is the general law, or rather liberty, which is their safe-guard. Thus it is precisely, because their interest is the universal interest, that it has no special representatives, or ravenous solicitors. It even happens that illusions divide them, and cause them to lose sight of the principal object; and that they solicit partially, and in different directions, against their real interest; for much knowledge is requisite to know it as it is general; and much justice to respect it, because the world lives on preferences. All those, on the contrary, who have a particular predominating interest, are united by it; form corporations; have active agents; never want pretexts to insist for prevalence; and abound in means, if they are rich, or if they are formidable, as are the poor in a time of troubles, that is to say when the secret of their force is revealed to them, and they are excited to abuse it.

At this moment it is not necessary to follow so far the consequences of the facts which we have established. Let us observe only, that the most necessary labours are the most generally demanded, and the most constantly employed; but, also, that it is in the nature of things, that they should always be the most moderately paid for. This cannot be otherwise. In effect, the things which are necessary to all men, are of an universal and continual use. But, for this reason alone, many occupy themselves constantly in their fabrications, and have soon learnt to produce them, by well known processes, and which require only common understanding; thus they have necessarily become as cheap as possible. Moreover it is indispensable they should not be dear; for almost their whole consumption is always made by people who have but few means, inasmuch as the poor are every where the most numerous, and are every where also the greatest consumers of necessary things, which indeed compose almost their whole expense. If then they were not at a low price they would cease to be consumed, and the poor could not subsist. It is on the lowest price to which they can be brought, that the lowest price of wages is regulated; and the workmen, who labour in their fabrication, are necessarily comprised in this latter class of the lowest wages.

Remark also, that there is nothing in what we have just said of manufacturing industry, which is not as applicable to agriculture as to all other species of fabrication. There are, in like manner, in agriculture, theory, application, and execution; and we find there the three kinds of labourers, relative to these three objects. But what applies eminently to agriculture, is the general truth which we have established, that labours the most necessary are, from this circumstance alone, the worst paid. In effect, the most important and most considerable productions of agriculture, are the cereal plants with which we are nourished. Now I ask to what price corn would rise, if all those employed in its production, were as dearly paid as those who labour in the arts of the most refined luxury? Certainly the poor workmen of all the common trades, could not attain it; they must absolutely die of hunger, or their wages must rise to a level with those of agricultural workmen; but then those of the others would rise likewise in proportion, since they are more sought after; thus the first would not be advanced. They would always be at the lowest possible rate; such is the law of necessity.

What is true of agricultural workmen comparatively with other workmen, is true of agricultural undertakers comparatively with other undertakers. Their processes are well known. It requires but a middling understanding to employ them. Results of a long experience; during the existence of which numerous essays have been made, and, more than is commonly believed, they are in general well enough adapted to the localities; and there are iew means of ameliorating them sufficiently, sensibly to augment their profits, whatever may be said by rash speculators who from time to time nearly ruin themselves. Thence it is, that, without extraordinary circumstances,* the profits of agricultural undertakers are very small in proportion to their funds, their risks, and their pains. Moreover, these well known and very simple processes, are nevertheless very embarrassing in practice; they require much care and time, so that in this state, one man can never be sufficient for the employment of large funds. He could not for example direct at the same time five or six farms even if he should have five or six times five or six thousand francs to stock them; and yet this is but a moderate sum, in comparison with certain lines of commerce. Thus this man, who cannot make great profits in proportion to his funds, is at the same time unable to employ considerable funds. It is then impossible that he should ever make a real fortune. This is the reason why there always are and ever will be few capitals employed in agriculture, in comparison with the quantity of those which exist in society. Let us prove this truth by facts; they will show us at the same time why agricultural operations often take different forms, which have not, or do not appear to have any thing analagous in the other arts. It is

* One of these circumstances, the most extraordinary, is, without contradiction, the discovery of the advantages of the propagation of Spanish sheep, instead of those of the country. This is the immortal glory of M. D'Aubenton, and the fruit of thirty years perseverance. Well! What has happened since this has been established? Even before the cultivator could procure these animals, and before he well knew the manner of deriving advantage from them, he gives already a much higher rent for lands on which he hoped to be able to raise them: That is to say, a part of the profits is taken from him in advance; the remainder will not fail to be taken from him at the next lease.

an interesting subject, which I have not yet seen well explained in any of our books on agriculture, or of economy.

You never see, or at least very rarely, a man having funds, activity, and a desire of augmenting his fortune, employ his money in buying a large extent of land, to cultivate it, and make of it his profession for life. If he buys it, it is to sell again; or to find resources necessary to some other enterprize; or to take from it a cutting of wood; or for some other speculation, more or less transitory. In a word, it is an affair of commerce, and not of agriculture. On the contrary, you often see a man possessed of a good landed estate sell it, to employ the price in some enterprize, or to procure for himself some lucrative situation. It is because culture is not really the road to fortune.

Accordingly, almost all the rich who purchase lands, if they are in business, do it because they have greater funds than they can employ in their speculations; or because they wish to place a part beyond the reach of hazard. If they are in public stations, or if they do nothing but live at their ease, it is to place their funds in a solid and agreeable manner. But neither the one nor the other propose to occupy themselves the land which they buy. Be it pleasure or business, they always have something which interests them more. They hope never to have any further trouble with them, than to rent them to undertakers of culture, as they would rent*

* It will be matter of astonishment to hear me say *rent* money, as we say rent lands, or a house; but I am more justly surprised, that when they say lend money, they do not also say to lend land—for it

the money which has served to purchase them, and receive the interest, without troubling themselves whether its employment has produced loss or profit to the borrower, who makes use of it.

It is perhaps fortunate that the rich thus purchase lands to rent them; for agriculture being a laborious and little profitable profession, those who devote themselves to it have generally small means, as we have just observed. If they were obliged to begin by buying the land they wish to cultivate, all their funds would be absorbed; there would nothing remain for the other advances necessary to culture, and still they could undertake but small enterprizes. It is then more convenient for them to find lands to be rented, than to be forced to buy them; but this is not more convenient to them than it is convenient to other undertakers, and to themselves, to find money to borrow, when they need it to give a greater extent to their enterprizes; and this is only advantageous to them under the same restrictions, that is to say it lessens their profits and renders their situation more precarious; for it is well known that a merchant, who does not carry on at least the greater part of his business on his own funds, is in a very dangerous situation, and rarely has great success. However, such is the situation even of those whom we call great farmers.

is the same thing. The truth is, we ought not to say lend but in cases o gratuitous loans.

When we have a property whatsoever, there are but six ways of using it To preserve or destroy it, to give or sell it, to lend or rent it. They do not precisely destroy lands, but they keep them or give them, or sell them, or lend them, or rent them, as they do every thing else. There is the same difference between a lending and renting, as between giving and selling.

In a word, proprietors who let lands are lenders, and nothing more. It is very singular that we have almost always confounded and identified their interest with that of agriculture, to which it is as foreign as that of the lenders of money is to all the enterprizes undertaken by those to whom they lend. We cannot sufficiently wonder to see that almost all men, and particularly agricolists, speak of great proprietors of land with a love and respect truly superstitious; regard them as the pillars of the state, the soul of society;* the foster fathers of agriculture,—while they most frequently lavish horror and contempt on the lenders of money, who perform exactly the same office as the others.† A rich incumbent who has just let a farm exorbitantly high considers himself as a very clever, and what is more, as a very useful man; he has not the least doubt of his scrupulous probity, and he does not perceive that he is exactly the same thing as the most pinching usurer, whom he condemns without hesitation, and without pity. Perhaps even his farmer, whom he ruins, does not any more than himself see this perfect similitude; so much are men the dupes of words. It is true that so long as they are so, they understand things badly; and, reciprocally, so long as they understand badly the things of which they speak, they but imperfectly comprehend the words which they use. I cannot

* If it is in considering them as men in general, enlightened and independent, it is just; but if in their quality of proprietors of land, it is absurd.

† The lenders of land have even a great advantage over the others, because when they have found a mean of obtaining a higher rent, they have by this circumstance augmented their capital: land is sold according to its rents. This does not happen to the lenders of money.

help returning frequently to this fact, for it is a great inconvenience to just reasoning: which, however, we must endeavour to attain in every matter.

However it be, much land being in the hands of the rich, there is much to be rented; and this, as we have said, is the reason why there may be a great number of enterprizes of agriculture, although there is not a proportionate mass of funds in the hands of the men who consecrate themselves to this state. In time these rented lands arrange and distribute themselves in the manner the most favourable to the conveniencies of those who intend to work them. Hence arise to great proprietors different kinds of rural work, which are not the effect of caprice or of hazard, as is believed without reflection, but which have their causes in the nature of things, as we shall see.

In fertile countries the fecundity of the soil does not turn directly to the profit of him who cultivates it, for the proprietor does not fail to demand a rent as much higher as they are more productive. But this land yielding a great deal, the quantity which a man can employ furnishes a considerable mass of production. Now all things being otherwise equal, as the profits of every undertaker are always proportioned to the extent of his fabrication, here the profits may be sufficiently great to attract the attention of men possessed of a certain degree of care and capacity. Once again, it is not the fecundity of the soil which has enriched and enlightened them; but it is this fecundity which attracts them, and prevents them from transferring their means to other speculations. These men wish to make a profit from all their means; they would not be satisfied with a small work, which would leave useless a part of their funds and personal activity, and would yield them, but small profits. For their convenience great properties are distributed into large masses of land, of commonly from three to five hundred acres, with a good habitation near them. They desire nothing else. They bring the gear, teams, cattle, provisions, sufficient to enable them to wait; they do not fear being long without receiving, to receive yet more in the end. They make essays, they sometimes discover new means of production, or of sale. In a word they fabricate, they trade, and hold their rank amongst the undertakers of industry. These are our great farmers, and this our great culture. Notwithstanding these fine names, a great farm is yet without doubt a sufficiently small manufactory; but if it is almost the minimum of fabricating industry in general, it is the maximum of agricultural industry in particular.

When the soil is less fertile, this industry cannot raise itself to this point. Put the same number of acres in a farm, and the productions will be insufficient. Put therein the double, and one man will not be sufficient by himself to work it;* besides the expenses and risks augment in a greater proportion—the enterprize is no longer worth the pains. You cannot then find the same kind of men to undertake it. And if there be capitals somewhat considerable, and intelligence in those cantons, they will be car-

* If he takes it, it will be to under-rent and divide it. Then he will be a parasite being a speculator and not a cultivator. This is done by the principal farmers of large farms where they are let on half-stocks. Their object is traffic.

ried elsewhere. What then happens? These lands, which already yield less, the proprietors divide into still smaller portions, to place them within the competence of more persons of those of slender means, and who often even do not make the cultivation of these lands their sole occupation. It is in these places that you often see small farms, or simply houses with very little land, or even lands without any buildings Yet these grounds are rented. Those who take them, even bring to them the instruments and animals indispensable. In short they make a profit from them, by their own labour; but it is not to be expected that they should display there the same physical and moral means, as the great farmers of whom we have just spoken. They are generally small rural proprietors who are found in these places, who join this work to their former occupations, and are contented if the whole together furnishes them with the means of living and rearing a family, without pretending much to augment their ease, and without the possibility of it, but by extraordinary chances. This is what many writers call small culture, in opposition to that of which we have just spoken. Yet we shall see that there are several cultures still smaller, or, if you please, more miserable than this. Observe always that this kind of small culture and even that by hand, of which we shall soon speak, ordinarily pay a higher rent to proprietors than the great, in proportion to the quantity and quality of the land, by the effect of the concurrence of those who present themselves in great numbers to work it, because they have no other industry within their reach; but it is precisely this high rent which irrevocably fixes these cultivators in that state of mediocrity, or penury, which renders their culture so indifferent.

When the soil is still more ungrateful, or when by the effect of different circumstances the small rural proprietors are rare, the great proprietors of land have not this resource of forming small farms; they would not be worth the trouble of working them and there would be no body applying for them. They adopt then another plan: They form what are commonly called domains or half-shares (metairies); and they frequently attach thereto as much or more land than is contained in the great farms, particularly if they do not disdain to take into account the waste lands, which commonly are not rare in these places, and which are not entirely without utility, since they are employed for pasture, and even now and then are sown with corn to give rest to the fields more habitually cultivated. These *metairies,* as we have seen, are sufficiently large as to extent, and very small as to product; that is to say they require great pains and yield little profit. Accordingly none can be found having funds who are willing to occupy them, and to bring to them domestics, moveables, teams and herds. They will not incur such expenses to gain nothing. It is as much as these metairies would be worth, were they abandoned for nothing, without demand of any rent. The proprietor is himself then obliged to stock them with beasts, utensils and every thing necessary for working them; and to establish thereon a family of peasants, who have nothing but their hands; and with whom he commonly agrees, instead of giving them wages, to yield them half of the product, as a recompense for their pains. Thence they are called metayers, workers on half-shares.

If the land is too bad, this half of the produce is manifestly insufficient to subsist, even miserably, the number of men necessary to work it. They quickly run in debt, and are necessarily turned away. Yet others are always found to replace them, because these are always wretched people who know not what to do. Even those go elsewhere, often to experience the same fortune. I know some of these metairies which, in the memory of man, have never supported their labourers on the half of their fruits. If the metairie is somewhat better, the half-sharers vegetate better or worse; and sometimes even make some small economies, but never enough to raise them to the state of real undertakers. However, in those times and cantons in which the country people are somewhat less miserable, we find in this class of men some individuals who have some small matter in advance; as for example, so much as will nourish them during a year in expectation of the first crop, and who prefer taking a metairie on lease, at a fixed rent, rather than to divide the produce of it. They hope by very hard labour to derive a little more profit from it. These are in general more active, and gain something if the ground permits, if they are fortunate, if their family is not too numerous, if they have not given too great a rent for the an d; that is to say if a number of circumstances rather improbable have united in their favour. Yet we cannot regard them as true farmers, as real undertakers; since it is always the proprietor who furnishes the gear, the beasts, &c. and they contribute only their labour. Thus it is still proper to range them in the class of half-sharers.

The mass of beasts, which the proprietor delivers and confides to the half-sharer, is called cheptel. It increases every year by breeding, in places where they raise the young, and the half-sharer divides the increase as he divides the harvest; but on quitting he must return a cheptel of equal value with that he received on entering; and, as he has nothing to answer, the proprietor or his agent keeps an active watch over him, to prevent him from encroaching on the funds by too great a sale. In some places, the proprietors not being willing or able to furnish the stock of cheptel, there are cattle merchants, or other capitalists, who furnish them, who watch over the half-sharer in like manner, and take half the increase as the interest of their funds; on the whole, it is very indifferent to the half-sharer, whether they or the proprietor do it. In every case we can only see in him a miserable undertaker, without means, weighed down by two lenders at high premiums, (he who furnishes the land and he who furnishes the cattle,) who take from him all his profits, and leave him but a bare and sometimes insufficient subsistence. It is for this reason that this kind of cultivation is also justly called small culture, although it is exercised on sufficiently large masses of property.

There exists still another species of work to which the name of small culture is also given. It is that of small rural proprietors, who labour their lands themselves. Almost all the nations of modern Europe have set out from an order of things, wherein the totality of the soil was the exclusive property of a small number of great proprietors; and all the rest of the population laboured solely for them as domestics, as serfs, or as hirelings. But by the effect of industry always acting, and of successive alienations, there has been found in almost every country a greater or less number of these small proprietors of land, who all have this in common, that they live on their land, and their trade is to cultivate it. However, with respect to culture, it is wrong to arrange them all in the same class—for amongst them are some who have a somewhat considerable extent of ground; and it is particularly on poor lands we find them, because it is these that the rich have alienated in preference, not being able often to draw any thing from them themselves. These certainly do not incur the same expenses in their culture as the rich farmers of great farms; but they labour with draught animals of a better or worse quality, and they have some flocks. In a word, their work is absolutely similar to that of the small farmers, of whom we have spoken before.* There are others again who possess a very small extent of ground, and who work it with their hands alone,—whether in vegetables, or in grain, or vines. These even positively require this manner of working—which,

* See what is the difference of the employment of funds. This man, who cultivates on a small scale, has perhaps an estate on which he could raise thirty thousand francs. If he would sell it he would have wherewithal to take a great farm in a good country; he would be much better, and would gain more: But perhaps he does not not know that this possibility exists far from him. Were he to know it he would fear the risks and his own inexperience: and, besides, man holds to his habits, and to the pleasure of property.

as we see, is very different from the preceding: besides the greater part of those who thus employ themselves cannot live solely on the produce of their soil, and undertake day labour a part of the year. We must assimilate to these latter all those who hold on leases from rich persons small habitations, with spots of ground attached to them; and who are known by the name of tenants, labourers, cottagers, &c. &c. Their industry is absolutely the same, and their existence quite similar; except that the small rent they pay represents the interest of the capital which the others possess: Here, then, is a third thing which is also called *small culture;* and which comprehends two kinds of it, very different from each other.

This is not all—there are many writers who call *great culture* that which is done with horses, and *small culture* that which is done with oxen; and who believe that this division answers exactly to that of farmers and half-sharers. But these two designations are far from being equivalent, for on one side the labourers work with their hands:—nothing prevents the cultivators of small farms, and the small proprietors of the first of the two species which we have distinguished, from labouring sometimes with horses or mules; and these cultures do not the less deserve the name of small. Moreover it may well be if such should be the local conveniences, that the great farmers may work with oxen; and I believe this is seen in several countries. On the other side, it is true that in general the half-sharers work with oxen: 1st. Because this method being less expensive, the greater part of proprietors prefer it. 2d. Because commonly the poor countries, which are those where we see half-sharers, produce bad hay, little or no oats, and are not susceptible of artificial meadows. 3d. Because these half-sharers being negligent and unskilful, it is difficult to confide to them animals so delicate as horses. But it is not this which constitutes them half-sharers, and which distinguishes between them and farmers. Their specific character is that of being wretched, without means, and unable to make any advances. It is that which reduces them to be half-sharers, and makes their culture really small; although by reason of the extent of their metairies, which commonly occupy a great deal of ground, there are some who still call it *great culture*, in opposition to that of small farmers or small labourers, or in opposition only to culture by hand.

Finally, that nothing may be wanting to the confusion of ideas, there are some angloman authors (as Arthur Young) who amuse themselves by calling small culture that of our greatest farmers, because they there see lands at rest, reversing exclusively the name of great culture for that system of rotation which themselves approved,—without reflecting that in the smallest of all cultures, that by hand, we most frequently see land that is never suffered to rest.

Thus we see by fair statement five or six different manners of employing the same words, of which two or three at least separate things absolutely similar, and unite others totally different; and these words are continually used without explaining in which sense they are taken. Proceeding thus, it would be a great miracle if they should understand one another.

I think if it is wished to write with some precision on agriculture, we must banish the expressions great and small culture as too equivocal; but distinguish carefully four sorts of culture, which have very distinct characters, because they are essentially different; and under which we can arrange all imaginable cultures.* These are first the *great farms*, or the culture of rich and intelligent undertakers, who make largely all the necessary advances. We see them only in places worth the trouble. 2dly. The *small farms*, or the culture of undertakers who likewise employ draught animals of their own, but whose means of all kinds are less extensive. They are generally found on poorer soils. (This class includes the small farmers, and the small proprietors, of the first of the two species which I have distinguished.) 3dly The metairies, or the culture by half-sharers, who also employ draught animals, but which do not belong to them. This is peculiar to bad soils. 4thly. Day labourers, or the culture by hand, as well that of proprietors as of tenants. We find these everywhere, and especially in vine countries. But they are in general less numerous in very good or in very bad

* If I dare to affirm this, it is not because I have travelled much; but I have had property for about forty years, in a country of great farms, a country of vineyards, and of bad half-shares. I have always followed their progress with attention; and more with a view to the general effect than to any particular interest. I have effected sensible ameliorations in the two latter, and I am persuaded that when we have thus a sufficient field of observation we gain more by thoroughly examining than by multiplying them.

countries: In the first because the rich have kept almost all the land, in the others because the land would not compensate them, and they prefer going to seek their livelihood by day labour elsewhere.—This division appears to me clearer and more instructive than all the others, because it shows the causes of the effects. Let us therefore use it as to what remains for us to say.

I think I have proved that the proprietors of lands, who do not work them themselves, have absolutely nothing in common with agriculture, nor with the laws which govern it, nor with the interests which direct it; that they are purely and solely annuitants and lenders of a particular kind; and, consequently, that having to give an account of the fabrication of the products, I ought to put them aside, and consider only the undertakers of culture.

Then I have shown that it is indispensable that the undertakers of the most necessary fabrications should be, of all others, those who make the most slender profits, in proportion to the quantity of their advances and productions; and further, that agricultural undertakings have this particular inconvenience, that one man is not sufficient to give them so great an extent as to compensate for the smallness of his profits by the greatness of his business.

I have shown afterwards—First, that the most fertile countries are those alone, in which the products of the quantity of land which one man can manage are sufficiently considerable to make the lot of the undertaker tolerable; that it is for these reasons that those countries are also the only ones in which we see undertakers of culture having sufficient means and capacity; and that they moreover seldom act on their own funds, but on those of others,—which is always a disadvantageous situation for fabricators. We call them, however, great farmers.

2dly. That when the lands are less good, the profits become so very slender, that we can no longer find but indifferent and insufficient undertakers. These are the *small farmers*.

3dly. That when the soil is still worse, the profits becoming absolutely null, the owner is reduced to the necessity of having no undertaker; for half-sharers are really but receivers of wages, since they make no advances and furnish only their labour.

4thly. and finally, That other circumstances render the enterprize so small that the undertaker and labourer are necessarily one and the same person, who employ no machine but their hands, and employ even them often elsewhere. Such are the day labourers. Such a business can scarcely tempt a capitalist.

There is, however, an exception to these general truths. It is in favour of the culture of very precious productions: such as certain drugs for dying, or wines highly esteemed. There great profits may be made. Accordingly we sometimes see great capitalists buy lands suitable to these productions, cultivate them themselves, draw from them all their profits, and make of them immense and fortunate speculations. But this exception itself confirms the rule; for these productions have the merit and the price of rarities. They are a real merchandise of luxury. Thus these speculations, although agricultural, are not in the class of fabrications of things of the first necessity.

If this picture is exact, if it is a faithful representation of facts, if it is true that agriculture, even under the most favourable circumstances, is not and cannot be but a laborious and not very profitable profession, we must not be astonished that it does not hold the first rank in society, and that capitals do not seek it. We should perceive that they are not and never will be so employed but by those who cannot or know not how to employ them otherwise. The only mean of causing numerous capitals to be employed in agriculture is, then, to cause them to superabound elsewhere. This evil, if it be one, is incurable; and it is very useful to know it. For however we may say that agriculture is the first of arts ; that it is the foster mother of man; that it is his natural destination ; that we are wrong in not honouring it more ; that the emperor of China ploughs a furrow every year, and a thousand similar fine things ; all this will amount to nothing, and will change nothing in the march of society :— These are vain declamations which do not merit our attention. Let us make only some short reflections on the first of these phrases, because it conceals an error. To bring it to light is to refute it.

Certainly agriculture is the first of arts in relation to necessity ; for before all things we must eat in order to live. If they mean to say this only, they say what is incontestible but very insignificant. If they understand by these words that agriculture is the only art absolutely necessary, the assertion is very inexact; for we have other very pressing wants besides that of eating, as for example that of being clothed and lodged. Moreover culture itself, in order to be in a small degree developed, needs the succour of many other arts, such as that of melting metals and fashioning wood; and its products, to be completely appropriated to our use, still require at least that of the miller and baker. Here then we see many other indispensable arts.

Finally, if they have pretended to affirm, as many will have it, that agriculture is the first of arts in relation to riches, the pretended axiom is completely false. In the first place we have seen, in respect to individuals, that those who devote themselves to agriculture are inevitably of the number of those who make the smallest profits: thus they cannot be of the richest. Now what is true of every individual cannot be false of nations, which are but collections of individuals. If you doubt the strength of this demonstration place on one side twenty thousand men occupied in the cultivation of wheat for sale, and on the other an equal number occupied in making watches. Suppose that both find a market for their produce, and see which will be the richest: Such are Geneva and Poland.

One of the things which has most contributed to the mistake of so manifest a truth is also an equivocal expression. We take very frequently our means of *subsistence* for our means of *existence*. These are two very different things. Our means of subsistence are without contradiction alimentary matters; and the quantity of these that can be procured in a country is the necessary limit of the

number of men who can live therein. But our means of existence is the sum of the profits we can make by our labour, and with which we can procure for ourselves both subsistence and other enjoyments. It is in vain that the Polander raises a great quantity of wheat: the overplus of what he consumes, which he is obliged to sell to foreigners at a low price, with difficulty supplies his other wants. He does not live the better on it, nor multiply more. The Genevan, on the contrary,—who does not gather even a potatoe, but makes great profit on the watches he fabricates,—has that with which he can buy grain and all other things necessary for him; on which he can bring up his children, and likewise economise. The first, notwithstanding the great quantity of his means of subsistence, has very few of the means of existence: The second, having great means of existence, procures abundantly the articles of subsistence which he has not, and whatever else he wants. It is therefore true that these are two things, which it is very wrong not to distinguish carefully. This fault shows itself in many otherwise excellent works, (particularly in that of Mr. Malthus on population) in which it casts an ambiguity over some explications, valuable in all respects. It is therefore a point which it was well to elucidate.

Let me not, however, be accused of mistaking the importance of agriculture, and of wishing that it should be neglected. In the first place I know very well that, although useful in itself, it is not the only thing to be desired either for individuals or for societies; and that a nation, notwithstanding great means, has but a precarious existence if it depends on strangers for its subsistence. I know, moreover, that although each single enterprize of culture cannot be regarded but as a very small manufactory, as in a large country their number is immense in comparison with that of all other fabrications, they compose a very great portion of the industry and wealth of a nation. The great details into which I have gone to analyse the operation of all the springs of agricultural industry, prove sufficiently the importance I attach to it; and certainly to show clearly that a profession is at the same time very necessary, and very unprofitable, is the best method of proving that it should be favoured. But we have not yet reached this point. The only object at present is to establish facts. We will afterwards draw their conclusions; and if the first of these operations has been well performed the second will not be difficult. Let us confine ourselves then to these generalities on fabricating industry, and speak of commercial industry.

CHAPTER V.

Of the change of place, or of Commercial Industry.

THE insulated man would fabricate to a certain point, because he would labour for himself; but he would not trade,—for with whom could he have trade? Commerce and society are one and the same thing. Accordingly we have seen in the first chapter, that society from its origin is essentially nothing but a continual commerce, a perpetual series of exchanges of every kind,—of which we have rapidly indicated the principal advantages and the prodigious effects. Commerce then exists long before there are merchants, properly so called.—These are agents who facilitate it, and who serve it, but who do not constitute it. We may even say that the exchanges which they make in their commercial capacity are but preparatory exchanges; for the exchange for use is not completed, has not fully attained its end, until the merchandise has passed from him who fabricated to him who wants it, whether to consume it or to make it the subject of a new fabrication; and the latter ought at this moment to be regarded as a consumer. The merchant, properly so called, interposes between these two persons, the producer and the consumer; but it is not to injure them. He is neither a parasite nor an inconvenient person: On the contrary, he facilitates relations, commerce, society; for, once again I repeat, all these are one and the same thing between this producer and this consumer. He is useful then, and consequently a producer also; for we have seen (Chapter II.) that whosoever is useful is a producer, and that there is no other way of being so. It is now to be shown how the merchant is a producer of utility. But previously let us give some preparatory explanations, which will be of service to us in the sequel. We have in the first chapter only shown the general advantages of exchange, and those of the commerce between man and man. Let us render sensible those of the commerce between canton and canton, and country and country; and for this purpose let us take France for example, because it is a very large and well known country.

Let us suppose the French nation the only one in the world, or surrounded with desarts impossible to be traversed. It has portions of its territory very fertile in grain; others more humid, which are good only for pasturage; others formed of arid hills, which are only proper for the cultivation of vines; finally others more mountainous, which can produce little else than wood. If each of those portions should be reduced within itself what would happen? It is clear that in the corn districts a tolerably numerous population could still be subsisted; because it would at least have the mean of amply satisfying the first of all wants, that of nourishment: however this is not the only want.—Clothing, shelter, &c. &c. are also necessary.—These people then will be obliged to sacrifice in woods, pasturage, and bad vines, much of this good land; of which a much smaller quantity would have sufficed to procure for them what they wanted by way of exchange, the remainder of which would still have nourished many other men, or served to provide better for those who live there. Thus this people would not be so numerous as if they enjoyed commerce, and yet they will want many things. This is still more true of those who inhabit the hills suitable to vines. If they are even industrious they will only make wine for their own use, not being able to sell it. They will exhaust themselves in unfruitful labours to produce on their arid hills some grain of inferior quality, not knowing where to purchase; they will want every thing else. The population, although agricultural, will be miserable and thin. In districts of marshes and meadows, too humid for corn, too cold for rice, it will be much worse. They must necessarily cease to cultivate, and be reduced to be graziers, and even to nourish as many animals only as they can eat. It is very true that in this situation—having beasts of burden, of draught, and for the saddle, to render themselves formidable,—they will soon become brigands, as all erratic people are; but this will be an evil the more. As for the country of woods there would be no mean of living but the chase, in proportion and so far as they would be able to find wild animals, without even thinking to preserve their skins; for what use could they make of them. This however is the state of France: if you suppress all correspondence between its parts, one half is savage the other badly provided.

Let us suppose, on the contrary, this correspondence active and easy, but always without exterior relations. Then the production proper to each canton would no longer be arrested for want of a vent, nor by the necessity of pursuing in spite of localities labours very unfruitful but necessary, for want of exchanges, in order themselves to provide either well or ill for all their wants, at least for the most pressing. The country of good land will produce as much corn as possible; and will send it to the country of vineyards, which will produce as much wine as can be sold. Both will supply the country of pasturage, in which the animals will multiply in proportion to the market, and the men in proportion to the means of existence which this market would procure for them. And these three countries united would feed in the mountains the most rugged industrious inhabitants, by whom they will be furnished with wood and metals. They would increase the quantity of flax and hemp in the north to send linen cloth into the south; which last would increase their silks and oils to pay for them. The smallest local advantages would be turned to profit. A district of flint would furnish gun-flints to all the others which have none, and its inhabitants would live on the produce of this supply. Another of rocks alone will send mill-stones into several provinces. A little spot of sand will produce madder for all the diers. Some fields of a certain kind of clay will furnish earth for all the potteries The inhabitants of the coast will set no bounds to their fishing, being able to send their salted fish into the interior; it will be the same with sea salt, with alkalies, with marine plants, with the gums of resinous trees. New kinds of industry will be seen arising every where, not only for the exchange of merchandise, but also by the communication of knowledge; for if no country produces all things none invents all things. When there is communication, what is known in one place is known every where; and it is much readier to learn, or even to perfect, than to invent; besides it is commerce itself which inspires the desire of inventing, it is even its great extension which alone renders possible many different kinds of industry. Yet these new arts occupy a multitude of men, who do not live on their labour, but because that of their neighbours having become more fruitful suffices to pay them. Here then is the same France, lately so indigent and uninhabited, filled with a numerous and well provided population. All this is solely owing to the better employment of every local advantage and of the faculties of every individual, without a necessity for the French nation to have made the smallest profit at the expense of any other nation, without even a possibility of its so doing, since our hypothesis supposes it alone in the world. We will see elsewhere what we should think of those pretended profits which one people makes at the expense of another, and how we ought to appreciate them.—But we may affirm in advance, that they are illusory or very small; and that the true utility of exterior commerce, that in comparison with which all others are nothing, is to establish between different nations the same relations which interior commerce establishes between different parts of the same nation, to constitute them, if we may thus speak, in a state of society with one another; to enlarge thus the extent of market for all, and by this mean increase likewise the advantages of the interior commerce of every one.

This commerce, without doubt, can and does exist, to a certain point, before there are *commercialists*, properly so called; that is to say men who make commerce their sole occupation; but it could not be much developed without their assistance.—When a man has fabricated, or is in possession of some useful thing, he may it is true exchange it himself, without an intermediary, for another useful thing which some other man possesses; but this is not often either easy or commodious. This other man may not have a desire of selling when we wish to buy; he may be unwilling to sell but a great deal at a time; he may not care for that which is offered in exchange; he may be very distant; we may even not know that he has that which we desire. In fine, in the course of life one has need of an almost infinite multitude of different things. If it were necessary to draw directly each of them from its immediate producer, one would pass their whole time in going backward and forward, and even in distant journeys; the inconveniences of which would greatly surpass the utility of the things which would be their object; it would therefore be necessary to do without them.

The merchant comes: He draws from all places the things which superabound therein, and carries thither those which they want. He is always ready to buy when any one wishes to sell, and to sell when any body wishes to buy. He keeps his merchandise till the moment it is wanted, and retails it if necessary. In short, he takes it off the hands of the producer, who is encumbered with it, places it within reach of the consumer who desires it; and all their relations have become easy and commodious: Yet what has he done? In his commercial capacity he has operated no change of form, but he has operated changes of place, and a great utility is produced. In effect, since values are the measure of degrees of utility, (see chapter 3d) it is manifest that a thing carried from a place where it is at a low price and brought to one in which it bears a high one, has acquired by its transportation a degree of utility which it had not before.

I know that this explication is so simple that it appears silly, and that all this appears written for children; for men are not supposed to be ignorant of facts so common and truths so trivial. But these trivial truths demonstrate another very much contested, which is, that whoever produces utility is a producer, and that the merchant is quite as much one as those to whom they have wished exclusively to give this title. Now let us search what is his recompense for the utility he has produced.

If we examine commercial industry it presents us the same aspect as fabricating industry. Here also, there is theory, application and execution; and consequently three kinds of labourers, the man of science, the undertaker, and the workman. Also, it is true that those whose labour is applied to the most necessary things are inevitably the worst paid; but it is not as in the enterprizes of agriculture.—

The undertaker can augment his speculations indefinitely as far as the market permits, and thus compensate the smallness of his profits by the extent of his business. Hence the proverb, there is no small trade in a large city. The head of a commercial enterprize also gives salaries to those he employs: He makes all the advances; and he is recompensed for his pains, his expenses, and his risks, by the augmentation of value which his labour has given to things—an augmentation which causes his sales to surpass his purchases. It is true that as the undertaker of fabrication he loses, instead of gaining, if being deceived in his speculations his labour is unfruitful. Like him, also, he labours sometimes on his own funds, sometimes on those he borrows. In short, the similarity is complete, and this dispenses me from entering into more details. It is not yet time to discuss delicate questions, nor to appreciate the merit of certain very complicated combinations. As yet we have had occasion to give a general glance of the eye only on the march of society and the train of affairs. If we have formed a just idea of them we shall soon see that many things which are thought very mysterious are merely perplexed by prejudice and quackery, and that mere common sense is sufficient to resolve difficulties which appear very embarrassing when we have not remounted to principles. To complete the laying our foundation let us say a word of money.

CHAPTER VI.

Of Money.

I have already spoken of the developement of industry, and even of that of commerce; and I have not yet said a word of money. It is because in effect it is not more indispensable to commerce than merchants. Those are its agents, this its instrument. But it can and does exist, to a certain point, before and without these two helps,—although they are very useful to it.

We have seen in the third paragraph of the introduction, and in the third chapter, which treats of *values*, that all useful things have a determinate value. They have even two; but at this moment I speak only of the conventional value, or market price. All these values are measured the one by the other. When, to procure any thing whatsoever, one is disposed to give a double quantity of any other thing whatsoever, it is evident that the first is twice as much esteemed as the second.—Thus the relation of their value is fixed; and one can exchange or negotiate these two things at this rate, without recourse to any thing intermediate.—We can give hay for corn, or corn for wood; a cart-load of potters clay, or of brick earth, for some plates or tiles, &c.; but it is evident that this is very inconvenient, that it occasions removals so troublesome as to render most affairs impracticable; that many of these merchandises are not divisible, so as to correspond well with the others; that many amongst them cannot be indefinitely preserved until the moment of finding employment for them, and that were they preserved we are still greatly embarrassed if, as must continually happen, what we have is not precisely that which suits him who possesses what we desire; or if he wishes but a very small quantity of ours, when we want a large quantity of his. In the midst of all these difficulties commerce then ought to be very languishing, and consequently industry also. It is proper to dwell a little on these inconveniencies, for we are always but little affected by those which we have never experienced. We do not even imagine them. Having never seen such an order of things, we have no lively idea of it; it appears to us almost chimerical. But it has existed, and probably for a very long time before that of which we still complain; and even with reason, although it is much better.

Happily amongst all useful things there is one kind which is distinguished, that of the precious metals. These like others are a merchandise, inasmuch as they have the necessary value which results from the labour their extraction and transportation have cost, and the market value given them, by the possibility of making them into vases, ornaments, or different conveniencies and instruments. But they have moreover the property of being easily refined; so that we know very exactly what quantity we have of them, and that all their parts are similar,—which renders them very comparable, and leaves no fear of their being of different qualities. Besides they are inalterable, and susceptible of being divided into portions as great or small as we wish. Finally, they are easily transported.—These qualities must cause every one to prefer these metals to every other useful thing, whenever we only wish to preserve the value we possess for an indefinite time until the moment of want. For every one who has any merchandise subject to damage, the quality of which may be uncertain or changeable, which is of great incumbrance, or little susceptible of being retailed on occasion, is naturally disposed to exchange it for another which has none of those inconveniencies. From this general disposition, it will naturally result, that the merchandise, which possesses so many advantages in this respect, should become by degrees the common measure of all others. This is also what has happened every where. This appears singular when the reason is unknown, but inevitable when known. It is the same in all cases. So soon as a thing is, be assured there are victorious reasons why it should be, which however does not mean that stronger reasons may not afterwards be discovered why it should no longer be. But here it is not the case. The precious metals once become the common and general measure, the universal type of all exchanges, acquire still an advantage which they had not before. It is first to have a greater market value, as they have acquired a new kind of utility; (but this would not affect the object which now occupies us) and next their market value their price becomes more constant than that of any other merchandise. Being in constant demand in all places, and on every occasion, they are not subject to the variations experienced by a thing sometimes sought sometimes refused: Besides they do not depend on the inconstancy of the seasons, and very little on that of events. Their total quantity does not change, but from causes slow and rare. They are then every day more confirmed in their character of being the common measure of exchanges. However they are not yet *money*. As yet they are transmitted only in bars and ingots, and at every change of hands they must be assayed and weighed; this is troublesome.

When society is a little more perfected, the competent authority intervenes to give to this mean of exchanges a greater degree of commodiousness. It divides these metals into portions adapted to the most ordinary uses. It impresses on them a mark which indicates the total weight; and in this weight the quantity of foreign matter which it has been convenient to leave therein for the facility of fabrication, but which is not to be counted for real value. This is what is called the weight and standard.—In this state the metals have become completely money; and authority has done a benefit in giving them this character. We shall see hereafter that it has but too often done evil by other acts of its power in this way.

This short explanation of the nature of money shows us, first, that there can only be one metal which can really be money, that is to say to the value of which we refer all other values; for in every calculation there can be but one kind of unit which serves as a basis. This metal is silver, because it is this which is best adapted to the greatest number of subdivisions, of which there is need in exchanges. Gold is too rare, the other metals too common.

Gold, however, comes in aid of silver in the payment of very great sums; as would, also, the precious stones if they were divisible without a loss of value. But it is only as a subsidiary that it is employed, and only by referring the value of gold to that of silver. The proportion in Europe is nearly as fifteen or sixteen to one; but it varies, as every other proportion of value according to the demand. In China it is commonly as twelve or thirteen to one; whilst in Indostan, on the contrary, we are told it is about as eighteen or twenty to one. Thus there is a profit in carrying silver to China, because for twelve ounces of silver you have there one ounce of gold, which on return into Europe is worth fifteen ounces of silver, whereby you have gained three ounces; and, on the contrary, there is a profit in carrying gold into Indostan, because for one ounce of gold you there have eighteen of silver, and thus you have gained three ounces of the latter metal. Political authorities may however very well coin money of gold and fix its proportion with that of silver, that is to say, determine that, whenever there are no stipulations to the contrary, one ounce of gold or fifteen or sixteen ounces of silver shall be received indifferently. It is as in judicial actions, they establish that when there are sums of money that ought to bear an interest which has not been stipulated by the parties, that interest shall be so much per cent. But they cannot, or at least ought not to prevent individuals from regulating between themselves the quantity of gold which they wish to give, or receive, for a certain quantity of silver, any more than from determining by agreement the rate of interest of the sum they lend or borrow. Accordingly, it is thus these two things are always arranged in the great operations of commerce, even in spite of all laws to the contrary; because without it business would not be done at all.

As to copper money, or that of billion,* wherever there is one of silver it is not real money. It is a false one. If it contained a sufficient quantity of copper to be really worth the quantity of silver to which it is made to correspond, it would be five or six times as heavy as it is, which would render it very inconvenient. Still this proportion would vary as that of gold, and more frequently, because of the more numerous uses for which copper is employed. Thus copper money is worth but the quantity of silver agreed to be given in barter for it.—Accordingly it ought only to serve for the facilitation of small fractions, in which this exaggeration of its value would be of no importance; because the moment after it is paid away at the same rate, in making it fulfill the same function. But when, as has happened sometimes, the payment of large sums of money with copper is authorized, it greatly wrongs him who receives it; as he can never find an opportunity of realising by agreement such large masses

* Billion is a mixture of a great deal of copper, and so little silver, that the extraction of the latter would not be worth the expense.

at their nominal value; but only at their real value, which is five or six times less. Let us conclude, then, that there can never be but one metal which may be the common term of comparison, to which may be referred all values; and that this metal is silver.

Since the utility of the impression, which makes of a morsel of metal, a piece of money, consists in the establishment of its standard and weight, we see further that it was very superfluous to invent, for the keeping of accounts, imaginary monies, such as livres, sous, and deniers, and others of this kind, which however are called money of account.* It would have been much clearer to say a piece of one ounce, of half an ounce, of a drachm, of a grain of silver; than a piece of six livres, of three livres; of twelve or of fifteen sous: We should have always known the quantity of silver of which we wished to speak. This idea presents itself so naturally, that I am induced to believe it would have prevailed, if all monies had been of the same standard: But, as their degree of purity has always been very different, the wish perhaps has been to have a mean of expressing that such an ounce of silver was worth a sixth more than such another, in saying that the one is worth six livres, and the other five. Perhaps, also, the expression of which I speak has been rejected precisely because it was too clear: For those who have participated in these matters, have always wished that others should understand

* Several of these denominations have been originally names of real monies, a Louis, Crowns and Ducats.

nothing of them, and they have their good reasons for it. We shall see many proofs of it.

However this may be, these arbitrary denominations being once admitted and employed in all the obligations contracted, we should take great care to make no change of them; for when I have received thirty thousand livres and have promised to repay them at a certain time, if, in the interval, the government says that the quantity of silver which was called three livres shall be called six, or which is the same thing, if it makes crowns of six livres, which do not contain more silver than was contained in the crowns of three, I who pay with these new crowns do not really return but the half of what I had received. This is merely an accommodation of which an indebted legislator wishes to avail himself with his numerous creditors; and it is to veil and disguise it that he gives me such an advantage with mine, and even with himself, if by chance I am his debtor. It is true, he knows well that he has none; but it has an air of generality and reciprocity which resembles equity and dazzles. In spite of this deception, let us speak plainly, this is permitting every one to rob to enable himself to rob; and it is, as we must acknowledge, what almost all governments have so frequently done with so much audacity and so little moderation, that, for example, what is now called in France a livre, and which formerly really was a *pound* of silver of twelve ounces, is scarcely one out of eighty-one parts thereof at present, when the mark is worth fifty-four livres; government, then at different times has stolen eighty parts out of eighty-one which it owed; and if there still exists a perpetual annuity of *one livre*, established in those ancient times in consideration of *twenty livres* received, it is paid at present with one part out of eighty-one of what was originally promised, and of what is honestly due. If at this time none of these annuities remain, it is because they have been successively reimbursed in the same manner as interests are at present. What is more frightful in such legal iniquity, is that it is not merely to permit injustice, it is to enjoin it, to enforce it. For, except in rare circumstances, an individual of the greatest probity is obliged to avail himself of the odious permission given him, since, every one using it against him, he would soon be ruined, and even insolvent. Thus he has but a choice between two bankruptcies, and he ought to decide in favour of that which the law authorises.

We will follow no farther the moral effects of such laws; this is not the place; and, besides, they are sufficiently sensible, their economical effects are these: First, all the creditors, who are reimbursed, are suddenly impoverished; and all the debtors, including the government, are enriched by their losses. Thus it is an extraordinary levy of money on a single class of citizens; which is even very unequally apportioned amonst them, and is further augmented uselessly by the whole portion which goes to the profit of other citizens, who find themselves in a position like that of the government, whose apparent interests are the motives of the measure.

Secondly, all the creditors who are not actually reimbursed their capitals are impoverished in like manner; because their rent is discharged with the same nominal value, but with a less real one. Here the thesis changes for the government. It is of the number of those creditors frustrated in the whole of what it receives in annual imposts; for they are paid with the same quantity of money, but with one-half less of effective silver, if it has diminished the value of money by an half. In truth, as it has the power in its hands, it soon doubles the existing imposts, and thus thinks itself at par; and that it has a clear gain of what it has avoided paying.

However, it is not so; for the third effect of this fine operation is to cause a fear that at every moment it may recommence, and that no further reliance can be had in plighted faith; to excite by this mean inquietude in all relations, and eventually to diminish all industrious and commercial speculations. Thus the public suffers, national riches diminish, and a great part of the imposts become ineffectual; for the labour which paid them is decreased, and he who gains nothing can contribute nothing. Moreover, the government has always need of being furnished with many supplies and advances; which it cannot exact by force. The price is doubled, if the value of the money is diminished one-half. This is quite plain. But, besides, every thing has become dear and scarce; and, what is more, in bargaining it is made likewise to pay for the fear it has created of its being a second time wanting in good faith. Thus its expenses are augmented in a greater proportion than its revenues, even after it has doubled the imposts.

In last result it has committed a robbery, which has caused to itself much more evil than it has produced good. Yet it is this which for a long time was very generally regarded as a wise operation of finance. It is here, then, we may well wonder how men are the dupes of words. To the shame of the human understanding, it would perhaps have been sufficient to preserve it from such an illusion, that the piecés of money should have been, as we have said, designated solely by their weight, instead of bearing insignificant names. It is very probable that then they would have seen, that half an ounce could never become an ounce.

Yet in truth, this becomes doubtful, when we see illusions, more gross and injurious than these, still succeed with many men, or at least be only imperfectly distinguished. This reflection leads us directly to paper money, with which Europe is inundated at the moment in which we are speaking; (1810) and to which recourse is always had, in spite of the constant experience of its inevitable effects.

To defend an injustice it is always necessary to rest it on an error. This is an universal rule. Those who have wished to defraud their creditors of a part of the money they owed them, by diminishing the quantity of silver contained in the money with which they expected to pay them, have all pretended that silver has no value in itself, as we cannot drink or eat it; that it is but the sign of of real values; that it is the impression of the monarch which gives it the quality of a sign, and that it is indifferent whether it be put on a greater or smaler quantity of metal. One might answered them, if silver has no value, why do you retain that which you owe? You have no occasion for it. Give it to us first, then you may put your impression on pieces of wood if you please, and you will see the effect it will produce. It does not seem necessary to be very sharp sighted to devise this overwhelming answer. Yet it has not been made because it was not so easy to prove directly that silver, as all useful things, has a proper and necessary value: indeed, to demonstrate this incontestably, it was necessary to remount, as we have done, and perhaps as has never been done before, to the first and only cause of all value, labour.

This foolish notion (we must call things by their names) that money is but a *sign* is then maintained, and still repeated every day. Many writers give no other name to money; and persons who think themselves historians and politicians gravely give you an account of the system of law and discuss it at full length, without perceiving, after a hundred years of reflection, that it is solely on this notion it was founded, and that all the rest consists but in accessories, imagined to mask this foundation.* The notable principle, then, of which we are speaking is neither abandoned nor proscribed. If they no longer avail themselves of it to degrade the coins, it is not because they are ashamed of it; it is because they have found a way of making a more complete application of it. For, in fact, in the most false of coins; there remains always a little silver. In that which is now substituted for it there is not any;

*It is for this reason that Law himself, when the Abbey Terrasson proposed to him to reimburse the Catholic Church with his paper, answered—the Roman Clergy are not such fools.

this is still better. They have not followed the counsel we just now gave, of putting the stamp of the prince on pieces of wood; they put it on paper, and this amounts to the same. The multiplied relations of perfected society have suggested this idea and likewise serve to mask the fraud. Let us explain this.

Paper, like every thing else, has no necessary value, but that which it has cost to fabricate it; and no market value, but its price in the shop as paper. When I hold a note, or an obligation of any kind, of a solvent person, to pay me at sight an hundred ounces of silver, this paper has only the real value of a piece of paper. It has not that of the hundred ounces of silver which it promises me. It is for me only the sign that I shall receive these hundred ounces of silver when I wish; in truth, when this sign is of an indubitable certainty, I am not anxious about realizing it. I may even, without taking this trouble, pass it by agreement to another person, who will be equally tranquil with myself, and who may even prefer the sign to the thing signified; because it is lighter and more portable. We have not yet either the one or the other any real value, (I count for nothing that of the piece of paper) but we are as sure of having it when we wish, as with the money we are sure of having a dinner when we shall be hungry. It is this that induces us both to say, that this paper is the same thing as the silver.—But this is not exact; for the paper only promises, and the silver alone is the value itself.

Proceeding on this equivoque, the government comes and says, you all agree that the paper of a rich man is equal to silver. Mine, for much stronger reasons, should have the same property, for I am richer than any individual; and moreover, you agree that it is my impression alone which gives to silver the quality of being the sign of all values; my signature communicates to this paper the same virtue. Thus it is in all respects a real money. By a surplus of precaution, they do not want inventions to prove that the paper about to be emitted really represents immence values. It is hypothecated, sometimes on a considerable quantity of national domains, sometimes on the profits of a commercial company, which are to have prodigious success; sometimes on a sinking fund, which cannot fail to produce marvellous effects; sometimes on all these together. Urged by arguments so solid, all who hope that this operation will enable government to grant them gifts, and all its actual creditors, who fear that without this expedient they will not be paid at all,—who hope to have this paper among the first, and to pass it away very soon, before it is discredited; and who moreover, calculating that if they lose something by it, they may amply indemnify themselves by subsequent affairs,—do not fail to say they are fully convinced that the paper is excellent; that it is an admirable invention, which will secure the safety of the state; that they are all ready to take it; that they like it as well as silver; that their only embarrassment would be if they should meet with persons stubborn and distrustful, as there will always be, who would not be willing to receive it; that to prevent this inconvenience it will be necessary to compel every body to do as they do, and that then all difficulties will have vanished. The public itself—prejudiced by so many sophisms, which have such numerous supporters,—at first relishes the measure, then desires it, and persuades itself that one must be absurd or evil intentioned not to approve it. Thus they make a real *paper money*, that is to say a paper which every one has a right to give and is obliged to take as good money; and it is not perceived that it is precisely the force they employ to render this paper better, which radically vitiates it.

In effect the government, which has only created it to liberate itself, makes in the first place enough to extinguish all its debts. It is commanded to be received, people are disposed to do it; it circulates with facility, it is in every one's hands concurrently with silver. It appears even at first to increase the activity of commerce, by multiplying capitals. Moreover it is only employed in large payments, and in the placing of funds. Thus the daily service and that infinite multitude of small exchanges which constitute the habitual march of society, continue as usual, and every body is satisfied.

Afterwards the same authority uses the same mean for its ordinary expenses. It observes necessarily less economy, conscious of resources always ready. It embarks in enterprizes, either of war, politics or administration, of which it would not have dared to think, knowing well that without this facility they would surpass its abilities. The paper is then greatly multiplied. The contractors for the government are the first to say that all things have grown very dear, that they must have much higher prices. They are careful not to avow, that it is because a promise is not silver, and that the promise begins to appear doubtful. They attribute this fact, at which they appear surprised, to a momentary encumbrance, which it will be easy to remove by slackening all payments except their own; to the intrigues of a party of mal-contents, which should be suppressed; to the jealousy of foreigners, who will only deal with them for ready money, for the objects they are obliged to draw from them.—It is impossible not to yield to such good reasons; and, above all, to necessity. The expenses are therefore augmented considerably, and the paper likewise.

People receive it still because they are forced; but every one demands much more of it for the same thing. Soon an acknowledged and known proportion is established between paper and silver. It becomes so disadvantageous to the paper, that those who live on salaries, annuitants, and the proprietors of leased estates, who are paid with this money are greatly aggrieved. Salaries are augmented particularly those of the officers of government; which is by so much the more burthened; the others suffer horribly. At this epoch, of the depreciation of paper, government already experiences the same loss in its imposts that individuals do on their annuities and rents. This embarrasses it, but this is not the moment to augment the public burthens. It is easy to create paper to supply the deficiency it experiences. It prefers this mean; hence a new cause of emission and depreciation.

The difference between paper and silver encreasing progressively, no one ventures to give any credit, or to make any loan; they do not even venture to buy in order to sell again; because they know not at what price they may be able to resell; all commerce languishes. The proportiou or rather the disproportion continually increases; it arrives to that point that the daily transactions for things of the first necessity, and which require only small sums paid in silver, become impossible—for an hundred francs in paper would be given rather than twenty-five in silver; and, for the same reason, if you owe twelve francs nobody will give you the change on a note of an hundred. There is universal outcry and complaint. Disputes are indeterminable, because both parties are right. The evil is supposed to be remedied by making notes for the smallest sums, and they are made,* but nothing is gained by this, for from this moment we no longer see a crown; and so soon as the most usual things are paid for with paper, they rise to a price proportioned to the discredit of the paper, that is to say, to such that nobody can afford them. The public authority is then inevitably forced to rate the necessaries of life.

Then society ceases and universal brigandage begins. All is fraud or punishment. The government lays requisitions every where, and the people plunder; for nothing but force can oblige a sale at loss, or to part with things which they fear soon to

* We have seen them even for five sous. You may judge whether it be possible to superintend them, and if three-fourths of them were not false.

want themselves. In fact a general want takes place; for no one makes new provisions, or new fabrications, for fear of suffering new spoliations. All trades are abandoned. There is no longer possibility of living on the produce of regular industry: every one subsists on what he can conceal, or on what he can lay his hands, as in an enemy's country. The poorest die in crowds. We may say in the strictest sense, that society is dissolved; for there is no longer any free exchanges.

There is no longer any necessity for small notes, for the largest hardly suffice for the smallest sums. We have seen three thousand livres paid for a pair of shoes, and been very happy to obtain them in secret at this price; for force may well oblige a thing which exists to be given for nothing, but it cannot oblige it to be made. Having reached this point, the government on the contrary must give a very high nominal value to every piece of its paper,—not merely that it may be of some use, but that, even to itself it may represent a little more real value than its fabrication has cost. This is the reason that in France, towards the last of the existence of paper money, government thought proper to make mandates, which were nothing but assignats of a new form; but to which was attributed a value an hundred times greater than that of the others, without which they would not have paid the cost of making them. Thus the process reached that pass that a note of a hundred francs in assignats, for example, had not effectively the real value of the piece of paper on which it was written; and it would have been worth more for him who received it if blank, or rather if he had received the price which it had cost.*

Such a fact appears incredible; yet we have all witnessed it, and it clearly proves two important truths: The one, that when we endeavor to go contrary to the nature of things, we are inevitably pushed to the most monstrous extremities; the other, that it is as impossible to give to things a real value which they have not, as to take from them the natural and necessary value which they have, which consists, (we cannot too often repeat it) in the labour which their production has cost.

In vain would it be said that paper money, may be used, without being abused to this excess, constant experience proves the contrary; and, independently of experience, reason demonstrates, that once abused, we are forced to abuse it more; and that it is not made *money*, that is to say having a forced circulation, but on purpose to be abused. For when you leave it to a free course, the moment in which a fear that you cannot fulfill your engagements occasions an unwillingness to receive it, indicates the moment in which effectively you begin to form engagements beyond your resources, that is to say to abuse it; when you give it a forced currency, it is because you are unwilling to be warned of that moment, and are determined to go beyond it, that is to say to enter into engagements which you cannot fulfill. In a word when your paper is good, it is useless to oblige people to receive it; when bad, it is iniquitous and absurd to force it to be received

*It is true that these mandats were the end of all; that they lasted but a few days; and that they never had a real currency: for no fear of punishment could determine any one to take them at any price.

as good. No solid answer can ever be given to this dilemma. Mirabeau had therefore great reason to utter the celebrated phrase, which he too much forgot afterwards : All paper money is a phrensy of despotism run mad.

We have seen that the consequences of the madness are still more fatal than those of the debasement of coins. The reason is simple. This debasement when not repeated, has but a momentary effect, by which many suffer as by a hail storm, and others profit as by a windfall ; but all things resume quickly their ordinary course. On the contrary, the gradual depreciation of paper money,d uring all the time of its existence, produces the effect of an infinite number of successive debasements continued to total annihilation; and during all this time, no one knowing on what to calculate, the progress of society is completely interverted. Add to this, that paper is made to much larger amounts than even bad money is coined. Thus the evil is still much greater.

Let us conclude, that paper money is the most culpable and most fatal of all fraudulent bankruptcies ; that the adulteration of *metallic monies* comes next; and that when a government is sufficiently unfortunate to be no longer able to pay its debts, it can do nothing better than declare frankly its insolvency, and compound faithfully with its creditors,— as an imprudent but honest merchant. The evil is much less; reputation remains, and confidence is soon renewed—three inestimable advantages.— Wherever there is candour, and probity, there is remedy for misfortune. This is one of the numerous points at which *economy* and *morality* are joined; and which render them but different parts of the same subject, the case of that one of our intellectual faculties which we call the Will.

After having thus spoken of silver, its uses, its real value, of the danger of pretending to replace it by fictitious values, it is proper to turn our thoughts for a moment to what is called the *interest of money*. This subject like many others would be very simple, if endeavours had not often been used to obscure it; and if it had never been treated on, but after the preliminaries with which we have preceded it.

Since we rent horses, coaches, furniture, houses, lands, in a word whatever is useful and has a value, we may well rent money also—which is likewise useful, has a value, and is exchanged every day for all these things. This rent of money is what is called *interest*. It is as legitimate as every other rent. It ought to be equally free. There is no more reason why public authority should determine its rate, than that of the lease of a house or a farm. This principle is so evident, that it ought never to have met with any difficulty.

There is nevertheless what is called legal interest; it is that which tribunals adjudge in judiciary cases, in cases in which the parties have not been able to agree, but in which it is still just that the debtor should pay some interest. It is very proper that the law should have determined it beforehand. It should neither be too high nor too low; not too high, that the debtor of good faith,—who wished to pay his debts, but has been prevented by circumstances not depending on himself,—should not be aggrieved for having been obliged to detain his money. Not too low, that the debtor of bad faith, who has had recourse to chicanery to defer payment, may not gain by having retained the disposition of his funds. In a word, it should be such that neither the creditor nor the debtor should be injured. For this purpose, the law should fix it as it is to be presumed that the parties would have agreed on, that is to say conformably to the most ordinary rate in analgous circumstances. But once again I repeat it, this *legal interest* should be of no consideration, whenever the parties have themselves been able to make their agreements. The public authority should never intervene in particular transactions, but to ensure their execution, and to lend its support to the fidelity of engagements.

It is true however, that it is the interest of society in general, that the interest of money should be low. First, because all the rents, paid by industrious men to capitalists, are so far funds taken from the laborious class for the profit of the idle. Secondly, because, when these rents are high, they absorb so large a part of the profits of industrious enterprises that many become impossible. Thirdly, because the higher these rents are, the greater the number of those who live without doing any thing. But all this is not a reason for government to fix the rate of interest; for we have already seen that society has absolutely the same motives for desiring that the rents of land should be at a low rate;* and yet no

* Agriculture is no where so flourishing and advancing as in those countries where the rents of land are as yet nothing; because there

one has ever proposed to declare usurious, and illicit the rents of farms which exceed a certain price. Moreover, to fix the rate of interest is not a mean of diminishing it; on the contrary, it is only in some manner to invite to dissimulation: for the lender will always require the most he can get for the enjoyment of his capital; and he will also be indemnified for the risque he runs in eluding an imprudent and even an unjust law. The only mean of diminishing the price of the interest of money is to make the mass of a nation rich, that thus there may be large sums to be lent, and that industrious men nevertheless have little need of borrowing.

Instead of fixing the rate of interest, we might perhaps extend to this kind of convention the principle of damage for more than the half, (lezion d'outre moitie) which, in certain cases, authorises the rescission of engagements; but the application of

are still lands belonging to nobody; for then all the produce of these lands is for him who cultivates them. See the western part of the United States of America.

This should teach us to appreciate the sagacity of those profound politicians, who pretend that it is highly advantageous to a natio a that its landed property should sell very high; because, say they, it follows that its soil, which is a large part of its capital, has a great value. They have no doubts on the subject.

However there are two ways of understanding the expression, very dear. Do they wish to say, that it is desirable that land should be sold high, in proportion to the rent which may be drawn from it? that is true; for this proves that the interest of money is low, and that the idle take but little from the laborer.

But do they wish to say that it is good that an acre of land should sell dear in proportion to what it will produce? that is false; for this price is so much taken from him who is going to work this acre, thus it is to say, that it is advantageous to take from this useful man a part of his means, and often to render his enterprize impossible by augmenting its expenses. Experience and reason declare equally against this mistake.

this principle would often be very embarrassing in matters of loan: it would require attention to many circumstances of difficult estimate, and especially to the degree of risk run by the lender in parting with his funds. At least, I would wish in this supposition for still stronger reasons, that the rents of land should be comprised under the same rule; for there is no risk of the funds being carried off. But I would always prefer that individuals should be left entirely free in their conventions.

To finish this chapter on money, and all that has relation to it, it remains for us to say a word on *exchange* and on *banks.* These are two very distinct things which are often confounded; let us examine them separately.

Exchange, or the service of an exchanger, is an operation the most simple. It is to barter money for money when it is required. It is only necessary to know how much pure gold or silver is contained by each of the two to render the same quantity he receives, and to take a stipulated reward for the small service he performs; or it is to barter ingots for money. This is still exactly the same thing. It is only necessary further to take into account the small increase of value which is given to the metal by the quality of money, impressed on it by the effigy or seal of the sovereign. If the standard value of metals were as easy to be established as their weights, the personal interest, the most inventive in fishing in troubled water, could not throw the least obscurity on a similar transaction; and, notwithstanding this small difficulty of the assay, it is still sufficiently clear when nothing else is mingled with it, because the two things to be exchanged are present. It is only requisite to value both and to barter. But the operation of the exchanger is often complicated with that of the banker. Let us now explain this.

The function of the banker is to enable you to receive in another town, the money which you deliver him in this in which you are. In this he renders you a service, for if you have need of your money in that other town, either to pay debts or to expend there, you must send or carry it thither; and this occasions expense and risque. The banker, who has a correspondent there, gives you a note called a *bill of exchange*, in virtue of which the correspondent remits you your amount. On an inverse occasion, the same correspondent gives to another person a like bill of exchange on your banker; thus they are quits, and they have obliged two persons; and, as every service merits a reward, they have retained at each time for their recompense a stipulated portion of the money transported. Such is the service and the profit of a banker.

I have always been astonished that writers, who have given long dissertations on this negociation, who know its utility, who have exaggerated its importance, have mistaken the increase of value, which a merchandise receives by a change of place; and have refused the quality of producer to the merchant, who transports it: for in this case, which is the most simple, it is very clear that when you, who live in Paris, owe an hundred francs at Marseilles, you would rather give your banker an hundred and one francs, than to carry yourself or send your hundred francs to Marseilles: and, reciprocally, if you had there an hundred francs, you would rather receive ninety-nine of them at Paris of the same banker, than go to Marseilles and receive the whole amount. Merchandise delivered at its destination has then really a value which it had not before; it is this which engages you to give your banker a recompence, although it costs him nothing to render you this service.

To this first profit he commonly adds another. You give him your money to day, the bill which he gives you in return will only be payable in fifteen or twenty days, more or less; time must be allowed for its arrival; the correspondent must be apprized; he might not have the funds; pretexts are never wanting to lengthen the delay. However it is not till the day of payment that the banker credits the sum to his associate. Thus, during all the interval, he enjoys your money gratuitously and can put it to use; and as money bears an interest it is a profit sufficiently considerable: for it is plain, that if he has successively eighteen or twenty similar commissions; he has gained the interest of the sum for a whole year.

To these calculations must be added a third.—when many Marseillese are indebted to the Parisians, they all demand bills payable at Paris.—These become scarce; the bankers may be embarrassed in furnishing them, their correspondents being already in advance with them. They take occasion hence to demand of you, independent of their commission, an hundred and two or three ounces of silver for procuring an hundred to your order at Paris; and you, who are under a necessity of acquitting yourself, will give it, not being able to do it for less. For a contrary reason, if Parisians have at the same time need of bills on Marseilles, the bankers of Paris might for an hundred ounces of silver give them a bill for an hundred and two or three ounces, since this is the price put on them at Marseilles. But as they alone are well acquainted with these fluctuations, they always combine to prevent the individuals from the whole profit, and to throw on them more than a necessary loss; and this is a new source of profit for them.

This is what is called—not very properly, in my opinion,—the course of exchange; and what ought rather, as I think, to be called the course of banking: for these two cities being in the same country, and employing the same money, there is no exchange, but merely a transportation of specie, which is the proper office of the bank. This course is said to be at par, when an hundred ounces of silver in one place are paid with an hundred in another; and that it is high or low, when it requires more or less,* always independently of the banker's commission.

* When less than a hundred francs are sufficient to pay an hundred elsewhere, it is said that the exchange is *low*. This is the case with the city which, compensation being made, still remains creditor, because apparently it has sent to the other more merchandise than it has received. This low exchange gives it an advantage in importation, for it can pay for the same things with less silver. But for the same reason it is disadvantageous if it continues to export, for it will require more money to pay them for the same quantity of merchandise. This is equivalent to a rise of price, and diminishes the demand.

This sole consideration, independently of many others, shows how ridiculous it is to believe that a country can always and constantly export more than it imports. It would be quickly arrested merely

The operation of exchange, on the contrary, mingles itself with that of banking, and complicates it when funds are to be transported from one country to another: for the sum which is received at Paris, and for which a bill is given on London, has been deposited in French money and will be paid in English money. We must ascertain then the concordance of these two monies, and determine how much pure metal is contained in each, according to the known laws of their fabrication. We must estimate too, at least approximately, what the pieces of money in the two countries may have lost since they have been in circulation. Hence it is that all other things being equal, less is demanded to pay the same sum in any country, when the money is ancient, and has consequently suffered much waste by use, and by the fraud of clippers, than when it is quite new and untouched: for in the latter case it contains really more metal, and the bearer of the bill will receive more for the same sum. This exchange is yet another source of profit for the bankers.

To this all the operations of exchange and banking are reduced, which as we see are very simple, and would be very clear if all coins bore the name of their weight and the mark of their standard value; and if pedantry and charlatanism had not concealed and disguised notions so common, under a multitude of barbarous names and cant terms, such as the initiated alone can understand.

by the course of exchange. But we are not yet come to the examination of the reveries on the pretended balance of commerce; it suffices to have made this observation.

Bankers render yet another kind of service.—When the bearer of a bill of exchange, not yet due, has need of money, they advance it to him, retaining the interest of the sum for the time remaining before the day of payment. This is called *discount.* Sometimes they receive from an individual effects not demandable other than bills of exchange; as bills of credit of long terms, title papers of property, and hypothecations on land; and guaranteed by these securities they advance money to him, making him pay an interest higher or lower. At other times, knowing a man to be solvent, they give him for a retribution a credit on them for a determinate sum; and they make themselves the agents of all his business, undertake to collect all his credits and to pay all his debts. These are so many ways of being useful; but in all these cases they are essentially *lenders* and *agents* for business, and not properly *bankers,* although bank services are mingled with these operations. All this, nevertheless, is ordinarily comprehended under the names of banks of discount, accommodation, credit, circulation, &c.

All these bankers, exchangers, agents, lenders, discounters, at least the richest and most accredited amongst them, have a strong tendency to unite themselves into large companies. Their ordinary pretext is, that transacting thus much more business they may be content with a smaller profit on each, and perform all the services on much better terms; but this pretextis illusory—for if they transact more business they employ more funds, and surely it is not their intention that every part of their funds should yield them a smaller profit. The truth is, that, on the contrary, they wish, by getting almost all the business into their own hands, to avoid competition, and make greater profits without any obstacle. Government, on their part, are much disposed to favor the establishment of these large companies, and to give them privileges to the detriment of their rivals, and of the public, with the expectation of receiving from them loans, either gratuitous or at a low rate which these never refuse. It is thus that the one sells its protection and the other buys it; and this is already a very great evil.

But these companies are of a much greater inconvenience. They emit bills payable at sight, bearing no interest, which they give for ready money. All those who depend on them, or are connected with them, (and they are very numerous) take their notes with eagerness and offer them to others. The public even which has great confidence in their solvency receives them willingly as very convenient. Thus they spread with facility, and are multiplied extremely. The company reaps in this an enormous gain, because the whole sum represented by these bills has cost it nothing but the fabrication of its paper, and yield it a profit as ready money. Howe-ver this is not yet an inconvenience, because these bills are always realized the moment they are demanded.

But soon the government, which has created it but for this purpose, asks of this company enormous loans; it dares not and cannot refuse them, because it depends on government to overthrow it by withdrawing its support for a moment. To satisfy this demand, s obliged to create an excessive quantity of new notes; it delivers them to the government, which employs them very quickly; the circulation is overdone with them; inquietude follows, every one wishes to realise them. It is evidently impossible, unless government repays that which it has borrowed; and this it does not do. The company can then but invoke its support. It asks to be authorized not to pay its notes, and to give them a forced circulation. It obtains its request, and society finds itself in the full state of *paper money*, of which we have seen the consequences. It is thus that the *caisse d'escompte produced the assignats in France. It is thus that the bank of London has brought England to the same state in which it is at this moment. It is thus all privileged companies end: they are radically vicious; and every thing essentially bad always terminates badly, notwithstanding its transient successes; all things hang together, and necessity is invincible. It would be easy to show that were these great machines so sophisticated not to produce the horrible danger which we have just described, the advantages promised by them would be illusory or very inconsiderable, and could add but very little to the mass of national industry and wealth. But it is not necessary to enter now into details; it suffices for us to have seen in a general manner the progression of affairs. Before going further, let us look back on the road over which we have travelled,—it is the mean of not going wrong as we advance.

* A bank existing at Paris at the commencement of the revolution.

CHAPTER VII.

Reflections on what precedes.

MANY readers will perhaps imagine that, so far, I have followed rather a whimsical course; that I have often ascended very high to establish truths very common; that I have disposed my chapters in an order which does not appear methodical; and, above all, that I have abandoned the subjects which I have treated without giving them all the developements of which they are susceptible. But I pray them to remark, that this is not a mere treatise on political economy. It is the second section of a treatise on our intellectual faculties. It is a treatise on the will, forming a sequel to a treatise on the understanding. My intention is much less to exhaust all the details of the moral sciences, than to see how they are derived from our nature, and from the conditions of our existence, in order to detect with certainty the errors which may have slidden into them by not ascending to this source of all we are and all we know. Now to execute such a design it is not the abundance of ideas we are to seek, but their severe enchainment, and a course uninterupted and without chasms. Still however I am persuaded that, without perceiving it, we are already much further advanced than we are aware.

In fact, we have seen that the property of being endowed with will, by giving us a distinct knowledge of our individuality, gives us thereby and necessarily the idea of property; and that thus property, with all its consequences, is an inevitable result of our nature. Here then is already a great source of rambling disquisition and of declamation totally drained.

We have afterwards seen that this same will, which constitutes all our wants, is the cause of all our means of providing for them; that the employment of our force, which it directs, is the only primitive riches and the sole principle of the value of whatever has one for us.

Before drawing any consequences from this second observation, we have likewise seen that the state of society is not only very advantageous to us, but is also so natural to us that we could not otherwise exist. Here then is another subject of common place notions, very false, exhausted.

Uniting these two points, the examination of the effect of the employment of our force, and of that of the increase of efficacy given to it by a state of society, has enabled us to discover what it is to *produce* for beings like ourselves, and what we ought to understand by this word. This, also, annihilates a great subject of ambiguity.

Strengthened by these premises, after some elucidations of the measure of utility of things, it was easy for us to conclude that all our industry reduces itself to a change of form and of place, and consequently that culture is a fabrication like every other; which dissipates many clouds obscuring this subject; and has enabled us to see very clearly the progress of every kind of industry, its interests, and the obstacles opposed to them. This likewise leads us to appreciate both men and things very differently from what is commonly done.

Finally, amongst all the things which have a value, we have remarked those which possess the qualities proper for becoming *money;* and we have easily recognised the advantages and the utility of this good and real money, and the danger of debasing it and of replacing it by another entirely fictitious and false in continuation; we have even cast a rapid glance on the small operations, commonly regarded as very great, to which the exchange of these monies and their economical transportation, under the name of banking, give place.

From whence it follows, if I am not mistaken, that we have acquired clear and certain ideas on all the important circumstances in the formation of our riches. Nothing then remains but to see in what manner their *distribution* amongst individuals is effected, and in what manner their consumption is effected, that is to say the use we make of them. We shall then have an abridged but complete treatise on all the results of the employment of our means of existence.

This second part, the distribution of riches in society, is perhaps that one of the three which gives place to the most delicate considerations, and in which we meet with phenomena the most complicated. However, if we have well elucidated the first, we shall see the obscurity of this fly before us, and all dissipate with facility. Let us endeavour to follow constantly the clue that guides us.

CHAPTER VIII.

Of the distribution of our Riches amongst individuals.

HITHERTO we have considered man collectively; it remains to examine him distributively. Under this second point of view he presents an aspect very different from the first. The human species, taken in mass, is rich and powerful, and sees a daily increase of its resources and its means of existence; but it is not so with individuals. All in their quality of animated beings are condemned to suffer and to die: All, after a short period of increase, should they even live through it, and after some momentary successes, should they obtain them, relapse and decline; and the most fortunate amongst them can do little more than diminish their sufferings and retard their term. Beyond this their industry cannot go. It is not useless to have this gloomy but true picture of our condition present to our minds. It will teach us not to desire impossibilities, and not to consider as a consequence of our faults what is a necessary result of our nature. It brings us back from romance to history.

There is more. These resources, these riches, so insufficient for happiness, are also very unequally divided amongst us; and this is inevitable. We have seen that *property* exists in nature: for it is impossible that every one should not be the proprietor of his individuality and of his faculties. The inequality in these is not less : for it is impossible that all individuals should be alike, and have the same degree of force, intelligence and happiness. This natural inequality is extended and manifested in proportion as our means are developed and diversified. While they are very limited it is less striking, but it exists. It is an error not to have recognised this among savage nations. With them particularly it is very grievous : for it is that of force without restraint.

If, to banish from society this natural inequality, we undertake to disregard natural property, and oppose ourselves to its necessary consequences, it would be in vain : for nothing which has its existence in nature can be destroyed by art. Such conventions, if they were practicable, would be a slavery too much against nature, and consequently too insupportable to be durable ; and they would not accomplish their purposes. During their continuance, we should see as many quarrels for a greater share of the common goods, or a smaller part of the common trouble, as can exist among us for the defence of the property of individuals ; and the only effect of such an order of things would be to establish an equality of misery and deprivation, by extinguishing the activity of personal industry. I know all they tell us of the community of property with the Spartans ; but I reply boldly it is not true because it is impossible. I know well that at Sparta the rights of individuals were very little respected by the laws, and totally violated in respect to slaves. But a proof that nevertheless they still had property, is that there were thefts. Oh! tutors, what contradictory things you have said, without being aware of it!

The frequent opposition of interest among us, and the inequality of means, are then conditions of our nature, as are sufferings and death. I do not conceive that there can be men sufficiently barbarous to say that it is a good; nor can I any more conceive, that there should be any sufficiently blind, to believe that it is an evitable evil. I think this evil a necessary one, and that we must submit to it. The conclusion which I should draw from it (but it is as yet premature) is, that the laws should always endeavour to protect weakness; while too frequently they incline to favour power. The reason is easily perceived.

After these data, society should have for its basis, the free disposition of the faculties of the individual, and the guarantee of whatever he may acquire by their means; then every one exerts himself. One possesses himself of a field by cultivating it, another builds a house, a third invents some useful process, another manufactures, another transports; all make exchanges; the most skilful gain, the most economical amass. One of the consequences of individual property is, if not that the possessor may dispose of it according to his will after death, that is to say at a time when he shall no longer have any will, yet at least that the law determines in a general manner to whom it shall pass after him; and it is natural that it should be to his nearest kindred. Then inheritance becomes a new mean of acquiring; and what is more, or rather what is worse, of acquiring without labour. However, so long as society has not occupied all the space of which it may dispose, all still prosper with care; for those who have nothing but their hands, and who do not find a sufficiently advantageous employment for their labour, can go and possess themselves of some of those lands which have no owners, and derive from them a profit so much the more considerable, as they are not obliged to lease or buy them. Accordingly care is general in new and industrious nations. But when once all the country is filled, when there no longer remains a field, which belongs to nobody, it is then that pression begins. Then those who have nothing in advance, or who have too little, can do no otherwise than put themselves in the pay of those who have a sufficiency.* They offer their labour every where, it falls in price. This does not yet prevent them from begetting children and multiplying imprudently; they quickly become too numerous. Then it is only the most skilful and the most fortunate among them who can succeed. All those whose services are in the least demand, can no longer procure for themselves but a subsistence the most strict, always uncertain, and often insufficient. They become almost as unhappy as if they were still savages.

* Once more I repeat, that hired labourers are not solely in the pay of the proprietors of land, but in that of all those who have capitals with which to pay their wages.

It is this class, destitute of the favours of fortune that many writers on economy call *non-proprietors ;* this expression is vicious in several respects. First, there are no non-proprietors, if by that we understand men entirely without the right of property. Those of whom we speak are more or less poor; but they all possess something, and have a need of preserving it. Were they but proprietors of their individuality, of their labour, and of the wages of this labour, they would have a great interest that this property should be respected. It is but too often violated, in many of the regulations made by men who speak of nothing but property and justice.— When a thing exists in nature, no one is without interest in it. This is so true of the right of property, that the felon, even, who is about to be punished for having violated it, if he is not entirely cut off from society, has an interest that this right should be respected : For the day after he had undergone his punishment, he could not be sure of any thing that remained to him, if property were not protected.

Secondly, the same writers, in opposition to the pretended non-proprietors, call by the name of proprietors those only who possess estates in land. This division is entirely false, and presents no meaning ; for we have seen that a landed estate is but a capital like another, like the sum of money which it has cost, like every other effect of the same value. One may be very poor, possessing a small field, and very rich without possessing an inch of land. It is therefore ridiculous to call the possessor of a poor inclosure a proprietor, and to refuse this title to a millionary. It would be more reasonable to divide society into poor and rich, if we knew where to place the line of demarcation. But if this division were less arbitrary, it would not be less illusory in relation to property. For, once again I repeat, the poor man has as much interest in the preservation of what he has, as the most opulent.

A distinction more real in respect to the difference of interests, would be between the hirelings on the one part, and those who employ them on the other, whether consumers or undertakers. The latter, under this point of view, may be regarded as the consumers of labour. This classification would, without doubt, have the inconvenience of uniting together things very different; as, for example, of classing among the hired, a minister of state, with a day-labourer, and of placing amongst consumers the smallest master workman with the richest idler. But in fine, it is true that all the hirelings have an interest in being paid high, and that all those who employ them have an interest in paying them low. It is true, however, that the undertaker who has an interest in paying little to the hired, has the moment after an interest in being paid high by the definitive consumer; and, above all, it is true, that we are all more or less consumers: for the poorest day labourer consumes articles produced by other hired persons; on which I make two reflections.

First, the interest of the hired being that of a very great number, and the interest of the consumers being that of all, it is singular enough that modern governments should be always ready to sacrifice first the hired to the undertakers, in shackling those by apprenticeships, corporation privileges, and other regulations; and afterwards to sacrifice the consumers to these same undertakers, by granting to these privileges, and sometimes even monopolies.

Secondly, I remark, that although each of us has particular interests, we change so frequently our parts in society, that often we have under one aspect an interest contrary to that which we have under another, so that we find ourselves connected with those to whom we were opposed the moment before; which fortunately prevents us from forming groupes constantly enemies. But, above all, I observe that in the midst of all these momentary conflicts, we are all and always united by the common and immutable interests of proprietors and consumers, that is to say, that we have all and always an interest, first, that property be respected; secondly, that industry should be perfected; or, in other words, that fabrication and transportation should be in the best state possible. These truths are useful, to comprehend perfectly the workings of society, and to be sensible of all its advantages. It was a desire of rendering them evident which induced me to enter into these details. Let us return to the subject of the distribution of riches, from which they have drawn us, although they are not foreign to it.

I have a little hastened above the moment in which distress begins to make itself felt in the bosom of new societies, by fixing it at the instant in which all land has a master, and at which it can no longer be procured, without being bought or rented.—

Certainly at this epoch a great mean of care is exhausted, labour loses an opportunity of employing itself in a manner extremely advantageous, and the mass of subsistence ceases to increase as rapidly; because there can no longer be a question of establishing new cultures, but only of perfecting the old, a thing always more difficult and less productive than is generally believed. However immense resources still remain. All the arts offer them in competition, especially if the race of men who form the new society have sprung from an industrious and enlightened nation, and if it has relations with other civilized countries: for then there is no question about inventing and discovering, which is always very slow; but of profiting and practising what is known, which is always very easy.

In fact, so long as agriculture offered such great advantages, all men unemployed, or not profitably enough employed to their liking, have turned themselves to that. They have only thought of extracting productions from the earth, and exporting them. Observe that without a facility of exportation, the progress of agriculture would have been much less rapid, but with this circumstance, it has employed all hands. Wages excessively high have scarcely been able to determine a sufficient number of individuals to remain attached to the profession of the other arts the most necessary. But for all those things, the manufacture of which has not been indispensable within the country itself in which they are consumed, it has been more economical to draw them even from a great distance, and they have not failed to do it! Accordingly the commerce of these infant nations consists at first solely in exporting raw products, and importing manufactured articles.

Now what happens at the epoch of which we are speaking, when all the territory is occupied? Agriculture no longer offering the means of rapid fortune, the men who have been devoted to it spread into the other professions; they offer their labour—they obstruct one another—wages lower in truth: But long before they have become as low as in the countries anciently civilized from whence manufactured articles are drawn, there begins to be a profit in manufacturing within the country itself the greater part of these articles: for it is a great advantage for the manufacturer to be within reach of the consumer, and not to fear for his merchandise either the expenses or dangers of a long voyage, nor the inconveniences which result either from the slowness or difficulty of the communications; and this advantage is more than sufficient to counterbalance a certain degree of dearness in the manufactory. Manufactories then of every kind are established. Several of them, with the aid of some favourable circumstances, open to themselves foreign markets after having supplied the internal consumption, and give birth to new branches of commerce. All this occupies a numerous population, who live on the produce of the soil, which then is no longer exported in as great quantities, because it has not augmented in the same proportion. This new industry is for a long time increasing, as was agricultural industry, which was the first developed, and so long as it increases, it affords, if not riches, at least ease to the lower classes of people.* It is not until it becomes stationary or retrograde that misery begins, because all lucrative employments being filled, without a possibility of creating new ones, there is every where more labour offered than demanded. Then it is inevitable that the least skilful and least fortunate among the labourers should find no employment, or receive but insufficient wages for what they do. Many of them necessarily languish, and even perish, and a great number of wretched must constantly exist. Such is the sad state of old nations. We shall soon see from what causes they arrive at it sooner than they ought, and by what means it might to a certain point be remedied. But previously some explanations are still necessary.

In fact, I am so bold as to believe that the picture which I have just traced, of the progress of societies from their birth, presents striking truths. There is in it neither a system made at pleasure, nor a theory established beforehand. It is a simple exposition of facts. Every one may look and see, if it is not thus they present themselves to the unprejudiced eye. It may even be observed that I have represented a nation, happily situated, enjoying all kinds of advantages, and making good use

* How very desirable it would be in such a case, that the superior class of society should be sufficiently enlightened to give to the inferior ideas completely sound of the social order, during this happy and necessarily transient period, in which it is the most susceptible of instruction. If the United States of America do not profit of it, their tranquility and even safety will be much exposed, when interior and exterior obstacles, and inconveniences, shall have multiplied. This will be called their decline and corruption. It will be the slow but necessary effect of their anterior improvidence and carelessness.

of them, and yet we come to this painful conclusion, that its state of full prosperity is necessarily transient. To account for a phenomenon so afflicting, it is not possible to stop at these vague words, of degeneration, of corruption, of the old age of nations, (as if an abstract being could be really old or young like a living individual,) all metaphorical expressions, which have been strangely abused, with which we have often been satisfied for want of better, but which in truth explain nothing, and which if they had a prevalence, would express effects rather than causes. We must then penetrate further. Every inevitable event has its cause in nature. The cause of this is the fecundity of the human species. Thus it is necessary to consider population; and afterwards we will resume the examination of the distribution of our riches.

CHAPTER IX.

Of the multiplication of Individuals, or of Population.

LOVE is a passion which so violently affects our heads, that it is not astonishing we should often be mistaken on all its effects. I acknowledge I no more partake of the zeal of the moralists, to diminish and constrain our pleasures, than of that of the politicians, to increase our fecundity and accelerate our multiplication. Each appears to me equally contrary to reason. At a proper time I may develope my opinions on the first point, at present the second is under consideration. Let us begin by establishing facts, by taking a view of all which surrounds us.

Under this relation, as under every other, we see nature occupied solely with the species, and not at all with the individual. Its fecundity is such in every kind, that if almost the totality of germs which it produces were not abortive, and if much the greater part of the beings brought forth did not perish almost immediately for want of aliment, in a very short time a single species of plants would suffice to cover the whole earth, and one single species of animals to people it entirely. The human species is subjected to the common law, though perhaps in a smaller degree than many others. Man is led to reproduction, by the most violent and imperious of his inclinations. A man and a woman, having attained ripe age, well constituted, and surrounded with the means of providing abundantly for all their wants, are able to raise many more children than are necessary to replace themselves on the scene of the world; and, if their career is not shortened by some unforeseen accident, they die surrounded with a numerous family, which continues always increasing. Accordingly the human race, when circumstances are favourable, multiplies very rapidly. The United States of North America furnish a proof of this, their whole population doubling in twenty years, and in some places in fifteen, and even in twelve years; and, that too where the emigration is almost nothing, and without the fecundity of women being greater there than elsewhere. And it is also to be remarked, on the contrary that, whatever be the cause, cases of longevity are rare in that country, so that the mean duration of life would be shorter there than in the greater part of Europe, without the great number of infants who perish from want in this same Europe. Here is an incontestable datum, on which we can rest.

If this be so, why then is population stationary, and sometimes retrograde, in so many places, even very healthy ones? Here we must recollect the distinction we have already established, in the 4th Chapter, between our means of existence and our means of subsistence. The latter are the alimentary matters with which we are nourished; they are the most necessary part of our means of existence, but they are only a part. By these last we are to understand, all which contributes to defend us against all the dangers and all the sufferings of every kind; thus they consist in all the resources, whatever, with which we are furnished by the arts and sciences, that is to say by the entire mass of our knowledge. This distinction, well understood, we may establish as a general thesis, that population is always proportioned to the means of existence; and this single principle will give us an explanation of all the facts, and all their circumstances.

Amongst savages population is not only stationary, but little numerous, because their means of existençe are very slender. Independently of their frequent want of subsistence, they have neither the conveniences sufficient, nor the attentions necessary for raising their children; accordingly the greater part perish. They neither know how to defend themselves against the severity of the seasons, nor the insalubrity of the climate; nor against the epidemics which frequently carry off three-fourths of a population. Having no sound ideas of the social state, wars are continual and destructive, vengeance atrocious; their women and old men are often abandoned. Thus it is misfortune and suffering, amongst them, which render the fecundity of the human species useless, and perhaps diminishes it.

Civilized people have all the resources which are wanting to the others; accordingly their population becomes numerous sooner or later; but we see it stops every where, when it has attained to that point, that many men can no longer procure by their labour sufficient wages to raise their children, and conveniently take care of themselves. If in general it is yet a little progressive, although very slowly in the actual state of our old societies, it is because the arts and sciences, and particularly the social science, being constantly cultivated there more or less perfectly, their progress is always adding from time to time some little facilities to the means of living, and open some new vents to commerce and industry. It is true that things proceed thus, that when from some causes, natural or political, great sources of profit are diminished in a country, population immediately becomes retrograde; and, on the contrary, when it has been suddenly diminished by great epidemics, or cruel wars, without knowledge having suffered, it quickly regains its level; because labour being more in demand, and better paid, the poor have more means of preserving their children and themselves.

If from these general observations we pass to particular facts, we shall find the reason for them with the same ease. Let us take Russia for the first example. I do not pretend to make either eulogy or satire on this nation, which I know not: But we may safely affirm that it is not more skillful than other European nations, yet it is proved that its population increases more rapidly than that of other states of Europe. It is because it has a great extent of land; which as yet, having no masters, offers large means of existence to those who go or are carried thither: and if this immense advantage does not there produce a multiplication of men as rapid as in the United States, it is because its social organization and its industry are far from being as perfect. Fertile countries, all things otherwise equal, are more peopled than the others, and easily repair their disasters, because their land furnishes great means, that is to say the labour applied to the land is there fruitful. Accordingly, Lombardy and Belgium, so often ravaged, are always flourishing. Poland however, which is very fertile, has a small population, and that stationary; because its inhabitants being cerfs, and wretched, have in the midst of abundance very slender means of existence. But suppose for a moment the small number of men, to whom these cerfs belong, and who devour their substance, driven from the country, and the land become the property of those who cultivate it, you would see them quickly become industrious, and multiply rapidly. Two other countries, in general tolerably good, Westphalia and even Switzerland, notwithstanding the latter has wiser laws, have small population through want of industry; while Geneva, Hamburgh, and all Holland have it in excess. On the contrary, Spain, which is a delicious country, has few inhabitants relatively to its extent. However it has been proved, that for the forty or fifty years, which preceded the present unhappy war, its population sensibly increased; because they had been able to free it's industry from some of its fetters, and in some degree to increase their information. It is then well proved, that *population* is always proportioned to the means of existence.

This truth has been already avowed by many political writers; but we see in their works, that they have not perceived all its extent. M. Say, whom I have already cited, and whom I may frequently cite, is I think the first who has clearly said, in his first book, chap. 46, "That nothing can increase population but what favours production; "and that nothing can diminish it, at least permanently, but what attacks the sources of production." And observe that by production M. Say understands production of utility. It is even after him that I have given this idea of it. Now to *produce* in this sense, is clearly to add to our means of existence, for whatever is useful to us is a mean of providing for our wants; and indeed nothing merits the name of *useful*, but for this reason. Thus the principle of M. Say is exactly the same with that which I have established. Accordingly he draws from it this very just conclusion, that it is absurd to attempt to influence population by direct encouragements, by laws concerning marriages, by premiums granted to numerous families, &c. &c. He justly laughs on this subject at the famous ordinances of Augustus, of Louis XIV. and of so many other legislators, so much boasted of. These are in effect very false measures, which could in no way augment population; and he added, very justly, in my opinion, that the smallest regulation hurtful to industry, made by these princes could and must have diminished the number of men. I think absolutely the same.

M. Malthus goes much further still. He is, at least as far as I am acquainted, of all the authors who have written on population, the one who has treated the subject the most profoundly, and has developed all its consequences. His work, singularly remarkable, should be regarded as the last state of science on this important object, and he leaves almost nothing to be desired. M. Malthus does not limit himself to prove, that though population is arrested at different degrees in different countries, and according to different circumstances, it is always and every where as great as it can be, having regard to the means of existence—He shows that always in civilised nations it is too great for the happiness of man; because that men, and above all the poor, who every where constitute the great number, urged by the stimulus so imperious to reproduction, always multiply imprudently and without foresight; and plunge themselves into inevitable misery by a multiplication of the men, who demand occupation, and to whom none can be given. All he advances is founded not only on convincing reasoning, but on tables of deaths, births, marriages, of the mean duration of life, and of the total population collected in different countries and discussed with care.

I add this latter point as very necessary: for it is to be observed first that all these data not only are often inexact, but that even when exact, they require to be examined attentively, and compared the one with the other, with much sagacity, before consequences are drawn from them; without which they would lead to serious errors. Secondly, that however imperfect these documents may be, they exist but in few countries, and within a short time only; so that in political economy, as in astronomy, we should calculate very little on ancient and distant observations. Even in France the simple registers of mortality deserve scarcely any confidence before the year 1700; and none of the other circumstances have been collected. Also, in the examples of population which I have above cited, I have made no mention of what is told respecting certain eastern countries, and of some nations antient or of the middle age. If China, if Spain, in the time of the Romans, are or were as populous as we are told, there must certainly have been local reasons for the fact. But we have no means of knowing it sufficiently to see the causes clearly, and to venture to draw consequences. It is the same case with all the parts of the political and domestic economy of the ancients, founded almost solely on the practice of slavery, and the profits or losses of war, and very little on the free and peaceful developement of industry. It is an order of things entirely different from our modern societies. As to the prodigious number of men which some authors pretend to have existed in France—for example under Charles V. or under Charles the IX. in the fourteenth and sixteenth centuries, that is to say at times in which industry was as unskilful and the social order as bad as we have seen it in Poland the eighteenth century—I believe the only answer to be made to these assertions is that which I have opposed to the marvellous union, which is said to have reigned at Sparta.—That is, that it is not true because it is not possible.

However it may be, all those who have reflected on these matters agree, that population is always proportioned to the means of existence. M. Say concludes therefrom, with reason, that it is absurd to think it possible to augment population otherwise than by an augmentation of these means; and Mr. Malthus proves further, that it is barbarous to endeavour to augment this *population always too great*, and the excess of which is the source of all miseries; and that, even in relation to power, the chiefs of nations lose by it: for since they cannot continue in life a greater number of men than they can at the same time subsist, by multiplying births they only multiply premature deaths, and augment the number of children in proportion to that of adults; which produces a weaker population, numbers being equal. *The interest of men, under every consideration*, then is to diminish the effects of their fecundity.

I will say no more on the subject, which is but too clear of itself; and which nevertheless has given occasion to such false opinions, before it was thoroughly explained. We leave them for time to destroy.

CHAPTER X.

Consequences and developments of the two preceding chapters.

Let us always return to the point of departure. An animated being, and especially man, is endowed with sensibility and activity,* with passion and action, that is to say with wants and means. While we were considering the manner in which our riches are formed, we might be charmed with our power and the extent of our means; in fact these are sufficient to render the species prosperous, and give it a great augmentation, both in number and in force. A man and woman, inept and scarcely formed, might end by covering the whole earth with a numerous and industrious population. This picture is very satisfactory; but it changes essentially its colour, when, from the examination of the formation of our riches, we pass to that of their distribution amongst the different individuals. There we every where find the superiority of wants over means; the weakness of the individual, and his inevitable sufferings. But this second aspect of the same object ought neither to disgust nor discourage us. We are thus formed—such is our nature; we must submit, and make the most we can of it by a skilful use of all our means, and by avoiding the faults which aggravate our evils.

* We might say with nerves and muscles, for it goes to that.

The two chapters which we have just read, although very short, embrace important facts; and, joined to prior explanations, give notions sufficiently certain on our true interests. It only remains to profit of them.

We have seen, that we must be satisfied to permit an opposition of interests, and an inequality of means to exist among us; and that the best we can do is to leave to every one the freest employment of his faculties, and to favour their entire development. We have moreover seen that this employment and development of faculties, although profiting unequally the different individuals, succeeded in conducting all to the highest state of well-being possible, so long as space, the greatest of all resources, was not wanting; and that when all the land is occupied, other subsidiary resources sufficed to support for a long time a high state of general prosperity.

We have also seen that, having once arrived to the period of being crouded and constrained, it is inevitable that those who have the smallest means will be able to procure by the employment of these means, but a bare satisfaction of their most urgent wants.

We have finally seen that, the multiplication of men continuing in all the classes of society, the superfluity of the first has been successively cast into the inferior classes; and that that of the last having no longer any resource, has been necessarily destroyed by wretchedness. It is this which causes the stationary and even retrograde state of population, wherever it is found, in spite of the great fecundity of the species.

This latter fact, population nearly stationary in all nations arrived to a certain degree of development, was for a long time scarcely remarked; because it is but lately, that we have begun to occupy ourselves with some success on social economy. It has ever been concealed by political commotions, which have produced disturbers of it; and has been disguised by the unfaithful or insufficient monuments of history, which have authorized mistakes. Finally, when it has been sufficiently observed and established, it has been with difficulty attributed to the real cause; because they had not an idea sufficiently clear of the progress of society, and of the manner in which its riches and power are formed. At this day, it appears to me we are able to put all this beyond a doubt.

Let us recollect that society is divided into two great classes, that of men, who, without having any thing in advance, work for wages—and that of men who employ them. This granted, it is evident that the first—taken in mass—live, daily and yearly, only on what the totality of the second has to distribute to them every day and every year. Now this latter class is of two kinds: the one lives on their revenue, without labour.

These are the lenders of money, the lessors of lands and houses—and in a word the annuitants of every kind. It is very clear that these men, in the long run, cannot give more in a year to those they employ than the amount of their revenue, or they would encroach on their funds. There is always a certain number who use them thus, and who ruin themselves. Their consumption diminishes or ceases; but it is replaced by those who become enriched, and the total continues the same. This is but a change of hands, of which even the ordinary quantity may be nearly estimated in the different countries. These men, taken in mass, make no profit; thus the sum total of their revenue, which is devided amongst the hired, is a constant quantity. If it makes some insensible progress, it can only be by the slow improvement in agriculture; which, by rendering land a little more productive, furnishes ground for a small augmentation of rents. For as to the hire of their money lent, it does not vary. If ever it did augment by a rise in the rate of interest, it would be an evil which, injuring many enterprises, would diminish much more the faculties of the second class, who feed those who work for wages.

This second kind of persons is composed of those who join to the product of their capital, that of their personal activity, that is to say the undertakers of any kind of industry whatsoever. It will be said that these make profits, and augment their means annually; but, first, this is not true of all. Many of them manage their affairs badly, and go to decay instead of thriving. Secondly, those who prosper, cease to labour after a certain time, and go to fill the void which is daily produced in the class of those who live without doing any thing, by the fall of spendthrifts withdrawing from it in consequence of having badly managed their fortunes. Thirdly, in fine, and this is decisive, this class of undertakers has necessary limits, beyond which it cannot go. To form any enterprize whatever, it is not sufficient to have the desire and means: it is necessary to be able to dispose of the products in an advantageous manner, which more than defrays the expenses they cost. When once all profitable employments are filled, no new ones can be created, unless others fall, at least unless some new vents are opened. This second fund for the support of the hired class is also, then, in our ancient societies, a quantity nearly constant like the first.

Things being thus, we see clearly why the number of hired does not augment, when the funds which might provide for their support, cease to increase. It is because all who are born beyond the requisite number perish through want of the means of existence. This is very easy to be conceived. We even comprehend that it is impossible for it to be otherwise, for every one knows that if four persons are daily to divide a loaf of bread, barely sufficient for two, the weaker will perish, and the stronger will subsist only because they quickly inherit the portion of the others.

If we further observe, that when the men who live solely on their revenues multiply so much that this revenue suffices for them no longer, they return into the class of those who join their labour to the product of their funds; that is to say of those whom we have called undertakers—and that when these, in their turn, become too numerous, many are received and link into the class of hirelings, we shall see that this latter class receives as we may say the too great plenitude of all the others; and that, consequently, the limits beyond which it cannot go are those of the total production.

This single point, well elucidated, gives us an explanation of all the phenomena relative to population. It shows why it is retrograde in one country, stationary in another, while it is rapidly progressive in a third; why it is arrested sometimes sooner sometimes later, according to the degree of intelligence and of activity of different people, and the nature of their governments; why it is quickly re-established after great calamities of a transient nature, when the means of existence have not been destroyed; why, on the contrary, without any violent shock, it sometimes languishes and perishes gradually, from causes difficult to be perceived, from the single change of a circumstance little remarkable. In a word, it gives us the solution of all the questions of this kind, and moreover furnishes us with the means of drawing therefrom an infinity of important consequences. I am only embarrassed with their number, and the choice of those which I ought to notice.

I will commence by remarking, with satisfaction, that humanity, justice and policy, equally require that of all interests, those of the poor should always be the most consulted, and the most constantly respected; and by the poor I mean simple hirelings, and every where those whose labour is worst paid.

First, humanity: for we should observe, that when it respects the poor, the word interest has quite a different degree of energy, from what it has when men are spoken of whose wants are less urgent, and sometimes even imaginary. We every day say, that the interests of one minister are contrary to those of another; that such a body has interests opposed to those of another body; that it is the interest of certain undertakers, that the raw material should sell high; and the interest of some others to buy them low. And we often espouse these motives with warmth as if they were worth the trouble. Yet this means no more than that some men believe, and often erroneously, that they have a little more or a little less enjoyment under some circumstances than under others. The poor, in his small sphere, has, assuredly, also interests of this kind; but they disappear before greater ones; we only do not perceive them—and, when we attend to him, the question is almost always on the possibility of his existence or the necessity of his destruction, that is to say of his life or his death. Humanity does not permit interests of this kind to be placed in the balance with simple conveniences.

Justice is equally opposed to it; and, moreover, it obliges us to take into consideration the number of those interested. Now, as the lowest class of society is every where much the most numerous, it follows, that whenever it is in opposition with others, what is useful to it, ought always to be preferred.

Policy leads us to the same result: for it is well agreed, that it is useful to a nation to be numerous and powerful. Now it has just been proved, that the extent to which the lower class can go, is that which determines the limits of the total population; and it is not less so by the experience of all ages and countries, that wherever this lowest class is too wretched, there is neither activity, nor industry, nor knowledge, nor real national force—and we may even say, nor interior tranquillity well established.

This granted, let us examine what are the real interests of the poor; and we shall find that, effectually, they are always conformable to reason and the general interest. If they had always been studied in this spirit, we should have acquired sounder ideas of social order, and we would not have eternized war—sometimes secret, sometimes declared—which has always existed between the poor and the rich. Prejudices produce difficulties, reason resolves them.

We have already seen, that the poor are as much interested in the maintenance of the right of property as the most opulent: for the little they possess is every thing for them, and of consequence infinitely precious in their eyes; and they are sure of nothing, but so far as property is respected. They have still another reason for wishing it; it is that the funds on which they live, the sum of the capitals of those who employ them, is considerably diminished when property is not assured. Thus they have a direct interest, not only in the preservation of what they possess, but also in the preservation of what is possessed by others. Accordingly—notwithstanding that from the fatal effects of misery, of bad education, of the want of delicacy, and of a sense of injustice—it would perhaps be true to say, that it is in the lowest class that most crimes are committed* it is, however, also true, that it is this class which has the highest idea of the right of property, and in which the name of thief is the most odious.

* This is very doubtful, if we take into consideration the difference in the number of individuals.

But when you speak of property, comprehend under this term, as the poor do, personal property, as well as that which is moveable and immoveable. The first is even the most sacred, since it is the source of the others. Respect that, in them, as you wish they should respect, in you, those which are derived from it; leave to him the free disposition of his faculties, and of their employment, as you wish him to leave to you that of your lands and capitals. This rule is as politic, as it is just and unattended to.

After the free disposition of his labour, the greatest interest of the poor man is that this labour should be dearly paid. Against this I hear violent outcries. All the superior classes of society—and in this view I even comprehend the smallest chief of a workshop—desire that the wages should be very low, in order that they may procure more labour for the same sum of money; and they desire it with so much fury, that when they can, and the laws permit them, they employ even violence to attain this end,—and they prefer the labour of slaves, or serfs, because it is still at a lower rate. These men do not fail to say, and persuade, that what they think is their interest, is the general interest; and that the low price of wages is absolutely necessary to the development of industry, to the extension of manufactures and commerce,—in a word, to the property of the state. Let us see how much truth there is in these observations.

I know it would be disagreeable that the price of workmanship should be so dear as to render it economical to draw from abroad all transportable things: for then those engaged in their fabrication would suffer, and would become extinct; it would be a foreign population which the consumers would pay, and support, instead of a national one. But, first, this degree of dearness would be no longer for the interest of the poor, since, instead of being well paid, they would want employment; and, moreover, it is impossible, or at least it could not continue; because, on one part, the hirelings would lower their pretentions so soon as they found themselves out of employ; and, on the other, if the price of a days's work still remained so high as to afford them a great degree of ease, they would soon multiply sufficiently to be obliged to offer their labour at a lower rate. I add that if nevertheless the price of workmanship should still remain too high, it would no longer be to the scarcity of workmen that it ought to be attributed, but to unskilfulness and bad workmanship; and then it would be the unskilfulness, ignorance, and laziness, of men which ought to be combated. These are effectually the true causes of the languor of industry, wherever it is remarked.

But where are these sad causes met with? Is it not always and uniformly there where the lowest class of the people is most miserable? This furnishes me new arms against those who believe it to be so useful, that labour should be badly paid. I maintain that their avidity blinds them. Do you wish to assure yourselves of it? Compare the two extremes, St. Domingo and the United States; or, rather, if you wish objects nearer together, compare in the United States the northern with those of the south. The first furnish only very common articles; workmanship is there at a rate that may be called excessive—yet they are full of vigour and prosperity, while the others remain in langour and stagnation, although they are adapted to productions the most precious, and that they employ the species of labourers the worst paid—namely slaves.

What this example particularly demonstrates we see in all times, and in all places; wherever the lowest class of society is too wretched, its extreme misery, and its abjectness—which is a consequence of it—is the death of industry, and the principle of infinite evils, even to its oppressors. The existence of slavery among ancient nations should be regarded as the source of their principal errors in economy, morality and politics, and the first cause of their continual fluctuation between anarchy, turbulent, and often ferocious or an atrocious tyranny. The slavery of the negroes, or aborigines in our colonies, which had so many means of prosperity, is equally the cause of their languor, their weakness, and the gross vices of their inhabitants. The slavery of serfs of the soil, wherever it has existed, has equally prevented the development of all industry, of all sociability, and of all political strength; and even in our own days, it has reduced Poland to such a state of weakness, that an immense nation existed for a long time only through the jealousy of its neighbors, and has ended by seeing its territory divided as easily as a private patrimony, so soon as the pretenders to it have come to an agreement among themselves. If from these extreme cases—without attending to the fury of the rabble in France, or to the excesses of John of Leyden and his peasants in Germany;—we come to the calamities caused by the populace of Holland, excited by the house of Orange; to the disquietudes arriving from the lazzarone of Naples, the transtiberians of Rome; and, in fine, to the embarrassments which even at this moment are caused in England, by the enormity of the poor tax, and the immensity of its wretched population, which nothing but punishments can restrain; I think all mankind will agree that when a considerable portion of society is in a state of too great suffering, and consequently too much brutalized, there is neither repose nor safety, nor liberty, possible even for the powerful and rich; and that, on the contrary, these first citizens of a state are really much greater, and happier, when they are at the head of a people enjoying honest ease, which developes in them all their intellectual and moral faculties.

On the whole, I do not pretend to conclude, that the poor ought to employ violence, to fix the price which they may demand for their labour. We have seen that their first interest is a respect for property; but I repeat that the rich ought no more to fix this price authoritatively, that it ought to leave to them the most free and entire disposition of their slender means. And here justice also pronounces in their favour; and I add, that they ought to rejoice if the employment of their means procure them an honest ease, for policy proves that it is the general good.

Observe, also, that if it is just and useful to allow every man to dispose of his labour, it is equally so—and for the same reasons—to allow him to choose his residence. The one is a consequence of the other. I know nothing more odious, than to prevent a man from emigrating from his country, who is there so wretched as to wish to quit it, in spite of all the sentiments of nature, and the whole force of habits, which bind him to it. It is moreover absurd: for since it is clearly proved, there are always in every country as many men as can exist in it under the given circumstances, he who goes away only yields his place to another who would have perished if he had remained. To wish that he should remain, is as if two men being inclosed in a box, with air but for one, it should be wished that one or both should be smothered, rather than suffer either one or the other to go out. Emigration, far from being an evil, is never a sufficient succour; it is always too painful to resolve on it for it to become in any degree considerable, the vexations must be frightful; and even then the void it operates, is quickly filled, as that which results from great epidemics. In these unhappy cases, it is the sufferings of men that ought to be regretted; and not the diminution of their number.

As to immigration I say nothing. It is always useless, and even hurtful, unless it be that of some men who bring new knowledge. But then it is their knowledge, and not their persons, that is precious; and such are never very numerous. We may without injustice prohibit immigration; and it is this precisely of which governments have never thought. It is true they have still more rarely furnished many motives for desiring it.

After sufficient wages—which is of first importance to the poor—the next is, that these wages should be constant. In fact it is not a momentary augmentation, or accidental increase, of his profits which can ameliorate his situation. Improvidence is one and perhaps the greatest of his evils. An extravagant consumption always destroys quickly this extraordinary surplus of means, or an indiscrete multiplication divides it among too many. When then this surplus ceases, those who lived on it perish, or those who enjoyed it must restrict themselves; and in the latter case it is never the consumptions least useful which cease first, because these are the most seducing. Then misery recommences in all its horrors, with a greater degree of intensity. Thus we may say, in general terms, that nothing which is transient is really useful to the poor; in this also he has the same interests as the social body.

This truth excludes many false political combinations, particularly if we join with it this other maxim equally true—that nothing forced is durable. It teaches us, also, that it is essential to the happiness of the mass of a nation, that the price of provisions of the first necessity should vary the least possible: for it is not the price of wages in itself that is important; it is their price compared with that of the things necessary for life. If for two sous I can buy bread sufficient for the day, I am better nourished than if I were to receive ten sous, when twelve would be necessary to complete my daily ration. Now we have before shewn (Chap. 4th. and elsewhere) that the rate of the lowest wages is regulated, and cannot fail of being regulated in the long run, by the price of the things necessary to existence. If the price of necessaries suddenly abates, hirelings without doubt profit momentarily; but without durable utility to them, as we have just said. This, then, is not desirable. If, on the contrary, this price augments, it is much worse; and the evils which result aggravate each other. First, he who has nothing more than what is necessary—has nothing to spare—thus all the poor are in distress: but, moreover, in consequence of this distress, they make extraordinary efforts; they are more urgent to be employed; or in other words, they offer more labour. Other persons who lived without labour, have need of this resource—there is no employment for them. They are hurtful to one another by this concurrence. This occasion is taken to pay them less, when they have need of being better paid. Accordingly, constant experience proves that in times of want wages fall, because there are more workmen than can be employed; and this continues till a return of abundance, or till they perish.

It is then desirable that the price of commodities, and above all that of the most important, should be invariable. When we shall come to speak of legislation, we shall see—that the mean of making this price as little variable as possible, is to leave the most entire liberty to commerce; because the activity of speculators, and their competition, makes them eager to take advantage of the smallest fall to buy, and the smallest rise to sell again; and thus they prevent either the one or the other from becoming excessive. This method is also the most conformable with a respect for property, for the just and the useful are always united. For the present let us limit ourselves to our conclusion, and extend it to other objects.

Sudden variations, in certain parts of industry and commerce, occasion—though in a manner less general—the same effect as variations in the price of commodities. When any branch of industry whatever takes suddenly a rapid increase, there is a greater demand for labour than in ordinary:—a profit here results to the labourers; and they use it as all other momentary profits, that is to say badly. But afterwards should this industry be relaxed or extinguished, distress arrives; every one must seek resources. In truth there are many more in this case than in that of a dearness, which is a universal misfortune. The unoccupied workmen here may go elsewhere. But men are not abstract and insensible beings. Their removals are not made without sufferings, without anguish, without breaking up imperious habits. A workman is never so adapted to the business he seeks as to that which he is forced to quit. Besides he is there superfluous—he produces repletion, and consequently a depression of the ordinary wages. Thus every one suffers. This is the great unhappiness of nations predominating in commerce, and the inconvenience of an exaggerated development of industry, a development which from being exaggerated is subject to vicissitudes, it is what at least should prove, that it is very imprudent for a political society to seek to procure a factitious prosperity by forced means. It can but be fragile, it is enjoyed without happiness, and is never lost without extreme evils.

It has been remarked that nations essentially agricultural are less subject to suffer from these sudden revolutions of industry and commerce, in consequence, the stability of their prosperity has been greatly vaunted, and to a certain point with reason. But I think it has not been sufficiently remarked, that they are more exposed than commercial nations to the most cruel of all variations, that of the price of grain: it seems that this ought not to be, and yet it is, it is even easy to find the reason. A people devoted to agriculture are spread over a vast territory. This territory is either entirely inland, or if it borders on some sides on the sea, it has necessarily a great portion of its extent deeply inland. When the crops fail their succours can only be carried by land, or by ascending rivers, a kind of navigation, always very expensive and often impossible. Now as grain and other alimentary matters, are articles of great burthen, it happens that when they are brought to the place in which they are wanted, their price from the expenses of transportation, is so high, that scarcely any one can purchase, accordingly it is known from experience that all importations of this kind in times of calamity, have merely served to console and calm the imagination; but have never been real resources: the poor then must absolutely restrict his consumption so as to suffer greatly, and the most destitute must perish. There is no other mean of preventing the whole from perishing, when the dearth is very great. It is in this case that in a besieged town, all the useless mouths if possible are sent away. It is the same calculation. The defence would still be prolonged, if they dared to rid themselves of all the defenders who are not indispensable ; but the consumption of war operates their destruction : and it is perhaps this cruel—but wise combination, which determines the otherwise useless sorties, made by certain governors near the end of a seige—sorties very different from those made at its commencement, in mere bravado.

Men would greatly augment the security of their existence, and the possibility of their occupying certain countries, if they could reduce alimentary matters to small bulk, and consequently to easy transportion. In truth, they would immediately abuse this faculty, to injure themselves, as Shepherd tribes avail themselves of the facility of transportation produced by the celerity of their beasts of burden, to become brigands : for nothing is so dangerous as a transportable man. We have only to observe the enormous advantage which temperance gives to armies in invasions. This is the power of the species badly employed ; but in short it is its power—and it is this power which, in case of dearth, is wanting to agricultural and peaceful nations, spread over a vast territory.

Commercial nations, on the contrary, are either insular, or extended along the coasts of the sea. Accessible every where, they may receive succour from all countries. In order that dearness should become excessive in these nations, for the price to become excessive with these people, the crops must have failed in all the habitable globe. Even then it would only rise to the mean rate of general dearness, and never to the extreme rate of the local dearness of the inland countries most destitute. These nations, then, are exempt from the greatest of disasters; and, as to the less general evils resulting from the revolutions which take place in some branches of industry and commerce; I observe that they are rarely exposed to them if they have left to this industry and to this commerce their natural course—and if they have not employed violent means to give them an exaggerated extension. I conclude, not only that their condition is better, but also that their misfortunes are produced by their faults, whilst those of the others proceed from their position; and that thus they have more means of avoiding these misfortunes. We were necessarily led to this result, and ought to have seen it in advance: for since society—which is a continual commerce—is the cause of our power and of our own resources; it would be contradictory, that where this commerce is the most perfect, and most active, we should be more accessible to misfortune.

If, therefore, it were proved that the prosperity of commercial nations was less solid, and less durable, (a fact I do not believe true, at least amongst moderns)* it would be necessary, first, to distinguish between happiness and power—and to re-

* The examples of the ancients prove nothing, because their political economy was entirely founded on force. The inland people were brigands, the maritime people pirates.—All wished to be conquerors. Then chance determines the destiny of a nation.

mark, that in the calamities of which we have just spoken—the happiness of individuals in agricultural nations is much at hazard, but their power subsists; because the loss of men, who perish in dearth, is quickly repaired by new births when it ceases—the habitual means of existence, not having been destroyed; whereas in a commercial nation, when a branch of industry is annihilated, it is sometimes annihilated without return, and without a possibility of being replaced by another; so that that part of the population which it brings to ruin cannot be again restored. But, as we have said, this latter case is rare, when not provoked by faults. If, independently of this, it were proved that the prosperity of commercial nations is frail, in proportion to the internal vices to which they are subject, it would not be proper to impute it to commerce itself, but to accidental causes—and principally to the manner in which riches are frequently introduced into these states, which favours extremely their very unequal distribution; and this is the greatest and most general of evils. On examination, we should find there, as every where, the human race happy from the development and increase of its means; but ready to become unhappy from the bad use it makes of them. The discussion of this question, in all its extent, will find its place elsewhere.

However, it may be, it is then certain that the poor are proprietors as well as the rich; that in their quality of proprietors of their persons, of their faculties, and of their product, they have an interest in being allowed the free disposition of their persons and labour; that this labour should produce them sufficient wages; and that these wages should vary as little as possible, that is to say they have an interest that their capital should be respected, that this capital should produce the revenue necessary for existence, and that this revenue if possible should be always the same; and in all these points their interests conform to the general interest.

But the poor is not only a proprietor, he is also a consumer: for all men are both the one and the other. In this latter quality he has the same interest as all consumers, that of being provisioned in the best and cheapest manner possible. It is necessary then for him, that manufacture should be very expert, communications easy, and relations multiplied: for no one has a greater need of being supplied on good terms than he who has few means.

What must be thought then of those who maintain that ameliorations of the methods and the invention of machines, which simplify and abridge the processes of art, are an evil for the poor? My answer is that they have no idea of their real interest, nor of those of society: For one must be blind not to see that when a thing which required four days labour can be made in one, every one for the same sum can procure four times as much; or, consuming only the same quantity, may have three-fourths of his money remaining to be employed in procuring other enjoyments—and certainly this advantage is still more precious to the poor than to the rich. But, say they, the poor gained these four days labour—and now he will gain but one. But, say I, in my turn, you forget then that the funds on which all the hirelings live are the sum of the means of those who employ them; that this sum is a quantity nearly constant; that it is always employed annually; that if a particular object absorbs a smaller part of it, the surplus, which is economised, seeks other destinations; and that thus, while it is not diminished, it hires an equal number of labourers—and that moreover, if there is a mean of augmenting it, it is by rendering fabrication more economical; because this is the mean of opening new vents, and of giving possibility to new enterprises of industry—which are as we have seen, the only sources of the increase of our riches. These reasons appear to me decisive. If the contrary reasons were valid, we should have to conclude that nothing is more beneficial, than the execution of useless labour, because there is always the same number of persons occupied; and that there would not remain fewer for the execution of the same quantity of necessary labour. I grant this second point. But, first, this useless labour would be paid with funds which would otherwise have paid for useful labour and which will not pay it—thus nothing is gained on this side. Secondly, from this unfruitful labour nothing remains; and, if it had been fruitful, there would have remained from it useful things for procuring enjoyments, or capable, by being exported, to augment the mass of acquired riches. It appears to me that nothing can be answered to this, when we have once clearly seen on what funds hirelings live. This series of combinations will occur when we shall speak of the employment of our riches. It is for this I have developed it: For so much reasoning appears unnecessary to prove that labour acknowledged useless is useless, and that it is more useful to execute useful labour. Now to this single truth is reduced the apology for machines and other improvements.

They have made against the construction of roads and canals, and generally against the facility of communications, and the multiplicity of commercial relations the same objections as those I have just refuted. I give them the same answer. It has moreover been pretended that all this is in another way hurtful to the poor, by raising the price of provisions. The truth is, that it raises their price at times when they are too low from the difficulty of exporting them; but it reduces their price, when too high from the difficulty of importing them. Thus it renders the prices more constantly equal; and I conclude, on the principles we have established, that it is a great benefit to the poor and to society in general.

I admit, however, that all these innovations, advantageous in themselves, may sometimes produce at first a momentary and partial restraint—it is the effect of all sudden changes; but, as the utility of these is general and durable, this consideration ought not to retard them. It is only requisite that society should give succour to those who suffer for the moment; and this it can easily do, when it is prospering in the mass.

It is then true that notwithstanding the necessary opposition of our particular interests, we are all united by the common interests of proprietors and consumers; and, consequently, it is wrong to regard the poor and the rich, or the hirelings and those who employ them, as two classes essentially enemies. It is particularly true, that the real interests of the poor are always the same as those of the society taken in mass. I do not pretend to say that the poor always know their real interests. Who is he that always has just ideas on these matters, even amongst the enlightened? But, in fine, it is much that things are thus; and it is a good thing to know it. The greatest difficulty, in impressing this, is, perhaps, to be able clearly to point out the cause. This I think we have now done. Arriving at this result, we have examined by the way several questions, which, without diverting us from our road, have retarded our march. Yet I have not thought it right to pass them by without notice, because, in things of this kind, all the objects are so intimately linked together that there is no one which, being well cleared up, does not throw great light on all the others.

But we are not only opposed in interests, we are also unequal in means. This second condition of our nature deserves also to be studied in its consequences, without which we cannot completely know the effects of the distribution of our riches among different individuals; and we shall but imperfectly know what we ought to think of the advantages and inconveniences of the increase of these same riches, by the effect of society. Let us at first establish some general truths.

Declaimers have maintained that *inequality* in general is useful, and that it is a benefit for which we ought to thank Providence. I have but one word to answer. Amongst sensible beings, frequently with opposite interests, justice is the greatest good: for that alone can so conciliate them, that none may have cause of complaint. Then inequality is an evil not because it is in itself injustice, but because it is a powerful prop to injustice wherever justice is in favour of the weak.

Every inequality of means, and of faculties, is at bottom an inequality of power. However, when we enter into detail, we can and ought to distinguish between the inequality of power, properly so called, and the inequality of riches.

The first is the most grevious—it submits the person itself. It exists in all its horror among brutal and savage men—with them it places the weak at the mercy of the strong. It is the cause why among them there are the fewest relations possible, for it would become insupportable. If it has not been always remarked among them, it is because scarcely ever accompanied by an inequality of riches; which is what strikes us most forcibly, having it always under our eyes.

The object of the social organization is to combat the inequality of power; and most frequently it causes it to cease, or at least diminishes it. Men shocked with the abuses still prevalent in society, have pretended that, on the contrary, it augments this inequality; and it must be confessed, that when it totally loses sight of its destination it justifies the reproaches of its bitterest detractors. For example wheresoever it continues slavery, properly so called, it is certain that savage independence, with all its dangers is still preferable. But it must be admitted nevertheless that this is not the object of society;

and that it tends, most frequently with success, to diminish the inequality of power.

By diminishing the inequality of power, and thus establishing security, society produces the development of all our faculties, and increases our riches, that is to say our means of existence and enjoyment. But the more our faculties are developed, the more their inequality appears and augments; and this soon introduces the inequality of riches, which brings with it that of instruction, capacity and of influence. Here, in a word, as appears to me, are the advantages and inconveniences of society. This view shows us what we have a right to expect from it, and what we ought to do to perfect it.

Since the object of society is to diminish the inequality of power, it ought to aim at its accomplishment, and since its inconvenience is to favour the inequality of riches, it ought constantly to endeavour to lessen it—always by gentle, and never by violent, means: for it should always be remembered, that the fundamental base of society is a respect for property, and its gurantee against all violence.

But it will be asked, when inequality is reduced entirely to an inequality of riches, is it still so great an evil? I answer, boldly, yes: For, first, bringing with it an inequality of instruction, of capacity, and of influence, it tends to re-establish the inequality of power and consequently to subvert society. Again, considering it only under an economical relation, we have seen that the funds on which hirelings live are the revenues of all those who have capitals; and among these it is only undertakers of industry who augment their riches, and consequently the riches of the nation. Now it is precisely the possessors of great fortunes who are idle, and who pay no labour but for their pleasure. Thus the more there are of great fortunes, the more national riches tend to decay and population to diminish. The example of all times, and all places, supports this theory: For wherever you see exaggerated fortunes,* you there see the greatest misery and the greatest stagnation of industry.

The perfection of society, then, would be to increase our riches greatly, avoiding their extreme inequality. But this is much more difficult at certain times, and in certain places, than in others. An inland agricultural people having few relations, living on a sterile soil, unable to increase their means of enjoyment but by the slow progress of its culture, and the still slower progress of their manufactures, will easily, and for a long time, avoid the establishment of great inequality among their citizens. If the soil is more rich—and especially, if in some places it produces articles in great demand—large fortunes will be more easily acquired: If it has mines of precious metals, many individuals will certainly ruin themselves by working them; but some will acquire immense riches: or, if the government reserves to itself this profit, it will soon be enabled to procure for its creatures an exaggerated opulence; and it is very probable it

* To judge of the exaggeration of certain fortunes, consider their proportions: for there may be Englishmen near as rich, or richer than the greatest Russian or Polish lords; but they live in the midst of a people generally in much more easy circumstances,—consequently the disproportion, though real, is much less.

will not fail to do it. Too many causes concur to produce this effect. Finally, if you suppose this people, still poor, to become conquerors, to seize on a rich country, and to establish themselves in it as conquerors, here is at once the greatest inequality introduced: First between the victorious and the conquered nation, and afterwards among the conquerors themselves: for where force decides it is very difficult to have equitable partitions. The lots of the different individuals are as different, as their degrees of authority in the army or of favour with the chief. Moreover, they are exposed to frequent usurpations.

The fortune of maritime nations is generally more rapid. Yet there we remark the same varieties. Navigators may be reduced to small profits—to carrying—to fishing—to commerce with nations from which great profits cannot be made. Then it is easy for them to remain long nearly equal amongst themselves. They may, on the contrary, penetrate into unknown regions; have in profusion the most rare articles; establish relations with people from whom they can derive immense profits; take to themselves great monopolies; found rich colonies, over which they hold a tyranical empire; or even become conquerors, and import into their country the productions of countries very extensive subjected by their arms,—as the English in India, and the Spaniards in South America. In all these cases, there is more or less of chance; but in all, a great probability that their enormous riches will be very unequally distributed.

Many other circumstances, without doubt, connect themselves with these, and modify their effects. The different characters of people, the nature of their government, the greater or less extent of their information, and, above all, of their knowledge of the social art in the moments which decide their fortune, occasion like events to have very different consequences. If Vasco De Gama and his cotemporaries had had the same views and misfortunes as Cook, or La Peyrouse, our relations with the Indies would be quite different from what they are. It is above all remarkable, how much influence the epoch at which a political society begins to be formed, has on the duration of its existence. Certainly empires founded by Clovis or by Cortez, or societies receiving their first laws from Locke or Franklin, ought to take very different directions; and this we clearly perceive, in every period of their history.*

It is these causes so different, and above all the last, which produce the infinite variety remarked in the destinies of nations, but the ground is every where the same. Society affording to every one security of person and property, causes the development of our faculties; this development produces the increase of our riches—their increase brings on sooner or later their very unequal division; and this unequal division occasioning the inequality of power

* This is so striking, that I imagine there is no one who does not regret that America was discovered three hundred years too soon, and who does not even doubt whether it would yet be a proper time for discovering it. It is true that these events, however deplorable, have promoted our ulterior progress; but it is buying them very dear. It appears that such is our destiny.

which society begun by restraining, and was intended to destroy, produces its weakness, and sometimes its total dissolution.

It is doubtless this vicious circle which historians have wished to represent to us by the youth and old age of nations, and by what they call their primary virtue, their primitive purity, then their degeneration; their corruptions, their effeminacy. But these vague expressions, against which I have already protested, paint the facts very badly, and often lead astray even those who employ them:—they tell us always of the virtue of poor nations. Certainly where equality renders injustice and oppression more difficult, and more rare, they are more virtuous from the fact itself—since fewer faults are committed. But it is equality and not poverty which is their protection. Otherwise the passions are the same there as elsewhere. Why incessantly represent to us commercial nations as avaricious, and agricultural people as models of moderation? Men every where hold to their interests, and are occupied with them. The Carthaginians were not more avaricious than the Romans; and the Romans, who were the most cruel usurers at home and insatiable spoliators abroad, were quite as avaricious in what are called their best times, as under the emperors. The state of society alone was different. It is the same with the word degeneration. Certainly when a part of mankind has been accustomed to resign itself to oppression, and another part to abuse its power, we may well say they have degenerated; but, from the manner in which this expression is often employed, we should be led to believe they are no longer born the same—that nature has changed—that the race is depreciated—that they have no longer force or courage :—all this is very false. We have a still greater abuse of the expressions effeminate and effeminacy. Montesquieu himself tells you gravely, that the fertility of the land effeminates its inhabitants * It nourishes them and this is all. To listen to certain authors, we should suppose that there comes a time when all the inhabitants of a country live amidst delights, as those famous Sybarites of whom we have been told so much. This would be very happy, but it is impossible. When you are told that a nation is enervated by effeminacy, understand that there is about an hundreth part of it, at most, corrupted by the habit of power and the facility of enjoyment; and that all the rest are debarred by oppression, and devoured by misery.† Nor are we less deceived in the sense of the expression, *poor nations;* it is there the *people* are at their ease—and the *rich nations* is where the *people* are commonly poor. It is for this reason that some are strong, and others often weak. We might multiply these reflections to infinity; but all may be reduced

* He says of it many other things. See his 18th book of laws, in the relation they have with the nature of the soil.

† And those famous delights of Capua! and all those armies suddenly effeminated, by having found themselves in abundance! Ask of all the generals if their soldiers have been the worse for having plentifully enjoyed the means of life for some time, unless they have suffered them to become pillagers, and undisciplined, by setting them the example; or the chiefs, having made their fortune, are no longer ambitious. If it is this which has happened to the Carthaginians, and others, this is what should have been said, and not in vain rhetorical phrases.

to this truth, which has not always been sufficiently perceived; the multiplication of our means of enjoyment is a very good thing; their too unequal partition is a very bad one, and the source of all our evils. On this point still the interest of the poor is the same as that of society. I think I have said enough on the distribution of our riches; it is time to speak of the use we make of them.

CHAPTER XI.

Of the employment of our Riches, or of Consumption.

After having seen how our riches are formed, and how they are distributed among us, we are arrived at the point of examining how we use them, and what are the consequences of the different uses we make of them. This is what will complete the illustration of the whole course of society, and show us what things are really useful or hurtful, as well to the public as to individuals. If in the two first parts, we have well ascertained and explained the truth, this will unravel itself, and every thing in it will be clear and incontestible. If, on the contrary, we have imperfectly viewed the first facts, if we have not remounted to first principles, if our researches have been superficial or led astray by a spirit of system, we are about to encounter difficulties on difficulties; and there will remain in all we shall say many obscure and doubtful things, as has happened to many others, and even to the most capable and learned. However the reader will judge.

We create nothing; we annihilate nothing; but we operate changes, productive or destructive, of utility. We procure for ourselves means of enjoyment, only to provide for our wants; and we cannot employ them in the satisfaction of these wants; but by diminishing and even destroying them. We make cloth, and, with this cloth, clothes, only to clothe ourselves; and, by wearing, we *wear* THEM *out*; with grain, air, earth, water, and manure, we produce alimentary matters to nourish ourselves; and, by nourishing ourselves with them, we convert them into gas and manure; which again produce more. This is what we call consumption. Consumption is the end of production, but it is its contrary. Thus all production augments our riches, and all consumption diminishes them.—Such is the general law.

However there are consumptions of many kinds. There are some which are only apparent; others very real, and even destructive; and some which are fruitful. They vary according to the species of consumers, and the nature of the things consumed. These differences must be examined and distinguished, in order clearly to see the effect of general consumption, on the total mass of riches. Let us begin by discussing the consumers. I hazard this expression, because it well expresses the end which I propose to myself.

We agree that we are all consumers, for we all have wants for which we cannot provide but by a consumption of some kind; and that also we are all proprietors, for we all possess some means of providing for our wants, were it only by our individual force and capacity. But we have also seen, that from the unequal manner in which riches are distributed, in proportion as they are accumulated, many among us have no part in these accumulated riches, and possess in effect but their individual force. These have no other treasure than their daily labour. This labour procures them wages, for which reason we have called them specially hirelings; and it is with these wages they provide for their consumption.

But whence are the wages raised? Evidently on the property of those to whom these hirelings sell their labour, that is to say on funds, in advance, which are in their possession,—and which are no other than the accumulated products of labour previously executed. It follows thence, that the consumption for which these riches pay, is truly the consumption of the hirelings in this sense, that it is them it subsists; but at bottom it is not they who pay it, or at least they pay it only with the funds existing in advance in the hands of those who employ them. They merely receive with one hand and give with the other. Their consumption, therefore, ought to be regarded as being made by those who pay them. If even they do not expend all they receive, these savings raising them to the ranks of capitalists, enable them afterwards to make expenditures on their own funds; but as they come to them from the same hands, they ought at first to be regarded as the expenses of the same persons; thus to avoid double reckoning of the same article in the economical calculations, we must consider as absolutely nothing the immediate consumption of hirelings, as hirelings; and to consider not only all they expend, but even the whole they receive, as the real expenditure and proper consumption of those who purchase their labour. This is so true, that to see whether this consumption is more or less destructive of the riches acquired, or even if it tends to augment them as it often does, depends entirely on knowing what use the capitalists make of the labour they purchase. This leads us to examine the consumption of capitalists.

We have said that they are of two kinds, the one idle, the other active. The first have a fixed revenue, independent of all action on their part, since they are supposed idle. This revenue consists in the hiring of their capitals—whether moveables, money or land,—which they hire to those who improve them by the effect of their industry. This revenue, is, then, but a previous levy on the products of the activity of the industrious citizens; but this is not our present enquiry. What we wish to see is, what is the employment of this revenue? Since the men to whom it belongs are idle, it is evident they do not direct any productive labour. All the labourers whom they pay are solely destined to procure them enjoyments. Without doubt these enjoyments are of different kinds: For the least wealthy they are limited to the satisfaction of the most urgent wants;—for the others they are extended by degrees, according to their taste and means, to objects of the most refined and unbridled luxury. But, in fine, the expenses of all this class of men are alike in this, that they have no object but their personal satisfaction; and that they support a numerous population, to which they afford subsistence; but whose labour is completely sterile. It is however true, that amongst these expenses some may be found which are more or less fruitful; as, for example, the construction of a house, or the improvement of a landed estate. But these are particular cases, which place consumers of this kind momentarily in the class of those who direct useful enterprises and pay for productive labour. After these trifling exceptions, all the consumption of this species of capitalists is absolutely pure loss, in relation to reproduction, and so far a diminution of the riches acquired. Also, we must remark, that these men can expend no more than their revenue: if they touch on their funds nothing replaces them, and their consumption exaggerated for a moment, ceases for ever.

The second class of capitalists, who employ and pay hirelings, is composed of those whom we have called active. It comprehends all the undertakers of any kind of industry whatsoever, that is to say all the men who having capitals of a greater or smaller amount, employ their talents and industry in improving them themselves, instead of hiring them to others; and who, consequently live neither on wages nor revenues but on profit. These men not only improve their proper capitals, but all those also of the inactive capitalists. They take on rent their lands, houses, and money, and employ them so as to derive from them profits superior to the rent.* They have then in their hands almost all the riches of society. It is moreover to be remarked, that it is not only the rent of these riches they annually expend, but also the funds themselves;

* Idle capitalists, sometimes rent houses and money to the idle capitalists: But the latter pay the rent only with their own revenues; and to find the formation of these revenues we must always remount to industrious capitalists. As to lands they almost always rent them to undertakers of culture, for what would the idle make of them?

and sometimes several times in the year, when the course of commerce is sufficiently rapid to enable them to do so: for, as in their quality of industrious men they make no expenditures which do not return to them with profit, the more of them they can make which fulfil this condition, the greater will be their profit. We see then that their consumption is immense, and that the number of hirelings whom they feed is truly prodigious.

We must now distinguish two parties in this enormous consumption. All which is made by these industrious men for their own enjoyment, and for the satisfaction of their own wants and those of their family, is definitive and lost without return, like that of the idle capitalists. On the whole it is moderate, for industrious men are commonly frugal, and too often not very rich. But all which they make for the support of their industry, and for the service of this industry, is nothing less than definitive,—it returns to them with profit; and, that this industry may be sustained, its profits must at least be equal not only to their personal and definitive consumption, but also to the rent of the land and money which they hold of the idle capitalists, which rent is their sole revenue, and the only fund of their annual expense. If the profits of the active capitalists were less than these necessary previous levies, their funds would be encroached on; they would be obliged to diminish their enterprizes; they could no longer hire the same quantity of labour; they would even be disgusted with hiring and directing this unfruitful labour. In the contrary case they have an increase of funds, by means of which they can increase their business, and their demand for labour, if they can find a method of employing it usefully.

I shall be asked, how these undertakers of industry are able to make such great profits, and from whom they can draw them? I answer, that it is by selling whatever they produce for more than it has cost them to produce it. And this is sold, first, to themselves for all that part of their consumption which is destined to the satisfaction of their own wants, which they pay for with a portion of their profits; Secondly, to hirelings, as well those in their pay as in the pay of the idle capitalists; from which hirelings they draw by this mean the whole of their wages, except the small savings they may possibly be able to make; Thirdly, to the idle capitalists, who pay them with the part of their revenue which they have not already given to the hirelings whom they employ directly, so that all the rent which they annually disburse returns to them by one or the other of these ways.

This is what completes that perpetual motion of riches, which although little understood has been very well called circulation: for it is really circular,* and always returns to the point from whence it departed. This point is that of production. The undertakers of industry are really the heart of the body politic, and their capitals are its blood. With these capitals they pay the wages of the greatest part of the hirelings; they pay their rents to all

* And why is it circular and continual? Because consumption continually destroys that which has been produced. If reproduction did not incessantly establish it, all would be finished after the first turn.

the idle capitalists, possessors either of land or money; and by them the wages of all the remaining hirelings;—and all this returns to them by the expenditures in all these ways, which pay them more for what they have had produced from the labour of their immediate hirelings, than the wages of these, and the rent of the land and money borrowed, have cost them.

But I shall be told, if this is really so, if the undertakers of industry in fact reap annually more than they have sown, they should in a short time obtain possession of all the public wealth; and there would remain in a state but hirelings without any thing in advance, and undertakers with capitals. This is true, and things would be effectively thus if these undertakers, or their heirs, did not retire from business in proportion as they become rich, and continually recruit the class of idle capitalists. And, notwithstanding this frequent emigration, it happens still that when industry has operated for a considerable time in a country, without too great disturbances, its capitals are always augmented not only in proportion to the increase of total wealth, but yet in a much greater. To be assured of this, we have only to see how slender these capitals were, through all Europe, three or four centuries ago, in comparison with the immense riches of all the powerful men, and how much they are multiplied and increased at the present day, while the others have diminished. We may add that this effect would be still much more sensible, were it not for the immense levies which all governments annually raise on the industrious class by means of imposts; but it is not yet time to occupy ourselves with this subject.

It is not necessary to observe, that at the commencement of society, before riches have become very unequal, there are scarcely any simple hirelings, and still fewer idle capitalists. Every one working for himself, and making exchanges with his neighbours, is a real undertaker, or momentarily a hireling when he occasionally works for another for a recompense. Even afterwards, when the different conditions have become more separate by the effect of inequality, the same man may and often does appertain to several at the same time. Thus a simple hireling, who has some small savings placed at interest, is in this respect an idle capitalist; as is also an undertaker who has a part of his funds realised in leased lands; while a proprietor of like lands, or a lessor who is a public functionary, is in this respect a hireling. But it is not less true, that those who live on wages, those who live on rents, and those who live on profits, constitute three classes of men essentially different; and that it is the last which aliment all the others, and who alone augment the public wealth, and create all our means of enjoyment. This must be so, since labour is the scource of all riches,—and since they alone give an useful direction to the actual labour, by a useful improvement of the labour accumulated.

I hope it will be remarked, how well this manner of considering the consumption of our riches agrees with all we have said of their production and distribution;* and, at the same time, how much

* In fact we here see clearly, why production is arrested, when the fruitful consumption of industry can no longer be augmented, and

light it throws on the whole course of society. Whence comes this accordancy and this lucidness? From this, that we have struck on the truth. This resembles the effect of those mirrors in which objects are represented distinctly, and in their just proportions when one is placed in the true point of view; and where every thing appears confused, and disunited, when one is too near or too distant. So here, so soon as it is acknowledged that our faculties are our only original riches, that our labour alone produces all others, and that all labour well directed is productive, every thing explains itself with admirable facility; but when, with many political writers, you acknowledge no labour as productive but that of culture, or place the source of riches in consumption, you encounter in advancing nothing but obscurity, confusion and inextricable embarrassments. I have already refuted the first of these two opinions—I shall soon discuss the second. For the moment, let us conclude that there are three kinds of consumers,—the hirelings, the lessors, and the undertakers,—that the consumption of the first is real and definitive; but that it must not be counted, because it makes a part of the consumption of those who employ them; that that of the lessors is definitive and destructive; and that that of the undertaker is fruitful, because it is replaced by a superior production.

If consumption is very different, according to the species of consumers, it varies likewise according to the nature of the things consumed. All represent truly labour; but its value is fixed more solidly in

why the number and ease of men increase or decrease as the industry, &c. &c.

some than in others. As much pains may have been taken to prepare an artificial fire work as to find and cut a diamond; and, consequently, one may have as much value as the other. But when I have purchased, paid for, and employed the one and the other,—at the end of half an hour nothing remains of the first, and the second may still be the resource of my descendants a century to come, even if used every day as an ornament of dress. It is the same case with what are called immaterial products. A discovery is of an eternal utility. A work of genius, a picture, are likewise of an utility more or less durable; while that of a ball, concert, a theatrical representation, is instantaneous and disappear immediately. We may say as much of the personal services of physicians, of lawyers, of soldiers, of domestics, and generally of all occasionally called on. Their utility is that of the moment of want.

All consumable things, of what nature soever, may be placed between these two extremes, of the shortest and longest duration. From this it is easy to see, that the most ruinous consumption is the most prompt, since it is that which destroys the most labour in the same time, or an equal quantity of labour in less time. In comparison with this, that which is slower is a kind of hoarding; since it leaves to futurity the enjoyment of a part of actual sacrifices. This is so clear that it needs no proof: for every one knows that it is more economical to have for the same price a coat which will last three years, than one which will last but three months; accordingly this truth is acknowledged by every body. What is singular, is that it should be so even by those who regard luxury as a cause of wealth: for if to destroy is so good a thing, it seems that we cannot destroy too much, and that we ought to think with the man who broke all his furniture, to encourage industry.

At the point to which we are now arrived, I do not know how to accost the pretended mighty question of luxury, so much and so often debated by celebrated philosophers and renowned politicians; or, rather, I do not know how to shew that it comprehends any matter of doubt, nor how to give the appearance of a little plausibility to the reasons of those, very numerous however, who maintain that luxury is useful: for, when preceding ideas have been well elucidated, a question is resolved as soon as stated; and this is now the case.

In effect, he who names luxury, names superfluous and even exaggerated consumption;—consumption is destruction of utility. Now how conceive that exaggerated destruction can be the cause of riches—can be production? It is repugnant to good sense.

We are gravely told that luxury impoverishes a small state and enriches a large one; but what can extent have to do with such a subject? and how comprehend, that what ruins an hundred men would enrich two hundred.

It is also said that luxury supports a numerous population. Without doubt not only the luxury of the rich, but likewise the simple consumption of all the idle who live on their revenues, supports a great number of hirelings. But what becomes of the labour of these hirelings? Those who employ them consume its result, and nothing of it remains; and with what do they pay for this labour? with their revenues, that is to say with riches already acquired, of which in a short time nothing will remain. There then is a destruction, not an augmentation of riches. But let us go further. Whence do these idle men derive their revenues? Is it not from the rent paid to them out of the profits of those who employ their capitals, that is to say of those who with their own funds hire labour which produces more than it costs, in a word the industrious men? To these then we must always remount, in order to find the source of all wealth. It is they who really nourish the hireling whom even the others employ.

But, say they, luxury animates circulation. These words have no meaning. They forget then what is circulation. Let us recal it. With time a greater or smaller quantity of riches are accumulated, because the result of anterior labours, has not been entirely consumed as soon as produced. Of the possessors of these riches some are satisfied with drawing arent and living on it. These we have called the idle. Others more active, employ their own funds, and those which they hire. They employ them to hire labour, which reproduces them with profit. With this profit they pay for their own consumption, and defray that of the others. Even by these consumptions their funds return to them a little increased, and they recommence. This is what constitutes circulation. We see that it has no other funds than those of the industrious citizens. It can only augment in proportion as they augment; nor be accelerated, which is still to be augmented, but in proportion to the quickness of their returns: for if their funds return to them at the end of six months, instead of a year, they would employ them twice a year instead of once; and this is as if they employed the double. But the idle proprietors can do nothing of this. They can but consume their rents in one way or another. If they consume more one year they must consume less another; if they do otherwise they encroach on their capitals. They are obliged to sell them. But they can only be purchased with funds belonging to industrious men, or lent to them, and who paid for labour, which they will no longer pay for, and for labour more useful than that employed by the prodigals. Thus this is not an augmentation of the total mass of expense, it is but a transposition, a change of some of its parts, and a disadvantageous change. Thus even in ruining themselves, the men who live on their revenues cannot increase the mass of wages and of circulation. They could do it only by a conduct quite opposite, by not consuming the whole of their rent, and by appropriating a part of it to fruitful expenditures. But then they would be far from abandoning themselves, to the exaggerated and superfluous consumption called luxury. They would devote themselves on the contrary to useful speculations, they would range themselves in the industrious class.

Montesquieu, who in other respects understood political economy very badly,* believes the profusions of the rich very useful; "because, says he, (book 7th, chap. 4th,) if the rich do not spend a great

* Montesquieu was a very great man, but the science was not built in his time; it is quite recent.

deal, the poor must die of famine." We perceive from these few words, and many others, that he did not know either whence the revenues of those whom he calls rich are derived or what becomes of them. Once more I repeat the revenues of the idle rich, are but rents levied on industry ; it is industry alone which gives them birth. Their possessors can do nothing to augment them, they only scatter them, and they cannot avoid scattering them. For if they do not expend the whole for their enjoyments, unless they cast the surplus into the river or bury it, which is a rare folly, they replace it, that is to say they form with it new funds for industry, which it employs. Thus even by economising they pay for the same quantity of labour. All the difference is that they pay for useful instead of useless labour, and that out of the profits procured, they create for themselves a new rent, which will augment the possibility of their future consumption.

Luxury, exaggerated and superfluous consumption, is therefore never good for any thing, economically speaking. It can only have an indirect utility. Which is by ruining the rich, to take from the hands of idle men those funds which, being distributed amongst those who labour, may enable them to economise, and thus form capitals in the industrious class. But first this would go directly contrary to the intention of Montesquieu, who believes luxury advantageous, especially in a monarchy; and who at the same time thinks, that the preservation of the same families, and the perpetuity of their splendor is essentially necessary to this kind of government. Moreover we must observe with M. Say, that a taste for superfluous expenses has its foundation in vanity, that it cannot exist in the superior class without gradually extending itself into all the others; that it is there still more fatal, because their means are less, and because it absorbs funds of which they made a better use; and thus it every where substitutes useless for useful expenses, and dries up the source of riches. All this is in my opinion incontestable.

Accordingly, our politicians no longer content themselves with vaguely saying, that luxury constitutes the prosperity of the state, that it animates circulation, that it enables the poor to live. They have made a theory for themselves. They establish as a general principle, that consumption is the cause of production, that it is its measure, that thus it is well it should be very great. They affirm that it is this which makes the great difference between public and private economy. They dare not always positively say, that the more a nation consumes the more it enriches itself. But they persuade themselves, and maintain that we must not reason on the public fortune as on that of an individual, and they regard those as very narrow minds which in their simplicity believe that in all cases good economy is to be economical, that is to say to make an useful employment of his means.* There

* See M. Germain Garnier, in his elementary principles of political economy abridged. Paris printed by Agasse, 1796. Page xii of his advertisement, he says, formally, "The principles which serve as guides in the administration of a private fortune, and those by which the public fortune should be directed, not only differ between themselves, but are often in *direct* opposition to each other." And page xiii, "The fortune of an individual is increased by saving; the public for-

is in all this a confusion of ideas, which it is well to dispel and to restore light.

Certainly consumption is the cause of production; in this sense, that we only produce in order to consume, and that if we had no wants to satisfy we should never take the trouble of producing any thing. Nothing would then be to us either useful or hurtful. It is also the cause, in this sense, why industrious men produce only because they find consumers of their productions. Hence it is said, with reason, that the true method of encouraging industry is to enlarge the extent of the market, and thereby augment the possibility of selling. Under this point of view, it is also true to say that consumption is the measure of production, for where vent ceases production stops. This has also made us say, that establishments of industry cannot be multiplied beyond a certain term; and that this term is where they cease to yield a profit: for then it is evident, that what they produce is not worth what they consume. But from all this it does not follow, for a nation any more than for an individual, that to expend is to enrich; nor that we may

tune, on the contrary, receives its increase from the augmentation of consumption." Page 130, in the chapter on circulation, he likewise says, "The annual production ought naturally to be regulated by the annual consumption." Also, in the chapter on public debt, page 240, he adds, "The amendment and extension of culture, and consequently the progress of industry and commerce, have no other cause than the extension of artificial wants;" and concludes from this that public debts are good things, inasmuch as they augment these wants. The same doctrine, joined to the idea that culture is alone productive, runs through his whole work, and his notes on Smith. All this is very superficial and very loose.

augment our expenses at pleasure; nor even that luxury augments them, for it only changes them. We must always return to production; this is the point of departure. To enjoy we must produce;—this is the first step. We produce only by availing ourselves of riches already acquired; the more we have of them, the greater are our means of producing; they are consumed in expenses of productions, they return with profit. We can expend annually but this annual profit. The more of it we employ in useless things, the less will remain for those which are useful. If we go beyond them, we break in on our capital; reproduction, and consequently future consumption, will be diminished. They may, on the contrary, be augmented if savings are made with which to form new capitals. Once more, then, consumption is not riches; and there is nothing useful, under an economical point of view, but that which reproduces itself with profit.

No sophistry can ever shake truths so constant. If they have been mistaken, it is because the effect has been taken for the cause; and, what is more, a disagreeable effect for a benificent cause. We have seen, that when a nation becomes rich a great inequality of fortunes is established, and that the possessors of large fortunes addict themselves to great luxury. It has been believed that this causes a country to prosper; and hastily concluded that inequality and luxury are two very good things. They ought, on the contrary, to have seen that these are two inconveniences attached to prosperity:* that the riches which cause them are acquired before they exist; and that if these riches continue still to increase, it is in spite of the existence of these inconveniences, and through the effect of the good habits of activity and economy which they have not been able entirely to destroy. But the strongest personal interests contribute to give credit to this error. Powerful men are unwilling to acknowledge that their existence is an evil, and that their expense is as useless as their persons. On the contrary, they endeavour to impose by pomp; and it is not their fault if we do not believe that they render a great service to the state, by swallowing up a great portion of the means of existence, and that there is much merit in knowing how to dissipate great riches.† On the other hand,

* We have already seen, in the preceding chapter, how inequality of riches is established, or rather increases in society; and, when we shall treat of legislation, we will likewise show that the excess of inequality, and of luxury, is still more the effect of bad laws than of the natural cause of things.

† It is incredible to what length of illusion self-love leads, and induces one to exaggerate to himself his personal importance. I have seen men obliged, by the troubles of the times, to quit their castles, who really believed that the whole village would want work—without perceiving that it was their farmer, and not themselves, who paid the greatest part of the wages; and sincerely persuade themselves that even if their peasants should divide their effects, or should buy them at a low price, they would only be the more miserable.

I do not pretend to say that it was well done either to drive them away, or to despoil them; nor even that such means can ever be the cause of a durable prosperity. I have made my profession of faith on the necessity of respect for property and justice in general. But it is not the less true, that the absence of an useless man makes no change in the course of things, or at most only changes the place of a part of his small personal expenses; and that the mere suppression of some feudal rights, produces more good to a country than all the benefits of him who levied them.

those who depend on them on whom they impose awe, and who profit by their expenses, care very little whether the money they receive from them would be better employed elsewhere, or if by being better employed it would enable a greater number of men to live. They desire that this expense on which they live should be very great; and they firmly believe that if it should diminish, they would be without resources: for they do not see what would replace it. It is thus that general opinion is led astray, and that those even who suffer from it are ignorant of the cause of their evils. Nevertheless, it is certain that the vicious consumption called *luxury*, and in general all the consumption of idle capitalists, far from being useful, destroys the greater part of the means of a nation's prosperity; and this is so true, that from the moment in which a country, which has industry and knowledge, is by any mean delivered from this scourge, we see there immediately an increase of riches and of strength truly prodigious.

What reason demonstrates history proves by facts. When was Holland capable of efforts truly incredible? When her admirals lived as her sailors did—when the arms of all her citizens were employed in enriching or defending the state; and none in cultivating tulips, or paying for pictures. All subsequent events, political and commercial, have united in causing its decline. It has preserved the spirit of economy—it has still considerable riches in a country in which every other people could with difficulty live. Make of Amsterdam the residence of a gallant and magnificient court, transform its vessels into embroidered clothes, and its magazines into ball rooms; and you will see if in a very few years they will have remaining even the means of defending themselves against the irruptions of the sea.

When did England, in spite of its misfortunes and faults, exhibit a prodigious development? Was it under Cromwell or under Charles the second? I know that moral causes have much more power than economical calculations; but I say that these moral causes do not so prodigiously augment all our resources, but because they direct all our efforts towards solid objects: Hence means are not wanting, either to the state or to individuals, for great objects, because they have not been employed in futilities.

Why do the citizens of the United States of North America double, every twenty-five years, their culture, their industry, their commerce, their riches, and their population? It is because there is scarcely an idler among them, and the rich go to little superfluous expense. Their position, I agree, is very favourable. Land is not wanting for their development: it offers itself to their labours, and recompences them. But if they laboured little, and expended much, this land would remain uncultivated—they would grow poor, would languish; and would be very miserable, as the Spaniards are, notwithstanding all their advantages. Their neighbours, the Canadians, do they make the same progress? They are gentlemen, living nobly, and doing nothing.

Finally, let us take a last example, much more striking still. France, under its ancient government, was not certainly as miserable as the French themselves have represented it to be; but it was not flourishing. Its population* and its agriculture were not retrograde, but they were stationary; or if they made some small progress, it was less than that of several neighbouring nations, and consequently not proportioned to the progress of the knowledge of the age. She was involved in debt —had no credit—was always in want of funds for her useful expenses—she felt herself incapable of supporting the ordinary expenses of her government, and still more of making any great efforts without: In a word, notwithstanding the genius, the number, and the activity of her inhabitants, the richness and extent of her soil, and the benefits of a very long peace, little troubled, she with difficulty maintained her rank among her rivals; and was of but little consideration, and in nowise formidable abroad.

Her revolution takes place: She has suffered all imaginable evils: She has been torn by atrocious wars, civil and foreign: Several of her provinces have been laid waste, and their cities reduced to ashes: All have been pillaged by brigands, and by the furnishers of the troops: Her exterior commerce has been annihilated: Her fleets totally destroyed;

* I desire it to be remembered, that I do not regard the augmentation of population as a good. It is but too often a multiplication of miserable beings. I should greatly prefer the augmentation of well being. I cite here the increase of the number of men as a symptom only, and not as a happiness. The abuse of competence is a proof of its existence.

though often renewed: Her colonies, believed so necessary to her prosperity, have been prostrated; and, what is worse, she has lost all the men and money lavished to subjugate them: Her specie has been nearly all exported, as well by the effect of emigration, as by that of paper money: She has supported fourteen armies in a time of famine; and, amidst all this, it is notorious that her population and her agriculture have augmented considerably in a very few years; and at the epoch of the creation of the empire—without any improvement in her situation as to the sea and foreign commerce, to which so great importance is commonly attributed, without having had a single instant of peace for repose,—she supported enormous taxes, made immense expenditures in public works,—she effected all without a loan; and she had a colossal power, which nothing on the continent of Europe could resist, and which would have subjugated the universe, but for the British navy. What then took place in this country which could produce such inconceivable effects! one circumstance changed has done the whole.

Under the ancient order of things, the greater part of the useful labour of the inhabitants of France was employed every year in producing the riches which formed the immense revenues of the court, and of all the rich class of society; and these revenues were almost entirely consumed in the expenditures of luxury; that is to say, in paying an enormous mass of population, whose whole labour reproduced absolutely nothing but the enjoyments of some men. In a moment almost the whole of these revenues, have passed partly into the hands of the new government, partly into those of the laborious class. They fed also all those who derive their subsistence from them; but their labour was applied to useful or necessary things; and it has sufficed to defend the state from without, and to increase its productions within.*

Ought we to be surprised when we consider that there was a time, of some length, during which, by the effect even of commotion and of the general distress, there was scarcely in France a single idle citizen, or one occupied in useless labours? Those who before made coaches, made carriages for cannon; those who made embroidery and laces, made coarse woollens and linens; those who ornamented boudoirs, built parks and cleared land. And even those who in peace rioted in all these inutilities, were forced to gain a subsistence by the performance of services which were wanting. A man who kept forty useless domestics left them to be hired by the industrious class, or by the state, and himself become a clerk of an office. This is the secret of those prodigious resources always found by the body of a nation in a crisis so great. It then turns to profit all the force which in ordinary times it suffered to be lost, without being aware of it; and we are frightened at seeing how great that is.

This is the substance of all that is true in college declamations on frugality, sobriety, abhorrence of ostentation; and all those democratical virtues of

* The sole suppression of the feudal rights and tythes, partly to the profit of cultivators, and partly of the state, enabled the one greatly to increase their industry, and the other to lay an enormous mass of new imposts; and these were but a small part of the revenues of the class of useless consumers.

poor and agricultural nations, which are so ridiculously vaunted without either their cause or effect being understood. It is not because they are poor and ignorant that these nations are strong; it is because nothing is lost of the little force they possess, and that a man who has an hundred francs, and employs them well, has more means than he who has a thousand and loses them at play. But let the same be done by a rich and enlightened nation, and you will see the same development of force which you have seen in the French nation, which has produced effects greatly superior to all that was ever executed by the Roman republic: for it has overthrown much greater obstacles. Let Germany, for example, during some years only, leave entirely in the hands of the industrious class the revenues which serve for the pageantry of all its small courts, and rich abbies, and you will see whether she will be a strong and formidable nation. On the contrary, suppose they should entirely re-establish in France the ancient order of things, that a great mass of property should return into the hands of idle men, that the government should continue to enrich favourites and make great expenditures in useless things, you would again see there immediately, notwithstanding its great increase of territory, languor in the midst of resources, misery in the midst of riches, and weakness in the midst of all the means of strength.

It will be repeated that I attribute solely to the distribution of riches, and to the employment of the labour they pay, the result of a multitude of moral causes of the greatest energy. Once more, I do not deny the existence of these causes; I acknowledge it as all others do; but I do more, I explain their effect. I agree that the enthusiasm of interior liberty and exterior independence, and the indignation against an unjust oppression, and a still more unjust aggression, have alone been able to operate these great revolutions in France; but I maintain that these have not furnished the passions with such great means of success, (notwithstanding the errors and horrors to which their violence led) but because they produced a better employment of all the national force. All the good of human society is in the good application of labour; all the evil in its loss; which, in other words, means nothing but that when men are occupied in providing for their wants they are satisfied, and that when they lose their time they suffer. One is ashamed to be obliged to prove so palpable a truth; but we must recollect that the extent of its consequences are surprising.

One might compose a whole book on luxury, and it would be useful, for this subject has never been well treated. It might be shown that luxury, that is to say the taste for superfluous expense, is to a certain point the necessary effect of the natural dispositions of man to procure constantly new enjoyments, when he has the means; and of the power of habit, which renders necessary to him the conveniences he has enjoyed, even when it shall have become burdensome to him to continue to procure them: that consequently luxury is an inevitable result of industry, the progress of which it nevertheless arrests; and of riches, which it tends to destroy; and that for the same reason, also, when a nation is fallen from its ancient grandeur, whether from the slow effect of luxury or from any other cause, it survives the prosperity which has given birth to it and renders its return impossible, unless some violent shock, directed to this end, should produce a quick and complete regeneration. It is the same with individuals.

It would be necessary to show, according to these data, that in the opposite situation, when a nation takes for the first time its rank among civilised people, it is requisite, in order that the success of its efforts may be complete, that the progress of its industry and knowledge should be much more rapid than that of its luxury. It is, perhaps, principally to this circumstance that we should attribute the great advances made by the Prussian monarchy under its second and third king, an example which ought to embarrass a little those who pretend that luxury is necessary to the prosperity of monarchies.* It is this same circumstance which appears to me to ensure the duration of the felicity of the United States; and it may be feared that the want of the complete enjoyment of this advantage, will render difficult and even imperfect the true prosperity and civilization of Russia.

It would be necessary to say which are the most injurious species of luxury. We might consider unskilfulness in fabrication as a great luxury, for it causes a great loss of time and of labour. It would above all be necessary to explain how the great for-

* If luxury is necessary in a monarchal state, it is for the security of the government, but not for the prosperity of the country.

tunes are the principal and almost only source of luxury, properly so called, for it could scarcely exist if they were all moderate. Even idleness in this case could scarcely have place. Now this is a kind of luxury; since, if it is not a sterile employment of labour, it is a suppression of it.* The branches of industry which rapidly produce immense riches bring then with them an inconvenience, which strongly counter-balances their advantages. It is not these we ought to wish to see first developed in a rising nation. Of this kind is a very extensive foreign commerce. Agriculture, on the contrary, is greatly preferable; its products are slow and limited. Industry, properly so called, (that of manufacture) is likewise without danger and very useful. Its profits are not excessive; its success is difficult to be attained and perpetuated; it requires much knowledge, and many estimable qualities; and its consequences are very favourable to the well being of consumers. The good fabrication of objects of first necessity is above all desirable. The manufactory of objects of luxury may also be of great advantage to a country; but it is when their produce is like the religion of the court of Rome—which is said to be for that court an article of exportation, and not of consumption; and there is always a fear of intoxicating ourselves with the liquor we prepare for others. All these observa-

* The only idle who ought to be seen without reprobation, are those who devote themselves to study; and especially to the study of man. And these are the only ones who are persecuted: there is reason for this. They shew how useless the others are; and they are not the strongest.

tions, and many others, should be developed in the book of which we are speaking; but they would be superfluous here. They enter in many respects into the reflections I have made before (chapter x,) on the manner in which riches are distributed in a country, in proportion as they are accumulated. Besides, my object is not to compose the history of luxury; I only wish to show its effects on general consumption, and on circulation.

I shall content myself with adding that if luxury is a great evil, in an economical point of view, it is still a much greater in point of morality; which is always much the most important, when the question is on the interests of men.

The taste for superfluous expenses, the principal source of which is vanity, nourishes and exasperates it. It renders the understanding frivolous, and injures its strength. It produces irregularity of conduct, which engenders many vices, disorders and disturbances in families. It leads women readily to depravity—men to avidity—both to the loss of delicacy and probity, and to the abandonment of all generous and tender sentiments. In a word, it enervates the soul, by weakening the understanding; and produces these sad effects not only on those who enjoy it, but likewise on all those who serve it, or admire it—who imitate or envy it. This will all be more clearly seen when we speak of our moral interests. I could not avoid indicating it here. We must not confound things however intimately connected they may be.

For the same reason it will not be expected surely that I should now discuss the question, whether luxury being acknowledged hurtful, we ought to combat it by laws or by manners; nor that I should examine by what mean we can favour production, and give a useful direction to consumption. This would be to encroach on the province of legislation; with which I may perhaps occupy myself some day. But in all this part of my work, I ought to limit myself to the establishment of facts.

I think I have solidly established, that since one can only expend what he has, production is the only fund of consumption; and that consequently consumption and circulation can never be augmented but by an augmenting production; and finally, that to destroy is not to produce; and that to expend is not to enrich. This small number of very simple truths, will enable us to see very clearly the effects of the revenues and expenses of governments on the prosperity of nations.

CHAPTER XII.

Of the Revenues and Expenses of a Government, and of its Debts.

THIS subject is still very vast, although it is but a part of that of which we have just treated. Many writers would divide it into three books, which they subdivide each into several chapters: but I prefer not to separate these matters, that I may not cause my readers to lose sight of their mutual dependance; and I feel the necessity for considering them principally in mass, and under a general and common aspect. This will not prevent me from entering also into details, and from distinguishing the particular cases which are really different, perhaps even with more exactitude than has been hitherto done.

In every society the government is the greatest of consumers. For this reason alone it merits a separate article in the history of consumption, without which it would be incomplete. But for the same reason, also, we can never perfectly comprehend the economical effects of government, and those of its receipts and expenditures, if we have not previously formed a clear and exact idea of general consumption, of its base, and of its progress.

The same errors which we have just combated will re-appear here. Those who think that agricultural labours alone are productive, do not fail to say that in the end all imposts fall on the proprietors of lands, that their revenue is the only taxable matter, that the territorial impost is the only just and useful one, and that there ought to be no others; and those who persuade themselves that consumptions can be a cause of direct riches, maintain that the levies made by government, on the fortunes of individuals, powerfully stimulate industry; that its expenses are very useful, by augmenting consumption; that they animate circulation; and that all this is very favourable to the public prosperity. To see clearly the vice of these sophisms, we must always follow the same track, and commence by well establishing the facts.

In the first place, there is no doubt but that a government of some sort must be very necessary to every political society; for its members must be judged, their affairs must be administered, they must be protected, defended, guarantied from all violence; it is only for this that they are united in society. It is no more doubtful, but that this government must have revenues since it has expenses to incur. But this is not the present question. The question is, to know what effects these revenues, and these expenses, produce on the public riches and national prosperity.

To judge of them—since government is a great consumer, and the greatest of all,—we must examine it in this quality, as we have examined the other consumers, that is to say we must see from whence it receives the funds of which it disposes, and what use it makes of them.

A first thing very certain is, that government cannot be ranked amongst the consumers of the industrious class. The expenditure it makes does not return into its hands with an increase of value. It does not support itself on the profits it makes. I conclude, then, that its consumption is very real and definitive; that nothing remains from the labour which it pays; and that the riches which it employs, and which were existing, are consumed and destroyed when it has availed itself of them. It remains to be seen from whence it receives them.

Since the moral person, called government, does not live on profits, it lives on revenues. It derives these revenues from two sources. It possesses estates in land, and it lays imposts. As to its estates in land, it is absolutely in the same situation as the other capitalists whom we have called idle. It leases them and receives a rent; or if they are forests, it annually sells the timber cut. The care taken of forests, and which principally consists in preserving them, does not merit the name of industrious labour. The real labour which gives them a value is that which consists in felling them, in selling and transporting them. If they belonged to him who fells them, he would receive all the profit. The price annually paid for the privilege of felling them ought to be regarded as a rent levied on the industry of the person who fells them: a rent absolutely similar to that derived from a fishery, yearly rented to him who has the industry to take the fish. Thus the revenues, derived from the estates belonging to government, are, like those of all other rural property, created by the industrious men who work them, and levied on their profits.

Many politicians do not approve of government having landed estates: it is very true, that as it is by no means a careful proprietor its managers must necessarily be very expensive and little faithful. Thus it does, with much unskilfulness, what another proprietor would do better. But it must be remarked, that this unskilfulness does not diminish, or diminishes very little, the total mass of the production of these estates: for the quantity of the production of the lands depends little on those who manage them, but almost entirely on those who work them. Now nothing prevents these lands being as well cultivated, and their timber cut down and sold, with as much intelligence as those of an individual. The defect in their management consists in employing a few more men than is necessary, and in paying them a little too dear. Now this is no very great inconvenience.

I, on the contrary, see many advantages in the governments having possessions of this kind. First, there are some kinds of productions which it alone can preserve in great quantity: such are forests of large timber, the productions of which must be so long waited for, that for the most part individuals prefer the same, or even a smaller quantity of more frequent returns. Secondly, it may be good that the government should possess cultivated lands. It will be better able to know more perfectly the resources and the interests of different localities; and, if it is wise and benevolent, it may even profit by this to diffuse a useful knowledge. Thirdly, when a great mass of landed property is in the hand of government, less remains at market. Now as this kind of possession is always greatly desired, all things otherwise equal, the less there is to be sold the dearer it will sell, that is to say that for a sum of one hundred thousand francs the buyer will be contented to receive four or even three thousand francs of revenue instead of five; and this will reduce the rate of interest of money in its various employments, which is a great advantage. Fourthly, and this consideration is the most important of all,—all that the government annually draws from these estates is a revenue, which it levies on no one. It comes to it from its own property, as to all other proprietors; and it is so much in diminution of what it is obliged to procure by imposts. In fine, in a case of necessity it may, as an individual, find a resource in the sale of its estates without having recourse to loans, which are always a great evil, as we shall soon see.

For all these reasons I think it very happy for government to be a great proprietor, especially of forests and large farms. One circumstance only would be to be regretted, that this would prevent these estates from falling into the hand of the industrious class. But we have seen on the subject of agricultural industry, that from the nature of things property of this kind can seldom be in the possession of those who work them, because this would take from them too great a portion of their funds. Now I had rather they should belong to government, than to any other capitalist living on revenue.

On the whole, our modern governments in general possess but little landed property. It is not that they have not almost all declared their domains inalienable, but they have also almost all sold or given a very great part of them. The true revenue on which they calculate is that of imposts; it is then this which we should take into consideration.

By means of imposts, the government takes from individuals the wealth which was at their disposition, in order to expend it itself; these then are always sacrifices imposed on them.

If this sacrifice bears on the men who live on their revenues, and who employ the whole of them on their personal enjoyments, it would make no change in the total mass of production, consumption and general circulation. All the difference would be, that a part of the wages which these men paid, would be paid by government with the money taken from them: this is the most favourable case.

When the impost falls on industrious men, who live on profits, it may only diminish their profits. Then it is that part of these profits which these men employ in their personal enjoyments which is attacked. It is these enjoyments which are diminished; and the impost has the same effects as in the preceding case. But if it goes so far as to annihilate the profits of the industrious men, or even to touch on the funds of their industry, then it is this industry itself which is deranged or destroyed; and consequently production, and in the end the general consumption are diminished by it. Suffering prevails every where.

Finally, where the impost falls on the hirelings, it is evident they begin to suffer. If the loss rests entirely on them, it is a part of their consumption which is suppressed; and which is replaced by that of those whom the government pays with the money taken from them. If they are able to throw it on those who employ them by raising the price of their wages, it is then necessary to know by whom they are employed ; and, accordingly as they are in the employ of idle or industrious capitalists, this loss will have one of the two effects which we have just described in speaking of these capitalists.

I think this preliminary explanation must appear incontestable, after the elucidations we have given in speaking of consumption. At present the great difficulty is to find on whom the loss occasioned by the impost really falls : for all imposts do not produce the same effects, and thus are so multiplied that it is impossible to examine every one separately. I think it best to arrange under the same denomination all those which are essentially of the same nature.

All imaginable imposts, and I suppose they have all been imagined, may be divided into six principal kinds,* viz. First, The impost on the revenues of lands, such as the real tax, the twentieth the manorial contribution in France, and the land tax in England. Second, That on the rent of houses. Third, That on the annuities due from the state. Fourth, That on persons, as the capitation and poll tax, sumptuary and furniture contributions, on patent rights, on charters and freedom of corporations, &c. &c. Fifth, That on civil acts and certain social transactions, as on stamps, and registers, on vendues, the hundredth penny, amortisement, and others ; to which we must add the annual impost on annuities charged on one individual by another, for there are no means of knowing of these investments, donations, or transmissions, but by the depositories which preserve the acts establishing them. Sixth, That on

* This is in my opinion the best method of classing them, to give a clear account of their effects.

merchandise, whether by monopoly or sale, exclusive, or even forced, as formerly of salt and tobacco in France; or at the moment of their first production, as the taxes on salt ponds and mines, and part of those on wines in France and on breweries in England; or at the moment of consumption, or on their passage from the first producer to the ultimate consumer, as the customs interior and exterior: the tolls on roads, canals, postage, and at the entrance of cities, &c. &c.*

* A note communicated to the Editor. Our author's classification of taxes being taken from those practised in France, will scarcely be intelligible to an American reader to whom the nature as well as names of some of them must be unknown. The taxes with which we are familiar class themselves readily according to the basis on which they rest. 1. Capital. 2. Income. 3. Consumption. These may be considered as commensurate; consumption being generally equal to income; and income the annual profit of capital, a government may select either of these basis for the establishment of its system of taxation, and so frame it as to reach the faculties of every member of the society, and to draw from him his equal proportion of the public contributions. And if this be correctly obtained, it is the perfection of the function of taxation. But when once a government has assumed its basis, to select and tax special articles from either of the other classes is double taxation. For example, if the system be established on the basis of income, and his just proportion on that scale has been already drawn from every one, to step into the field of consumption, and tax special articles in that, as broadcloth or homespun, wine or whiskey, a coach or a waggon, is doubly taxing the same article. For that portion of income, with which these articles are purchased, having already paid its tax as income, to pay another tax on the thing it purchased, is paying twice for the same thing. It is an aggrievance on the citizens who use these articles in exoneration of those who do not, contrary to the most sacred of the duties of a government, to do equal and impartial justice to all its citizens.

How far it may be the interest and the duty of all to submit to this sacrifice on other grounds, for instance, to pay for a time an impost on the importation of certain articles, in order to encourage their manufacture at home, or an excise on others injurious to the morals or health of the citizens, will depend on a series of considerations, of another order, and beyond the proper limits of this note. The reader, in deciding which basis of taxation is most eligible for the local circumstances of his country, will of course avail himself of the weighty observations of our author.

Each of these imposts has one or several manners, peculiar to itself, of being burdensome.

At the first glance, we may see that the tax on revenues from land has the inconvenience of being difficult to assess with justice, and of annihilating the value of all those lands whose rent does not exceed the tax or exceeds it by too little, to determine any one to incur the inevitable risques, and the expenditures requisite for putting these lands into a state for cultivation.

The tax on house rent, has the defect of lessening the profit of speculations in building; and so of deterring from building houses to rent, so that every citizen is obliged to content himself with habitations less healthy, and less convenient, than those he might have had at the same rent.*

A tax on annuities due from the state is a real bankruptcy, if established on annuities already created, since it is a diminution of the interest promised for a capital received; and it is illusory if

* I do not avail myself against this impost of the pretentions of some economists, that the rent of houses ought not to be taxed, or at least but in proportion to the nett revenue which would be yielded by the cultivation of the land occupied by these houses, all the rest being only the interest of the capital employed in building, which according to them is not taxable. This opinion is a consequence of that which considers agricultural labour as alone productive, and that the revenue of land is the only thing taxable, because there is in the produce of land a part purely gratuitous and entirely due to nature; which portion, according to these authors, is the only legitimate and reasonable subject of taxation.

I have shown that all this is false, therefore I cannot avail myself of it either against this or any of the following imposts; which are all not only reprobated in this system, but are declared illusory, as never being nor possible to be, any thing but an impost on the revenue of lands, disguised and additionally charged with useles expenses and losses. Such a theory is untenable when we know what is production.

established on them at the moment of their creation, for it would have been more simple to have offered in the first instant an interest lessened by the amount of the tax, which would have come to the same thing.

A tax on persons gives occasion to disagreeable scrutinies to assess it justly, according to the fortune of every one; and can never rest but on arbitrary bases and very uncertain knowledge, as well when attempted to be assessed on riches already acquired as when intended to bear on the means of acquiring them. In the latter case, that is to say, when it is predicated on the supposition of any kind of industry whatever, it discourages that industry, and obliges it to rise in price or to be abandoned.

The tax on civil acts, and in general on social transactions, cramps the circulation of real property, and diminishes their market value, by rendering their transfer very expensive; augments so much the expenses of justice that the poor dare no longer defend their rights; renders all business perplexing and difficult; occasions inquisitorial researches, and vexations by the agents of the revenue; gives rise in these acts to concealments, and even to the insertion of deceptious clauses and valuations, which open the door to much iniquity and give rise to a multitude of contentions and misfortunes.

As to taxes on merchandise, their inconveniences are still more numerous and complicated; but are not less disagreeable nor less certain.

Monopoly, or a sale exclusively by the state, is odious, tyrannical, contrary to the natural right which every one has of buying and selling as he pleases, and it necessitates a multitude of violent measures. It is still worse when this sale is forced, that is to say when government obliges individuals, as has sometimes been done, to buy things they do not want, under pretext that they cannot do without them, and that if they do not buy them it is because they have provided themselves by contraband.

A tax, levied at the moment of production, evidently requires on the part of the producer an advance of fund, which being long without returning to him greatly diminishes his means of producing.

It is not less clear that all imposts levied either at the moment of consumption or during the transportation from the producer to the consumer, cramp or destroy some branch of industry or of commerce; render scarce, or costly, necessary or useful articles; disturb all enjoyments, derange the natural course of things; and establish, between the different wants and the means of satisfying them, proportions and relations which would not exist but for these perturbations, which are necessarily variable, and which render the speculations and resources of the citizens inevitably precarious.

Finally, all these taxes whatsoever on merchandise occasion an infinity of precautions and embarrassing formalities. They give place to a multitude of ruinous difficulties, and are necessarily liable to be arbitrary; they oblige actions indifferent in themselves to be constituted crimes, and inflict punishments often the most cruel. Their collection is very expensive, and calls into existence an army of officers, and an army of defrauders, men all lost to society, and who continually wage a real civil war, with all the greivous economical and moral consequences which it brings on.

When we attentively examine each of these criticisms on the different taxes, we see that they are well founded. Thus, after having shown that every impost is a sacrifice, we find that we have also shown that every impost has, besides, a manner peculiar to itself of being hurtful to the contributors. This is already a great deal, but it does not yet teach us on whom precisely falls the loss resulting from the impost, nor who it is that really and definitively supports it. Yet this latter question is the most important, and absolutely necessary to be resolved in order to judge of the effects of taxes on the national prosperity. Let us examine it then with attention, without adopting any system, and adhering scrupulously to an observation of facts, as we have done hitherto.

As to the tax on the revenues of land, it is evident that it is he who possesses the land, at the moment in which the tax is established, who pays it really without being able to throw it on any one. For it does not give him any means of augmenting his productions, since it adds nothing either to the demand for articles, or to the fertility of the soil; and does not in any degree diminish the expense of cultivation. All assent to this truth. But what has not been sufficiently remarked, is, that this proprietor ought to be considered less as having been deprived of a portion of his yearly income, than as having lost that part of his capital, which would produce this portion of income at the current rate of interest. The proof is, that if a farm, yielding annually five thousand francs nett rent, is worth an hundred thousand francs—the day after it shall have been charged with a perpetual tax of a fifth, all other things equal, it will not command more than eighty thousand if offered for sale; and it will be stated but at eighty thousand francs, in the inventory of an inheritance which contains other articles whose value have not been changed. In effect, when the state has declared that it takes in perpetuity the fifth of the income of lands, it is as if it had declared itself proprietor of the fifth of the capital, for no property is worth but the utility which may be derived from it. This is so true, that when, in consequence of a new impost, the state opens a loan, for the interest of which it pledges the revenue it has seized, the operation is consummated; it has really received the capital, it had appropriated, and has made away with the whole at once, instead of annually expending its income. It is as when Mr. Pitt took at once from the proprietors the capital of the land tax with which they were charged: they were liberated and he swallowed his capital.

From hence it follows, that when once all the land has changed owners since the establishment of the tax, it is no longer really paid by any one. The purchasers having bought only what was left, have lost nothing; the heirs having succeeded but to what they found, the surplus is to them as if their predecessors had expended or lost it, as in effect they have lost it. And, in case of inheritances abandoned as of no value, it is the creditors who have lost the capital taken by the state from the property which was security for their debt.

It follows likewise from this, that when the state renounces the whole or part of a territorial tax, anciently established as a perpetuity, it purely and simply makes a present to the actual proprietors of the lands of the capital of the revenue which it ceases to demand. It is as to them a gift absolutely gratuitous, to which they have no more right than any other citizens. For none of them calculated on this capital, in the transactions by which they became proprietors.

It would not be absolutely the same, if the impost had been originally established only for a determinate number of years. Then there would really have been taken from the proprietor but a part of the capital corresponding to this number of years. The state, likewise, would have borrowed but this value from the lenders, to whom it might have pledged this impost for the payment of their principal and interest; and the lands would have been considered in the transaction but as deteriorated to this amount. In this case when the tax ceases, as when the corresponding dividends of the loan are exhausted, it is on both sides a debt extinguished, because it is paid. On the whole the principle is the same, as in the case of a tax and of a perpetual rent.

It is then always true, that when a tax is laid on land, a value equal to the capital of this tax is taken at once from the actual proprietors, and that when all have changed owners, since the establishment of the tax, it is really no longer paid by any one. This observation is singular and important.

It is absolutely the same with the tax established on the rent of houses. Those who possess them at the moment it is established support the entire loss, for they have no means of indemnifying themselves. But those who buy them afterwards pay for them but in proportion to the charges with which they are incumbered. Those who inherit them, reckon them, in like manner, but at the value which remains; and as to those who build subsequently, they make their calculations according to the state of things as they are established. If no room is left for useful speculation they defer building until the effect of scarcity raises rents. As, on the contrary, if it was extremely advantageous there would soon be funds enough employed therein to make it no longer preferable to any other employment of them. We conclude again that the proprietors on whom the impost falls, lose the entire capital, and that when all are either dead or expropriated, this impost is paid but by those who have no right to complain of it.

We may say the same of the taxes which governments sometimes permit themselves to impose on annuities which they owe for capitals formerly furnished. Certainly the unfortunate creditor from whom this deduction is made suffers the entire loss, not being able to throw it on any one; but he moreover loses the capital of the sum retained. The proof is that if he sells his annuity he gets so much the less, as it is more encumbered if otherwise the general rate of interest on money has not varied. Whence it follows that subsequent possessors of this annuity no longer pay any thing: for they received it in this condition and for its remaining value in virtue of a purchase freely made or of successions voluntarily accepted.

The effect of a tax on persons is not at all the same. We must distinguish between that which is supposed to bear on acquired riches, and that which is meant for the means of acquiring them, that is to say on industry of some sort. In the first case it is certainly always the person taxed who supports the loss resulting from it, for he cannot throw it on any other. But as the tax on every one ceases with his life, and every one is successively subject to it, in proportion to his presumed fortune, the first person taxed loses only the dues which he pays, and not the capital, and does not liberate those who come after him; thus at whatever epoch the tax ceases, it is not a pure gain to those who are subject to it, it is a burthen weighing really on them and which ceases to be continued.

As to a tax on persons, which has for its object industry of some sort, it is equally true that he who first pays it does not lose the capital nor liberate those who are subjected to it after him; but it gives room for considerations of another kind. The man who exercises a branch of industry at the moment in which it becomes burthened with a new personal tax, such as the establishment or increase of patent rights, the freedom of corporations, masterships, or other things of the same kind, this man I say has but two courses to pursue, either to renounce his occupation, or to pay the tax and support the loss resulting from it, if notwithstanding this it still holds out a prospect of sufficient profits. In the first case he certainly suffers, but he does not pay the tax; therefore I shall not now occupy myself with it. In the second case, it is he assuredly who pays the imposition, since neither augmenting the demand, nor diminishing the expense, it does not give him any immediate mean of increasing his receipts or lessening his expenditures. But taxes are never all at once laid so heavy as to oblige inevitably all of the same occupation to quit it: for all industrious professions being necessary to society, the total extinction of any one would produce general disorder. Thus after the establishment of a tax of the kind we speak of, none but those who are already rich enough to consider a diminished profit as no object, or those who exercised their profession with so little success, that no profits would remain to them after paying the tax, would renounce their occupation. The others continue it; and these, as we have said, really pay the tax at least until rid of the competion of many of their brethren, they could avail themselves of this circumstance to levy it on the consumers by making them pay more for the articles than before.

It is thus with those who exercised the profession at the moment of the establishment of the tax. The case is different with those who embrace it after the tax has been once established. They find the law made; we may say that they engage themselves on this condition. The tax is for them among the expenses required by the profession, as the necessity of renting a particular situation, or of buying a particular utensil. They only enter on this profession because they calculate that, notwithstanding these changes, it is still the best employment they can make of the portion of capital and industry they possess. Thus they certainly advance the tax, but it does not really take any thing from them. Those to whom it is a real loss are the consumers, who without this change could at less expense have made up the income with which they are contented, and which was the best in their power to procure in the present state of society. From hence it follows, that, if the tax be removed these men really make a profit on which they did not calculate, at least until this advantage produces new competitors. They find themselves gratuitously, and fortuitously, transported into a class of society more favoured by fortune than that in which they were placed; while to those who exercised it previously to the tax, it is but a return to their first state. We see that a tax on persons, founded on industry, produces very different effects; but its general effect is to diminish the enjoyments of consumers, since their furnishers do not give them merchandise for that part of their money which goes into the public treasury. I cannot enter into more details; but we cannot too much accustom ourselves to judge of the different reverberations of a tax, and to follow them in thought, in all their modifications. Let us pass to the imposts on papers, deeds, records, and other monuments of social transactions.

This requires also a distinction. The portion of this impost, which goes to augment the expenses of justice, and which makes a part of it, is certainly paid by the parties on whom the judgment throws the expense; and it is difficult to say to what class of society it is most hurtful; however, it is easy to see that it burdens particularly the kind of property most liable to contention. Now, as this is landed property, the establishment of such an impost certainly diminishes its market value. Whence it follows that those who have purchased lands, since the existence of the tax, are a little compensated, in advance, by the smaller price of their purchase; and that those who possessed them before bear the entire loss if they have any law-suit, and even sustain a loss without any law contest, and without paying the tax, since the value of their property is diminished. Consequently if the tax ceases, it is but a restitution for the latter; and there is a portion of gratuitous gain for the others, for they find themselves in a better situation than that on which they had calculated, and according to which they had made their speculation.

All this is yet more true, and is true without restriction, of that portion of the tax on transactions which regards purchases and sales, such as fines on alienation, the hundredth penny, amortisement, and others. This portion of the tax is entirely paid by him who possesses the property at the moment it is thus encumbered: for he who buys it subsequently pays him but accordingly, and consequently pays really nothing. All that can be said, is that if this tax on deeds of sale of certain possessions is accompanied by other taxes on other transactions which affect other kinds of property, other employments of capitals, it will happen that these possessions are not the only ones lessened in value; and consequently that proportion is preserved, at least in part, and that thus a part of their loss is prevented by that of others, for the market price of every kind of revenue is relative to that of all the others. Thus, if all these losses could be exactly balanced, the total loss resulting from the impost would be exactly and very proportionably distributed. This is all that can be asked: for it must necessarily exist, since impost is always a sum of means taken from the governed, to be placed at the disposition of those who govern.

Imposts on merchandise have effects still more complicated and various. To unravel them well, let us recollect that all merchandise, at the moment it is delivered to the consumer, has a natural and necessary price. This price is composed of the value of what has been necessary for the subsistence of those who have fabricated and transported this merchandise, during the time which they were employed about it. I say that this price is natural because it is founded on the nature of things independently of all convention; and that it is necessary, because if the men who execute a labour whatsoever do not obtain subsistence they perish, or apply themselves to other occupations, and this labour is no longer executed. But this natural and necessary price has scarcely any thing in common with the market or conventional price of the merchandise, that is to say with the price at which it is fixed by the effect of a free sale. For a thing may have cost very little trouble, or if it has required much labour and care it may have been found or stolen by him who offers it for sale; in these two cases he may sell it very low, without losing; but it may at the same time be so useful to him, that he will not part with it but for a very great price; and, if many people want it, he will obtain this price, and make an enormous gain. On the contrary it is possible that a thing may have cost the vendor infinite trouble, that not only it may not be necessary to him, but that he may have a pressing call to dispose of it, and that yet no body is desirous of buying it. In this case he will be obliged to part with it for almost nothing, and will sustain a very great loss. The natural price is then composed of anterior sacrifices made by the vendor, and the conventional price is fixed by the offers of buyers. These are two things, in themselves foreign to one another. Only when the conventional price of any labour is constantly below its natural and necessary price, it ceases to be performed. Then the produce of this labour becoming scarce, more sacrifices are made to procure it, if it is still desired, and thus however little it is really useful the conventional or market price re-ascends to the level of the price which nature has attached to that labour, and which is necessary to a continuance of its execution. It is thus all prices are formed in a state of society.

It follows hence that those who exercise a labour, the conventional price of which is inferior to its natural value, ruin themselves or disperse, that those who execute a labour, or in other words exercise an industry whatsoever, the conventional price of which is strictly equal to the natural price, that is to say, those whose profits balance nearly their urgent wants, vegetate and subsist miserably and that those who possess talents the conventional price of which, is superior to absolute necessaries, enjoy, prosper, and in course multiply. For the fecundity of all living, even among vegetables is such, that nothing but a want of nourishment for the germs disclosed arrests the increase of numbers of the individuals. This is the cause of the retrograde, stationary or progressive state of population, in the human kind. Momentary calamities, such as famine and pestilence have little effect. Unproductive labour, or productive in an insufficient degree, is the poison which deeply infects the sources of life. We have already made nearly all these observations, either in the fourth paragraph of our introduction, in speaking of the nature of our riches, or in the chapters in which we have spoken of values and population. But it was well to bring them again into view in this place.

Now it is easy to perceive that imposts on merchandise, affect prices, in different ways, and in different limits, according to the manner in which they are levied, and according to the nature of the articles on which they bear. For example in the case of monoply or exclusive sale, by the state, it is clear that the impost is paid directly immediately and without resource by the consumer, and that it has the greatest extension of which it is susceptible. But this sale, if forced cannot however, either in price or quantity exceed a certain term, which is that of the possibility of paying it. It stops whenever it would be useless to exact it, or when it would cost more than it would bring in. This is the point at which the tax on salt was in France and it is the maximum of possible exaction.

If the exclusive sale, be not forced it varies according to the nature of the merchandise, if it be on articles not necessary in proportion as the price raises the consumption diminishes; for there is but a certain sum of means in the whole society, which is destined to procure a certain kind of enjoyment: it may even happen, that a small increase of price may greatly diminish the profit because many renounce entirely this kind of consumption, or are even able to replace it by another. But the impost is always effectively paid by those who persevere in consuming.

If on the contrary the exclusive sale made by the state, but by mutual agreement bears on an article of the first necessity, it is equivalent to a forced sale, for the consumption, diminishes truly in proportion as the price rises, that is to say, people suffer and die, but as in fine it is necessary, it always rises with the means of paying, and it is paid by those who consume.

After these violent means, if we examine others, more mild, we shall find their effects analagous, with a less degree of energy. The most efficacious of these is a tax imposed on merchandise at the moment of production, for no part escapes, not even that consumed by the producer himself, nor even that which may be damaged or lost in warehouses, previously to being employed. Such is the tax on salt levied on the salt ponds; that on wine at the instant of the vintage, or before the first sale, and that on beer at the breweries. We may also range in the same class the impost on sugar, coffee, and other such articles levied at the moment of their arrival from the country which produces them: for it is not till this moment they exist, for the country which cannot produce them and which is to consume them.

This tax levied at the moment of production, if established on an article little necessary is as limited as the taste we have for it. Thus, when it was wished to derive a great revenue from tobacco, pains were taken to render it a necessary to the people. For if society is instituted for the more easy satisfaction of the wants given us by nature, and from which we cannot withdraw ourselves, it seems that fiscality is destined to create in us artificial wants, in order to refuse us one part, and make us pay for the other.

When this same impost, at the moment of production, is established on an article more necessary, it is susceptible of a greater extension; however, if this article costs much labour and expense in its production the extent of the impost is likewise soon stopt, no longer through want of a desire to procure the article, but by the impossibility of paying for it: for there must always reach the producers a sufficient portion of the price for their subsistence; thus there is less remaining for the state.

But an impost displays all its force when the article is very necessary and costs very little, as salt for example: there all is profit for the treasury; accordingly its agents have always paid a particular attention to salt. Very rich mines produce also the same effect to a certain point, but in general governments have taken the property to themselves, which saves the trouble of taxing, and is equivalent to the process of exclusive sale. Air and water, if they could have appropriated them would have been objects of taxation very heavy and very fruitful for the treasury; but nature has diffused them too widely. I do not doubt but, in Arabia, revenue farmers would draw great profit from a tax on water, and so that no one should drink without their permission. As to air the window tax accomplishes as much on that as is possible.

Wine is not a gratuitous present from nature. It costs much trouble, care and expense; and, notwithstanding the necessity and the strong desire we have to procure it, we should with difficulty, believe it could support the enormous charges with which it is burthened at present in France, at the moment of its production. If we were not apprised that a part of this burden falls directly on the land planted in vines, and operates only as a great reduction of the rents paid. In that way it has the effect of a land tax, which is, as we have seen to take from the proprietor of the soil a portion of his capital, without influencing the price of the products or encroaching on the profits of the producer. Thus the capitalist is impoverished.

but nothing is deranged in the economy of society, and this capitalist is obliged to sustain this loss, whenever the land would yield him still less by a change of culture.

Corn like wine, might be the object of a very heavy tax, levied at the moment of production, independently even of the tenth, with which both are burthened almost every where. A part of this impost would operate in like manner in diminution of the rent of the land, without touching the wages of the production, and consequently without increasing the price of the article. If in general they have abstained from this tax, I am persuaded it is not from a superstitious respect, for the principal nourishment of the poor, which has otherwise been charged in many ways which enhance the price, but because they have been prevented by the difficulty of superintending the entry into every barn, a difficulty which in effect is still greater than that of entering every cellar. In other respects the similitude is complete.

Let us observe, in finishing this article, that an impost thus levied, at the moment of production, on an article of indispensable use all over the world, is equivalent to a real capitation; but of all capitations it is the most cruel, for the poor. For it is the poor who consume the greatest quantity of articles of the first necessity, there being for them no other substitute; and they constitute almost the whole of their expenses, because they can only provide for their most pressing wants. Thus such a capitation is distributed, in proportion to misery and not to riches in the direct ratio of wants-

and the inverse of means. In this way we may appreciate imposts of this kind. But they are very productive: for it is always the poor who constitute the great number, and by this great number great sums. They little affect those who could make their complaints be heard; and this determines in their favour. It cannot be dissembled, that these are the two only causes of the preference given to them.

As to imposts levied on different merchandises, either at the moment of consumption or at their different stations, as on the public roads, in the markets, in ports at the gates of cities, in shops, &c. &c. their effects have been already indicated by those we have just seen resulting from exclusive sale, or from a tax at the moment of production. These are of the same kind, only they are commonly less general and less absolute; because they are more various, and seldom embrace so great an extent of country. In fact the greatest part of these imposts are local measures. A toll affects only the goods which pass along the road or canal on which it is established. At the entrance of towns it affects directly only the consumption made within their interior. (I suppose its transit exempt from duty.) A tax levied in a market or shop does not affect what is sold in the county, or at extraordinary fairs. Thus it deranges prices and industry more irregularly, but always deranges them in the points on which they bear. For so soon as an article is charged the condition either of the producer or the consumer is deteriorated. It is here that we meet again relatively to products and the effects of taxation, the consequences of two important conditions proper to all merchandise, the one being of the first necessity, or only agreeable or of luxury, the other that their conventional or market price be greater than their natural or necessary one, or merely equal to it, as to being lower, we already know that impossible in the long run.

If the article taxed be of the first necessity it cannot be dispensed with, it will always be bought while there are means; and, if its conventional price be only equal to the natural one, the producer can make no abatement;—thus all the loss will fall on the consumer. Whence we are to conclude, that if the sale and the product of the tax diminishes, it is the consumer who suffers and perishes.

We must remark that in our old societies occupying a territory circumscribed long ago, and able to acquire only lands already appropriated, this is the case with all merchandises of the first necessity; for, by the effect of the long contention between the contrary interests of the producer and consumer, every one is posted in the social order according to his degree of capacity. Those who possess some talent, in sufficient demand to enable them to exact payment beyond their absolute necessities, will devote themselves to the employment so preferred. None but those who cannot succeed in them devote themselves to the indispensable productions; because these are always in demand. But they are not paid more than is strictly necessary; because these are always inferior persons who can do nothing else.

It is even necessary it should be so: these articles of first necessity are the urgent wants of all, and especially of the poorest of all the other classes who consume without producing them, being occupied in other productions; thus the poor can subsist only in proportion as these articles are easy to be procured.

The more indispensable then a profession is, the more inevitable it is that those who devote themselves to it for want of other capacity should be reduced to the strictly necessary. The only direct means of ameliorating the condition of these men, the last in rank in society from their want of talent, would be to persuade them to multiply less, and to leave them always free to go and exercise their feeble talent whenever it would be the most profitable. For this reason expatriation should always be permitted. There are still some other political measures which might indirectly concur in defending extreme weakness against extreme misery; we will speak of them elsewhere. On the whole these men, whom we compassionate with justice, suffer still less than they would in the savage state. The proof is that they vegetate in greater numbers, for man extinguishes but through excess of suffering.

We have already said all this elsewhere, as occasions presented themselves; but it was very necessary to repeat it here on the subject of taxation. For the history of the revenues and expenses of government is the abridgment of the history of production and consumption of the whole society; since under this point of view government is but a very great annuitant, with whom authority stands instead of capital. Without too much forcing the similitude between the circulation of riches and that of the blood, we might say that the circulation operated by government in society, resembles entirely the pulmonary circulation in an individual. It is extracted from the total mass, and returns to diffuse itself there again after having performed its functions separately; but in a manner absolutely similar.

If the article taxed is not of the first necessity, and if nevertheless its conventional price is but equal to its necessary one, it is a proof that the consumers hold feebly to this enjoyment. Then, the tax superve-ning, the producer has no choice but to renounce his occupation, and endeavour to find wages in some other profession; in which he will increase misery by his concurrence, and in which he likewise is under disadvantage from it, not being his own. Thus they perish, in a great measure at least. As to the consumer, he loses but an enjoyment, to which he was little attached apparently, because he easily replaces it by another; which gives occasion to other wages. But the produce of the tax becomes null.

If, on the contrary, merchandise of little necessity, stricken by a tax, has a conventional price greatly superior to its necessary one—and this is the case with all articles of luxury, there is scope for the treasury without reducing any one precisely to misery. The same total sum is expended for this enjoyment, unless the taste diminishes which has occasioned it to be desired: and it is the producer who loses almost the whole of what the impost takes from this total sum; but, as he gained more than the necessary, he is not yet below it. However it must be observed that this is only true in general. For in this trade, supposed generally advantageous, there are individuals who through want of skill or good fortune, obtain only the slender necessary; and the impost supervening, these are obliged to abandon their profession; which is always a great suffering.

It is thus we may represent to ourselves with sufficient accuracy the direct effects of the different imposts, local and partial, levied on merchandise in their passage from the producer to the consumer. But, besides these direct effects, these imposts have others that are indirect, foreign to the first, or which mix with and complicate them. Thus a heavy duty on an important article, levied at the entrance of a city, diminishes on one hand the rent of its houses, by rendering its habitation less desirable, and on the other it diminishes the rent of land which produces the dutied article, by rendering the sale less considerable or less advantageous. Here then idle capitalists, although they should be absent and not consumers of any thing, are affected in their capital, as by a land tax while it is believed that only the consumer or producer is affected. This is so true, that these proprietors, if it were proposed to them, would make sacrifices to pay off a part of the funds of this impost, or directly furnish a part of their annual produce. This we have seen a thousand times.

What is more, in our economical considerations we often regard as real consumers of an article those only who effectively consume it for their personal satisfaction; yet they are by no means the only buyers of the article. Often the greater part of those who procure it purchase it as a first material of other productions, and as a material of their industry. Then the tax on these articles affects all these productions, and all these occupations. It is what particularly happens to articles of very general use, or of indispensable necessity. They make a part of the expenses of all producers, but in different degrees.

Finally, we must likewise observe, that the imposts of which we are speaking never fall altogether on a single article. They are at the same time levied on many different kinds of goods, that is to say on many species of productions and consumptions. On each, according to its nature, they operate some of the effects we have just explained; so that all these different effects reciprocally clash, balance and resist each other. For the new expenses, with which any kind of industry is burdened, lessen the promptitude to engage in it, in preference to another which has also experienced an injury of the same kind. The burden which oppresses one kind of consumption, prevents its becoming a substitute for that which we wish to renounce. Whence it results, that if it were possible so completely to foresee all these reverberations as to be able perfectly to balance all the weights and to place them all at the same time, so as to produce every where an equal pressure, no proportion would be changed by them. They would produce all together no other effect than the general one inherent in all imposts, namely that the producer would have less money for his labour and the consumer less enjoyment for his money. We might consider imposts as good when to this general and inevitable evil they do not join particular evils too distressing.

I shall follow no farther this examination of the different kinds of imposts. I think I have said enough to enable all to judge of them, and especially to show as clearly as that is possible on whom the loss occasioned by them really falls.

In effect, we see first, that the tax on annuities due by the state and that on the income of land, are not only annually paid by those on whom they fall without their being able to throw any part of them on others but that they lose even the capital; so that after them nobody really pays any thing. Secondly, that it is the same with the tax on the rent of houses; but that moreover it restrains speculations in building, and diminishes the comfort of tenants. Thirdly, that a personal tax, having acquired riches for its object does no wrong but to those from whom it is demanded; but does not liberate those who are to pay it after them. Fourthly, that the loss resulting from a tax on the instruments of social transactions is really supported by those from whom it is demanded, whenever the occasion of paying it occurs; but that its existence alone is injurious to others, by reducing the price of several things and shackling several kinds of industry. Fifthly, that a personal tax which has for its object any kind of industry whatsoever, and all taxes on merchandise, burden first all those from whom they are demanded; and, moreover, that they derange all prices and all kinds of industry; and that, by the effect of their numerous reverberations they end by falling on all the consumers, so as that we cannot precisely ascertain in what proportions.

I know that these results, separated, distinguished, modified, will appear less satisfactory than a very dogmatical decision which, treating the series of the interests of men as a row of ivory balls, should affirm that which ever is touched the last only is put in motion; but I could only represent things as I see them, and not as they may be imagined. If extreme simplicity pleases the understanding by relieving it, if even it is for this that it creates abstractions, a good understanding ought not to forget that this extreme simplicity is found only in itself; and that even in mechanics, as soon as there is a question of real bodies, it is necessary to have regard to many considerations, which have no place so long as we reason on mathematical lines and points. Nevertheless, urged by the desire of arriving at a positive principle, I shall be asked perhaps, as I have been already asked on a similar occasion, what is my conclusion, and what is the tax which I prefer. Having exposed the facts, I might leave to the reader to draw his own consequences. But I will give my opinion with its reasons, warning however beforehand that it will never be absolute, but always relative; for a tax is never good when it is exaggerated, nor even when it is not in proportion to all others.

First I remind, that the consumption of industrious men, that which I have called productive consumption, being the only one that reproduces what it destroys, and being therefore the only source of riches, it is that above all which we ought to endeavour not to derange.

Setting out from this truth, the tax on the annuities due by the state would appear to me the best of all; but it is impossible to think of it, since we have seen that it is a true bankruptcy. It is not that I think it useful to cherish the public credit. I think, on the contrary, it is an evil for the government to have credit, and to be able to borrow; I will give the reason when I shall speak of its debts. Moral considerations alone determine me invincibly. Society being entirely founded on conventions, it is impossible that it should not be pernicious to give an example of the violation of plighted faith. No pecuniary calculation can counterbalance such an inconvenience. Its consequences are immense and fatal. The true method of taxing annuitants is to administer well. This causes them to receive but a low interest for their money.

After this tax, of which we cannot think, the best in my opinion are those which resemble it the most, that is to say the taxes on the income of land, and on the rent of houses, to which we may join that personal tax which has for its object riches already acquired. It will be seen, that if I prefer the tax on the income of land, it is not for the reasons of the ancient economists. It is on the contrary, because I regard the proprietors of land as strangers to reproduction. Moreover, I consider these three imposts, which bear principally on the rich, as a compensation for the imposts on merchandise, which necessarily oppress principally the poor. I have no need to say that the tax on land ought not to be such that much land would be neglected.

The tax on deeds and social transactions, notwithstanding its inconveniencies, appear to me admissible also, provided it be not exaggerated. Extending to many things, it bears on many points, which is always an advantage; and it does not press immediately on the first wants of the poor, which is also a great good.

As to taxes on merchandise, to which we must join the personal tax which has presumed industry for its object, I begin by rejecting absolutely all exclusive sales; and yet more, all forced sales, as well as every measure tending to shackle the freedom of labour, and to injure individual property, that is to say the entire disposition of personal faculties. These excesses provided against, I see nothing to forbid the establishment of taxes on merchandise. First, all those on articles purely of luxury are excellent, and have nothing but advantages without any inconveniencies. They diminish the effects of the excessive inequality of fortunes, by rendering more costly the enjoyments of extreme luxury. They are the only sumptuary laws which can be approved. But these are the taxes against which powerful men exclaim the most; besides they are always of very slender product, for in all cases it is the great number, though too much despised, which constitutes the force. We must therefore have recourse to taxes on more useful merchandise, and even on those of first necessity: for, in short, there must be a public revenue. These, as we have said, bear principal ly on the poor; but, as we have also said, they are balanced by those which bear solely on the proprietors of land, and they justify them. Besides, levied at the gates of cities, they contribute to desseminate the population over the whole extent of the territory, levied at the frontiers, they may be useful on some diplomatic combinations, so long as sound policy has not their entire direction. I do not think then we should blame these impositions. I confine myself to the recommendation, that they never be so heavy as to crush any kind of industry; and that they be very various, that they may bear on all. All are taken care of when all are so charged as that each will sustain its part of the common burden, for it must not be forgotten that our only question here is ever how, to do the least evil possible; and that when we have well distributed the necessary evil, we have attained the maximum of perfection in this art.

The expense of collection and the necesity of punishments are likewise two accessory evils of taxation, to which, some it is true are more subject than others; but on which I have nothing to say. But that neither the one nor the other are carried to extremes when the taxes are not excessive and when not enforced by tyrannical forms. Thus I regard them only as secondary considerations.

This is what I think of imposts. But is a more precise conclusion desired? Here it is. The best taxes in my opinion are, first, the most moderate, because they occasion fewer sacrifices, and less violence. Second, the most various, because they produce an equilibrium of the whole. Third, the most ancient, because they have entered into all prices and that all are regulated in consequence.

Once more I fear that this decision will not be satisfactory. It is not sufficiently striking to be brilliant; but except in its moderation, (which is often wanting through necessity) it is sufficiently conformable with what is practised every where; and if it be just as I think it is, it will be a new example of an intellectual phenomenon very common, but which has not always been sufficiently remarked: that in matters somewhat difficult the practice is, provisionally, sufficiently reasonable long before the theory becomes so; and, when the subject is thoroughly examined, we perceive that the good sense of the public (I might almost say the general instinct) has less wandered from the right road than the first scientific speculations. The reason is simple. In practice we are close to the facts; they present themselves every moment, they guide us, they retain us, they continually bring us back to what is, to the truth. Whereas in speculative combinations, which consist all in deductions, one first false supposition suffices to lead us very consequently into the greatest errors, without any thing apprizing us of it. This is the cause of the blind attachment so generally manifested for whatever is in use, and the great distrust inspired by every new truth too contrary to it. This disposition is without doubt exaggerated, but it is sufficiently founded in reason. However this may be, we have said enough on the revenues of government. Let us occupy ourselves with its expenses.

We have little to say on this subject. We have seen that government in every country is a very great consumer, and a consumer of the kind of those who live on revenues, and not on profits; that it is a very great annuitant with whom authority is instead of capital. Consequently all we have said of this species of consumers is applicable to it. Its expense does not re-produce itself in its hands, with an increase of value, as in those of industrious men. Its consumption is real and definitive. Nothing remains from the labour it hires. The riches it employs, and which did exist before they passed into its hands, are consumed and destroyed when it has made use of them. In effect, in what consists the much greater part of its expense? In paying soldiers, seamen, judges, and officers of every kind, and in defraying all the expenses required by these different services. All this is very useful without doubt, and even necessary in the whole, if the desirable economy is employed in it; but nothing of all this is productive. The expenditure which government may incur to enrich the favourites of power is equally sterile, and has not the excuse of necessity nor even of utility. Accordingly it is still more disagreeable to the public, which it injures instead of serving. It is quite otherwise with funds employed in public labours of a general utility, such as bridges, ports, roads, canals, and useful establishments and monuments. These expenses are always favourably regarded, when not excessive. They contribute in effect very powerfully to public prosperity. However they cannot be regarded as directly productive, in the hands of government, since they do not return to it with profit and do not create for it a revenue which represents the interest of the funds they have absorbed, or if that happens, we must conclude that individuals could have done the same things, on the same conditions, if they had been permitted to retain the disposal of the sums taken from them for this same use; and it is even probable that they would have employed them with more intelligence and economy. Finally, we may say the same things of what the government expends, on different encouragements of the sciences and arts. These sums are always small enough and their utility is most frequently very questionable. For it is very certain that in general the most powerful encouragement that can be given to industry of every kind, is to let it alone, and not to meddle with it. The human mind would advance very rapidly if only not restrained; and it would be led, by the force of things to do always what is most essential on every occurrence. To direct it artificially on one side rather than on another, is commonly to lead it astray instead of guiding it. Nevertheless let us also admit the constant utility of this kind of expenses; not very considerable in relation to money, it is not the less true that, like all the preceding, they are real expenses which do not return.

From all this I conclude, that the whole of the public expenses ought to be ranged in the class of expenses justly called sterile and unproductive, and consequently that whatever is paid to the state, either under the title of a tax or even of a loan, is a result of productive labour previously executed, which ought to be considered as entirely consumed and annihilated the day it enters the national treasury. Once more I repeat it, this is not saying that this sacrifice is not necessary, and even indispensable. Without doubt it is necessary that every citizen, from the product of his actual labour, or the income of his capital which is the product of more ancient labour, should give what is necessary to the state; as it is necessary to keep up his house, that he may lodge in it in safety. But he should know that it is a sacrifice he makes; that what he gives is immediately lost, to the public riches, as to his own; in a word, that it is an expense and not an investment. Finally, no one should be so blind as to believe that expenses of any kind are a direct cause of the augmentation of fortune; and that every person should know well that for political societies, as well as for commercial ones, an expensive regimen is ruinous, and that the best is the most economical. On the whole, this is one of those truths which the good sense of the people had perceived for a long time before it was clear to the greatest politicians.

If, from the examination of the ordinary expenses of government, we pass to that of its extraordinary expenses and of the debts which are their consequence, the same principles will guide us. This is likewise a subject on which the general good sense has greatly preceded the science of the pretended adepts. Simple men have always known, that they impoverished themselves by spending more than their income, and that in no case is it good to be in debt; and men of genius believed and even wrote, not long since that the loans of government are a cause of prosperity, and that a public debt is new wealth created in the bosom of society. However, since we are convinced, first, that the ordinary expenses of government add nothing to the general mass of circulation, and only change its course in a manner most often disadvantageous; Secondly, that they are of such a nature, also, as to add nothing to the mass of riches previously produced, from which they are taken, we ought to conclude that the extraordinary expenses of this same government being of the same nature as its ordinary expenses, are equally incapable of producing either the one or the other of these good effects. As to the ridiculous idea, that in issuing certificates of dues from the state a new value is really created, it does not merit a serious refutation: for if those who receive these certificates possess a certain sum the more, it is evident that the state which issues them must possess an equal sum, the less; otherwise we must say that as often as I subcribe an obligation of a thousand francs, I augment the total mass of riches by a thousand francs, which is absurd. Thus it is very certain, that in no case have we reason to rejoice at the increase of the consumption of government, and the greatness of public expenses.

But, finally, when these expenses are very considerable, ought we to felicitate ourselves on being able to meet them by loans, rather than taxes? or, in other words, is it happy for the governed, that the government should make use of its credit, or even that it should have credit? This is the last question which remains to be treated, before finishing this chapter. I know it is resolved for many statesmen, and even for may speculative writers, who firmly believe that public credit constitutes the force and safety of the state; that it is a great cause of prosperity in ordinary times, and the only efficacious resource in urgent necessities; and thus that it is the true palladium of society.

Yet I think I have good reasons for combatting their opinion. I will say nothing of the grevious effects of loans on the social organization, of the enormous power they give to the governors of the facility they afford them of doing whatsoever they please, of drawing every thing to themselves, of enriching their creatures, of dispensing with the assembling and consulting the citizens; which operates rapidly the overthrow of every constitution. These things are not now my subject. I consider in loans at this moment but their pure economical effects; and it is solely under this point of view that I am going to discuss their advantages and inconveniencies.

The first thing said in favour of loans is, that the funds procured by these means are not taken involuntarily, from any one. I think this an illusion. In effect it is very true, that when government borrows it forces no one to lend; for we must not regard forced loans, as loans, but as contributions. When, therefore, the lenders carry their money to the public treasury it is freely and voluntarily; but the operation does not end there. These capitalists have lent, not given; and they certainly intend to lose neither principal nor interest. Consequently, they force the government to raise, one day or other, a sum equal to that which they furnish and to the interest which they demand for it. Thus, by their obligingness, they burthen without their consent not only the citizens actually existing, but also future generations. This is so true, that the kind of easement, which their service produces for the present moment, only amounts to a rejection of a part of the burden on future times.

This circumstance, in my opinion, gives room for a great question; which I am astonished to have seen no where discussed. A government of any kind, whether monarchical or polyarchical, in a word of men now existing, has it a right thus to burden men not yet in existence, and to compel them to pay in future times their present expenses? This is not even the case of a testament; against which it has been said, with reason, that no man has the right of being obeyed after his death. For, in fine, the society which for the general good takes so many different powers from its individual members may well grant them this, and guarantee it if it is useful to them; and the heirs of the testators are always at liberty to accept or to refuse their inheritances, which at bottom belong to them only in virtue of the laws which give them, and under the conditions prescribed by the laws. But when there is a question of public interest the case is quite different. One generation does not receive from another, as an inheritance, the right of living in society; and of living therein under such laws as it pleases. The first has no right to say to the second, if you wish to succeed me, it is thus you must live and thus you must conduct yourself. For from such a right it would follow that a law once made could never be changed. Thus the actual legislative power, (whatever it be) which is always considered as the organ of the actual general will, can neither oblige nor restrain the future legislative power, which will be the organ of the general will of a time yet to come. It is on this very reasonable principle that it is acknowledged in England that one parliament cannot vote a tax but until the commencement of another, or even until a new session of the same parliament. I know well that to apply this principle generally to the debts of a country where it is not admitted, and where prior engagements have been entered into bona fide, would be to violate public faith; and I have heretofore sufficiently manifested my profound belief that such an act can never be either *just* or *useful*, two terms for me absolutely equivalent to *reason* and *virtue*. But it is not the less true, to return to the example of England, that it is contradictory, and consequently absurd that a parliament should think it could not vote taxes but for one year, and should think it could vote a loan on a perpetual annuity or on long reimbursements: for this is to vote a necessity for taxes sufficient to pay these annuities or these reimbursements, without a right to refuse them. I find the principle formerly admitted in Spain much more sensible and honourable, that the engagements of one king are not binding on his successor. At least those who contract with him know the risques they run and have no room for complaint of what may happen to them. We shall soon see that this principle, put in practice, is as beneficial as it is reasonable.

For the present I only maintain, that, since definitively the principal and interest of a loan can never be paid but by taxes, the funds which government procures by this mean end always in being involuntarily taken from individuals; and, what is worse, from individuals not obliged, because they have never engaged either by themselves or by their legitimate or *legal* representatives. I call *legal,* those whom the existing law authorizes; and whose acts are valid, even if the law is not just.

The second advantage which is found in loans, is that the sums which they furnish are not taken from productive consumption: since it is not undertakers of industry who place their funds in the hands of the state; but idle capitalists only living on their revenue, who choose this kind of annuity rather than another. I answer that this second advantage is not less illusory than the first. For although it be true that those who lend to government are not, in general, the men who have joined their personal industry to their capital, to render them more useful in productive employments; yet it happens that there are many of these lenders whom the facility of procuring a sufficient existence, without risque or fatigue, has alone disgusted from labour and thrown them into idleness. Besides, even admitting that all were equally idle if the state had not borrowed, it is certain that if they had not lent it their money they would have lent it to industrious men. From that time these industrious men would have had greater capitals to work on, and, by the effect of the concurrence of lenders, they would have procured them at a lower interest. Now these are two great goods of which the public loans deprive them. In fine it cannot be denied that without a bankruptcy, when a sum is borrowed it must be repaid; and, to repay it, it must be levied on the citizens. Thus, sooner or later, it affects industry as much and in the same manner as if it had been levied at first. Moreover, there must be added to this all the interest paid by the state till the moment of reimbursement; and it is easy to see that in few years these interests have doubled the capital, and consequently the evil.

But at this day, in Europe, we are so habituated to the existence of a public debt, that when we have found the means of borrowing money on perpetual annuities, and of securing payment of the interest, we think ourselves liberated and no longer owing any thing; and we do not or will not see that this interest absorbing a part of the public revenue (which was already insufficient) since we have been obliged to borrow, is the cause that this same revenue still less suffices for subsequent expenses; that soon we must borrow again to provide for this new deficit, and load ourselves with new interest; and that, thus in but a short time it is found that a considerable portion of all the riches annually produced is employed, not for the service of the state, but to support a crowd of useless annuitants. And to fill the measure of our evils, who are these lenders? Men not only idle, as are all annuitants; but also completely indifferent to the success or failure of the industrious class to which they have lent nothing: having absolutely no interest but the permanence of the borrowing government, whatsoever it be or whatsoever it does; and at the same time having no desire but to see it embarrassed, to the end that it may be forced to keep fair with them and pay them better. Consequently natural enemies to the true interests of society, or at least being absolutely strangers to them. I do not pretend to say that all the annuitants of the state are bad citizens; but I say that their situation is calculated to render them such. I add further, that life annuities tend moreover to break family ties; and that the great abundance of public effects cannot fail of producing a crowd of licentious gamblers in the funds. The truth of what I advance is manifested in a very odious and fatal manner in all great cities without commerce; and especially in all the capitals in which this class of men is very numerous and very powerful; and has many means of giving weight to their passions, and of perverting the public opinion.

It is then as erroneous to believe that the loans of government are not hurtful to national industry, as it is to suppose that the funds which they produce, are not taken from any individual involuntarily. In truth these are not the real reasons which cause so much importance to be attached to the possibility of borrowing. The great advantage of loans, in the eyes of their partisans, is that they furnish in a moment enormous sums, which could only have been very slowly procured by means of taxes, even the most overwhelming. Now I do not hesitate to declare that I regard this pretended advantage as the greatest of all evils. It is nothing else than a mean of urging men to excessive efforts, which exhaust them and destroy the sources of their life. Montesquieu perceived it well. After having painted very energetically the state of distress and anxiety to which the exaggeration of the public expenses had already, in his time, reduced the people of Europe, who ought by their industry to have been the most flourishing, he adds, "And, "what prevents all remedy in future, they no longer "count on the revenues; but make war with "their capital. It is not unheard of* for states "to mortgage their funds even during peace, and "employ to ruin themselves means which they "call extraordinary; and which are so much so "that an heir of a family the most deranged could "with difficulty imagine them.†"

It will not fail to be said that this is to abuse its credit, and not to use it; and that the abuse which may be made of it does not prevent its being good to have it. I answer, first, that the abuse is inseparable from the use, and experience proves it. It is scarcely two hundred years since the progress of civilization, of industry, of commerce, that of the social order, and perhaps also the increase of specie, have given to governments the facility of making loans; and in this short space of time these dangerous expedients have led them all either to total or partial bankruptcies, some-

* He ought to have said, 'it is frequent'.

† Spirit of laws, book 13th. Chap. 17.

times repeated, or to the equally shameful and more grevious resource of paper money, or to remain overburdened under the weight of a load which daily becomes more insupportable.

But I go farther. I maintain that the evil is not in the abuse; but in the use itself of loans, that is to say that the abuse and the use are one and the same thing; and that every time a government borrows it takes a step towards its ruin. The reason of this is simple: A loan may be a good operation for an industrious man, whose consumption reproduces with profit. By means of the sums which he borrows, he augments this productive consumption; and with it his profits. But a government which is a consumer of the class of those whose consumption is sterile and destructive, dissipates what it borrows, it is so much lost for ever; and it remains burdened with a debt, which is so much taken from its future means. This cannot be otherwise. In several countries they have commenced, by being long without feeling the bad effects of these operations; because the progress of industry and the arts being very great at this epoch, their advance has been found more rapid than that of the debt; and the means of the government have not failed to augment also. Many have even concluded that a public debt was a source of prosperity, while it only proved that individuals did more good than the government did evil; but this evil was not the less real; and nobody now undertakes to deny it.

These cogent reasons are answered by the excuse which is usual where no other remains. *Necessity*;

but I insist, and affirm, that in the present case necessity itself is no excuse: for it is this very remedy which creates the obligation we are under to have recourse to it. I will explain myself. When a nation is once engaged in a perilous situation there is no doubt but that there is a necessity for it to make the greatest efforts to free itself from it. But a body politic does not naturally find itself placed in such a situation. Always some anterior cause has brought it to this. Or it has very badly managed its internal affairs; and thereby encouraged some unquiet neighbour to attack it, to profit by its weakness; or, if it has well conducted its own affairs, it has sought to avail itself of it to meddle unreasonably with those of others: it has abused its own prosperity to trouble that of others, to undertake too great enterprises, to raise exaggerated pretensions; or merely to assume a menacing attitude, which provokes hostile measures and produces hatred. These are, in effect, the faults which commonly bring on the necessity of making excessive efforts, and of having recourse to loans; and if it is true that it is by the foolish confidence inspired by this pernicious resource, that governments have been led into these faults, it will be agreed that the credit which is regarded as a remedy to these evils is their true cause. Now history teaches us that it is in fact since governments have had what is called credit, that is to say the possibility of employing in an instant the funds of several years, that they have no longer set bounds either to their prodigality, or their ambition, or their projects, that they have augmented their armies, multiplied their intrigues, and that they have adopted that intermeddling policy with which it is impossible to avoid war or enjoy peace. These are the effects of this public credit which is regarded as so great a good. But, at least, is it useful in imminent dangers? No. There is no imminent danger for a nation, except a sudden invasion of its territory. In this extreme case it is not money which saves it, it is the concourse of force, it is the union of wills. Requisitions supply necessaries, levies in mass furnish men; loans are of no use. The end answered by credit is the maintenance of distant wars, that is to say their prolongation. It also fails when they become disastrous that is to say in the moment of necessity. Then peace is made. It would have been sooner made if the government had not had credit, or rather there would have been no war. And, when this tardy and forced peace is signed, it is perceived that of all the losses sustained, that most to be regretted, after the useless sacrifice of men, is that of the sums they would have preserved had they not had the unfortunate facility of borrowing them. The conqueror himself is never indemnified by his successes for the sacrifices they have cost him, and the debts with which he remains burdened. From all this I conclude anew, that what is called public credit, is the poison which rapidly enough destroys modern governments.

I will not, however, advise a law which should forbid a government ever to borrow, and the governed ever to lend. Such a law would be absurd and useless:—absurd—for it would be founded, like the evil which it is meant to destroy, on this false principle: that the actual legislative power can bind the legislative power of futurity:—useless because the first thing that would be done by those who, in the sequel, should wish to borrow would be to abolish the law which forbids them; and thus would have a right to do it. I should wish then quite a different course to be pursued. I should wish them, on the contrary, to recognise and proclaim this principle of eternal truth: that whatsoever is decreed by any legislature whatsoever, their successors can always modify, change, annul; and that it should be solemnly declared, that in future this salutary principle shall be applied, as it ought to be, to the engagements which a government may make with money lenders. By this the evil would be destroyed in its root: for capitalists, having no longer any guarantee, would no longer lend; many misfortunes would be prevented, and this would be a new proof that the evils of humanity proceed always from some error, and that truth cures them. It is by this wish that I will terminate what I had to say of the revenues and expenses of government, and that I will finish this first part of the treatise on the will. Only, before passing to the second I will yet present to the reader some reflexions on what we have so far seen.

CHAPTER XIII.

Conclusion.

We are now arrived at a remarkable point on the road over which I had proposed to travel. I ask permission to stop here for a moment. I will again repeat to the reader, that what he has just read is not properly a treatise on political economy. It is the first part of a treatise on the will, which ought to have two other parts; and which is itself but the sequel of a treatise on the understanding. Every thing here then ought to be co-ordinate with what precedes, and what will follow. Thus it ought not to excite surprize that I have not entered into the details of political economy; but it should have done so if I had not ascended to the origin of our wants and of our means, if I had not endeavoured to show how these wants and means arise from our faculty of willing, and if I had neglected to point out the relations of our physical with our moral wants.

It is that I may not merit these reproaches that I have commenced by a very general introduction, which no more belongs to economy than to morality or to legislation; but in which I have endeavoured clearly to explain what are the ideas for which we are indebted to our faculty of willing, and without which these three sciences would not exist for us. I shall be told that this introduction is too metaphysical. I answer that it could not be otherwise, and that it is precisely because it is very metaphysical that there is no bad metaphysics in the rest of the work. For nothing can so effectually preserve us from sophisms and illusions, as to begin by well elucidating the principal ideas. We have not been long without proofs of this.

In fact after having well observed the manner in which we know our wants, our original weakness, and our propensity to sympathy, we were no longer in any doubt on the nature of society. We have seen clearly that it is our natural and necessary state, that it is founded on personality and property, that it consists in conventions, that these conventions are all exchanges, that the essence of exchange consists in being useful to both the contracting parties, snd that the general advantages of exchanges (which constitute the social state) are to produce a concurrence of force, the increase and preservation of knowledge, and the division of labour.

After having examined in like manner our means of providing for our wants, we have also seen that our individual force is our only primitive riches; that the employment of this force, our labour, has a necessary value, which is the only cause of all the other values; that all our industry consists in fabrication and transportation; and that the effect of this industry is always and solely to add a degree of utility to the things on which it is exercised, and to furnish objects of consumption and means of existence.

Ascending always to the observation of our faculties, since personality and property are necessary it is evident that inequality is inevitable. But it is an evil. We have seen what are the causes of its exaggerated increase, and what its fatal effects.

These have explained to us in a very precise manner what has commonly been said very vaguely of the different states through which the same people successively pass.

Since we all have means, we are all proprietors; since we all have wants, we are all consumers. These two great interests always re-unite us. But we are naturally unequal; from whence it happens, in process of time, that some have property in advance, and many others have not. These latter can only live on the funds of the former. From thence two great classes of men, the hired and the hirers, opposed in interest in the respect, that the one selling their labor wishes to sell dear, and the other buying it wishes to buy cheap.

Amongst those who buy labour, some (the idle rich) employ it only in their personal satisfaction; its value is destroyed. The others (these are the undertakers of industry) employ it in a useful manner, which reproduces what it has cost. These alone preserve and increase the riches already acquired; these alone furnish to the other capitalists the revenues which they consume, since doing nothing, they can derive no benefit from their capitals, whether moveable or immoveable, but by hiring them to industrious men in consideration of a rent, which the latter pay out of their profits The more the industry of the latter is perfected the more our means of existence are augmented.

In fine, we have remarked that the fecundity of

the human species is such, that the number of men is always proportionate to their means of existence; and that wheresoever this number does not continually and rapidly augment, it is because many individuals daily perish for want of the means of life.

Such are the principal truths which follow so immediately from the observation of our faculties, that it is impossible to dispute them. They lead us to consequences no less certain.

After having seen what society is, it is impossible not to reject the idea of foregoing it absolutely, or of founding it on an entire renunciation of one's self, and on a chimerical equality.

After having well unraveled the effects of our industry, it is impossible not to see that there is nothing more mysterious in agricultural industry than in any other, but we discover the inconveniences which are proper to it, and which are the cause of the different forms which it takes according to times and places.

When we have recognized the necessary cause of all values, we must conclude that it is absurd to pretend that money is but a sign; and odious to undertake to give it an arbitrary value, or forcibly to replace it by an imaginary value; and that every establishment which tends towards this end is dangerous and pernicious.

When we have seen how the formation of our riches is operated and their continual renovation, which we call *circulation*, we necessarily see that consumption in itself can never be useful, and that the exaggerated consumption, called luxury, is always hurtful; and we cannot otherwise than find rediculous, the importance ascribed to men who have no other merit but of being consumers, as if that were a very rare talent.

Just views of consumption give necessarily just ideas on that greatest of consumers, government; on the effects of its expenses, its debts, and the different imposts which compose its revenues, and lead us clearly to trace the different reflections of these assessments, and to estimate the greater or less evil they do, according to the different classes of men on which they fall.

All these consequences are rigorous. They will not be the less contested. It was necessary then, to arrive at them methodically. But those above all, which will experience the greatest opposition, are what lead us to determine the degrees of importance of the different classes of society. How persuade the great rural proprietors, so much cried up, that they are but lenders of money, burdensome to agriculture and strangers to all its interests? How convince these idle rich, so much respected, that they are absolutely good for nothing; and that their existence is an evil, inasmuch as it diminishes the number of useful labourers? How obtain acknowledgement from all those who hire labour, that the dearness of workmanship is a desirable thing; and that, in general, all the true interests of the poor are exactly the same as the true interest of the whole society. It is not merely their interests, well or ill understood, which oppose these truths, it is their passion; and among these passions, the most violent and antisocial of all, vanity. With them demonstration, or at least conviction is no longer possible; for the passions know how to obscure and entangle every thing; and it is with as much reason as ingenuity, that Hobbes has said, that if men had a lively desire not to believe that two and two make four, they would have succeeded in rendering this truth doubtful; we might produce proofs of it.

On many occasions, then, it is still more difficult to conciliate to truth than to discover it. This observation discovers to us a new relation between the subject we have treated of, and that which is next to occupy us, between the study of our actions and that of our sentiments. We have perceived, and said, that we should know well the consequences of our actions, to appreciate justly, the merit or demerit of the sentiments which urge us to this or that action; and now we see that it is necessary to analyze our sentiments themselves, submit them to a rigorous examination, distinguish those which being founded on just judgments always direct us well, and those which having their source in illusions, and rising from the obliquities of our minds, cannot fail to lead us astray and form within us a false and blind conscience, which always removes us further from the road of reason, the only one leading to happiness. This is what we shall next investigate, and if we have well exposed the results of the actions of men, and the effects of their passions, it seems that it will be easy to indicate the rules which they ought to prescribe to themselves. This would be the true spirit of laws and the best conclusion of a treatise on the will.

Book II

PSYCHOLOGY OF POLITICAL SCIENCE

With Special Consideration for the Political Acumen of Destutt de Tracy

BY THE SAME AUTHOR

The Foundations of Human Nature (Longmans, Green and Co., 1935).

Living Consciously, with Walter H. Seegers (Detroit: Wayne State University Press, 1959).

The Growth of Self Insight (Detroit: Wayne State University Press, 1960).

The Jefferson-Dunglison Letters (Charlottesville, Va.: University of Virginia Press, 1960).

Illness or Allness (Detroit: Wayne State University Press, 1965).

American Government, Conscious Self Sovereignty (Detroit: Center for Health Education, 1969).

Psychology of Emotion (Detroit: Center for Health Education, 1971).

Psychology of Language (Detroit: Center for Health Education, 1971).

Monographs

Science of Sanity (Detroit: Center for Health Education, 1954).

Living Education (Detroit: Center for Health Education, 1957).

Discovering My World of My Mind, A Conscious Way of Life (Detroit: Center for Health Education, 1965).

Book II

PSYCHOLOGY OF POLITICAL SCIENCE

With Special Consideration for the Political Acumen of Destutt de Tracy

by

John M. Dorsey, M.D. LL.D.

Published by
Center for Health Education
4421 Woodward Avenue
Detroit, Michigan 48201

Printed by Edwards Brothers, Inc.

CONTENTS

PREFACE

> If we are inexorably alone when we sink down to rock-bottom, the wisest life is a life "tenon'd and mortis'd" upon loneliness.
>
> John Cowper Powys
> (*A Philosophy of Solitude*)

Through making my Tracy's self insights my own, by consciously feeling and thinking as my Tracy's literary efforts seem to reflect his consciously feeling and thinking, I have grudgingly, gradually enriched my living with appreciation for my unique individuality, including appreciation for my unique world. Only in this kind of life-cult, viewing my existence afresh, have I been able to emerge from dangerous heedlessness for my immeasurable wholeness to a condition of mind well informed with appreciation for the integrity of my being. This way of life requires no particular intelligence or cleverness. Merely as American citizen I may teach myself to declare, "I do not belong to my Government, rather my government belongs to *me*." John Stuart Mill personified his government thus:

> A state which dwarfs its men, in order that they may be more docile instruments in its hands—even for beneficial purposes —will find that with small men no great thing can really be accomplished.

My *new economy* based upon the cynical principle that the enormity of my *national debt* is the measure of enormous economic strength, is terrifying to consider earnestly. Terrifying, for I see it is built solidly upon my disregard for the truth of the allness and wholeness of concrete *individual man* in the name of abstract *national security*. All I can find helpful to do about it is my utmost in my holding my self to my government's original principle of full appreciation for the dignity of human individuality. My negating the wholeness of my being, instead of affirming it, disregards what health *is*. Only when my individuality is extolled by me *as all that can be Americanized* does my Americanism live itself freely.

It is my living, itself, that is all-sacred for me, regardless of what names, such as "politics" or "government," it may appear under. Despite its seeming to have, my political science has no life or meaning of its own. Only by steadfastly heeding that I am all that I live, under whatever terminology, can I make a "success" of my life that is biologically adequate. It is my life that I need, and it is all that I can need. Love of life requires conscious cultivation. It is my freedom to help myself by restraint that reconciles freedom and restraint.

Most timely is my orientation of my government of whatever description, as being necessarily my self government. *The fact that my government is not necessarily conscious self government, including the most awful consequence of my not making it my conscious self government, is the immediate motivation for this present book.* I fervently hope that it may serve as a companion volume to my *American Government,* in which I refer to the most precious and urgently useful political genius I discover in my Tracy.[1] In all of my recent major works I have painstakingly observed the profound meaning my Thomas Jefferson cherished for his Destutt de Tracy (see Appendix).

It is further to be noted that my main study of my Destutt de Tracy is limited largely to literature about his adult living. Unable to shift my personal responsibility for being all of my self and unable to absolve my reader from being all that he reads; but able to feel certain that I cannot follow any life course but the stream of my mind, I recognize pretty clearly that my declared solipsistic literary production has little chance to reach other than a rare reader. I cannot but shudder when I let my self be aware of three soul-shaking thoughts: 1) How far my governmental representative has wandered from his sane principle of conscious self government; 2) How only he can ever reveal to himself this fateful plight; and 3) How

[1]Detroit: Center for Health Education, 1969.

ideally his military can serve any of his desperate resort to dictatorship.

If I speak I soliloquize; if I write I diarize. Yet despite my unfaltering conscious resolve to write in an evidently self continent way, I realize that my unconscious word habit can lead me into the beguiling byway of so-called popular communication involving my solitude in illusional multitude instead of self-evident multitude in my solitude. However the unwavering providence of conscious integrity of my mind (or soul) can spare me drawn-out mortification for such lapses of linguistic reality. The true helpfulness of my mind is obscured by any of my language that does not seem to me to exalt it.

It is not that conscious self government has been tried by the American citizen and found wanting, not at all. It has been rarely tried wholeheartedly, for a *consciously* whole person is most rare. Nevertheless I have made some attempt at it, and I have found it most rewarding although correspondingly exacting. However, I realize that I must ever choose between conscious self sovereignty and unconscious self sovereignty (seeming authoritarianism), truthfully recognizing real achievement to awaken to my life-revering truth: self-sovereignty, either conscious or unconscious, is the only sovereignty possible. It is my will to choose *conscious* self sovereignty, that is, the essence of my Americanism. How to preserve my consciousness for the inviolable integrity of my individuality is becoming increasingly difficult and rewarding as I live simultaneously the tremendous increase of my true fellowman and the immense decrease in my illusional space.

This present writing upholds the arduous cultivation of every American citizen's ideal of conscious self sovereignty as being his self discipline that he needs most. Its absence fully accounts for the troublous functioning of his American government. However, I recognize that every individual's *conscious* self development is as difficult to achieve as it is correspondingly great. Therefore my whole intention throughout this description of the benefit of self conscious life appreciation is merely to indicate the *direction* I must begin to give my self if I would free my government from its apparent authoritarianism by steadily freeing my mind from its unconsciousness for the truth that *all* of my obedience is self obedience just as *all* of my command is self command.

I hear my fellowman's cry, "I want the helpfulness of self consciousness to reach the man on the street," "Your message does not reach the common man," "If only what you have to offer could be put into simpler words," "*Everybody* needs the kind of conscious self-knowledge you describe." However the obstinate and inevitable reality is: only my fellowman can reach, teach, or otherwise influence his self. My conscious originality discloses my heresy as helpful faultfinding.

Although my friend seems impatient to see to the widest distribution of my statements of *how* I help my self, this subject of my writing is really simple, elementary, obvious: I achieve *all* of my self helpfulness by my self alone. My daily demonstrated fact is that I really work with my struggling, underprivileged, unsophisticated and uneducated fellowman on terms of identity. He always finds his Dorsey-living helpful and consistently wishes to grow more of it to unite it with the rest of his conscious power. With my Byron,

> I wish men to be free
> As much from mobs as kings—from you as me.

Contrary to any such pleasing expectation, the wisdom of the world's great thinkers of today cannot form the creed of educated men tomorrow and of all men on the day after. Only the man of tomorrow who has already heedfully grown his own wisdom can be capable of appreciating the wisdom of his forefather.

Arthur O. Lovejoy insightfully records the special resistance of the individual to recognizing his wholeness and allness: "The identification of self-sufficiency with the supreme good . . . a good for God but not for man—is one of the most influential and widely-ramifying ideas in Western thought."[2]

[2] *Essays in the History of Ideas* (Baltimore: Johns Hopkins Press, 1948), p. 25.

George Washington observed in his farewell to his troops: "Government is not reason, it is not eloquence—it is force! Like fire, it is a dangerous servant and a fearful master." As a fully qualified psychiatric specialist I trace mental trouble to its source in the illusional alien control begun in each individual's misconception of parental authority and then continued throughout all of his authoritarian public schooling. Above all else I consider it my public educator's first concern (and I am a public educator) to renounce kindly his every powerful pretension to this magic control. There can be no possible education but self education and this truth must be actively practiced constantly in order to be sufficiently effective. It is not a complicated truth; it is a simple truth that a child can feel is true. My conscious sociableness is my helpful extension of my conscious solitude.

The whole principle and point of this writing is that the basic justification for any and every so-called government of a human being is specifically its indispensable efficacy as a device for his purposefully, continuously and thoroughly demonstrating this truth: All government can only be of the individual, by the individual and for the individual whose own mind creates the only meaning of whatever he chooses to call government.

My self-evident theme that economics is made for individual man, not individual man for economics, may be one of those mighty ideas whose time has finally arrived. I have just finished studying six interesting accounts describing my countryman's established economics, each written by an expert: Leonard Silk, editorial writer for the *New York Times*, Daniel R. Fusfeld of the University of Michigan, Robert Lekachman of New York State University at Stony Brook, Marc J. Roberts of Harvard, Robert A. Solo of Michigan State University and Charles L. Schultze of the Brookings Institute (director of the Bureau of the Budget when Lyndon B. Johnson was president).[3] Every contributor but Schultze addresses his views directly to his realization of the humane necessity to build

[3] "Does Economics Ignore You," *Saturday Review*, Jan. 22, 1972, pp. 33-57.

his economic program solidly upon full respect for the nature and needs of human *individuality*, specifically as a self rather than a cipher. Schultze also considers economics as a discipline dealing with man as he is, at best intending to align man's "very human motivations" with the public weal.

I am the sole *problem of existence* that can ever concern me. Insofar as my sense of personal conviction includes belief in the wholeness and allness of my individuality, I can understand my Aristotle's dictum: Man is by nature a political animal. All of my sensing, such as seeing or hearing, is merely a form of my own mental activity. Thus my listening to what my fellowman says is my yielding of my own mind to experience itself in this particular form. I am still guided by the activity of my own genius in all such so-called passive experience. Merely by hearing my fellowman out, seeing him hog the scene or road, watching his doing all of the socializing, heeding his comment regarding his Dorsey, or whatever else, I am thereby responsibly providing all of the activity that I am experiencing. I have cultivated my mind to be able to indulge its activity of this kind consciously, observing the degree to which otherwise it is possible for me to furnish my mind its distracting appearance of activity without being conscious that all of its whole experience is its own. Of such is the rarely cultivated art of unapparent self-assertion (pure selfishness). My *self consciousness* provides the full expression of my activity; my self unconsciousness provides the full expression of all of my activity I name passivity.

My judging any of my sensory experience as being not my own is always an instance of my relieving my mind of too much conscious responsibility by deluding my self temporarily. I must always think for myself, be my own only authority for whatever I am mindful of. Whether I acknowledge that truth by affirming *it* or by denying *it*, in either case that "it" is equally mine. Without this insight I find my self fitting my H. L. Mencken's conception of *homo boobiens*, unable to set my self up as conscious God in order to be God conscious.

The firm foundation upon which the maxims of *my* political science rest cannot go deeper than my insight that it is all mine. That balancing political orientation is the only one that proves to be ever new and ever valuable. It feels like wistful living of the unquestioned and undivided wholeness of the mind of my earliest self-discoveries. The common denominator of all of my political shortcoming is my limited ability to deal with the real world of my self in the light of *its* possibilities.

How I shirk conscious self government is understandable only on the basis of my fearing the awesome weight of responsibility. My experience demonstrates that I will suffer every kind of feeling of indignity rather than consciously acknowledge that all government must be self government.

In seeing my identity in my living that seems new my strongest temptation may be to ignore or depreciate what was formerly new in my development, particularly if the new new-look seems to be able to oppose or rule out the former one. Therefore I place in my Preface this sanifying, mind-balancing truth: my development of a new mental horizon always involves all of my previously attained mental advancement as being equally precious; never excludes any of my earlier efforts to help my self; ever honors each former access of my development as necessary foundation for the present one. Furthermore, regardless of the extent of my self development, my daily living requires the full functioning of all of my power,—my wriggling toe or my self insight.

By increasing my own conscious self possessiveness as much as I can, thus enabling my self-sufficing mind to feel the glorious gusto of my existence, I can willfully concentrate my mental power accurately upon just where all of the action is of which I am capable. Thus my guiding my life according to its nature, seeing and feeling where *my* political living must really occur, unquestionably cannot remove me from politics *in any respect.* Rather my recognition that *all* of my meaning for my political science is naturally grown by me in, of and by my mind is essential, for it alone can make me as careful and caring as I need to become in all of my political activity.

It is most helpful of all to keep heedful that my view of all government as being self-government (either conscious or unconscious) does not and cannot rule out my every other previous view of government as equally precious living of mine, quite as it may be the only precious political living of my external-world oriented fellowman.

The point at issue is political. My individual life is necessarily solitary, but it is *consciously* solitary only to the extent that I have arduously disciplined my mind with its self-consciousness. It is my nature to want to live my sociableness whether I am aware that it *is* all mine or not. It is my nature also to have to live my politics, my economy, my science, whether I am aware that each *is* all mine or not. Here I come to my bed-rock advantage in realizing that whatever I live is entirely my living of my self: With this insight I can feel my way in my living, e.g., of politics, thus deriving self satisfaction safely where I can, while avoiding hurting my self under cover of the impersonal seeming of politics. I can imagine few more health hazardous vocations than that of my government official who is unaware that his political living is all his own! *I can well imagine how rare is the official who can take this fateful warning to heart as being his own wisest health counsel.*

As my loving, stoical slave Epictetus decided before me, when his Domitian tyrannically ostracized all philosophers from Rome (94 A.D.), it is only natural and desirable that I expect my fellow-citizen to resist with all his might, and even take offence against, any citizenship discipline requiring his extending self consciousness at its heavy cost, self responsibility. I may certainly be absolutely sure to find this resistance in my fellow-citizen who feels that he must preserve his life by diligent, brow-beating persecution, intolerance and ready violence.

Hurting is the prerogative of hurt. Pain, like the external props or former convictions of my life, instead of being healed by time, forgetting or some other distraction, is relieved by my recognizing that I keep myself alive by it, by my reverence for the sufficient truth accounting fully for it, by my realizing that I am deriving strong virtue of hardihood from it, by understanding my painful humility as invitation to my conscious-self cultivation.

Ever since Sigmund Freud, my modern psychiatric diagnosis, treatment and research have been based solidly upon realization that man's uncontrolled functioning of his mental power which he has specifically rejected (as not being his own) provides the force underlying *all* of his mental trouble, including every form of his criminality (e.g., injurious political conduct). The question of course arises, Why cannot the combined works recorded by great political minds of the past, by our own illustrious American forefathers and even by the modern scientists of the mind serve to endow at least our academic political scientist of today with the guidelines by which he may preserve his mental equilibrium while he addresses his interest to the political nature and needs of his government?

I tell my self the answer, namely, the political view of my self conscious citizen does not and cannot serve the turn of his mostly self unconscious fellow citizen. The former's ground self-introspection seems hopelessly impractical (unpolitical) for the grand external-world orientation of the latter. The latter understands little of the unfathomable power of the individual mind to create its own political living.

I lovingly refrain from trying to classify conscious truth of the allness and wholeness of individuality by the name mystic or any other than a synonym for oneness. Whatever is, mystically is. It is my self-consciousness that gives me my most convincing right to say to myself: I am alive. It alone resolves all of my histrionic effort to ignore that I am responsible for making my own life history as I will. *Beginning with my embryological conception, my only possible power has been my power of growing my self as an individual.* My every function is basically understandable only as a specific form of my growing my self.

Hardest of all has been my fond renunciation of each illusion of the cosmogonic presence of a functioning anyone or anything but my self. It often seems too trying to seek and find my own level on account of all of my protean unconscious living. I am glad that I shrewdly recognize the futility in my asking my fellowmen to do it. For nearly forty years my voluminous writing has been an effort to record my intensifying my willful devotion to conscious self-helpfulness. Daily I renew my faith in my self thus: I am my own original all-there-is! Whatever I live, is the generating soul of me! My life is all and only about its living itself! Meanwhile everyone of my world also is willfully living as he (she) originally deems best. But I find that what my mind can do, my fellowman's mind can also do, once he can find and feel for himself the benefit in such being and doing.

I know of no sure way to create order out of disorder in politics other than to begin by renouncing kindly the whole conception of "disorder" as being based upon faultfinding, not fact-finding. The true *order* in alleged "disorder" becomes sun-clear as the psychological forces sufficiently accounting for so-called disorder become fully appreciated by the observer whose mind is incorrupt enough to recognize that he is his own dislikes quite as he is whatever he lives with liking. *I corrupt my mind by denying that it is mine and just to the extent to which that denial reaches any of the working of my mind.* In *The Rebel*[4] Albert Camus heeds the infinite initiative of his self-helpful mentality, "The Kindgom of Heaven is within the mind of the person, not within the collective mindlessness of a crowd."

I help myself most by considering "the American Idea" (Theodore Parker, 1850) to mean *the Individual Idea,* the ever new ordering principle of my mind. My experience has taught me that this way of living is most natural of all, that even the preschool child can beget it. It is only every other kind of understanding of learning that proves difficult, for it appears to the young learner that he is supposed to "get" it rather than grow it.

Indeed, since the only way in which conscious self sovereignty *can* develop is through its being arduously grown by each citizen, it stands evident to observation that such precious self-control cannot be achieved merely through reading a book about it. Creative reading, that is, the reader's recognizing that he is the creator of all that he reads (thereby authoring

[4]New York: Vintage Books, 1960, p. 78.

the work), although mighty, is as rare as it is self rewarding. However, for what it might be worth, it is my intention to see to it that this volume is widely distributed, as was my *American Government,* especially to educators and to administrative, legislative and judicial government officials. *The ability to consider kindly any educational effort, describes the consciously mature mind.*

Here is to my contemporary politician or statesman who can make the sanifying observation that he has already identified himself *as his self* very fully!

ACKNOWLEDGEMENTS

The author wishes to thank the following for permission to quote from the works listed: Dr. Mary A. B. Brazier, for "Some Early Concepts of Anxiety in Relation to Brain Mechanisms"; Dover Publications, Inc., for *The Analysis of Sensations* by Ernst Mach, 1959; Farrar, Straus and Giroux, Inc., for *Memoirs of an Egotist* by Henri Beyle (Stendhal), The Noonday Press, 1958; Harper and Row, Publishers, Inc., for *The Age of Discontinuity* (1969) and *Landmarks of Tomorrow* (1957) by Peter F. Drucker; Little, Brown and Company, for *Thomas Jefferson, The Apostle of Americanism* by Gilbert Chinard, 1929; McGraw-Hill Book Company, for *Adrienne, The Life of the Marquise de La Fayette* by André Maurois, 1961; Oxford University Press, for *Thomas Jefferson and the New Nation* by Merrill D. Peterson, 1970.

I would also like to thank Barbara Woodward for her most valuable editorial work and Dorothy Maskal for her very valuable assistance in editing and typing. I appreciate greatly the help of William Runge, Curator of Rare Books at the University of Virginia Alderman Library, for securing the two photographs of Tracy's original manuscript; Roger Viollet, Documentation Générale Photographique Pour la Presse, L'Édition et la Publicité, for the photographs of the bust of Destutt de Tracy by David d'Angers; and Michael Sibille and George Booth for the photographs of Tracy's ancestorical chateau. My American Philosophical Society, Library of Congress, Bibliotheque Nationale Suisse, and Bibliotheque Nationale of Paris were of great assistance in securing valuable information. Of indispensable help to me through my Parisian friend, Iris Hartman, has been Mme. de Lepiney of the Bibliotheque Nationale. Special appreciation goes to Iris Hartman for her valuable translations from the French.

For years now Douglas Dow has kindly upheld his valuable interest for my publishing Tracy's book and my own. This volume would not be possible were it not for the financial and kind support of each trustee of the Center for Health Education of Detroit: H. Walter Bando, Mrs. William D. Crim, Robert L. DeWitt, Mrs. George C. Edwards, Dwight C. Ensign, Mrs. Carl B. Grawn, Robert F. Grindley, Miss Emilie G. Sargent, Walter H. Seegers, and Frank J. Sladen.

My wife, Mary Louise Carson Dorsey, has provided constant inspiration for this whole achievement.

INTRODUCTION

> The law perverted! And the police powers of the state perverted along with it! The law, I say, not only turned from its proper purpose but made to follow an entirely contrary purpose! The law become the weapon of every kind of greed! Instead of checking crime, the law itself guilty of the evils it is supposed to punish!
>
> If this is true, it is a serious fact, the moral duty requires me to call the attention of my fellow-citizens to it.
>
> Frederic Bastiat (1801-1850), *The Law*

There can be no fully satisfying purpose of law other than that of protecting and furthering the nature and needs of perfect human individuality. Individual life must maintain itself *alone.* Every man must be law unto himself either consciously or unconsciously. Immeasurable responsibility! However, it is the rare man, whose self consciousness is adequately tried, who finds that he is capable of cultivating his consciousness for this responsibility. Nevertheless my gradually growing my self with full appreciation for my consciousness as being all and only self consciousness, is indispensable to my acknowledging that all of *my* government must be *self* government, that all of *my* fellowman is my living of my fellowman, that all of *my* altruism is my consciously grown up egoism! *My ideal constitutional government is patterned upon the nature and needs of my consciously disciplined human constitution!*

Marvin Bristol Rosenberry, Chief Justice of the Supreme Court of the State of Wisconsin beginning in 1929, declared:

> It would not be difficult to accumulate a mass of evidence showing that what the members of the Continental Congress had in mind when they referred to "schools and the means of education," was educational opportunity for all citizens. Illiteracy and ignorance were regarded as a continual threat to the perpetuity of democratic institutions . . . unless the people of the country could be made to understand the fundamental principles of government and to realize that in the past almost

> every conceivable form of government had been tried without securing to the people as a whole those inalienable rights referred to in the Declaration of Independence, the people might waiver in their devotion to the Constitution. . . . It is probable that general education has not been as efficacious in government as it was expected to be in the early days of the Republic.[1]

There is only one possible kind of education, namely *self* education. However, that one and only kind of education may be either 1) conscious or 2) unconscious. Unconscious self education is by far the easiest for the student to assume as sufficient, for the teacher to administer as discipline, for the school board member to overlook as enough, for the tax payer to provide as worthy and for the government official to determine as *politic*. Unconscious self education, fortunately and steadily, can result only in the individual's terrifying "cry for help" indicating that his not-self schooling is hardly worth living for it is necessarily favoring his dying. *Unconscious self education specifically unfits any and every student for democratic government.*

Conscious self education is absolutely essential for human health. Only *conscious* self education *can* help a student to biologically adequate self respect. Conscious self education seems difficult, even too difficult, but whoever would gradually become master of his immeasurably powerful individuality must painstakingly cultivate it. *Conscious self education is indispensable to democratic civic spirit.*

For all of my psychological study I find my Sigmund Freud's *insightful* science most enlightening and my Ralph Waldo Emerson's consciousness most illustrative, with regard to my appreciating my psychic reality. Herman Grimm (1828–1901) records that "it is necessary to stand on the defensive now-a-days against books and people, if we would reserve time and inclination for our own thoughts."

Upon starting to read Emerson's essays, Grimm wrote, "The construction of the sentences struck me as very extraordinary.

[1] *A University Between Two Centuries,* Wilfred B. Shaw, ed. (Ann Arbor, Michigan: University of Michigan Press, 1937), p. 100.

I soon discovered the secret: they were real thoughts, and individual language, a sincere man, that I had before me; naught superficial—second-hand . . . I have never ceased to read Emerson's works, and whenever I take up a volume anew it seems to me as if I were reading it for the first time." He goes on to describe Raphael and Goethe also as "standing in the closest affinity to nature . . . they show us things as they are . . . as they would and must appear to candid observers, *had not our eyes been injured and abused by a false education until they are no longer capable of discerning without help these primal glories* . . ." (my italics). "Emerson possesses this power in the highest degree . . . [his] theory is that of the 'sovereignty of the individual' . . . ."[2]

Emerson begins his essay "Politics" thus:

> In dealing with the State, we ought to remember that its institutions are not aboriginal, though they existed before we were born: that they are not superior to the citizen: that every one of them was once the act of a single man: every law and usage was a man's expedient to meet a particular case: that they are all imitable, all alterable; we may make as good; we may make better. Society is an illusion to the young citizen. . . .[3]

He continues:

> The law is only a memorandum . . . so is its force. . . . Society always consists, in greatest part, of young and foolish persons. The old, who have seen through the hypocrisy of courts and statesmen, die, and leave no wisdom to their sons. They believe their own newspaper, as their fathers did in their age. . . . Whenever I find my dominion over myself not sufficient for me, and undertake the direction of him (my neighbor) also, I overstep the truth and come into false relations to him. . . . This undertaking for another, is the blunder which stands in colossal ugliness in the governments of the world. . . . Of all debts, men are least willing to pay the taxes. What a satire is this on government! . . . . Hence the less government we

[2] *Essays On Literature,* 1888, "Ralph Waldo Emerson," First Essay, published in 1861. Also see *Psychology of Language.*
[3] *Essays: Second Series.*

> have, the better,—the fewer laws, and the less confided power. The antidote to this abuse of formal Government, is,the influence of private character, the growth of the Individual; the appearance of the principal to supersede the proxy; the appearance of the wise man, of whom the existing government is, it must be owned, but a shabby imitation. . . . We think our civilization near its meridian, but we are yet only at the cock-crowing and the morning star. . . . Surely nobody would be a charlatan, who could afford to be sincere. . . . What is strange too, there never was in any man sufficient faith in the power of rectitude, to inspire him with the broad design of renovating the State on the principle of right and love. . . .

In *The Law,* Bastiat defends the thesis of conscious self sovereignty as his own. His wording as translated is choice indeed:

> If each man has the right to defend, even by force, his person, his liberty, and his property, several men have the right to get together, come to an understanding, and organize a collective force to provide regularly for this defense.
>
> Collective right, then, has its principle, its *raison d'être,* its legitimate basis, in individual right; and the collective force can rationally have no other end, no other function, than that of the individual forces for which it substitutes.
>
> Thus, as an individual cannot legitimately use force against the person, liberty, or property of another individual, for the same reason collective force cannot legitimately be applied to destroy the person, liberty, and property of individuals or classes.
>
> For this perverse use of force would be, in the one case as in the other, in contradiction with our premises. Who will dare to say that force has been given to us, not to defend our rights, but to destroy the equal rights of our brothers? And if this is not true of the use of force by each individual, acting separately, how can it be true of the collective force, which is nothing but the organized union of the separate forces?
>
> Hence, if anything is self-evident, it is this: Law is the organization of the natural right to legitimate self-defense; it is the substitution of collective force for individual forces, to act in the sphere in which they have the right to act, to do what they have the right to do; to guarantee security of person, liberty, and property rights, to cause *justice* to reign over all.
>
> And if there existed a nation constituted on this basis, it seems to me that order would prevail there in fact as well

> as in theory. It seems to me that this nation would have the simplest, most economical, least burdensome, least disturbing, least officious, most just, and consequently most stable government that can be imagined, whatever its political form might be.
>
> For under such a regime, everyone would comprehend clearly that the full enjoyment of his life, as well as complete responsibility for it, was his and his alone.[4]

My particularizing growth in my conscious self-interest of my Tracy helps to explain why I have chosen his Ideology as a telling illustration backing up my own observations regarding safe and sane political economy. True, I might have chosen for this purpose the economic clarities of a book already famous, *The Wealth of Nations* (1776), for which contribution its author, Adam Smith (1723-1790), earned the title "The Father of Political Economy." Both Smith and Tracy, as do I, derive great helpfulness from studying the psychological (individual, subjective) nature of language. Beginning in 1763 Smith spent two-and-a-half years on the Continent living ten months in Paris, where he too became interested in the novel economic science being worked up by the Physiocrats, Turgot, Helvétius, and Quesnay. During his eighteen months in Toulouse, Smith had commenced his writing of *The Wealth of Nations*, then requiring a ten year period to complete this masterpiece of political exactitude.

George S. Montgomery, Jr., records many a profound self observation in his slender volume, *The Return of Adam Smith*, e.g., "It may be said in general of the social coercionist that his eagerness to manage the affairs of others varies directly with his inability to manage his own."[5] And quoting Smith directly:

[4]Frederic Bastiat, *Selected Essays on Political Economy*, trans. from the French by Seymour Cain, ed. by George B. de Huszar (Irvington-on-Hudson, New York: The Foundation for Economic Education, Inc., 1964), pp. 52–53.

[5]George S. Montgomery, Jr., *The Return of Adam Smith* (Caldwell, Idaho: The Caxton Printers, Ltd., 1949), pp. 104, 105, 139.

> It is not from the benevolence of the butcher, the brewer, or the baker, that we expect our dinner, but from their regard to their own interest. We address ourselves . . . to their self-love. . . . . The property which every man has in his own labour, as it is the original foundation of all other property, so it is the most sacred and inviolable. The patrimony of a poor man lies in the strength and dexterity of his hands; and to hinder him from employing his strength and dexterity in what manner he thinks proper without injury to his neighbour, is a plain violation of this most sacred property. It is a manifest encroachment upon the just liberty both of the workman, and of those who might be disposed to employ him. As it hinders the one from working at what he thinks proper, so it hinders the others from employing whom they think proper. To judge whether he is fit to be employed, may surely be trusted to the discretion of the employers whose interest it so much concerns. The affected anxiety of the law-giver lest they should employ an improper person, is evidently as impertinent as it is oppressive.
> . . . . There is no art which one government sooner learns of another, than that of draining money from the pockets of the people.

My collectivist (unconscious individualist) deems such self wisdom to be impractically ideal at best. Smith's other writings reveal his extraordinary interest in, and insight about, his own *united* mental power. His *A Dissertation on the Origin of Language* was added to the second and following editions of his *The Theory of Moral Sentiments.*

Both Smith and Tracy considered America the choice place in the world for the development of the citizen's rational (self conscious) economic liberty. Each recognized the cost in human benefit of the innumerable studies based upon seeming divisiveness of mental power (e.g., science and religion, whole and part, mind and body, subject and object) and the human economy in respecting the unity of necessary personal identity underlying all apparent "difference."

Neither Smith's nor Tracy's political wisdom has ever been applied systematically by the governmental officials of any nation. However, Smith's writings, unlike Tracy's, have already been given widespread and lasting publication. Tracy's works have not been adequately publicized, either in France or in the United States where his political insights proved helpful to my American forefathers. Tracy and Smith each cultivated his own understanding of the holistic life appreciation of (his) Auguste Comte (1798–1857).

Obviously my collectivist (unconscious individualist) colleague must try to rid his mind of responsible insight for the allness of his own mentality. This can be accomplished by his "classifying" the lifesaving economic wisdom of every self conscious individualist as being obsolescent, or impractical, or whatever pejorative description may temporarily serve.

Furthermore, individual freedom of his personal enterprise, the biologic birthright of my collectivist, thoroughly and defensibly justifies his subordinating every other principle of living, beginning with that of conscious self interest, to his necessity to live his fellowman unconsciously (that is, *as if all of his meaning for his fellowman really is not entirely the production of his own creative living*). Anew, my experience teaches me that it is only the rarest of all individuals who has succeeded in making his mind fit and ready for conscious individual freedom. "Your book is impractical, unpolitical," decides my popular critic.

Hence it is, every possible form of unconscious political science (unconscious self politics) can prove temporarily to seem "the obvious choice." Also, my citizen's public schooling cannot remedy this situation as long as his education can continue to pass as if it is not *conscious self-education only.*

> Government surely has never been more prominent than today. The most despotic government of 1900 would not have dared probe into the private affairs of its citizens as income-tax collectors now do routinely in the freest society. Even the Czar's secret police did not go in for the security investigations we now take for granted. Nor could any bureaucrat of 1900 have imagined the questionnaires that governments now expect businesses, universities, or citizens to fill out in ever-mounting number and ever-increasing detail. At the same time, government has everywhere become the largest employer. . . .
>
> The young are right when they protest against the tendency of organization to look upon an individual as a tool. But they

> are wrong when they blame organization for this. They have never asked themselves: "How can I make this or that organization serve *my* end and *my* needs?" "How can I make it enable *me* to perform, to achieve, to contribute?"[6]

Realizing how difficult it is to scale the self heights of calling my political science (that is, my ideal government) my own and really meaning it, I also realize the dangerous disadvantage, for example, in calling *my social coercionist* (dictator) the enemy of freedom. Rather he is actually trying to compensate for his limitation in recognizing all that he means by his fellowman as truly being the product of his own living (of that fellowman of his). This same caution against self hurt, and it is a most desirable one, applies to my temptation to depreciate my own living in the name of (my) somebody else I may wish to disown as being a communist, bureaucrat, anarchist, or whatever. My finding helpfulness in extending my self interest to subsume my fellow-citizen with communist or anarchist leanings, in no sense means that I consider his unconscious enslavement as harmless or symptom-free. Quite the contrary, I regard each such citizen as not only needing help but also crying out (instead of *in*) for help. Humane treatment is indicated for him as it is for any "carrier" of distress. My official political scientist *must* be incompetent to the extent that he cannot recognize the true comprehensiveness of his individuality.

Only my self conscious (self insightful) citizen can sense that his mind needs its consciousness most for whatever living of his he most resists acknowledging as his own. *I find consistently that my fellowman is most resistive of all when it comes to his disciplining his mind with consciousness for its purely solipsistic nature.* Certainly, I find that my own continuing cultivation of the lifesaving benefit in my conscious solipsism is all that I ever do resist working up. Yet I recognize

[6]Peter F. Drucker, *The Age of Discontinuity* (New York and Evanston: Harper & Row, 1968), pp. 212 and 258, respectively. Government forms now estimated to be well over 700,000 (*Detroit Free Press*, August 13, 1972, p. 3E).

clearly that my conscious individual liberty is *my* only possible source of development of my responsibility for the general welfare of *my* world.

Self consciousness is the only mental condition that cannot be used to attempt to undermine this unalterable truth: All that can possibly be of importance in all of humanity is each human individual. My solipsism is the necessary doctrine of my intact integrity. However, reasoning can be, and is, used for the express purpose of trying to show how *the world* has become entirely too complex to be subordinated to "the ideal" of the human individual. Over and over I find my fellow citizen asserting: "Self help is no longer adequate, the individual must resort to impersonal state aid or even impersonal federal aid." My fellowman helps himself with this effort as I do with mine. Of his author's singular devotion to conscious self responsibility he may even say, "He appears to be carried away with this idea." The fact is that the practice of conscious self responsibility proves itself to be the kind of mental functioning that specifically enables its practitioner to, so to speak, stand on his own feet to call his soul his own and his all his soul.

Again here only the insightful citizen has worked up his appreciation for his life to detect the life-negating (life-risking) assumption underlying such a purportedly soft solution, namely, that his "state" or his "federal government" is some kind of an extra-human or superhuman agency capable of looking out for his own private-and-personal best interests. *Nothing could be further from the truth of the greatness of being human. My* state or federal government is entirely and only an existent occurring in my own existence. Only my own identity can be found in it, and that is the only possible (biological) basis for my being interested in it. All of my helpfully imagining a government external to me, is made up entirely of my own living of that imagining.

> In a time of change and challenge, new vision and new danger, new frontiers and permanent crisis, suffering and achievement, in a time of overlap such as ours, the individual is both all-powerless and all-powerful. He is powerless, however exalted

> his station, if he believes that he can impose his will, that he can command the tides of history. He is all-powerful, no matter how lowly, if he knows himself to be responsible.[7]

In fact, there can be nothing more meaningful for my welfare than the kind of political science I create and propagate for my self. But again, only my self consciousness can reveal to me that open secret. Thus, as laborer I am my own capitalist; as capitalist I am my own laborer. "Division of labor" cannot mean: separation of a part, or parts, from the whole that provides it with its only existence. But, whenever this separatistic (instead of unifying) meaning is assumed by "division of labor" my true single identity underlying my whole corporation (or organism) is obscured. The resulting illusion of plurality clears the way for seeming conflict or dissidence creating the illusion that the gain or loss of one "division" can mean respectively the loss or gain of the other. Such illusional significance of division may be the product of reasoning,—not of self consciousness, the one-maker. A true definition of any present person, thing or word can be secured only from an accurate account of the full history of his, or its, whole development up to now.

My reasoning, alone, cannot serve the best interest of my whole self,—only my self consciousness can protect my wholeness and allness. Reasoning is an excellent tool but self consciousness *only* can master the integrity of my being. From the beginning of life, despite all of the apparent evidence to the contrary, self helpfulness (not *conscious* self helpfulness) is all that is possible for each individual. Despite appearance to the contrary, whatever I do is momentarily my only way to try to help my self. However, my consciousness for my self helpfulness does not begin until I first start to sense that I am an individual capable of feeling my personal identity. With my consciousness for being an individual grows my appreciation for my individual authority and responsibility.

[7] Peter F. Drucker, *Landmarks of Tomorrow* (New York: Harper and Brothers, 1957), p. 270.

I naturally resist sensing my identity in my living until I can feel strong minded enough to acknowledge being responsible for it.

Too much cannot be made of this understanding of the evolution of the true comprehensiveness of human individuality, and I shall return to it over and over, for that is my way of helping myself. For every person is wonderfully great whether or not he can consciously acknowledge his true greatness. Every being is constantly helping himself wonderfully in innumerable ways, from conception on, whether or not he can consciously acknowledge his true self helpfulness. Every man is always doing his very best at present. Until he really knows self he cannot add to his conscious self helpfulness.

However, each person tends to conduct his life according to his own *conscious opinion* of its worth, its true wonderfulness, its complete helpfulness. If my conscious self esteem approximates its maximal adequacy I have no difficulty sensing divine helpfulness in my living. If my conscious self esteem approximates its minimal adequacy I have no difficulty sensing merely helplessness, worthlessness, or meaninglessness in my living.

Political implication of my *conscious* self helpfulness is evident. I am my own electorate, government, mass unemployment, taxation, public debt, monopoly, waste, or whatever political. I benefit my self by realizing that my approach to economics from the side of conscious solipsism is the only ethical one possible for me. *Naturally, I hope some day to see the subject of human liberty presented to my American student by a conscious solipsist,*[8] *rather than only by an unconscious solipsist (collectivist).* I see some of the current restive movement of my American youth largely as his instinctive effort to return to his devotion to the ideal of individual freedom that he vaguely believes gave birth to his nation.

There can be no industrial development except in the mind of each industrialist creating such a conception. There can

[8]My *American Government* (Detroit: Center for Health Education, 1969) is just such an attempt.

be no class-consciousness,—only *self* consciousness. The property a man has in his own self consciousness, the original founder of all his self possession, is his only demonstrable commodity, his only real goods. So-called society has absolutely no possible foundation other than that in the mind of the individual giving it meaning.[9]

My purpose in my educational ideal of *conscious* self education to conscious self helpfulness becomes manifest. Thus, my conscious meaning for my State or Nation or World develops true perspective in the range of my whole self order, and the economic consequence of all of my behavior becomes a conscious responsibility of mine.

However, regardless of the greatness of this advantage I could not add it to my conscious benefit as long as I felt sure that I was most comfortable only without it. A hardly noticeable resistance takes this form: my barely accepting any of my living as really being mine so that I can comfort my self with a degree of feeling that I already am quite insightful about it.

I find that it is not true (untrue) that the idea of unique helpfulness of self consciousness is too complex to appeal to the undisciplined mind of my self unconscious fellowman. Quite the contrary, I find he is ever willing, even eager, to try to begin to feel justification for his omnipresent need to revere his own individuality, to "think more of himself" than he can.

My fellow citizen will certainly vote for his political candidate whose platform really, consistently, stands for: Renounce all dismal self respect that supplants ideal individuality-appreciation with the illusion of collectivity or society or any other form of individuality-concealing "people." Economically stated: A billion owes all of its meaning only and entirely to each single one constituting it.[10] I discover the amazing, hence avoided, fact: *Law becomes the legislator's indomitable force of self-in-*

[9]Charles Horton Cooley, *Human Nature and the Social Order* (New York: C. Schribner Sons, 1902).
[10]See, *American Government.*

justice precisely to the extent that it is not consciously based upon full appreciation for the wholeness and allness of his human individuality!

Seeing my own identity, only, in my official political scientist is all that can spare me from hurting my self in his name, thus continuing my age-old addiction of the pot calling the kettle black. My incontinent "ouch" reaction to my hurt feeling (e.g., about my taxation without competent representation) can only amount to my helpfully hurting my self further. Therefore all of this writing is as free from accusation or guilt as I can make it. *It reports only how greatly I have been able to strengthen my political economy by finding out exactly where all of it is operating, namely, in my self.* Thus, I am grateful to my self for helping my self by studying the conscious self helpfulness of each conscious political competent, such as Destutt de Tracy, Adam Smith, Frederic Bastiat, Sigmund Freud, Albert J. Nock, Henry Hazlitt, Dean Russell, Leonard E. Read, Ludwig von Mises, Robert M. Hutchins, Henry M. Wriston, and many another one.

Each writer is most self helpful who does not lose track of his individuality when he looks at his political or economic woods.[11] Sumner H. Slichter properly emphasizes the fact that his American economy "is a far better economy than most people realize." Describing transformation of American economy "from a capitalistic to a laboristic" one, he cites powerful truth of the gain to the employee in his developing "effective policies for stimulating enterprise." Of course, there can be no possible enterprise but that of an individual, but this is the truth of truths remaining to be *constantly* upheld by my every economist in all of his writing, reading and computerizing.

[11]Just for example, Sumner H. Slichter's *The American Economy: Its Problems and Prospects* (New York: Alfred A. Knopf, 1948), is still a trenchant analysis of his subject, but my reality-respecting term "individual" is conspicuously absent. The author does mention the "spirit of enterprise" which, of course, can be only an individual's spirit. He also mentions "self-employed." The truth that I need to *feature* is: *There can be no employment but self employment.*

Only this lifesaving orientation in *conscious* self continence gives my present work its unique quality, placing it directly in the front of my economic literature. I must make my peace with the truth that I do not expect it to be read very much, if at all, by my kindly and fully respected public official, governmental or educational. I can expose my economic fallacies or facts only to my self,—*that* I am both sure of and glad about. For example, my economist's term "exchange" implying more-than-one is renounced by me in favor of my term "identity" implying the truth of individuality: each employer being *his* own employee; each employee, *his* own employer; each buyer, *his* own seller; each seller, *his* own buyer; and so on, ever reducing seeming plurality to real unity.

My consciously preserving my self sovereignty, my revered self control, is all that can enable me to develop the unrestricted use of my functioning carefully and caringly, without any implied expense to my fellowman. I can live and satisfy all of my wants safely only by laboriously giving birth to my self consciousness as I proceed considerately to indulge my wishes, ever seeing only my own identity in whatever I live. *Obedience to the law codifying my own individual nature is my only possibility and it is my most important lifesaving task to work up my consciousness for this law of laws.*

This immense discovery of the inviolable wholeness of my life is now the consummate fulfillment of my self understanding, derived from my *growing* it. I cannot create in any way except by my growing my creation. How far this precious realization must be removed from any such helpful illusion as "communication" or "imparting of information"! How self helpful is my originating (growing) my Frederic Bastiat's *What Is Seen and What Is Not Seen,* or *The Law,* or *The State,* or *The Petition of the Candlemakers Against the Competition of the Sun*!

Bastiat insightfully defines "the law" as the organization of the natural right of individual man, specifying that this force is to do only "What the individual forces have a natural and lawful right to do . . . to cause *justice* to reign over us all.''[12] This definition allows for *individual me* to cultivate my mental strength ultimately to be able to imagine consciously and kindly every feeling and thought that is humanly possible, thereby fully developing my potential self helpfulness to possess all the privileges as well as all the responsibilities of my existence. It is my precious birthright to be able to thank my self for my wonderful self activity.

I remind my self often of Emerson's world citizenship which he could express freely as American Citizen, even amidst hisses,—his fierce comment upon his erstwhile hero, Daniel Webster, when that great worthy disappointed him by not proclaiming immediately the divine insensibility underlying slavery, ''Every drop of his blood has eyes that look downward. He knows the heroes of 1776, but cannot see those of 1851 when he meets them on the street.''

In 1844 black citizens of Massachusetts were taken to prison from ships in southern ports. Delivering an oration in Concord on the anniversary of West Indian emancipation Man showed his hurt civic spirit with successful results. Impassioned Emerson pictured the ''infinite wrongs'' the black man endured with ''godlike patience'' and asserted his heroic practicality:

> If such a damnable outrage can be committed on the person of a citizen with impunity, let the Governor break the broad seal of State; he bears the sword in vain. The Governor of Massachusetts is a trifler; the Statehouse in Boston is a playhouse, the General Court is a dishonored body, if they make laws which they cannot execute. The great-hearted Puritans have left no posterity.[13]

He then demanded the representatives of the State to demand of Congress the instant release, by force if necessary, of the imprisoned black seamen, and their indemnification, ''As for dangers to the Union from such demands, the Union is

[12] *The Law.* Irvington-on-Hudson, New York: The Foundation for Economic Education, Inc., 1970, p. 7.

[13] Moncure D. Conway, *Emerson At Home and Abroad* (Boston: James R. Osgood and Co., 1882), p. 233.

already at an end when the first citizen of Massachusetts is thus outraged."

Being all and only about my self my writing upon my political science cannot be accurately construed as having anything whatsoever to do with so-called official *external* government or institution. I fully realize and tenderly appreciate that every one of my imagined government officials is properly doing (being) all possible at present to be consciously and unconsciously self helpful. It is my sincere intention to honor the law of my country as it is now in force. Certainly I am most profoundly interested in the necessary vicissitudes in my wonderful American experiment.

I see all of my American legislator's governmental experience as just. For example, it is only by his own living of law based upon *any* disrespect for human individuality that he can ever grow this essential understanding: It is exactly this overlooking of the biological comprehensiveness of human individuality that can clearly account for the exaggerated importance any individual must ascribe to his conscious political passion, at the enormous expense of his duly appreciating his self importance.

Surely this life-depreciating consequence of the law, making it my instrument of injustice, is best felt keenly by me (painfully unhappy though that must be). Again my Emerson, Man must be healed by a quarantine of calamities before he can declare, "I am free." To a Boston orator who described the Declaration of Independence as a series of "glittering generalities," he countered, "They are blazing ubiquities." During the Civil War in which many a dear friend of his was slain and his only son wounded, he underwent terrible trial and no man served his country better "with voice, pen, and means. . . .

> Emerson was about to give a lecture (in Boston) on the condition of the country . . . I said to him "the accident of my being born in the South enables me to give a practical suggestion. You remember how Thoreau used to catch bream . . . this fish had the peculiarity of hastening to defend its spawn, and by placing his hand under the spawn (he) pulled up a fish. Well the spawn of the South is its slaves; we have

only to put our hands on it, and these armies now resisting us will hasten back to hold on to its slaves. As long as we do not touch slavery, the negroes till the fields, and it is they who point the soldier at us as the soldier points his gun." Emerson proceeded at once to say this in his lecture . . . and added, *"I hope that it is not fatal to this method that it is entirely moral and just."* He also, I believe, urged the same plan in Washington, where his lecture was attended by the President and his Cabinet. . . . Thus did the President of the literary, respond to the President of the political Republic. . . . When the war had ended . . . in Boston . . . he uttered the true American faith.

America means opportunity, freedom, power. . . . Let us invite every nation, every race, every skin; white man, black man, red man, yellow man. Let us offer hospitality, a fair field, and equal laws to all. . . . Let us educate every soul!

It was a sign 'gracious as rainbows' that, in the centennial year of American Independence, Emerson delivered the oration before the literary Societies of the University of Virginia.[14]

Above all plunder, indeed my only possible political spoliation, is my robbing my life of its conscious self-respect to pay off its unconscious self-respect called "the Law." *The properly specific concern of my Law is my vigilant recognition and prevention of just such organized injustice.*

What is my Liberty except the conscious unity of all my power: my appreciating all that my whole life can consciously or unconsciously mean to me as an individual, born free, capable fully of activity of my own being, methodically liberating my self from trying to reject my very own personal identity in *whatever* I live. When I become consciously free then I can at last declare my soul my own and my all my soul, acknowledging faith in the harmonious order and peaceful functioning of my conscious self interest.

There can be the seeming of inequality in my world only to the extent that I can succeed in refusing to see nothing but the sameness of my own real identity in all of it,—hence the necessity for my *extending* coverage of my self consciousness for *all* of my living. I cannot really, justly, accurately,

[14]Ibid., pp. 313 and 314. My italics.

view any living of my world impersonally. I am actively all of my mankind and I truly cannot divide the same me into "haves" and "have nots." I can pretend to do so only at the cost of serious mental (i.e., soul-of-body) trouble derived from my self injustice.

When I first discovered my Tracy, a single-minded man who not only sensed his self comprehensively as an individual but also sensed this life orientation as being the only one upon which to construct a constitutional government reconcilable with human welfare, I encouraged my self to try to find some degree of application of this really workable political economy to the grievously critical affairs of my own American Government. First, I published and distributed widely my book on American citizenship.[15] This present volume records my further approach to revealing the benevolent providence in conscious self sovereignty as well as the awful cost in civil liberty of *all* unconscious self sovereignty.

The absolute political necessity for human individuality is: self sovereignty, either conscious or unconscious. The added absolute truth that such self sovereignty need not be conscious accounts fully for the existence of all of my other governmental forms, including even the democratic one wherever it is not intended to be strictly synonymous with conscious self sovereignty. And that "wherever" is everywhere, since it is only by cultivating all knowledge as only and entirely conscious *self* knowledge that the necessary ingredient for conscious self sovereignty can be provided. There can be no political magic merely in the name Democracy. All conscious human power derives only from the working of the conscious spirit of human individuality.

Conscious self orientation towards my American Government is specifically what I mean by my Americanism. I find it to be the one citizenship orientation most needed by me (including *my* every fellow citizen), quite as I clearly realize that it is the most difficult one to attain and maintain.[16] It

[15] See, *American Government, Conscious Self Sovereignty.*
[16] Ibid.

reminds me of Thomas Jefferson's observation: A single good government is a blessing to the whole earth. And I find it in complete unison with my Adam Smith's feelingful conception of his national spirit:

> The natural disposition of every individual to better his own condition, when suffered to exert itself with freedom and security, is so powerful a principle that it is, alone and without assistance, not only capable of carrying on the society to wealth and prosperity, but of surmounting a hundred impertinent obstructions with which the folly of human laws too often encumbers its operations.

Michael Montaigne observed, "There never was in the world two opinions alike, no more than two hairs or two grains; the most universal quality is diversity." The only witness upon whom Tracy could rely as being true to his truth was his self. Living a world in which his fellowman seemed to consider life to be cheap, he seemed most unpopular, and by this illusional unpopularity I measure his conscious greatness. Particularly in my study of government I have helped my self by noting the extent to which the writing of this seemingly ignored genius of government records his living in accordance with the seminal principle of sanity: conscious self sovereignty. His psychology requires no "externality" except that necessarily *imagined*, consciously imagined by him. He is consciously his own mediation, delegation, representation, communion, all-in-all. He realizes that his mind cannot be comprehended by what it comprehends, or subsumed by what it subsumes, except in that mind's imagination.

In *American Government* I refer to Tracy's extraordinary insight regarding his conscious self sovereignty and its historic significance for my every American citizen. However, expectably this book does not prove the least bit "popular," as far as I can tell, with my governmental official or fellow citizen at large. Its theme makes heavy demand upon its intended reader, namely his working up the conscious emotional continence to be able to renounce his illusion of authoritarianism in favor of his realism: recognizable self-government. Although in the main my fellow citizen does seem too far "gone" in the direction of unconscious authoritarianism, nevertheless I do sense his beginning to show helpful signs of awakening to the marvelous, potential power for guaranteeing human happiness in his customarily taken-for-granted American Constitution.

It is with fervent hope for my fellowman's capacity for *conscious* self government that I undertake the glorious task of bringing to conscious life, from the dust of old shelves and files of rare books, 1) the wonderful love of, and wisdom regarding,the source and course of human freedom of the independent integrity of the soul of man; and 2) the tremendous self insight of each founding father of the United States that enabled him to appreciate and identify his own comprehensive understanding with that of his Destutt de Tracy.

Most meaningful self observation in this Introduction is:

1) Man's natural constitution is a law unto itself providing the ideal paradigm for his biologically adequate political science.

2) There can be no education but self-education, conscious or unconscious.

3) Every citizen's most urgently needed personal (including political) innovation is his thorough work up of his understanding of the kind of education absolutely necessary for his developing his *conscious* self control, the foundation essential for his clearly evident self sovereignty providing his one and only foolproof political freedom.

4) My first self deception, my rejection of my living as if it could be not-mine (repression) occurred when I had to help my self to want to be my self by repudiating my living that I was unable to feel was desirable (calling it not-I, not-me, not-mine, not-self or some other name indicating my effort to alienate it).

5) I dignify such and other illusional mentation by innumerable grammatical terms unwittingly hypostatizing unreality (e.g., plurality, pejoration, melioration, externality, impersonal, etc.).

6) I equate individuality with reality thus: Whatever is, individually is.

7) All help is self help, either acknowledged or unacknowledged.

8) Understanding of conscious self control preparing for conscious self government can begin in early childhood, as well as any time thereafter. No one can effect my *political individualism* but me.

9) My civic spirit is identical with my selfish spirit.

10) My law is as my law does. Eternal vigilance is the cost of just law.

11) My fellowman, rarely responsible for the truth that he is the only law unto himself, is therefore justly dependent upon *his* fellowman whose experience has worked up this degree of his conscious freedom.

12) Unconscious self-education (so-called impersonal experience) is helpfully heralded by the appearance of signs and symptoms usually called sickness, or crime, or "accident."

13) Illness, or crime, or accident, as a rule is depreciated as harmful rather than appreciated as helpful.

14) My every sickness, or crime, or accident can be truly understood merely as necessary experience that not only protects my life but also reveals how the present character of my living requires such unhappy development.

15) *Every* instance of my faultfinding means only that I must create a phantom problem for I am presently unable to do the fact-finding that would disclose that faultfinding as unjust.

16) My mind is my only real estate; conscious free-mindedness is my only possible freedom.

17) Conscious or unconscious solipsism is my (including my every fellowman's) only possible kind of living.

18) My reasoning without self consciousness creates the run-away self, responsible for my bewildering political plight.

19) The nature of the psychogenesis of his individuality is the specific conscious self-education that is indispensable for American citizenship.

20) Every school child is capable of teaching his (her) self the precious benefit in observing how his own wonderful mind develops itself.

21) My life is positive living of lovable sensibility that can terminate itself but not negate itself except in the form of its unconscious affirmation.

22) My Destutt de Tracy is a conscious individualist aware for the organic integrity of his wholeness.

BRIEF HISTORICAL NOTES

It is clear that in whatsoever it is our duty to act, those matters also it is our duty to study.

Thomas Arnold

I discovered Vera Stepanowa's doctoral dissertation (University of Zurich) on Destutt de Tracy[1] through Professor Stanley Kirschner while he was abroad on his sabbatical leave from Wayne State University. The microfilm which he sent me was then enlarged in attractive monograph form by my long-time friend, Eugene Power of Ann Arbor.

Stepanowa finds Tracy an enthusiastic student of John Locke, particularly in his *Elements of Ideology* where Tracy seeks to have his findings of the human soul organized along the principles of natural science. To begin with, he favors the way in which Descartes began his philosophic work, feeling that Descartes later departed too far from his beginning orientation of strict subjectivity. Stepanowa observes the great extent to which Tracy found his identity helpfully in his Condillac.

This author devotes the fourth and last division of her dissertation to a discussion of the significance of Tracy's work for her contemporaries, *concluding that it presents many interesting viewpoints and correct observations applying to her present study of psychology.* With rare insight she records her appreciation of her de Tracy's development of his mental power as an independent self observer. Most lifeworthy is her recognition of the identity of the development of Tracy

[1] *Destutt de Tracy, eine historisch-psychologische Untersuchung,* (Zurich: Druck von Zurcher & Furrer, 1908). Author Stepanowa was born in Moscow in 1883. Her education in Moscow was along the lines of history and philosophy. In 1902–1903, she continued her formal education in Zurich, specializing in philosophy, psychology, art history, history, and literature. On account of its positive treatment of her Tracy and his works I find it helpful to include following detail from her treatise.

the psychologist and the growth of Tracy the self conscious man.

She points out that the works of Tracy are little known by her contemporaries apart from Picavet's book, *Les Idéologues*, which gives some description of Tracy's life and his work, including a short account of his psychological orientation. She finds no other work of Tracy in her recent literature. In his lifetime he was one of the most popular French philosophers. In the beginning of the 19th century, his fame extended into many lands. His importance for the history of psychology lies especially in his effort to construct a positivistic psychology as such, a development which accorded with the views of Stepanowa's contemporary psychologists.

The appreciation for the physiological as representing the unconscious psychological is especially important to Tracy. Thus Stepanowa notes he has asserted that the will is fundamentally an effective and constant accompaniment of physiological movements, which are completed within the organism and which determine so-called voluntary movements. Out of the fulfillment or unfulfillment of wishing, respectively, issues all joy and sorrow. If I wish a definite movement, I tend to exercise it. If it suddenly is inhibited through an "outer" influence, it nevertheless continues despite there being opposition to it which hinders its action. Tracy declares that this "something" cannot belong to my ego, that the idea of another being responsible for this resistance may not appear as a result of first frustration but builds itself when my experience of frustration is repeated.

(However, whatever I live consciously, of necessity belongs to my ego. *This realization is essential in order that I may be able to appreciate that I am all that I live as my "other one.")*

Stepanowa further observes that Tracy considered idea, sensation and perception to be synonymous. He used the term *intellectual* as a synonym for *mental.* His ardent wish is to base science upon observation alone for he trusts the evidence of his senses as such, rather than as modified in imagining, wishing, reasoning or judging. He sensed (felt) all observation to be self observation but he also realized just opposition to feeling it consciously as self observation: "To think is to sense"; "An unfelt thought would be no thought." Nevertheless he wonders that such a simple method as observing is so long in establishing itself, and then so weak.

With keen understanding Stepanowa recognizes that Tracy's writing reflects his own psychogenesis, varying in its indication of his self consciousness as he gradually developed this life-affirming self orientation. Thus he comes to regard motility as sensation of his over-all category of sensibility (living, itself). Also he attributes essential functioning to it: sensory feeling in the narrower sense, memory, judgment, will and mobility. His indispensable meaning of this conscious importance of mobility for constructing comprehensive unity of the whole individual, is awe inspiring. Tracy dutifully observes the fact that no form of sensibility is excited in isolation from the rest, that all is in one and one is in all. Quite as sensation is found in every movement, so movement resides in all sensation. *Thus my entire mental activity may be conceived as a sequence of sensible motility constituting my real existence from which I may hypothesize my personal identity*[2] (Logic IX, S. 351).

Tracy courageously conceived sensibility to be based upon movement in the nerve itself (or in its ending), pure sensation arising peripherally (centripetal); remembering, judging and wishing arising in the brain (centrifugal). He renounced the assumption of inborn idea. One must work up one's mental competence individually through living (experiencing) sensibility. As might be expectd Tracy studied the nature of language, realizing "conventional" language to be an abstraction, indeed every word amounting to an abstraction drawn from the linguist's sensing his wording.

Cabanis contributed a very important supplement to Condillac's psychology by observing organ sensation. Stepanowa observes that Tracy consciously appropriated this new idea in his Ideology, Chapter II, including therein *inner sensation*

[2] My italics.

providing visceral mentality. This unifying conception of living, including all mental experience, as consisting of the same generative sensibility, can be my creation only if I attain appreciation for the self-fulfilling, lifesaving importance of my self consciousness. Without my devoting my attention to the unique power of my self sensing, self feeling, or self idea, I cannot achieve abstracting my sensing the specific wholeness-nature of my wholeness.

Discerning Stepanowa remarks that, although Tracy posits four forms of mentality (beginning with unmodified sensibility and then memory, judgment and will or wish), he feels great concern lest such modification seem to resemble a division of mental force thus obscuring its intact wholeness in its one power, namely, sensibility. By "I" or ego he refers to *all* of the sensibility he has experienced. However, consciousness for being (living) my ego is my personifying this mental unity as an abstraction. My will (wish) plays an important role in my feeling my personal identity. Stepanowa records how Tracy felt strongly the importance of the effect of habit on sensibility in its four forms. In each experience of sensation (elementary, memory, judgment and will) repetition worked the same way, constituting a general law: the activity became easier, its timing faster, and its conscious meaning less noticeable.

The significance of Tracy's responsible self observation for the development and functioning of lifesaving self consciousness, as indicated by Stepanowa, is both clear and strong. The dread consequence to character or disposition of rote learning, contrasted with conscious self activity, is awful to consider,—sufficiently frightening to account for its being overlooked. I fear for my self world as I feel the necessity that justice, truth and love are thoroughly compatible with pain and suffering of every kind and degree.

Dr. Mary Brazier traces the first experimental scientist to the 17th century, his work then becoming based upon empiricism instead of rationalism.[3] John Locke (1632–1704) traced all

[3] "The Growth of Concepts Relating to Brain Mechanisms." Reprinted from the *Journal of the History of the Behavioral Sciences* 1 (1965) No. 3.

knowledge to sensory observation, claiming the mind capable of creating ideas from no other source but the senses. Abbé Condillac contended that the mind itself has the power to reflect on the ideas formed from sensations. He explained all aspects of human consciousness on the unifying foundation of all his understanding, namely, sensation, putting great emphasis upon touch. He also declared pleasure and pain constituted the principle determining all the soul's activities. Destutt de Tracy was one of Condillac's most ardent students, having read Condillac's works while in prison. He developed his science of ideas, *ideology*, feeling the science of perception to be vital to it. D'Alembert wished "to reduce metaphysics to that which it ought to be, namely, the experimental physics of the mind." Dr. Cabanis favored this orientation.

Dr. Brazier relates a classic description of habituation, given by Destutt de Tracy:

> . . . when it (the sensation) has been repeated frequently, it should then evoke in us a sensation often experienced but less vivid; and this is what is observed. It no longer produces in us a feeling of the surprise which excited us so much the first times; the more it is repeated the less it attracts our attention. And finally, if repeated too frequently and for too long, it ends up by being no longer perceived, as when we sense for too long the same odor or the same taste or the same degree of light or of temperature.

Dr. Brazier brings her comprehensive article right up to date in observing the role of electrophysiology in the search for understanding of the physiology of the nervous system.[4]

As noted, Tracy prized most highly his growing his psychology through study of his Condillac, especially appreciating the latter's empirical method. He considered Condillac to be the first to give a systematic presentation of the operation of the human mind, never presenting probability as capable of substituting for true fact. Tracy felt himself to be the elucidator

[4]This discussion is of special interest to me for I conducted extensive research in this particular area with Dean Lee Edward Travis and Dr. Samuel T. Orton at the University of Iowa (1927–1934).

and augmenter of his Condillac's thoughts, naming him "the great ideologist."

Condillac assumed a mental substance, attempting to account for all mental process on the basis of sensation. He characterizes sensation as possessing specificity of its own nature (redness, sweetness, hardness); affectivity (pleasant or unpleasant); duration; unique distinctiveness. As mentioned, touch was his most important sensation. He also considered the mind as passively sensing rather than as actively creating its sensory living, sensation being intrapsychic. Repetition of sensation strengthens its faculty so *that* peculiarity of faculty tends to depend upon habit. Habit rather than self consciousness seems to occupy the important role in Condillac's psychology.

Although Tracy considered mind to be biologically organic he was not satisfied either to regard his living as essentially passive or as non-psychologically physiological. However, he did recognize and cherish the truth that the conception of man strictly as a biological organism does stress the fact of his inviolable individuality, for example, by excluding every wishful claim that man is not really an individual or ever a part of a larger whole named society.

Crudely put, Condillac illustrates his theory by constructing a statue, first with the capacity to experience only the sensation of smelling. He then describes how this strictly limited mind might conduct all mental activity in an elementary way. When in moving, the statue touches its own body in two places it is sensing its being; but when it senses resistance only in one place it can conclude that it is touching something other than itself. Tracy elaborated upon this argument, observing that if his mind is nothing but sensation, then all reasoning must be a sensing in disguise. The conscious solipsist's teacher, Dr. Cabanis, described physical sensibility as the power of organic matter to react to stimulus, as the fundamental fact of the physiologist. Therefore he claimed the physiologist aware of the role of sensibility would hold in his hands the secrets of all human living.

Condillac defined attention as the quality of sensitivity that enabled it to be selectively excited. Thus he attempted to account for the developmental stages of every psychic process. For example, once a sensation stops being the immediate subject of attention it retains that potential, thereby being *memorable*, thus accounting for "memory." Now if the statue can possess both sensation and memorable sensation, each as the subject of attention, then the possibility of comparison arises and the condition for judgment is present. Yet judgment involves sensing of pleasure and pain providing also the condition essential for wishing.

Condillac's psychology names sensing of pleasure or unpleasure its leading principle, constantly present in all sensation. He derives the power of abstraction from experiencing the sense of a generality in a complex of sensations, e.g., each one pleasing or unpleasing. Before the statue can develop "I want" it must first have developed "I" out of immediate and potential sensing. The *sine qua non* for the structuring of this ego-idea, self consciousness, is its sensing its changing but still finding itself to be the same, namely, "I." Sensing "I" sequence underlies the ideas of timing, spacing and moving.

Ernst Mach (1838–1916), physicist, made the basic psychological study, *Contributions to the Analysis of Sensations* (1886), his comprehensive methodology being conceived on the model of (his) Theodor Fechner's *Psychophysics:*

> To bring together elements that are most intimately connected with pleasure and pain in one ideal mental-economical unity, the ego; this is the task of the highest importance for the intellect working in the service of the pain-avoiding, pleasure-seeking will. . . . The primary fact is not the ego, but the elements (sensations). . . . The elements constitute the I.
>
> *Bodies do not produce sensations, but complexes of elements (complexes of sensations) make up bodies. If to the physicist, bodies appear the real, abiding existences, while the elements are regarded merely as their evanescent, transitory appearance, the physicist forgets, in the assumption of such a view, that all bodies are but thought-symbols for complexes of elements (complexes of sensations).*
>
> On a bright summer day in the open air, the world with my

> ego suddenly appeared to me as one coherent mass of sensations, only more strongly coherent in the ego. Although the actual working out of this thought did not occur until a later period, yet this moment was decisive for my whole view.[5]

Mach specifies his using the term sensations to describe the elements, rather than

> . . . particles of mass that are considerd as physical elements, to which the elements, in the sense here used, are attached as "properties" or "effects." In this way, accordingly, we do not find the gap between bodies and sensations . . ., between what is without and what is within, between the material world and the spiritual world.[6]

For this solipsistic heroism, Mach willingly endured the self scathing criticisms of his less self-conscious contemporary.

> *The facts given by the senses . . . are alike the starting-point and the goal of all the mental adaptations of the physicist. The thoughts which follow the sense-given fact are the most familiar, the strongest, and the most intuitive. . . . The man of science is not looking for a completed vision of the universe; he knows beforehand that all his labor can only broaden and deepen his insight.*[7]

As did Tracy before him, for his psychological self growth (continuity), Mach ventured beyond the illusional security of so-called objectivity as being the basis of scientific truth.[8] In building my new system of life orientation by seeming to be able to destroy my preceding one, I am already trying to lay foundation upon non-existence. My creative activity is (i.e., must be) ever an outgrowth of its previous existence. Thus my so-called destruction reveals its nature as self-destruc-

[5] Ernst Mach, *Contributions to the Analysis of Sensations*, Trans. C. M. Williams (Chicago: Open Court Pub. Co., 1897), pp. 22, 23, 29, 30. My italics.
[6] *History of Mechanics*, p. 17.
[7] *Contributions to the Analysis of the Sensations*, pp. 327, 358. My italics.
[8] *The Analysis of Sensations*, revised and supplemented from the Fifth German Edition by Sydney Waterlow, with a new Introduction by Thomas S. Szasz, M.D. (New York: Dover Publications, Inc., 1959.)

tive. In his *Autobiographical Notes,* Albert Einstein said of his Mach: "I see Mach's greatness in his incorruptible skepticism and independence."

Although my sense of touch does aid me in my working up sensibility for outlining my body ego, I may also deceive myself with it. Thus when I feel opposition to my touch without sensing also my "being felt" in that opposition, I may delude my self to conceive that I thereby can feel something or somebody other than my own body, whereas such cannot be the case. I am also all of *my* opposition in which I cannot again experience feeling my body, quite as I am my opposition in which I can experience my self as "being felt." *This correct observation of touch is absolutely essential for my fully appreciating the inviolable wholeness and allness of my individuality.*

All I can resist is nothing but my self consciousness. Whenever I live touch or any other feeling without self consciousness then my reasoning takes over and can appear to be my supreme guide. *As only a reasoner I can dispense with solipsistic reality (the reality of solipsism) with superb ease, merely by judging it to be absurd.*

My healthful process of living *consciously* amounts to ongoing self analysis. Thus my mind is always engaged in free association in the sense that, instead of only verbalizing its emotionality, its stream of consciousness may also use sensation or perception, as such, for freely venting emotionality. In my own self analysis, of this extended definition, I can make most important discovery from my free association. For instance, I notice that I use my mind in a distinctly unique way depending upon what kind of person I consider to be present while I use it. Stated inaccurately but conventionally, my mind works itself differently depending upon whom I am "with." If I wish to develop my mind with augmenting self consciousness I can help my self attain that cultivation by being "with" an individual whom I deem to be devoted to working up his own self consciousness. It is this finding that helps to explicate why it makes such great difference exactly whom I am consciously conceiving as present while I am free associating (e.g., my so-called analyst).

WORKING FORMULATIONS

> If right and wrong are to be determined by majority vote, then slavery itself can easily be justified. But since no *individual* has the right to enslave another individual, then no group of individuals can possibly have such a right.
>
> Dean Russell, *Frederic Bastiat: Ideas and Influence*

I have consciously created this work *organically*, by necessity, i.e., as a growth of my own burgeoning insight about my governmental economy, without reference to "conventionality" or "popularity" or similar undependable "standards of soundness." I present it remorselessly as nothing but a true diaristic history of my own psychogenesis in the direction of politics, the science and art of government. For want of this perspective I cannot know my own mind.

My political economy, the study of man's wants, work, and wealth[1] does not lend itself readily to scientific method. A so-called science of economics implies that *men* generally, if not invariably, behave in the same way when put into the same circumstances. I note well the scientific illusion of making an object out of completely subjective man in this so-called scientific treatment of him. Any communal problem of economic life, of whatever magnitude, can occur only and entirely where whatever is lived must always occur, namely, in the unique individual whose mind creates it, e.g., any and every consideration of "monetary, fiscal and commercial

[1]John M. Gregory, *A New Political Economy* (New York: American Book Co., 1882), p. 40. Also see, Frederic Bastiat's *Economic Harmonies:* "The subject of political economy is MAN. . . . Economic Science does not possess a standard that can be used to measure the intensity of desires, efforts and satisfactions of individual man. As Aristotle recorded: 'there is no science except of the general'." And all that can be meant by "the general" is to be found only in the individual mind creating that image in and of its own likeness.

policies of governments," or of "production, distribution and consumption of wealth," or of "maladjustments in the mechanism of production and trade," and so on. Any science of humanity is incomplete which does not clearly indicate itself to be wholly and solely the production of the scientist working it up!

It is precisely by my observing each truth of my political science as I live it consciously in my mind that I can succeed in working it up into an exact science. Only in my own acknowledgeable living can all that I mean by natural law be appraised at its true worth, as my law of my nature. What I call my legislative law can be no exception to my natural law, but if I overlook that reality I involve myself in illusional diversity rather than in the real organic unity of my mind's wholeness. This perspective, namely, my *consciously* living all of my politics, economy and science exactly where all of it really is, *in me*, is my supreme political ideal. It can be formulated only from the standpoint of conscious mental integration.

Naturally I enjoy seeing my fellowman discover in his own highly refined mental development all that he can possibly mean by his political economy or political science. Certainly there is absolutely no way for me to impart, communicate, transfer, inform, telepathize, or otherwise extend to anyone but my self the ownership of this, or any other, lifesaving truth. I possess by birth the inviolable copyright of *whatever* I live. *My needful work is not the learning of more and more so-called impersonal data about so-called external political or economic organization, but rather a continuous clearing up of my perception of the comprehensiveness of my truly amazing self identity.* With this whole self appreciation I can reveal my spiritual starvation expressed in my dispirited objectivity as hidden hunger for conscious living.

My finding that I am, in my Aristotle's terms, the political animal capable *by nature* of recognizing all of my political activity as my own, highlights the indispensable benefit to my mankind in my everyone's conscious self discipline (self education) duly cultivating this only reality: *subjectivity.* It is all that I (including *my* every fellowman) can ever discover in any of my mental activity.

No one of my world was ever able to tell me about my wholeness and allness, in any sense of any seeming effort to do so. My undeniably helpful sights of what I may call so-called external world I now artistically recognize as illusional, reminding me of the plight of those spirits created by Dante, doomed to see only the remote, all near to them being invisible. My need to acknowledge my self in all of my conscious as well as unconscious being (doing) is well extended to my seeing only my unique identity in all of my political and economic action. By identity, of course, I mean my self's subjectivity where all of my actuality occurs, seeming external "impression" becoming evident as my life's real fruitage, and so on. I have finally wised up to the realization that my only safeguard against a theory-blinded mentality is my steadfast devotion to self consciousness, the source of all quickness of my so-called moral sense. Political economist Charles Gide records: "The ethics of political economy are justice."

Thus G. Stanley Hall created a concept helping him to integrate his living: "We must find, or make and ascend a new outlook tower high enough to command the whole earth."[2] My vital need is to be able to use my mind in the unique way that must reveal itself to me as actually being my mental functioning, a production of insight rather than outlook. Albert Schweitzer described the efficacy of this psychic process of conscious self observation:

> The man who, with the help of epistemological idealism, has made his way through to the higher rationalism, is safe from losing his optimism, even though he goes through the cruellest experiences. . . . What is essential he knows: that what is real in the world is not matter, but spirit only.[3]

[2] *Life and Confessions of a Psychologist* (New York: D. Appleton & Co., 1923).
[3] *The Philosophy of Civilization,* trans. C. T. Campion (New York: Macmillan Co., 1950), p. 203.

My grave concern for all that I mean by *science*, or *politics*, or *economics* is the direct outgrowth of my heeding the enormous extent to which I see each vital interest controlled by one authority after another who never seems to be able to appreciate that his own mind contains all of the only meaning he has to work with. His single alternative is to treat each subject as if he can and must be "out of his mind" to do it. His method fully accounts for his disastrous results.

As Leonardo da Vinci remarked, I can have neither a greater nor a less dominion than that over my own being. My reality necessitates that in all of my experience I cannot go beyond the role of observing subject. Therefore, I begin my Psychology of Political Science by responsibly defining what I mean by each of its terms, starting with my psychology of science itself. My mind creates within itself *all* of its own observant character.

By "psychology" I mean: my study of my keenly sensible mind's existence itself. By "science" I mean: my emotional self-continent mind's self-activity systematically directed towards developing my potential manpower. My science of any subject includes study of its developmental history. *My greatest possible scientific contribution to human welfare is my responsibly locating all of my scientific living, itself, in my mind.* The highest reach of human science is the clear scientific recognition of the scientist's psychological world. Othcrwise the scientist must be defined as: one who knows more and more (of illusional externality) about less and less (of his own personal development). "Learned ignorance," the consciousness of his ever expanding room for his further self development, is the mind-conscious scientist's reward for "hanging on" to his scientific self, for feeling equal to his growing individuality.

Science may be clearly conceived as the systematic working of the principle of self revelation, the progress of this process varying directly with the scientist's spirited devotion to it. The lowest common denominator of everything that can exist in the name of his science must be the scientist's own irreducible being. Furthermore, I can measure the purely scientific nature of my science by the extent to which I am able to feel my own identity in it. For only to the degree that I can appreciate my own self identity can I ascribe unique individuality to anyone or thing of my world.

This holistic conception of scientific orientation is in accord with Aristotle's study of being (ontology, metaphysics):

> There is a science which investigates being as being and the attributes which belong to this in virtue of its own nature. Now this is not the same as any of the so-called special sciences; for none of these others treats universally of being as being. They cut off a part of being and investigate the attributes of this part.

My scientific approach to understanding, for any direction of my research, duly considers the complete subjectivity of every subject *thus featuring its essential individuality,* indicating my imagined external universe to be a great solipsistic unity quite as is my own directly experienced individuality.

As Ruskin recorded, "there is no wealth but life." My only discovery worthy of the name is of a growth of my mind. Sigmund Freud indicated scientific observation to be characterized specifically by its thoroughness. Only when any observation, including any sensation or emotion, is felt by me as self observation, can I describe it as thorough. I can be sure of my ground really if I can recognize it as mind, otherwise not. It is my scientific discipline which I can see as my inner working, which commits me to a kind peaceful search for the attainment of human well-being, to a careful and caring observance of every law that concerns the furtherance of life.

Every "system of scientific procedure" is an outgrowth of a "system of psychology," quite as every system of psychology is an outgrowth of life's "human system." An educator who appreciates the basic fact that his psychological orientation decides his educational orientation, finds it necessary to do some research upon the order of his mind. Regularly he discovers that he has obscured, almost to the vanishing point, these mind-strengthening feelingful truths: 1) all of his "facts of life" are nothing but evidence of the impassioned *fact of his life,* 2) all of his scientific data are nothing but his own heartfelt self data, 3) all of his research (learning) experience is nothing but his own ardent self-activity furthering his own self-development, 4) all of his refinement of himself as if a scientific instrument (means), has been at the expense of his fervent appreciation of himself as truly an *end,* 5) all that *can* reveal his life as worth living, is his realization that it *always* is helpful, 6) all that *can* support disesteem for his life is his (piling up) anaesthetic disregard for his experience, calling it "impersonal," 7) all of the health benefit of his scientific effort is safeguarded, if he steadily heeds it as augmenting his (ever increasing) enthusiastic estimate of his own worth, 8) all humanization of science (the counter-vailing force now needed to prevent scientific suicide) can derive only from the scientist's cultivating the reverent self insight enabling him to call his scientific soul his own, 9) all educational programs are decided ultimately by what the educator has been able to achieve of the insight: My magnificent mind-consciousness decides the limits of my educational perspectives, 10) all that *can* be of any importance to anyone is his life, hence the advantage of growing to be able to feel my world as my own *lovable* living.

Systematically observing myself as a fount of creative power, methodically studying my human being as a growing life which is everyday in the making, crediting myself with the realization that I have a truly creative mind which works scientific wonders for me,—all such getting to work of this special part of my mind, this highest helpfulness which I call "self-consciousness," is a lifesaving kind of accounting. My possession of my vitality is my one and only true possession, any other claim of property being my true illusion. Laboratory work, experimental project, scientific discovery,—each is wholesomely lived only as fully *appreciated* mental development of *my* scientific discipline.

All of my basic wisdom consists in my proper appreciation of my whole self, as being that power which alone can make anything possible for me. What makes my presence of mind is my momentary awareness for my self as of genuine solid worth, my regard for my self as a growing individual, a developing person, a treasure of my own production. What every scientific meaning is in terms of *my own mind's creating it*,—therein is its only truth (reality, scientific validity) to be found.

I find psychotherapy (the process of appreciated self-discovery essential for wholesome self-esteem) to be the specific antidote for scientific training (and for all other formal and informal education) based upon disregard for the inviolability of human individuality. Discovery of the vastness of my world must spell out for me my own seeming littleness, each of my scientific developments must dwarf my own recognition of my magnanimity, unless I develop the habit of mind of noticing that all of my life experience (including my scientific research) consists of my self-knowledge enhancing my appreciation for my own worth. May the day come when every American citizen can teach himself only such public schooling.

Although all that can be proved about any event is that it is in perfect accord with all of the forces bringing it about, nevertheless this sanifying appreciation for the power of truth is most difficultly cultivated and correspondingly a rare achievement. For example, a life-orientation based upon this realization (that nothing can happen unless all of the truth required for its happening is present) would be endowed with the virtue of observing the existence of nothing but perfection everywhere and all of the time. Walt Whitman sang,

> I say no man has ever yet been half devout enough,
> None has ever yet adored or worship'd half enough,
> None has begun to think how divine he himself is, and how
> certain the future is.

Of such realization is composed the most comprehensive conception of man's most highly prized understanding that he names reality, itself. It helps me to find fault in order to assert my will-to-live despite any experience of pain.

Hence it is though that I trace all of my life's woe to its single source in my faultfinding, the omnipresent alternative to undertaking the hard work of fact-finding that alone can reveal to me all is always exactly as it should be, including my present intention to see to it that additional truth will be able to modify it in a direction desired. This faultfinding has innumerable names. My parent calls it disobedience; my teacher calls it error or failure; my clergyman calls it wrongdoing; my attorney, crime; my politician, corruption; my bereaved, loss; my life-despairing, death; and so on.

J. H. van der Hoop observed that the most careful construction of thought-systems is found in the sciences, adding: "Only by recognizing the subjective aspect of all scientific methods is it possible to envisage the organic unity that exists in two kinds of psychology: the psychology of consciousness, and the natural science of psychology."[4] His so-called scientific discovery has steadily revealed the appearance of each scientist in a new light thrilling him mostly as unbounded admiration for his whole law-abiding world. Poincaré pointed out that a beclouding of his earth sufficient to obscure astronomical uniformities might have permanently beclouded man's mentality. Certainly my beclouding my mind with incomplete sensory experience (misreporting self as if it could be not-self) has been sufficient to hinder my developing scientific appreciation for my own full and whole self identity as a wonderful individual.

How excitingly new my life became for me, once I found the specific way to discover its true extent! I refer to my completing my already started (but discontinued as too difficult) teaching my self precisely how to use each of my senses so that I can find that it does report my own augmenting personal development of my manpower. Thus I have disciplined my mind to recognize that my sense of touch, hearing, sight, smell, taste, feeling or consciousness of any kind, reveals only my own living, for my own magnificent mind's conscious cultivation. It is this far-reaching scientific unification of my conscious self identity that fully restores the free functioning of my biologically adequate life-appreciation, a rare sanity

[4] *Conscious Orientation*, trans. Laura Hutton (New York: Harcourt, Brace and Co., 1939), p. 261.

indeed. Walter Bagehot conceived a sobering self observation, "Every trouble in life is a joke compared with madness."[5]

My *heeding* that my sensing, perceiving or observing is always an instance of my growing my self, enables me to look within me, whence all of my help cometh, for any knowledge I seek. This looking within rather than without distinguishes my idealistic from my materialistic self, my sciolistic from my scientific self. Such self insight (i.e., self consciousness) is my largest truth justifying cultivation of my science in its complete expression. Any fact of mine is impossible until it is generated as an individuation of my own individuality, the star of all of my stars. Ralph Waldo Emerson, scholar of scholars, divined "The Informing Spirit":

> There is no great and no small
> To the Soul that maketh all:
> And where it cometh, all things are;
> And it cometh everywhere.
>
> I am owner of the sphere,
> Of the seven stars and the solar year,
> Of Caesar's hand, and Plato's brain,
> Of Lord Christ's heart, and Shakespeare's strain.

My scientific exertion must rely upon the vital energy in my self development as its driving force, every discovery of my research work being the awesome issue of my consciously revealing my own mind creating its own conception. I feel my self conscious research also as deeply religious experience thus achieving precious conscious integration. To the solid ground of my own nature, only, can I trust any of my mental development from all of my research. It is my conscious manpower that "makes for righteousness" as I rightly assume responsibility for my own conscious and unconscious making of me. A valuable word now about the new significance of this report for my political living.

[5] *Bagehot's Historical Essays*, ed. Norman St. John-Stevas (New York: New York University Press, 1966), p. vii.

The lifesaving principle of conscious individualism is ignored at the cost of life. At this moment immeasurable difficulty in my world is directly traceable to disregard for the inexorable fact that whatever is named political, national, international, or racial can exist *only* in the mind of the individual naming such a meaning. Rightly every individual who witholds from himself consciousness for any of his individuality seeks proportionate redress from whatever living of his he names "external help."

I can and must expect or demand help (financial assistance or whatever) only from that government or society of mine that I cannot fully acknowledge is my creation of my own mind. Specifically, only as a white citizen unable to recognize that I live all that I name black can I know of my black's dire need without feeling pain or unhappiness; only as a black citizen unable to recognize that I live all that I name white can I believe my "white" to be responsible for my plight. Only as a black or white citizen rejecting enormous living of my own can I believe it possible to classify myself either as a black minority or white majority, blind for my personal identity in absolutely *all* living I experience.

Horace Kallen aptly described his freedom in the few words: "Freedom begins where economic necessity ends."[6] Whether impoverished or a millionaire I must live all of my experience whether I name it wealth or want. The lot of the wealthy one certainly looks easier but it cannot be healthful except to the extent that he can feel acutely his responsibility for his living of *his* needy fellowman so that he can intentionally will its relief. Otherwise he must immediately suffer the grievous health consequence of his self neglect, seldom enjoying the ability to trace his troubled living to its true source. I find that most of what I loosely call individual or social illness is of this derivation: disregard for the necessary fact that all living is, must be, individualistic living. Whatever I conclude is not-I is as much my true self as is whatever I have come

[6] *Individualism: An American Way of Life* (New York: Liveright, 1933), p. 200.

to believe is I. Furthermore, to make the most of myself consciously is my only way of learning how to take care of myself dutifully. In *Romola,* George Eliot stated this necessity that each one be his own salvation, here and now.

> We can only have the highest happiness, such as goes with being a great man, by having wide thoughts, and much feeling for the rest of the world as well as ourselves; and this sort of happiness often brings so much pain with it that we can only tell it from pain by being what we would choose before everything else, because our souls see it as good.

Self consciousness disciplines my mind, being the unique focal point for generating the systematic unity of its seemingly diverse rays of mentality. It is the oneness-principle with which I can master all of my experience. Whatever is, *individually* is. With this guiding enlightenment I have been able to look anew at all of my life's meaning, finding nothing old under my sun. Without it, I lose my most valuable sense of direction.

My precious satisfactions of original creativity and of boundless interest are directly traceable to their sources in my extending the lovable content of my mind by my hardy practice of conscious self observation. I firmly believe my fellowman entirely capable of enjoying this kind of inexhaustible wealth from his self cultivation, hindering himself from it only by the form of self education he experiences, namely, his *self unconscious education.* However even against such odds as I have made for my self by practicing "self unconscious education" I have been able to stay alive, as well as sense the biological inadequacy of so-called impersonal science.

The living force acting to produce a troubled mind is negation, the denial of right of certain mentation to be. Feelingful thought is always associated with negation, and originality begins to show its power not only in creating anew but also in the mind's unencumbering itself of its fettering limitations. My wisdom of most worth is how to manage my mental power most economically. This reality cannot be relegated to party politics; it is lifesaving originative necessity in each individual.

A. N. Whitehead noticed the possibility of a correct solution issuing from wrong premises:

> It is this possibility of being right, albeit with entirely wrong explanations as to what is being done, that so often makes external criticism—that is so far as it is meant to stop the pursuit of a method—singularly barren and futile in the progress of science.[7]

It is essential for clearly felt thinking on every subject of humanity to distinguish these two terms thoroughly: 1) *individuality* and 2) *conscious individuality.* They are not at all interchangeable. The former refers to all that can exist: whatever is, individually is. The truth that *it* is conceived mentally is ordinarily completely unobserved, to the accumulating disadvantage of the observer. The latter however is indeed a name for my self development ultimately enabling my acknowledging my self identity in my meaning for my every experience. *Whenever I am not acknowledgeably conscious I am unacknowledgeably unconscious.* Above all else for ordering my mind sanely I need to be able to realize that only my mind can account for all of my life's meaning. Meaning is solely a psychic construct, naming the basic unit of my mental activity.

The fact that this evident distinction of conscious and unconscious is seldom made, that hardly ever is this definition of consciousness used, deserves closest heed, for immeasurable mental trouble is traceable to it. *My idea of politics must remain unscientific to the extent that is is only unconsciously mine.*

For example, my mere reference to any of my political experience, without respect for the conscious aspect of it, introduces irresponsibility for its only reality as being entirely a mental event in my own self. Thus I can use my mind for coping with any of my world interest without realizing that it *is* all and only mine. My vocabulary of so-called impersonal words supports me in this unrecognized madness.

[7] *An Introduction to Mathematics* (New York: Henry Holt & Co., 1911).

Meanwhile I can warily resist considering my mind's inherent hold of evidence that all I can ever touch is my own sensible being, or can see in a test-tube is my own visual subjectivity, or can measure or count in any way is my mental activity.

Not until with the help of my consciousness I was able to work my own recognizable way to increasingly conscious self development was I able to discover the biological adequacy of using all of mind for the purpose of revealing my self as my only possible reality. Ever since then I have found thorough life satisfaction in using my wealth of power economically, understanding at last my Aristotle's definition of politics as minding my own business and extending this insight to define economics similarly as my socially responsible self-accounting.

My fellowman who may be unable thus far to live his altruism consciously as his grown-up egoism has no recourse other than to live that abiding truth of his human nature unconsciously. Largely unconscious conduct of my life constitutes my greatest health risk. *Without question, my unconscious living of my fellowman is my number one public health problem.* Only my costly ignorance of *its* existence can prevent me from devoting my self unfalteringly to its solution. My ignorance of this law of my human nature is the source of all of my mental trouble underlying all of my political, economic, or whatever social trouble.

A new and wonderfully efficacious method of self-help for every human being became potentially available ever since my Jean Martin Charcot (1825–1893) created his conception, *the organicity of the idea,* and my Sigmund Freud elaborated and systematized this lifesaving insight in his psychoanalytic research, psychology, and self-analysis. I record my, including my fellowman's, resistance to living this truth of truths, namely that *any* mental activity—whether an idea or feeling or whatever—is always significantly effective energy duly accounting for the intact organic integrity of human individuality. Whoever willingly creates this special mind-consciousness by himself enjoys his life's greatest pleasure: his sensing his greatening of his own manpower. Resistance to any form of altering my already established sensing of my own identity is traceable to my ever-present wish to preserve my life's *status quo.*

Hence even my idea of extending my conscious self-identity may be associated with fear. It requires real daring to be able to grow up mentally, to be able to cultivate conscious responsibility for being all of my self, beginning with my own parent and extending to include my every fellowman. But such *is* the greatness of my human being, and my greatness cannot be ignored without my developing signs and symptoms of my extreme self disregard.

Conscious self-education to consciousness for being all of my self is my definition of conscious American education. And this is an idea of such magnificent self-benefit that I thoroughly enjoy realizing fully its organic power. I know no limit to my (always including my fellowman's) capacity for developing insightful appreciation for my life's worth.

Whoso would deserve well of himself in the care of his life will guard lovingly the purity of his appreciation for the organic force of any thought, notion or vagary he may experience. It *is* his living; it is a vital element of his organic constitution, as is his so-called bone or muscle. It helps to unify his living into a whole quite as does his conscious act of self-preservation or unconscious metabolism.

I turn to my so-called physical sciences to observe how my lunar capsule or computer was constructed by so-called thousands of disinterested impersonal scientists, heed how my so-called thousands of dispassionate legislators in or out of committee created millions of good laws, consult my so-called government's millions of employees despite deficit financing, read occasional and seemingly hurried accounts about so-called individualists, personalists, freethinkers, solipsists or some other classification of the unclassifiable,—and I do not wonder that my mostly self-unconscious fellowman will have "no truck with such a hare-brained scheme" for survival and wish-to-live as *the practice of self consciousness.* However, my only alternative to self conscious work for building or producing anything by human effort is my practice of self unconsciousness. Whether I live my fellow laborer consciously as my own living of all that he can mean to me, or unconsciously as not my own living of all that he can mean to me, decides respectively whether I enjoy the enlivening benefit of conscious self devotion or suffer the sickening consequence of unconscious self sacrifice.

I know full well that *all* that (my) fellowman ever *thinks of* as being "outside of him" can be nothing but his very own lifesaving thinking that he cannot even credit himself with. I fully know it and I fully approve it as his very best presently available way of staying alive. I want no faultfinding to blind me for the necessity: whatever is, truly is.

Necessity is a name for *whatever is.* Complete organic unity of my individuality necessitates self-relationship only. I must be my own whatever-I-name-other. My every so-called materialistic-machine conception *is* demonstrably my subjective-dynamic psychic process only.

I want *my* fellowman to be able to think in every possible way. I also want him to be able to add to his thinking as well as to his way of thinking whenever he finds it possible to do so.

Whenever I use the diremptive power of my mind to segregate some of my mental content so that I can focus my attention upon it, I tend then to indulge the illusion that such a division can actually exist autonomously in my nature.

This kind of apparent separating of my mentality has its most consequential significance in my developing and practicing my illusion that a divided element can function by itself without the need for my organic wholeness to originate all of that functioning. Thus I can actually proceed to live my mind as if one part of it can be opposed to another, be in conflict with another (see *Psychology of Emotion*). Illustrations are innumerable, involving any so-called opposites such as pleasure and unpleasure, love and hate, or consciousness and unconsciousness.

To this source of my making mental trouble for my self may be traced my notion that my scientific creation must be either qualitatively or quantitatively superior or inferior to my artistic creation, or pure science to pure philosophy, or pleasure in scientific discovery to pleasure in creating a poem, or undirected joy of living to joy of a life of research, or youthful carefree gratification in spontaneity to adult caring satisfaction in self-insight.

I trouble my mind with whatever feeling or thought I have not been able to claim as my psychic functioning that is subject to my will power. Thus I may let a thought or feeling "come over me," appear to "take me over," without realizing that I am allowing it to happen as if it is beyond my responsibility or control. I can resolve any such problem only by modifying my mentality itself rather than by using my mind, as it is, for the solution.

For example, my painful meaning for all that I name "my enemy" as being a merely hateful person must remain an insurmountable hurdle just as long as I am unable to include all that I mean by my "hateful enemy" as constituting helpfully functioning pain in my lovable self. It is only power of mine that I can recognize as mine that makes up my self consciousness, voluntary emotional control and acknowledgeable mentality. My "hateful enemy" is solely: inhibited lovable living of mine.

The basic advance in scientific thinking is not merely the result of the scientist's additional observation of his subject but rather a new ordering of his mentality itself. The latter *altering of his way of using his mind* is of a most specific nature, namely the scientist's fully realizing through his self consciousness that his research finding is the creation issuing from the growth of his own mental process. This ideal research method develops when it occurs to the scientist that his freely functioning imagination grows in the direction of the devotion of his interest.

Each access of my self consciousness involves a gain in my voluntary emotional control; and with every increase of my conscious emotional control I open up new reaches and realms of consciously constructive thought. In other words, every increase of my self identity that I can sense as mine provides me with the enlivening experience of being able to put on a new thinking cap.

However, it is insightless of me to expect my reader to be able to extend the range of his conscious self identity by reading all about the desirability of that extension. It is only the conscious work of an individual's mind that can prepare him for an extension of that work. It is only my devotion to conscious work of cultivating my mental potentiality, itself, that can further my consciously growing my mentation in that direction of my devotion.

Cicero recorded that the very foundation of the whole commonwealth is the proper bringing up of the young. I can diligently teach my self all about the subject of political science or civics without developing my mind in the direction of accruing conscious self sovereignty. Furthermore what passes for either my public or private schooling regularly enhances the importance of so-called subjects of study at the direct expense of my appreciating all of my living as being entirely the vitalistic subject of my own sovereign self. *All of my education unrecognizable as conscious self education imposes arbitrary limits to my achieving biologically adequate appreciation for my life itself, disciplining me for mental slavery, not freedom.*

For nearly forty years now I have studied my mind *consciously* for the express purpose of being able to recognize it as being my own. I thus began to renounce kindly my previous method of studying my mind, namely, with little or no appreciation for the truth that there could be nothing else possible for me to study. Gradually I became strong minded enough to acknowledge 1) that my first method of study was gratefully comforting from the standpoint that it appeared to absolve me from too heavy responsibility for being my self, and 2) that my second method of study is apt to be distressing from the standpoint of its fixing upon me heavy responsibility for being my self.

To illustrate, by not acknowledging all that I can mean by political science as consisting entirely of my own mentality I can appear to rid my self of overwhelming feeling of responsibility for its being all and only about me and, thereby, find helpful vent for my discontent by accusing my government official of economic irresponsibility or whatever ineptitude.

In 1901 my beloved mentor, Sigmund Freud, pointed out the need for the increasing understanding of all that passes for memory.[8] *All of my living is always now-living.* Hence all that I can mean by "past" (or by "future" for that matter) *must* concern my *present* living only. I am right now all that I can mean by whatever occurrence I name past or future.

I find now *all* that I mean by memory I use with the intent of displacing my present responsibility for some of my now-living upon my so-called past. It is pure illusion, quite as my projecting any of my responsibility for my sensation or perception upon my so-called externality or otherness is illusion. Each device serves the purpose of my relieving my already overburdened but acknowledgeable mind of further conscious responsibility. My feeling of responsibility for being all of my self *now* is the specific emotion absolutely indispensable for my being able to integrate the lifesaving psychic unity I recognize as my personal identity.

I must live my self-experience with responsibility, either consciously or unconsciously. My unconscious responsibility I feel consciously too, but only in its form I name guilt or self-accusation. When I cannot live my guilt consciously it assumes the form of blaming my disowned self such as my fellowman. As a young child incapable of supporting much responsibility in my conscious self-identity I can attack my toy or any inanimate object in revenge for its hurting me.

Just as I had to live most of my childhood self-experience irresponsibly, thus accumulating feeling of guilt and blame, so limitedly must I continue to use my mind precisely to the extent that I have not undertaken the difficult mental discipline of acknowledging and cherishing all of its activity consciously as my immediate own. The language I have taught myself plays into this purpose of hiding (dissociating) anything resembling my magnificently whole mind from my all-too-

[8] *The Psychopathology of Everday Life, The Standard Edition of the Complete Psychological Works of Sigmund Freud*, trans. John Strachey in collaboration with Anna Freud, vol. VI (London: Hogarth Press, 1953), p. 134.

meager mentality that I can consciously claim to be all mine right now (see *Psychology of Language*). Franz Alexander noted one's "desperate need for self-justification is an irrefutable proof that man is not only asocial but that he is also at the same time a socially minded being."[9]

"I remember" implies my living my past now so that the *presence* of the so-called remembered, as such, thereby must be negated. Why I "recall" any specific event rather than another, is fully explained only by my present need. Invariably such seeming displacement of present to so-called past, is traceable to my intention to soften the meaning of the "past" mental posture for the particular purpose of applying it to my present living. Thus instead of directly stating my present strong disapproval for my companion's behavior, my words can seem to dispose of the whole matter of my dissatisfaction by my relating a temper-tantrum of my childhood.

Like every other discovery of the nature of my mind, so with this one about memory—i.e., past is only of the same actuality as anticipation (future), namely, the substance of my *present* mind—once I became able to see it clearly, then it seemed as if it always had been an understanding of mine. In fact, my notion that so-called re-call could truly enable me to live "in the past" seemed hardly creditable at all except for my addiction to it. Memory is not warmed-up death, it is present vitality. Much difficulty in "establishing priority" for a discovery is traceable to this actual timelessness of psychic reality. "I know histhry isn't thrue, Hinnessy, because it ain't like what I see ivry day in Halsted Sthreet . . . histhry is a post-mortem examination. It tells ye what a counthry died iv. But I'd like to know what it lived iv."[10]

In speaking with my fellowman I find it helpful to heed how I can use my (illusional) memory to make statements that would seem obviously offensive were they not disguised

[9] "Psychology And The Interpretation Of Historical Events," *The Cultural Approach To History*, ed. Caroline F. Ware (New York: Columbia University Press, 1940), p. 56.
[10] Finley Peter Dunne, *Observations By Mr. Dooley* (New York: R. H. Russell, 1902), p. 271.

as if impersonal recollections. If I feel my conversationalist as difficult I seem to *recall* difficult life-experience; if he seems troublesome my "*memory*" serves me by my *reminiscing* on hard times; if he is grief-stricken I seem to *remember* (rather than immediately live) unhappy incidents.

From my self-analysis while speaking my mind as freely as possible I discovered some of the enormous extent to which I could employ my illusion I call memory, for instance, to escape conscious responsibility for living 1) my utterly now while indulging temper-tantrum feeling towards my fellowman, including *my* government official, 2) my all of my transference emotion in terms of my specific psychoanalyst and 3) my saving my face by allowing my linguistic habit of using words in which I could not recognize my self at all to front for my conscious intention to consider my self observantly.

Gradually I have taught my self to be able to use my illusion that I am remembering, instead of always living my self *anew*, to discover past areas of my mentality that I am now treating with varying degrees of dangerous irresponsibility. I refer now specifically to what I have named Psychology, Science, Politics and Economy, even endowing each such complex of my own mind's meaning with imaginary power, and that power supposedly extendable over my whole world! I, including my every fellow scientist, am guilty of (not responsible for) innumerable verbal efforts to belittle the immeasurable, unquantifiable, indefinable mind of the scientist in order to exalt his illusional world. On account of its extreme consequence in making human life seem cheaply expendable I shall list illustrations of this effort to make the creation of man seem greater than the man. In each instance of using my mind to deny the existence of my mind, I am helpfully using my imagination to posit the reality of a world that is not a construction of my imagination but rather of its own make-up apart from me:

We live in a world vastly improved by science. All of my world's meaning lives only in me. Science can have no function except in the mind of the scientist.

In 1945 my atomic bomb changed the scale of man's inhumanity to man. My 1945 is only in me, as is all that

I can mean by my atomic bomb. Living my self consciously I can be human to my self. Living my self unconsciously enables my inhumanity to my self.

I define science as the organization of our knowledge so that it can control more hidden forces in nature. My science consists of my self-knowledge only, helping me to manage the only nature I can ever know anything about, my own nature.

The scientific revolution began in the sixteenth century. No scientific revolution ever did or ever can exist except in the mind of the individual living whatever he (she) means by the words, and then not in the sixteenth century but rather exactly when he (she) lives that meaning.

Science as it is finds marvelous order and meaning in our experience. Science as it is consists of nothing but meaning labelled science in the mind of the individual labelling it. Science finds nothing; only the given scientist can find anything, and that only in his very own experience. "Our" also exists only and entirely as a meaning in a single person's mind. Scientific libraries, laboratories, leads, and lasts can further no scientific research whatsoever except in and by the mind of each worker.

The Sonnets of Shakespeare belong to this world. Nothing can belong to anyone or anything but one's self or its self. "This world" has *all* of its possible meaning in the mind of any one person using it.

The works of art and the discoveries of science are one. There can be no work of art or discovery of science. Only one individual mind can work or discover itself merely.

The sanction of truth is the sanction of fact. All that can be known by sanction, or truth, or fact is known only by the one person knowing it in his own mind.

Many schools of psychology are suspicious of solipsism. A school of philosophy has all of its existence only in the mind of the one creating whatever he means by it. Only a mind can use its meaning. A school of philosophy is not a whole mind but rather a complex of meaning in the mind conceiving it.

Four hundred years in the field of science have taught us

something of how the mind works. Time is a useful illusion of a given mind. Only the learner can teach himself (herself) anything about mind, and that mind must be his (her) own.

Society, classless or not, holds together by the respect honored between its members. Society is nothing but an abstraction in the mind of the individual using the term. "Between" is nowhere. Innumerable are such abstractions being used irresponsibly by me (including my every fellowman): "the Internal Revenue Service," "the State," "the Government," "the Underworld," "the City Hall," "Congress," "the White House," "the Supreme Court," "the social question,"—even such an impossible as "the individualist schools" or "the fellowship of scientists."

We ought to be able to rely on other people, to trust their word. All reliance is self-reliance; all trust is self-trust; all help is self-help. Whatever *is*, ought to be. What "ought" to be cannot usurp the right to be of whatever is. Whatever is, truly is, individually is, necessarily is.

My discovering the singular oneness underlying apparent duality in opposites (e.g., love-hate, conscious-unconscious, reality-unreality, right-wrong, and so on) clarified many a paradox for me, such as "one out of many." Merely by recognizing plurality as opposed to singularity I can see that my conscious individuality upholds the illusion of manyness. My early psychogenesis involved my constantly indulging my illusion of manyness for I had not then evolved any conception of my individual self identity. Even after I did begin to conceive my self as an individual I also continued to judge most of my living as not mine, thereby requiring my illusion more-than-one (or less-than-one).

My only way of conceiving either more or less than one is by seeming to be able to make more or less than one out of my own (individual) living. Then, therefore, I must seem to my self to be subject to *alien* control, to need it and seek it just to the extent that I cannot consciously recognize my own living as being entirely my own and therefore only subjectively controllable by me. The profound political implication of self consciousness for complete American citizenship thus becomes clear: *I can make my mind ready for conscious self sovereignty only to the extent that I can discover how to discipline it with self consciousness.*

The only motive possible to an individual is one that he generates in his own living. As well demand that an infant stop crying for his milk so that his mother can sleep, as expect philanthropy from an individual who has not thus far been able to identify it with his self interest. Willingly cultivated self interest is the only safe and sensible foundation of all of my interest, for it only consists of my own living, although it even be named so that I cannot recognize my self in it (Father, Mother, Sister, Brother, Neighbor, God, Another, Society, Government, Political Economy, Law, and so on).

Nowhere is disregard for the necessary allness of my individuality more grievously consequential than in my orientation to whatever I may mean by government, for right here rises the issue of my personal responsibility for my societal living. Furthermore my concern for the necessary inviolability of *my* self sovereignty must include the same concern for the allness, wholeness and self identity of *my* every fellow creature. I cannot satisfy my self very much with the notion that right now my fellowman may feel incapable of assuming his self sovereignty and therefore it is safe for me also to ignore his unpreparedness. Quite the contrary. *I cannot misprize my fellowman's greatness on account of the fact that he seems to do so, except at the cost of misprizing that much of my own greatness.*

Augmenting disregard for my own wonderful being is fatal, for *I can only take due care of my marvelous self exactly to the extent that I can feel my whole life to be worth living.* This truth is the essential foundation for whatever self discipline I may refer to as *political science.* Hence this book, in which I record how I work my mind to help my self facilitate conscious love of life. There can be nothing for me to be unwilling to consider lovingly ("resist") except my self consciousness.

As my most developed form of sensibility, my self consciousness merits my most careful (wisely loving) cultivation. I am certain of this fact. Therefore I willingly speak and write about the importance to me of my cherishing my life appreciation in my conscious individuality, thus: My way of life depends upon my discovering my life's real nature. I find that nature well described as self sensible, self lovable, self desirable. Therefore my idea of successful living consists of finding just how to make self love purposefully, out of any and all of my living, difficult and easy alike.

Without noticing it my life depreciation can occur as a result of my mind's power of denial. The first and simplest form of my conscious life negation occurs as my otherness (unconscious life), namely, my own mental activity that seems different from my avowable self.[11] Negation derives all of its entity of not-being from the life affirmation of which it is the negate. All of my existence *positively* exists. Therefore, to deny that some of my existence is mine necessarily involves me directly in asserting not only that there is existence other than my own but also that I can attest this assertion by means of my own experience, an obvious impossible. The factuality of the matter is merely this: my assertion that I am pure white, is one way in which I can use my mind; my assertion that I am not white at all, is also a way in which I can use my same mind. Each assertion is entirely about itself only and each consists merely of the same nature, namely, my living it in my mind's creating it. My objection to the right-to-be of either assertion is just the same as my objection to the right-to-be of that much of my own existence. Goethe identified his devil as the spirit of denial, the opposite of the spirit of truth. "Opposite" always means merely my unreadiness to recognize sameness, e.g., hate is hurt love (see my *Psychology of Emotion*).

Once I can see clearly that all of my mental activity is the life of my mind creating its own content, then I shall be able to recognize that content's right to be as such, namely, mental life of mine. Then only can I be able to understand

[11] See *Existence and Inquiry*, Otis Lee (Chicago: University of Chicago Press, 1949), p. 109.

that my negating my mental content cannot mean my ridding my mind of that specific living of itself. However, as long as I merely assume that, instead of consisting only and all of my mind's productivity, my declared world orientation can somehow consist of anything external to it, then with complete disregard for that life worth I can continue to indulge my illusion of affirming or denying the right to exist of my every so-called impersonal meaning such as Politics, Education, Religion, Physics, or Whatever.

PERSPECTIVE

> One of the most urgent tasks for human welfare—I recommend it to the Ford Foundation—is the development of a view of man which reconciles scientific method and the creative imagination.
>
> Lancelot Law Whyte, ("A Scientific View of the Creative Energy of Man")

Before going on with my describing the obvious source of the economic distress overburdening my American citizen living his land of plenty, I wish to make a matter of conspicuous record my certain expectation that my exposition, if at all considered somewhat soberly by *my* economic expert, will not be considered creatively by him (that is, as being authored by him). Rather, I fully expect my individuality-oriented account of political economy to be considered lightly, even with levity, if at all, by my political economist, each one, whose appreciation for the allness of his own individuality has largely gone underground (unconscious) where it functions in its negative form of collectivity (statism, nationalism, or some other disguised and disowned selfism). Archibald MacLeish, life-oriented patriot, writes:

> Mihajlov, Yugoslav writer, watching the human disintegration in the East—"the desperate longing to leave the solitary cell of one's own soul" and run with the totalitarian herd—asks whether there are forces in the West capable of resisting this massive modern sickness. If there are, he says, he cannot make them out from the far shore of the Adriatic. . . . The opposite of the longing to lose one's self in a totalitarian herd or in a deterministic theory or in a vast despair is, of course, the stubborn belief in man. And little is said about that belief in Washington these days or in the universities or in the advanced reviews.[1]

[1]Guest editorial, *Saturday Review* (November 13, 1971), p. 40.

Briefly, I find the one infallible criterion of the excellence of any expert's political science in the detail with which it observes each individual citizen's biological necessity to consider his own best interests in all of his political activity, most importantly in the laws codifying his system of political *economy*. Only to the extent that he can acknowledge the wholeness and allness of his self, thereby actually feeling *his* fellowman as his own being of his fellowman, can he avoid extravagance, waste, or any other depreciation of the true worth of his money. Whoever is inclined necessarily, by virtue of his limited appreciation for the truth that he *is* all that he names and means by *his* fellowman, to spend his money unwisely, must pay the consequence in terms of oppression of his health, no less.

This demonstrable fact (already stated and deserving further statement) that I impair my health by ignoring *my* fellowman's good is rarely realized of course, so that I then have no choice other than to go on hurting my self, with or without awareness, by refusing to recognize *my* needy fellowman as my own self experience. While I suffer the inevitable health consequence of such deficiency of coverage of self consciousness in innumerable forms and signs of life discontent, *my* fellowman goes on suffering his own variety of unrelieved deprivation including hidden hunger for biological adequate nourishment. "Love thy neighbor as thyself," is a safe economic principle only insofar as one's own conscious self love subsumes *all* of his living, e.g., *his* own fellowman living. The diffusion of wealth essential for the good of individual man (for man is, first and last, individual) must safeguard a basis upon which his life interest also rests: the welfare of *his* very own individual fellowman.

In *The Wealth of Nations*, self conscious Adam Smith clearly recorded his hard-earned conviction that self-love, individual self appreciation, is the only safe and sane governing principle for his living of his fellowman,—societally, governmentally, economically, or however. However, through this same power of self love I can resist my letting my self be influenced by the way my fellowman is conducting his self love, and thus avoid suffering the feeling that I am losing any of my freedom, independence, or self reliance. Such feeling of conscious self sufficiency is indispensable for my enjoying the truth of my inviolable wholeness. All influence must be self influence, but not necessarily *conscious* self influence, and that distinction explains as it explicates all of my illusional alien influence, such as suggestibility.

In his "Ethics of Belief" mathematician William Kingdon Clifford states of belief:

> It is the sense of power attached to a sense of knowledge that makes men desirous of believing, and afraid of doubting. . . . The sense of power is the highest and best of pleasures when the belief on which it is founded is a true belief, and has been fairly earned by investigation . . . no belief is real unless it guides our actions, and those very actions supply a test of its truth. . . . It is hardly in human nature that a man should quite accurately gauge the limits of his own insight. . . . We must rest in our experience and not go beyond it at all.[2]

My majority rule is necessarily always most meaningful for me despite even my most strongly dissenting vote, since by definition it provides the only device for respecting individuality the most. Therefore it behooves me to examine carefully my democratic principle in my so-called majority conception with particular concern for the nature of *this* role of each individual's self-sovereignty in it.

In the first place every citizen of every government can be capable only of self-sovereignty for he alone lives (creates) all that he can ever mean by his government, whether democratic, communistic, despotic, or whatever. Since this truth may be most easily disregarded it is well to make it conspicuous.[3]

It is customary to attribute the governmental power of self-sovereignty only to the individual who pledges his allegiance

[2] *Contemporary Review*, Jan. 1877.

[3] See Leonard E. Read's *Government—An Ideal Concept* (Irvington-on-Hudson, New York: The Foundation for Economic Education, Inc., 1954.)

to some form of democracy providing him a voice and vote in his political affairs. However, every citizen or subject of the most tyrannical government is also the sole creator of whatever tyranny he alone experiences. Man *is* a political individual by nature capable of developing all that he can possibly mean by his social, civil, political, or governmental experience.

What then is the specific advantage in my democratic government? Is it inherent in the fact that my Constitution specifically records the ubiquitous truth of self sovereignty? Is it that the all-important truth of my inviolable individuality is revered by my Bill of Rights? Is it that my democracy favors the possibility that I may become conscious for the necessity that all my sovereignty naturally must be self-sovereignty? Is it that inherent in my democratic form of government, although scarcely at all activated, is the law of my nature enabling me to find out for my self my lifesaving truth precisely by disciplining my mind with free acknowledgement that it is *all* mine. This hardy discipline (e.g., my freely acknowledging that I am my dislikes as well as my likes) specifically enables me to augment my conscious self identity sufficiently to recognize that *my* government exists in, of and for individual me.

It does appear that my consciousness for my self sovereignty is the uniquely vital principal of my American Government. However, whether or not I ever grow that realization and how much I may be able to cultivate it are entirely my own responsibilities. That is, as a natural born citizen my becoming a voter depends largely upon my coming of age, not at all upon my understanding the tremendous biological importance in my difficultly cultivating consciousness for my personal identity until it evidently includes my government along with my fellowman and whatever else enters into my life experience. *E Pluribus Unum.*

In his highly interesting book, *Benjamin Franklin of Paris 1776–1785*, Willis Steell describes how in 1779 the United States Congress voted the presentation of a sword to Lafayette, and Franklin had engraved on its elegantly designed arm the words,

E Pluribus Unum, thinking it to be the first time this phrase was applied to designate the thirteen original states.[4] It may have been its first *public* application. However, the French statesman and financier, Turgot (Baron de L'Aulne) reminded Franklin that he, Turgot, had shown him this nice description, and also had found *E Pluribus Unum* in Virgil's little poem, "Moretum."

An ominous oversight in my American Constitution is its omission of declaring the peril to my life associated with my not obligating my self to work up, however difficultly, my conscious appreciation for being an absolute individual capable of self sovereignty only. Right here, I assert that *every* citizen able to vote is capable of working up this *natural* conception of self appreciation. I speak accurately of government-by-consent precisely as far as I am able to speak for my whole self, rather than merely for any limited amount of my self that I can freely claim responsibility for being. *My amount of self freedom varies directly with the amount of my self I can consciously claim!*

To the extent that I cannot consciously claim that I am *my* every fellowman my democracy takes on the resemblance of a mobocracy. Majority vote escapes the paradox of seeming cruelly despotic only to the extent that each voter succeeds in seeing his own personal identity in all of his living of his fellow citizen.

Certainly a greatly self conscious monarch may be willing and able to observe the rights of his own individual subject in whom he feels his own personal identity, whereas a limitedly self conscious but official representative of his democratic electorate may be unwilling and unable to observe that same humaneness in his political living.

The natural consideration rises: Why keep trying to make Democracy work, why not let thinly disguised governmental compulsion continue to wax as conscious self control wanes, especially since conscious self-sovereignty is most difficult of governmental attainment in either a citizen or a subject?

[4]New York: Minton, Balch and Co., 1918, p. 82.

Why indeed, since my limited self conscious sovereignty already leads to the innumerable shortcomings of bureaucracy seeming successfully tolerated right now in my living of my American Government; since the practicality of my self discipline for enlarging my self consciousness, the prerogative of every citizen, is only most rarely recognized; since the outlook is most unpromising for any voluntary undergoing of such hardy discipline by my fellow citizen who already feels that he is enjoying the benefit of living "in a free society," rather than that all he calls society or anything else can live only in him? Such earnest inquiry deserves thorough study.

Weighty as such protest undoubtedly is, it overlooks entirely the all-important fact that *my human constitution itself cannot tolerate such self deception as alien control without manifesting grievous signs and symptoms that the truth of my nature is being ignored, disregarded, rejected and otherwise oppressed by me.* All that I name "governmental" is wholly and solely my own living of me, requiring the same kind and degree of biologically adequate living that every other functioning of my economy requires, e.g., my digestion, the circulation of my blood, or the activity of my respiration. I can no more neglect the truth of my absolute self control with impunity than I can safely ignore the nature and needs of any of my physiological living.

In other words, my obligation to develop my full self control, in the only way possible, by arduously enlarging my appreciation for the true extent of my individuality, is not merely an impersonal civic responsibility of mine by any means. *Rather, this constant growing of my conscious self identity is my most basic health concern, the only source of my sanity and the requirement of my biologically adequate hygiene.* Hence it is I prudently grow my mental strength to recognize that my government, whatever the kind, is nothing but my own creation of it. Thereby I can conceive the true worth in my fellow citizen's heedfully creating his own government also.

Thus I find my self having to make my peace with whatever degree of conscious self identity I have been able to work up thus far, for it is only upon this foundation that I can proceed to evolve further living of mine needing to be appreciated as mine. Certainly I can consciously control only my living that I can freely acknowledge is mine, and that realization is helpful motivation for my taking the trouble to see only my own self identity in experience I associate with dislike of one kind or another, e.g., collectivist statism, galloping government ownership and enterprise, bureaucratic and socialist regimentation, unendingly increasing public debt,[5] irresponsible federal economy, invisible governmental activity, administrative agency decision diluting majority rule, constantly threatening national emergency justifying skyrocketing taxation, ever stupendous increase of national population depending for livelihood upon the world's greatest payroll (local, state and national government), price control, governmental indecision, political medicine, centralization of civic authority, on and on. Winston Churchill felt the need to limit the growth of his governmental population: "We must beware of trying to build a society in which nobody counts for anything except the politician or the official—a society where enterprise gains no reward and thrift no privileges."

The stubborn fact is that, except in the form of an individual's illusion, there cannot even be such a possibility as "bureaucratic" bungling, ineptitude, waste, ignorance, gluttony or whatever. *The saving truth is that all human competence or incompetence can be found only in individual human being. Therefore it is not difficult to be able to imagine the consequent difficulty when concrete human individuality is lost sight of in the name of any abstract collectivism which cannot exist except in the mind of the individual creating this abstraction!*

I and I alone am all of my collectivism. In all of my own personal psychogenesis I lived and depended upon a collectivist form of my self control too. In fact my conscious self-sovereignty is an outgrowth of it based firmly upon ever earlier

[5]The amount of health trouble I can sustain without ending my life also may be conceived as a kind of measure of the power of my resourcefulness.

forms of my unconscious self control. Furthermore being an American citizen I can legitimately claim all of *my* bureaucratic living as being entirely my own. This privilege is a tremendous advantage, for by feeling all of my governmental regulation as being my own living of it I not only spare my self dangerous hurt from attacking my self without feeling it but also I enjoy honoring my governmental activity 1) for being as helpful as it is and 2) for providing me with a base for my further working towards its biologically adequate development.

Ever since growing self consciousness for the truth of self consciousness I have considered this life orientation to be the most complete act of my mind. My living *I* cannot even exist except to the extent that I am uniquely endowed with sensibility for my one-being. What Plato calls *misologia*, hatred of reason, may well be understandable as motivation resisting the usurpation of authority for being one's self by that very self's reasoning power. My aspiration after my full feeling of being my conscious self enables me to appreciate as much as possible the unity I actually am. All that Plato calls the higher self and lower self is thus born of the same living individuality. Organic wholeness is the law of human growth. My consciousness is my unifying attribute ultimately empowering my capacity for feeling my divinity in my humanity. My Emerson words his soul beautifully, defining revelation: "the announcements of the soul, its manifestation of its own nature."

My *consciously* living in my present existence, acknowledging my every innovating self activity as my own creation, instead of consciously reserving my feeling of self identity merely for my illusional sense of pastness, is my most effective way to realize such an ideal as "gaining my soul by losing it." My illusion of selflessness must derive entirely from my not acknowledging my self's identity in my *present* living, including any illusional "pastness" I may be presently activating. However my expanding-but-also-intensifying way of life requires unfailing devotion to my ever present living itself as the source of my conscious individuality, rather than to any "recalled" accumulation of my historical "facts of living."

I can never either "remember" or "forget" my self, for all that can ever be possible is my *being* only my self now. Nevertheless, my *illusion* past or future, quite as of "somewhere else," is essential for my being able to keep my *presence of mind* whenever my mental activity becomes too exciting in one way or another for me to be able to feel that I can consciously control it. Merely by attributing whatever emotionality I am feeling to "sometime else" or "some place else" I can "save my face" (assume a consciously controllable self identity). My ability to mobilize whatever conscious sense of self identity I possibly can is of lifesaving importance. Without it I cannot mobilize my caring whether I live or die.

My Norbert Wiener has aptly described his psychology to be "like a tapeworm that keeps losing its segments to physiology," and well it may be, in that all I can accomplish as a physiologist is clarification of the functioning of the body nucleus of my mind. I might prefer to see my psychology as a tapeworm that keeps *finding* its segments (individuations) in physiology. Certainly my every term signifying nomenclature of my physiology exists only as meaning of my mind. Further, by rescuing all of my body meaning that I may be habitually designating as non-mental material and restoring it to its rightful conscious reality as integral psychic functioning, I can at once honor all of my physiology as being fundamental mental functioning of mine. My physiology, as such, cannot create for me my conscious self realization. I find it helpful to use my imagination to conceive non-mental reality external to my own being, but I also am quick to make my self conscious for the fact that any and all such imagining is none the less integral being of my being.

Only by incessantly revering my mind's inviolably intact wholeness can I remain consciously true to the oneness, allness and wholeness of my life itself. I feel strongly my Leonard W. Levy's declaration: "The finest moments of American liberty occurred when men defied popular prejudices and defended right and justice at the risk of destroying their own careers."[6]

Professor Howison thus described the individual dignity of Alcott and Emerson in greeting each other:

> I was fairly taken off my feet to see the cold reserve with which they approached each other and passed their greetings as one sovereign might to another, with no warmth in their manner whatever. Mr. Emerson rather enjoyed this all through his being, I think.[7]

In his Personal Idealism, Howison nobly recorded wisdom most needed in my to-day's world:

> . . . the actual history of philosophic thought, even after philosophy attains to the view that rational consciousness is the First Principle, exhibits a singular arrest of the movement toward putting complete personality at the center of things. Historic idealism is, in fact, far from being personal; rather, it is well-nigh overwhelmingly impersonal.[8]

My experience has demonstrated that nearly always I select my literature of every kind with the wish that it may add valuable knowledge merely to the *status quo* of my conscious self image, thus reinforcing my currently firm conviction that my already worked-up conscious self identity alone is quite sufficient for my life's purposes. Thus, if a brief scanning of sample pages proves to be a pleasing result I may then safely assume that my further reading will not prove disturbing to my dearly cherished and comforting illusion that my presently conscious self identity adequately resembles the truth of my whole being. Furthermore, my *conscious* self observation is my only accurate reflection or meditation.

Why must I guard so zealously merely what ever extent

[6] *Jefferson and Civil Liberties. The Darker Side* (Cambridge, Mass.: The Belknap Press of Harvard University Press, 1963), p. 160.
[7] See, *George Holmes Howison, Philosopher and Teacher,* by John Wright Buckham and George Malcolm Stratton (Berkeley: University of California Press, 1934), p. 64.
[8] Ibid., p. 125.

of my self identity I can now acknowledge as mine, regardless of whether or not it approximates the vitally necessary truth of the native spontaneity of my whole self? Why must my *conscious* self development be as difficult as it is rare?

First of all, my feeling of my wholeness is my *only* feeling that I can sense in any and every extent of my acknowledgeable being, so that it is only natural that I do prize it in my every element as a quantity of me made up entirely of my wholeness. Analogously, I cherish as my life every area of the body nucleus of my mind, for each one (finger, toe, organ, etc.) is an individuation of my sensed individuality. Sense is the substance of all that I consciously mean to my self. My Tracy also builds his psychology upon his sensory living.

Furthermore, in my acknowledgeable self identity, however restricted, is resident my only already established executive interest in my being an organic political individual who must heed the nature of my constitution in order to stay alive. Not by finding fault with my politician but by minding my own business, i.e., attending to my growing of my mentality, can I serve my self most helpfully. My health (ideal wealth) lies in my conscious self love derivable from my observable use of my own functioning. I, including my every I, can use what is in me to grow further love or wisdom of me. Consciousness for that truth makes daily bread of my otherwise rare fare of self esteem essential for life appreciation. To become hardy I must discipline my self to bear disappointment cheerfully, thus recovering from it speedily. This purification of my mind with responsible consciousness is the source of any political sagacity I may claim.

Emerson said it best, "In self-trust all the virtues are comprehended. Free should the scholar be—free and brave." *Complete adulthood means my measuring my full living in no hours but those of self consciousness.* I find that I cannot realize my ideal except by idealizing the real allness of my mentality. I *am* whatever I live. Every law of my life is generated from the elements of my nature.

My source of conscious self preservation is *whatever* extent of my wholeness I can already claim as being my own. Therefore

I feel I must preserve my *conscious status quo* regardless of how much of the rest of my living it may not include. Hence it is I can fully *justify* to my self my unwillingness to withdraw my attention from safeguarding the present stage of development of my conscious self identity, even in the interest of trying to augment it. Like the storied man wishing to build his new house out of the materials of his old one, I do not want to tear down the old one until the new one is finished. Although I am not as happy as I would like to be with my present limit of self consciousness, I fear extending it as if that would surely cost me my life.

Spinoza, as did Plato, taught himself that self-conscious living is as difficult as it is rare. *Consciously* choosing my self vitalizing experience on an ever ego-enlarging scale, is the ideal way of life with which I can preserve my sanity while living personally that most hazardous profession I call self analysis, conscious self education.

Hence my creating every access of conscious self identity has been dreaded and avoided as long as possible, despite the fact that it is the one development uniquely and specifically needed by me for my *extending* my loving treatment of my self (including my fellowman). Hence it is, I *must* fear awakening to every truth about my self that will provide me with increasing awareness of the real extent of my wholeness. Hence it is, I avoid even the occasion of such living that seems to force me to attend to any of my painful or unhappy "past" I have succeeded in ignoring.

Therefore, I may hate the idea of my physically (psychologically) examining my self, detest the word "psychiatry," praise mental health as long as it is intended for someone else, consider religion an anachronism, welcome child guidance so long as I am not the child. On and on, I do all that I can to maintain my *status quo,* valuing my refusal to tolerate additional self awareness as my only means of keeping my "mental balance," escaping "depersonalization sensations," guarding against "feelings of strangeness," thereby staying "loyal to my family traditions," "true to my past," "devoted to my upbringing," or even "faithful to my religion."

The truth is that my working up additional conscious self identity is never at the cost of my giving up any previously cultivated self awareness. I now live with the same love the self observations I lived and loved as a child. Justice Benjamin Cardozo observed, "In breaking one set of shackles let us not substitute another."

The excellence of anything is inherent in the way it works itself. My work, rightly regarded, is the doing (functioning) of my being. My idealizing my present being (functioning) is most favorable to ongoing development of my being. However my prevailing attitude towards my working is that it is slavish, exactly to the extent that I cannot recognize my own self development in it. Only my self conscious living enables me to feel the torture in my idleness, to realize that lack of life worthy occupation for any of my power leads to my downfall, that all of my gainsaying means merely my temporary unpreparedness to consciously affirm my own mind's productivity. Conscious self industry is essential to conscious mental integrity, genuine morality and clean politics.

However much my specious theories of short working hours, controlled production, wage freeze, or whatever, may seem to prevail, my individual mind's augmenting self consciousness always remains the sole basis for my valuing my service. As workman my life-affirming goal is to feel that I already am the only proprietor I can ever know, rather than merely to feel my ambition to become that proprietor someday. My everyman is like Goethe's Prometheus, either consciously or unconsciously:

> Here do I sit, and mould
> Men after mine own image.

My looking in the only place where I can really see, namely in my world of my mind, provides the only adequate foundation for my economic, or any other, confidence. Only self consciousness of a biologically adequate inclusiveness, comprehensive enough for the range of my mental development, can free me from uncontrollable ambition or despair.

I can justify any of my political organization only on the basis of (my) its helpfulness to each individual citizen. I can see the goodness, truth and beauty in my political work in the proportion that I can see my duly enlarged soul in it. My consecration to my politics will not be the desecration of the remainder of my wholeness to the extent that I can convert the law of my self love into the law of my self's world. There is for every citizen a statement of this nature so incisive and compelling that he can see his own identity in it, but only he can make it. Each student is his only helpful teacher but only he can evolve that insight. How wonderful Emerson's conscious self identity! The story is told, a fanciful acquaintance once brought him the fearsome news, "The end of the world is at hand." He replied, "I am glad of it; man will get along better without it."[9] He said, "to me the universe is all a spiritual manifestation."

What is not *biologically* adequate cannot be really adequate at all. And *my* biological adequacy occurs only and entirely in the functioning of my own whole individuality. Any legislation which tends to impair the conscious freedom of my individual (inherent) contract with my self-welfare must be enacted or enforced at the awful cost of my conscious self sovereignty. My human constitution cannot endure such injustice without showing helpful signs and symptoms of its distress in the form of evident disrespect for such tyrannous law. *My self is all I am (have) but I resist with all my might exploring any of its allness that I have not already owned up to as constituting my conscious self identity.* My creating this self orientation seems like a miracle; but it also seems that I believe in nothing but miracles.

As a clergyman I am lovingly aware of my fellowman's resistance to considering earnestly trying to do what he can briefly imagine is certainly good for him. As a physician I can observe my patient's fear of finding a cancer as sufficient to block out his fear of cancer itself. As an educator I am often astounded by my fellow student's tremendous resistance

[9]Conway, *Emerson At Home and Abroad,* p. 233.

to acknowledging that *his* knowledge is all and only his knowledge of his own mind. I hear often seemingly paradoxical assertions: "There are enough physicians, There are enough medical schools, hospitals, clinics, outpatient services and the like." "Paradoxical" each such claim is against the background of ever-increasing population. However, there is widespread reluctance of my fellowman to *use* his already existing health facility. Fear of self examination beyond what is comforting is fear of augmenting self consciousness.

I observe deep and powerful resistance of my fellowman against his assuming *any* further conscious responsibility for his own healthful development. This overwhelming resistance extends even to his unwillingness to relegate any of his responsibility to his health official if that means his having to alter his conscious *status quo*. In his political living he chooses to put up with a show of democracy; in his religious living, a show of divinity; in his education living, a show of learning;—and so on, all in his lifesaving interest of preserving his *status quo. No accounting other than this one is needed to explain the helpfully sorry state of my nation.*

The warning woes of every description of *my* body politic are increasingly aggravating. I am seriously troubled upon every governmental level, everywhere finding conspicuous signs and symptoms of (my) hurt human individuality crying out for relief of any and every kind, often settling for chemical analgesics, medically prescribed or unprescribed. To be sure I sense all of my social and political upheaval as beneficially indicating not only the source of trouble but the specific help needed, namely, *my* working up conscious love for my difficultly livable (since difficultly lovable) self. Self preservation warns me that I cannot afford to indulge the temptation, ascribed to a caricature of Thomas Carlyle, of loving all of mankind but hating every man.

Yet all of my mental content having to do with whatever I call the subject of political science may seem to be broken from the only connection in which it can mean anything (my own mentality) and then be misunderstood to be the *mindless* ground of its own condition! Thus my facts about my subject of political science become distorted and falsified from the start in order to serve the *status quo* of my anxiously circumscribed, lifesaving sense of personal identity. I, my self, am the only subject of all of *my* subjects!

My mind is the generating whole that constitutes and composes its every interest. Its consciousness enables even momentary focus upon the specific meaning of its organic wholeness, the nature of the essence of individuality, thus disclosing the very purpose of human existence as being the realization, including fulfillment, of its own nature. For this meaning of my life to operate consciously I must keep working up my feeling of identity in my organic unity, in close keeping with my living (that is, with my continuing self growth). Kant, insightfully identifying with his Aristotle, defined pleasure as the feeling of furtherance, and pain as the feeling of hindrance, of individual life. I feel pleasure whenever I live self consciously. Even my realizing that all of my suffering is of my own creating, immediately pleases, thus reducing my pain.

The significance of my free imagination for the far reaches of my mind is not always obvious so that I resort to such fixating self-identity devices as, "I can't even imagine such an extreme notion," or "His imagination runs away with him," or "I'll imagine only what I please, thank you," and so on. The fact is that I seem to spend my mental life largely in my imagination,—thus I must *imagine* whatever I happen to be thinking, feeling, willing, perceiving, or sensing about my so-called external world.

It is tempting to comfort my self with the illusion that my financial, political, or industrial advancement amounts to successful living, but all such show of success actually must neglect my best interests exactly to the extent that it ignores my identity in *any* of my wholeness. *My experience proves to my complete satisfaction that my withholding my feeling of my identity from painful want or despair in any of my world must take its exact toll upon my health, quite as my withholding biologically adequate nutrition from my diet must do so.* Whoever reads this soul-shaking truth can benefit from it only to the extent that he can consciously originate (author) it. It is rare for one to realize as did Henry Thoreau in early life that the sure road to wealth lies in wanting what one is, in truly assessing the riches of his unadorned human nature. Asked on his deathbed to speak of a future life, he replied simply, "One world at a time."

As a rich man, my ignoring my identity in my poor man has its exacting effect upon my metabolism so that every tissue and organ of my economy reflects such lack of interest in my living. As a poor man, my ignoring my identity in my rich man similarly results in my hurting my self metabolically in some area of my living of my wholeness. My neighbor, parent, child, spouse, stomach, tumor, back, skin, eye, or whatever trouble,—each has the same source in the way in which I ignore or reject some of my self identity. As employer it is morally, economically and sanitarily profitable to me to feel my identity in *my* employee; as employee it is morally, economically and sanitarily profitable to me to feel my identity in *my* employer. Self consciousness as an ideal furnishes ever-present living of excellence. I (including my every fellow-man) can prosper only as my reverence for life extends to *all* of my living. Reliance upon blame, or praise, or popularity spells "failure" in conscious self continence (see my *Psychology of Emotion*).

From all of this sophisticated orientation to the necessity for *whole* self helpfulness all of the way to *conscious* whole self helpfulness, it may become evident for my rare reader that his Dorsey writes as he does solely and selffully for the purpose of developing his mind with his discipline of self consciousness, his one and only sovereign remedy he has ever been able to discover for all of his unrecognized illusions, including his illusion of helping somebody else. I would be perfectly comfortable arguing for the sanity of my life scheme but I am certain that argument can only beget itself.

I can associate nothing with fear except whatever true living of itself my own mind creates, either consciously or unconsciously. It follows that I can consciously associate with fear only some activity of my own self consciousness. My fellowman's associating his fear, and dislike in general, with his self consciousness, accounts for his difficulty in claiming his painful living as his own, in view of his enormous resistance to developing further conscious self identity. The same powerful resistance accounts for my (including my fellowman's) *laissez faire* attitude towards my unheedingly indulging local, state, federal and world political living that deflates my conscious self of its real coin of life consciousness and inflates my unconscious self with its counterfeit money of not-self.

Since my writing must be dereistic insofar as it is not diaristic, it records only my effort to sense my way back to my sane political economy based safely upon consciously cultivating my wholesome appreciation for the wholeness and allness of my (including my fellowman's) sovereign individuality. I discovered that my Destutt de Tracy also consciously cultivated his sense of self identity in the world of his mind, including his generating lovingly his Thomas Jefferson's governmental ideal of self sovereignty. Deeming this true-to-life self-orientation the one most needed by me today I help my self by bringing my Tracy to conscious life.

Complete self government being the only form possible for individual man, and *conscious* self government being only rarely, if at all, considered by him, nevertheless grievous consequence of this disregard is too seldom recognized by him. The demonstrable truth is that all human trouble is individual trouble only, always traceable to biologically inadequate self control. In 1925 Thorsten Veblen published his ominous "Economic Theory on the Calculable Future" describing a bleak prospect that may be helpful also right now:

> Things have taken such a turn that nations, national interests, national policies, and national armaments no longer have any other use, serve no other purpose, than the differential gain of business concerns doing business in competition with outsiders. The war and that peace of suspicion, bitterness, and bickering in which it has eventuated have made all that plain . . . and such economists and commissions of economic inquiry as are drawn into the service of the national establishment are drawn in for no other purpose and on no other qualifications than

such as are presumed to serve bankers and traders against outsiders. Economic science, insofar as it enters into the training of the nation's civil servants is perforce of this complexion.[10]

It is imperatively noteworthy that only the most insightful political scientist can uphold the all important truth of the comprehensive allness and wholeness of the individual citizen. If this truth (namely, all government is self government) would become conscious truth, that is, *if every sovereign individual would recognize his self as such, that would mean not only certain end to all governmental extravagance but also no possibility at all for spoils or red tape or any other such enormous costs of citizen government that is figuratively but not literally representative in form.* Therefore to the extent that an author's scientific literature about government stresses the one and only political reality, namely human individuality (conscious and unconscious), he knows better than to expect other than exceedingly limited reading of it, with excellent prospect for its early rejection.

Again and again I have discovered in the rare references to Tracy's political insight the question politely raised as to why his uniquely helpful writings have been overlooked consistently by nearly every government official, supreme court justice included. The answer is obvious to anyone who understands his own powerful need to resist the arduous mental discipline of enlarging his current image of his self identity by extending his awareness of the actual comprehensiveness of his individuality.

To be sure I do not expect to find any such esoteric, mystic and subjective political principle as the sovereignty of human individuality elaborated in any of my current literature, scientific or otherwise. And whatever is, is exactly what it should be. Once I taught my self *that* lesson I was able to renounce my addiction to faultfinding, e.g., to hurting my self, as if unfeelingly, in the name of my very own governmental representative.

[10] *American Economic Review*, Vol. XV, No. 1, Supplement.

By appreciating that my governmental representative is always doing his very best, I discovered my most helpfully workable understanding of him. However, for me to be unwilling to see myself in my government official experience is tantamount to my willingness to vote for a candidate who is unwilling (unable) to recognize his own personal interest in each one of his well-called constituency. *The absence of the expressed private opinion of everyone grown capable of calling his government his own is a most serious omission in my American politics.* Emerson, first American scholar to renounce slavery as slavery of every citizen, rallied his so-called public opinion to the cause of the brave, "Whoso is heroic will always find crises to try his edge."

Whoever could observe clearly his panic of '29 as his own mental shock did not have to seem subject to it, for the clear observer is his clear observed. However many an individual of my world who "lost his money in the exchange" had identified such wealth as meaning his whole life. To his question, "What am I worth?" he could not reply that he was worth his whole world.

The beauty of my charity (my feeling the unity of my mankind) can be felt only when I can consciously attribute to my mind the meaning of the allness of my living that rightfully belongs to it. *My every so-called panic or financial crisis of any kind can become fully understandable only as being the result of my attempted violation of the natural law of growth of the oneness, allness and wholeness of my human individuality.*

The present day has no vital issues, and can have none. The United States has no recession or depression, and can have none. The nation cannot profit from a book such as Tracy's, or from any other book ever. There are no great social and economic problems of the day, and there can be none. The time is not out of joint, or ever can be. There is no labor problem, or capital problem or money problem, or can there ever be one. There is no aid from courts or judges or welfare, or can there ever be. A corporation can never commit treason or be outlawed. *There is no natural law possible but the law of individual man's biological constitution.*

There is no beaten path, only each person's individual footstep. There can be no genius in education, the trade, philanthropy, or whatever, for all genius lies only in individual genius. To be consciously *alone* is to feel the allness in my oneness. My having is its own wanting; my wanting is its own having; my being is its own all; all of my doing is only my being; all of my credit is self investment. With all due apology to Morris, united I stand, divided I fall. Quite as my world-Shakespeare felt it, one conscious touch of my nature, makes my whole world kin. Man cannot be his own master without being his own servant.

If there were such an easy way as so-called communication available for me to acquire my conscious self knowledge, the only real product of so-called effective learning, then indeed I would be unable to explain the total failure of any such effort to impart my teacher's wisdom to me. None of it ever had the slightest effect in my directing my educational growth to the sanity of consciously feeling my self in my mental activity. Where the law of conscious self activity seems to end, there some form of necessary tyranny seems to begin.

I cherish as my real educator every one who seems to recognize that all of his teaching must be only his own mind's learning about itself. His mind-wise study of his society, political science, government, dynamics, geography or economy is only possible in the light of its only possible importance for him, namely his very own personal living of all of it. Thus Cicero divined the truth of his need to grow his own knowledge as self-knowledge, "It is especially harmful to those who wish to learn to be under the authority of those that teach."

As a mind unconscious scientist I have seemed to make what I call fast progress in science by overlooking all that can be possibly real in it, namely my own living. I have gloriously divided "the" atom and united "the" earth and moon, and may yet sustain my supreme discovery, my life revering recognition that *my* atom or *my* moon is all and only mine; that my team-work is all and only my mind's team-work; that motion, distance, space, time,—each is a helpful illusion of my mind's creating; that my soul (mind) does not, need not, travel.

Neither millions of miles nor millions of signatures can in any way efface the infinite identity of human individuality. It is the *only* possible human force and furthermore it is constantly vindicating its unique power. I can only *seem* to fail to assert that my individuality is my only possible political entity. Really I am constantly exerting my self sovereignty, either consciously or unconsciously, as constituting my only possible nature. *Life-wise indeed, and incapable of political failure, is my political scientist who can make the most of this truth of all truths of his being.*

My ignorance for my truth that I create all that passes for political economy or the science of politics in my own mind, to my great good fortune does not exempt me from paying for that ignorance in whatever form of pain or unhappiness, for *if I could transgress the law of my being without its costing me any disturbance I would surely lack any motivation for studying my true nature and needs.* Each transgression of law of my human constitution exacts full payment in terms of my enraged wholeness, in either conscious or unconscious emotional coin of hurt living. My economic self suffers financial crisis following unwise spending, quite as my headache may follow my drunkenness. But all of this recording of self responsibility was very well stated and widely acclaimed in the last century:

> That physical disease, the effect of which is to gradually thin the blood toward a watery condition, when it continues unchecked, is no less certain in its logical results than will be the degradation of our monetary system to a silver or greenback basis, if at any time a process of dilution indefinitely continues. Legislation may for a while prevent the full assertion of law, but it is nevertheless an active, living force, unceasingly pressing in the direction of its natural fulfilment.[11]

[11]Henry Wood, *The Political Economy of Natural Law* (Boston: Lee and Shepard, 1894), p. 20.

My organized effort, political, social, economic, or of whatever name, derives from my (including *my* every fellowman's) living only. My personality is the *only* one in any organization of mine. I am all of it from bottom to top but I may be rarely aware for that reality. And it is that ignorance which is my most grievous mental condition, quite as it is my appreciation for my allness and wholeness that is my most felicitous mental condition. The magnificence of human being necessitates augmenting self responsibility in keeping with its consciously evolving greatness. But I will never seek difficult living consistently until I can feel the life-importance in doing so.

I find there can be no motive, law or purpose in any self development except non-interfering self interest. For me unselfishness is necessarily inhuman for it would be tantamount to my nonexistence. What passes for unselfishness must be a selfishness that is unrecognized, such as a mother's caring for *her* child, a soldier's dying for *his* country, or a martyr dying for *her* God. I earnestly labor for my seeing *my* identity alone in whatever I live as being my only way to fulfill and appreciate my self development. I now find that any other life course is fatal to my methodically honoring my wholeness and allness and thereby practicing lifesaving hygiene.

Most helpful in this consciously responsible way of life has been my making peace with, and finally living contentedly, my every feeling of pain or unhappiness as being nothing but lovable living, the truthful providence of which becomes undeniable once I discover the sufficiency of fact necessitating it. Out of pure self defense for whatever conscious self identity I have thus far been able to cultivate (by honoring my pain and unhappiness as lifesavingly life worthy) I may try to locate my distressing experience as if *it* could be outside of me, until I can mobilize sufficient conscious self love to feel *it* as all my own.

I am certain that my self regeneration to conscious self continence has safeguarded my living, and I observe my fellowman's consciously personal regeneration has been his salvation. I record this constant finding of mine as identical with my Aristotle's observation that politics consists of everyone's minding his own business, in the only way that he can, either consciously (responsibly) or unconsciously (as if irresponsibly). The only real rule for individual living must be created by that individual in terms of the presenting condition of his conscious self love (see, *Psychology of Emotion*). With love consciously active in his living he is functioning with the power of his recognizable wholeness, willingly obedient to whatever he observes *is*, recognizing that it is affording him subjective (inspiring) sustenance. But my words mean too little unless I see feelingly in them self helpful signs of my own unfathomable vitality (creativity). I believe in my self, the creator of my heaven and earth, the pantheon of all of my divine fellow being, the author of my every authority, the source of my every sensible. Emerson worded it well: If one cannot trust one's senses there is nothing and nobody he can trust.

My greatest genius for political living became mine when I discovered the potential identity in my national citizenship and my world citizenship, recognizing that my highest civic ideal must depend upon my mental development in the specific direction of calling not only my soul my own but also my world my soul. My greatest aid in this arduous exertion has been my finding the enormous amount of my self concealment hidden in my language, especially my vocabulary, itself (see my *Psychology of Language*).

As my *conscious self* education then became my purposeful way of study, I realized why and how my revered Thomas Jefferson's inspired plan for public school education-to-responsible-citizenship could not realize its avowed intention of effective citizen emancipation from mind neglect, limited self knowledge, emotional incontinence and compensatory illusional dependence. There can be no so-called objective approach to my necessarily private self activity named subjectivity. I can never understand, or be understood by, anyone but my self.

The moral education needed for my competent American citizenship is (my) each citizen's educating his self (disciplining his mind) with consciousness for the marvelous greatness of his own individuality. *The only possible road to good citizenship is: enlarging conscious self appreciation.* Every attempt to picture subjectivity objectively may be likened to an effort to make nothing out of something. Conversely every attempt to picture objectivity subjectively may be likened to an effort to make something out of nothing. I see my identity instantly in my Wilhelm von Humboldt's conscious self wording, "for me the essential nobility of man lies in the sobriety which honors the autonomy of the purely inward will."[12]

Every collective noun lends itself to disregard for the truth that its arbitrarily assumed plurality can be only a *seeming* manyness, must be always and only one mental construct in the *individual* mind creating it usually as its illusion that there can be more, or less, than *one* of anything. Even the term "individuals," signifying a plurality of unique ones, assumes that individuality itself can be sensed objectively (rather than subjectively) somehow. Sensing is entirely and only subjective however. Only I can sense me.

The unified allness of the wholeness of my organic being necessitates that my nature be constituted of my internality alone. Being all-of-my-self requires my ever being "next" only to my self, never "next" to another so-called all. My only "externality" accessible to my sensing therefore must consist only of my unconscious *internality*, a case of my being able to help my self by using my imagination to conceive existence other than my self which I then inaccurately nominate external world, not-I, somebody else, objective reality, and so on.

I can only feel my own identity (consciously or unconsciously) wherever my sensibility is. The measured functioning of my self sensibility, including my every passion, is a development deserving my life concern. Only my conscious self love is capable of willing its moderation, for with this self love consciously accessible to all of my living its moderation is

[12] *Humanist Without Portfolio.* Translated from the German with an Introduction by Marianne Cowan (Detroit: Wayne State Univ. Press, 1963).

assured, in the interest of my allness and wholeness.

As (my) Tracy asserts, all sensibility must be self sensibility only, with its single source in the wellspring of (my own) organic being. *My realizing that my every activity must be nothing but my growing of my self reveals all of my negation as an effort to inhibit my self development.* Fully developed Emerson once described man as the dwarf of himself, implying the arrest of development of his self consciousness. I define self consciousness as living with the sense, or appreciation, of being that living. My life choice is self consciousness or autohypnosis (making my self experience unconscious and thereby overlooking that my sensibility is mine).

Most meaningful self observation in the Perspective is:

1) I must *grow* all of my knowledge for it consists only of my organic self experience, quite as does my hand or foot. All of my linguistic reality is in my mind only.

2) Therefore, my only possible *real* political science cannot be around some subject that seems to exclude my self but must be right through my conduct of my own life somehow.

3) My political science cannot be exact at all except to the extent that I can observe its every term as being a name for a meaning occurring in my own mind only. This same assertion holds true for any other so-called science of mine.

4) My earnestly trying to solve my political problem by increasing my efforts to secure valuable external data by way of a so-called brain-trust, idea-pool, imagination-bank or whatever, is a specific instance of solving my problem of going in the undesired direction merely by redoubling my speed.

5) My economic expert is consciously dedicated to his present habit of mind-unconsciousness, with which by the way he has thus far succeeded in keeping himself alive, so that his senses are set to grow self knowledge further in that self-unconscious direction (not to his growing new self observation as to how his Dorsey or any of his like has painstakingly discovered the sanity of his political science).

6) Daily I demonstrate to my self and validate my observation that I must and do impair my health to hasten my death precisely to the extent that I neglect my acknowledged fellow-

man's good (for certainly all that I can conceive of him becomes entirely rejected living of my own). I can experience no selfless ground.

7) Far wiser am I to "stay out of politics" or social living of any kind, to live as one quarantined, to the extent that I cannot live my fellowman with the same responsible care with which I can realize I need to live whatever I can consciously recognize as my own life.

8) My majority rule is my choice political device for discovering where the greater (and lesser) amount of my own wholeness is involved.

9) The amount of my conscious self control varies directly with how much of my living of my world I can consciously recognize as being mine.

10) The amount of my conscious self control decides how much or how little conscious self control I shall require of my governmental representative.

11) My governmental representative is always doing his level best with whatever political acumen he possesses (his own worked-up conscious self control determines the biological adequacy of that acumen).

12) My imagination, my term for all of my mental activity, functions unconsciously when I believe I can know other-than-myself (e.g., an external world), and consciously when I can observe all of my world as the world my mind creates for my helpfulness.

POLITICAL HUMAN INDIVIDUALITY

> There is no substitute for original material in the study of American political thought.
>
> Andrew M. Scott. *Political Thought in America*

Woodrow Wilson's declaration holds good: "Politics is a business of interpretation." As stated, over the past decade I have had in mind the writing up of this study and this particular mindfulness has been of generative significance for other works I have published meanwhile. Unless I can insightfully observe that I am my only subject, object, predicate, or whatever, I must conduct my life as if I am mostly "out of my mind." *Having discovered the genetic helpfulness in my Tracy's insightful political and economic orientation, and the general theoretical and practical neglect it has been accorded to date, my intention to try to do something about it has continued to grow sufficiently strong for that purpose.*

There is ever a need for a psychology that reveals everyone's Democracy to be grounded solidly on the ideal principle of the worth of every individual's life itself.

There is no government at all possible except individual government. There is no freedom possible except individual freedom. And it cannot be taken for granted; there is no life but individual life. As long as I am unprepared even to try to find all of my living in my self where it must be, I must suffer fearfully despairing loneliness for whatever of my living I cannot consciously claim to possess already. This *illusional* mental condition "individual loneliness" can be so painful that it obscures my appreciation for the true worth of my individual freedom and factually makes me prefer servitude as liberation. Hence "the mass surrenders which sanctioned the victories of totalitarian parties in several countries."[1] My increasing recognition for my individuality is ever

[1]Yves R. Simon, *Philosophy of Democratic Government* (Chicago: University of Chicago Press, 1951), pp. 307-308.

the complete resolution of such distressing loneliness, my nostalgia always based upon my illusion that all of my living that I cannot recognize as my own therefore somehow becomes not-my-own.

Conscious self government builds most healthful citizenship; unconscious self government necessarily entails helpful signs and symptoms pejoratively called sickness or crime, warning the citizen of the life endangering self disregard he is requiring of his constitution.

The goal ever hovering before man of attaining a divine state of perfection has been really his dim perception of his already existing perfection. Only his believing awareness for his absolute perfection is lacking, on account of his inability to appreciate his unhappiness (pain of any kind) as also constituting his divinely inspired helpfulness. Ignatius Loyola sensed this truth and in his *Book of the Spiritual Exercises* recorded how man can discover his godliness through his own will and purpose. He also indicated the importance of sensing with "the eye of the imagination."

My fellowman sometimes credits his Dorsey with being a great teacher. Voltaire sensibly commended, "If you wish to converse with me, define your terms." There can be only subjective definition. My teaching is limited strictly by conscious reverence for the truth that all teaching is entirely the learner's own (conscious or unconscious) self-activity.[2] *My consciousness for that truth is my greatest educational, including religious and political, attainment, the pivot for all of the functioning of my mind.* My most precious birthright I deem to be my development of certainty that I *am* all of my own living. Furthermore, if my education is *for* anything it is that I learn to appreciate the wonderfulness of my life, the true knowledge of the good. My living is all that *can* be adorable, godly, for me. All of the mischief of my world comes from my

[2]By "reverence" I mean conscious devotion to the fullest self appreciation. All my learning is my growing of my self-knowledge and I must revere that truth before I can be conscious for the illimitable greatness of my own individuality, as such. With *conscious* self-learning comes awe for my own life.

not realizing *that*. And as Stevenson brightly declared, there is no self obligation I may tend to underrate as much as the duty of being happy.

In my self analysis (through steadily practicing examination of my mind) I see that my every mental element appearing to signify not-self (more or less than one, e.g., impersonal otherness) continues to serve the purpose of my creating my illusion of limits in my mind, analogous to those described in my illusion of boundary in my body ego. My liking to deceive my self with platitudes that some of my living may somehow have something to do with somebody else or something else seems essential for my conscious presence of mind, on account of my mind's undeveloped love-capacity for fully appreciating the abiding grace of its solipsistic nature, on account of my need to avoid burdening my mind with the overwhelming truth that its own inherent nature enables it to realize its own infinity, eternity, divinity, or whatever unlimited. Whatever is mental is naturally individual and therein is its excellence.

I cannot believe in even the existence, let alone the action, of any social or political organization, from committee to congress, except insofar as I can recognize it as *my* best available device for protecting the security of my social or political self. I can live my politics as being always the very best possible at present and work with it as such without finding fault with my occasional faultfinding indicating my unpreparedness for appreciating its immediate necessity. In Will Durant's elegant phrasing I can get along with my political dynamics as "the distilled mediocrity of the land"[3] without forfeiting my sane recognition of its excellence.

What an access of life appreciation I recognized when I first realized clearly the mere fact that I learned difficultly only when I was not able to be lovingly interested in studying whatever therefore must seem hard to learn! What a relief from distressing mystification I enjoyed when I first realized fully the extent to which I was cultivating strong self disesteem

[3] *Harpers Magazine*, 153 (November 1926): 746.

simply by giving bad names to the helpfulness in biologically indispensable power of sickness, crime, accident, and even dying itself! What a joyous release I found in learning (for my self, in my self, and about my self) that all of my conscious unhappiness is just unconscious happiness, that all of my conscious badness is merely unconscious goodness, that all of my conscious accident is unconscious design,—that the only desideratum in any and all of my conscious faultfinding is sufficient strengthening of my love to be able to live my fact-finding, conscious self difficultly! (See my *Psychology of Emotion.*)

For maintaining my comforting illusion of a measurable mind that I can quantify, it is essential that I be able to negate the truth that I am the *all* of my being. Once again, all of my negation is my effort to make nothing out of something by consciously disowning the latter as integral existence of mine. Obviously if any of my living can be judged to be spontaneity that is not mine, if I can claim to experience anything or anybody other than my own identity, then my illusion of plurality must come to my aid at the enormous expense of my appreciation for the unity, wholeness and allness of my individuality. All of my judgment or reasoning, all of my mentation *except self consciousness,* employs this useful but illusional device (negation), especially my notion of plurality underlying so-called "opposites." I can further obscure the ever singular identity of my living by even opposing affirmative and negative, as if my negative could exist somehow except in the form of my inhibited (unconscious) affirmative.

Each emotion supports my easy illusion of plurality. Only consciousness for my own individuality supports the whole truth of my united oneness. Fidelity for my own inviolable integrity is my unfailing source of relief from the helpful hurt of jealousy ever ready to protect my love of living. Individuality can never be dropped out of consideration at all, for it alone is all there can be to consider.

I find the only possible law of my political science originating and operating wholly in my own human constitution. It is merely the *that in my self* which I can see anywhere in my world. The human law of selffulness is all that can be natural law. Ideal political economy emerges from this pure *natural* legislation: every individual is a law unto his self. Responsible consciousness for that truth is most distressfully overlooked. Appreciation for that truth is the essential mental development needed even to understand the love of his mankind inherent in Louis D. Brandeis's conception: the *living law* arising from full knowledge of the facts out of which a just law arises. Even brooding over my unhappiness is my only available way of helping my self whenever I resort to it. The Right Reverend Frederick B. Fisher recorded:

> Brooding over ills, the brooding soul
> Creates the evil feared, and hugs its pain.[4]

My widespread wish to minimize or even deny the all-inclusive significance of my individuality is thoroughly understandable for it alone enables me to be unaware about my full responsibility for being my self. Powerful emotion (e.g., hatred, jealousy, guilt, fear) is necessary to make me live my self unconsciously rather than consciously. However my most wonderful development, namely, my self consciousness, can enjoy only limited functioning in such a psychological system. My true magnanimity must be expressed some way but I can always relegate all that I mean by it to my alienated divinity, or any such self-disclaimed consciousness. All of my self helpfulness called either psychotherapy or religious healing owes its efficacy to my purposefully furthering my appreciation for my true worth, in the only way possible, by consciously tracking it to my self through self consciousness.[5]

Idealism is all that is possible in economics as in every other scientific discipline. *Conscious* idealism is the rarest mental condition and, as might therefore be expected, the greatest. Certainly I find it understandable for me to resent

[4] *Personology, The Art of Creative Living* (New York: Abingdon Press, 1930), p. 71.
[5] See my *Illness or Allness* (Detroit: Wayne State University Press, 1965).

the demand that my skill and effort be expended upon my lifting my self consciousness to behold the true meaning and extent of my individuality further than I presently can. Just maybe I can get by as I now think I am constituted. After all, nobody ever gets out of his troubles alive. Maybe *my* lying to my self won't prove unhealthy, etc.

To be sure, conscious idealism is (my) everyone's most vital concern, and precisely *there* is the competent-citizenship issue. I must make all of *my* world that is already (perforce, by definition) mine, *consciously* mine, in order to appreciate fully what my life's worth amounts to, before I can develop my adequate American citizenship. My schooling can only fit me, or unfit me, for my self esteem. Henry Wood, self-mindful economist, recorded:

> Political economy is the outward expression of the play of the forces of the mind. . . . Man is One; and just in the measure that that grand fact is installed in human consciousness, are *all* the natural principles found to be altruistic.[6]

The complete selffulness of an infant, child or so-called immature adult is rarely appreciated for its right to be. Thus it is either lovingly or unlovingly tolerated as unworthy, described pejoratively as undesirable selfishness, and thereby emphasized in the form of a prohibition always striving to actualize itself. My longsuffering reader may now properly exclaim, "Do you recommend that a childish adult be allowed to carry on all of the mischief of which he is capable? Foolish *one* do you never read your newspaper responsibly? Have you no pity for the victim of your consciously selfful maniac? (and so on). You will say my opposition to you does not inspire me with the tongue of an angel. Go ahead!"

Yes, I continue to live all of the hurt you describe, feeling quite as you do. Forbearance or endurance does not mean the absence but rather the presence, of what is to be tolerated

[6] *The Political Economy of Natural Law* (Boston: Lee and Shepard, 1894) pp. 294, 295.

as difficult helpfulness. My most precious virtue, my discipline in ability to love what can only be loved difficultly, requires the presence of hardship which is the source of whatever hardihood I can command. My discovering the lifesaving power of pain and unhappiness of any kind enabled me to possess my self consciously of vast reaches of my living which I had seemed to be able to disclaim as if not constituting my own living only.

Whatever I live is lifesaving exactly to the extent that I succeed in living it *by living it.* My ceasing to live that *whatever* must mean my ending my life. Life is a continuum sustaining no suspension of its continuity. *I continue to live all of my previous ways of conducting my life along with any new design that I discover to be also helpful.*

Yes, I do read my newspaper responsibly, seeing my personal identity in my victim and victor alike. Furthermore I realize that every victor is his own dying or dead victim, quite as every victim, alive, is his own victor.

Yes, I live my victimized fellowman as well as my victor with pity until I can live each one with my conscious love that enables me to understand and fully appreciate that truth is always on the side of whatever happens; that whatever is, justly is.

Yes, I do see my immediately urgent need to recognize that my child, or childish adult, often must cry "out" (instead of *in)* for help to control his tremendous power and that his only way of crying "out" is often that of shortsighted violence. Also I recognize it is my responsibility to see to it that he does help himself fully by living his consciously self controlled Dorsey for the purpose of restraining himself. Furthermore (and here the going may be most difficult for my reader) I consider it most essential to this due process of natural law that my infant, child, or childlike adult be allowed to carry through all of his violent but natural thoughts and feelings *in his mind's imagination to completion,* for it is only by this experience of being able to see fully the consequence of his emotional incontinence that he can will his voluntary emotional control.

It is fatal to my health to permit my parental disobedience to allow me to ignore the lifesaving lesson of absolute self-interest I can observe in my infant's honest living of his sincere selfishness.

Idealism consists of full consciousness for this true worth of what already *is: whatever is, in anyone's living, is human life.* The only established order is entirely in the mind considering it. *Wherever human legislation deflects from this standard of value (namely: whatever is human, is individual living) it becomes economically extravagant.* Whatever *is,* having all of the meaning of eternity and infinity in it, honorably is.

Love is my only primary feeling (see my *Psychology of Emotion*). If I cannot live it consciously, as such, on account of being unable to sense my helpful self identity in my experience associated with my love's hurt condition, then I must live it unconsciously, calling it hate or jealousy or some other name signifying that it is associated with living that I cannot, as yet, consciously identify as my desirable own.

No matter how much I can deceive my self about being able to live not-self, by virtue of the illimitable power of my mind, the truth of *all* of my being continues to exert its due force without my magically going in and out of my mind. My belief in any or all of my meaning presupposes my mind which creates and organizes it as either consciously mine or unconsciously mine. My developed ego is the development of the unity of my meaning of my mind's experiencing itself. All that my mind can be capable of is the appearing of itself to itself, either consciously or unconsciously. All of my experience is in the activity of my experiencing my self-functioning.

The entire content of my government consists only of my mind's experiencing itself. My construction of all of my world's meaning is the consequence of my organizing my mind. Rarely do I find my fellow citizen capable of understanding this self-evident truth on account of the fact that he has never taught himself that all of his education is his cultivating his mind with knowledge about itself. I find consistently that I (including my he, *unum et idem*) pay enormously for this extravagant self squandering on account of its natural consequence in my depreciating the true extent and worth of my individuality.

I cannot yield to belief in my own self-evidence as long as I can declare it as alien to me. My so-called empty jumble of words contains just as much precious living of mine as does a profound utterance of the same extent. When I seem to break up my life's unity by seeing my identity in one political direction but not in another I cannot feel at one with my self. The uneasiness that I then experience indicates that unhealthiness results from my neglecting to use my self consciousness for recovering my pacific sensing of my wholeness. Discovering the wonder of my nature through living it was the starting point of my mental activity quite as it remains its goal. Therefore I must either cultivate symptom-free self *conscious* political science or symptom-ridden self *unconscious* political science.

George Washington observed the danger to the union of his United States inherent in so-called political parties, the member of each party supposedly the adversary of the member of every other one. In every dichotomy, or division of any kind, the truth of the absolute identity of the original wholeness constituting all of each so-called division is rarely, if ever, consciously acknowledged. All psychic conflict is symptomatic of this self deception. As republican I am all that I can mean by my democratic or socialistic fellowman.

Whatever can have any meaning for my mind must be a product of my wonderful mind. I find it most helpful therefore to cultivate my awareness for doctrine of my own organic being. Only consciousness for my present necessary perfection, my being perfectly all and only whatever I am, can provide the basis I need to further consciousness for my excellence. Too good to be true? Rather, too true not to be also good. To be sure, any one mental position is all about itself and therefore cannot rule out (or rule in) another. Only consciously valuing the perfection of my own mind can spare me from exciting compensationally helpful feeling of envy, jealousy, hatred, rivalry, competition or external cooperation and collaboration. Mine is the lever and mine is the fulcrum upon which I must lift *my* world, either consciously or unconsciously.

To the extent that I cannot feel distinctly the law of my being, the design of all of my own allness, I must rely upon compensatory laws which seem to be able to preempt it (the law of my unique allness). Then I seem to lose my self in my own conceptions of commerce involving cooperation, collaboration, loss, gain, transaction, etc. This seeming (to be able to lose my self in a larger or smaller whole) is inconspicuous in its operation so that I tend to remain unconscious for its ubiquity (wherever I am not self conscious). Thus all that I call "organization" is the consequence of my self unconscious fellowman's seeming to be able to lose his self identity in what he calls a union, or trust, or whatever classification of his own creating. Mind wise Irwin Edman noted the universal tonic needed:

> In an age given over to regimentation by external things, and regimentation by governmental agencies, one welcomes all movements . . . which reaffirm the quality of individual life . . . or irreducible personality. . . . Something speaks to our own wistful and constricted hearts when . . . in one way or another, an individual tries to make his life bear unmistakably his own signature, bespeak his own vanities.[7]

Man's blind fear associated with absolute solitude is responsible for rejection of his truth that whatever is, is *all* of itself. Most of the unpleasantness in feeling lonesome would be resolved if I could locate my living of my fellow creature just where I have developed it, in my own mind. John Dewey indicated how craving for sociability is largely an effort to find a substitute for the truth that all social union occurs only within each individual.[8]

All of my so-called relationships occur in my mind only.

[7] "The Autobiography of a Symptom," *Under Whatever Sky*. New York: The Viking Press, 1951, p. 191.
[8] See, *Individualism Old and New* (New York: Minton, Balch and Company, 1930).

But I may be sorely tempted to content myself with my conventional habit of losing my conscious mind in my so-called social contact rather than to dare to find that much of my mind where it always must be. Surely, the former system of self accounting usually seems easier.

Mind-honoring Thomas Davidson spoke of education as "conscious evolution" for he knew that conscious self education always evolves the student's life appreciation. The more of my life's experience I can succeed in living with conscious love, the more psychic energy I integrate into my conscious mind to be controlled by my conscious will. The more of my mental activity I acknowledge as being my own, the more my sense of personal identity subsumes responsible living of my wholeness.

It is tempting to make an analogy between the development of the mind and the building of any other kind of structure, but every such effort can only apparently succeed, and then at the expense of understanding the mind's true nature (that is, consisting of anything and everything but whatever is claimed to be nonmental). To illustrate, in the imagined "external" world denial, opposition, and destruction seem necessary. For example, I must demolish the old building and clear the ground in order to erect the new. Not so with my acknowledgeable mental creations. Mental development is always positive. In the mind *everything* is possible. I do not have to get rid of one idea in order to develop another. All of my self-experience continues to exist helpfully along with my most recent mental developments.

Furthermore all of my behavior that is rejected as "asocial" because it might lead to my making trouble "with my fellowman"—all of it, if it is considered to be "non-mental"—must be condemned as "inhuman," as unfit for my living, so that I cannot claim it as precious self possession. However, once any of my living is recognized by me as occurring only and entirely in my mind, it thereby becomes safe and sane self possession properly augmenting my sense of my true personal worth. *For getting along well with my fellowman, seeing my identity in my living of him is all that it takes, but it does and must take that and no less than that.*

My reasoning may be dispassionately considered to be my crowning glory, so that I may not feel incentive to study its grievous limitations and therefore lack precious incentive to examine my mental power to discover its wholly self-contained nature as being my only reality. I cannot arrive at appreciating my integral individuality by way of my reasoning since it is all and only about itself. Reasoning, I can feel only reasoning. For attaining evidence of my intact organic being I need specific sensing of my identity as a unity. First my lifesaving power of using my mind self consciously must become evident, and this discovery occurs as I proceed to *feel* mentally active, imaginative, observant.

To begin with I am not aware that all of my observing is really mine, in the sense of my creating my self observation only out of my own being. This conscious-selfness-truth seems to evolve somewhat as follows. Gradually heeding my wishing (willing) as the beginning of my acknowledgeable self identity I begin to unify my wishing with my heeding to form an awareness that is to become evident as my acknowledgeable self awareness (self observation, self consciousness). With this development I start activating my vivid sense of being the boundless individual whole and all that I am, rather than the seemingly pitiful accident of mortal strife that my life experience may otherwise make me appear only to be.

While directing my present attention to observe my personal development I fully recover conscious appreciation for my immeasurable potentiality and absolve my self of the guilt helpfully dislocating life meaning of mine I was formerly unable to appreciate as precious self possession. I feel gratefully the peace and plenty derivable from realizing how I *always* helped my self in the only way possible for me, namely, by conscious or unconscious self help. I can now observe that any and all of my present marvelous living is based solidly upon any and all of my preceding living, despite the greatly varying evaluation I would then consciously assign it (such as Triumph and Disaster, Success and Failure, Perfect and Imperfect, throughout all so-called opposites). Strong is my pain-saving illusion that I can build my self up without the foundation of *all* of my preceding being. "Looking down" upon *any* of my past can only mean unconscious difficulty in my present living. I can live only as present whatever I am meaning about my history.

When my good fellowman turns historian to attempt to give a fair and just account of historical events he seems to be totally unaware 1) that his history consists of his own mind's abstraction, 2) that it is all and only about his own self and 3) that it describes only whatever is present, not past, in his mind. The consequence of his self unconsciousness is his (unnoticed) delusion that his historical production is impersonal, dispassionate, objective, matter-of-fact living of his past.

When this worthy recorder does not seek to make his history as emotionless (meaningless) as possible by restricting it largely to colorless dates, places and names, he assumes heavier responsibility by introducing his reasoning power to explicate his course of events. Then his self unconsciousness shows most conspicuously in his resort to faultfinding through pejoration, melioration, prejudice, or some other form of (unconsciously) incontinent wish fulfillment. His theme ever seems to him to be far away from his own being, in the long lost past and distant places, so that he has no recognizable opportunity to *feel* personally the pain (unhappiness in any form) he is inflicting upon his own living by any of his faultfinding treatment of it.

The point must be made over and over, my historian's so-called faultfinding is presently his only possible way of helping his self and, as such, is as perfectly ideal, as perfectly practical as it can presently be. His consciously creating his literary career of perfectly recording solidly *all* of his past experience would indicate his appreciation for his literary development as being his continuous growth process. *All of my present living includes at once all of "the new life" that was formerly mine.*

However, by-passing my power of self consciousness and thereby becoming insensitive for the personal consequence of my (consciously) undisciplined judgment, logic and reasoning,

I can hurt my self without feeling it by depreciating what is only within, and of, my life itself. *Being born an individual, my real life orientation requires my experience to individualize my self consciously.* This heeding of my life as my growing only of my self is my only way of living that can enable me to invest my conscious love in all of my world of my own mind's creating. I practice self hypnosis (autosuggestion) for, by far, the greatest extent of my living, habitually saying to my self of my very own so-called external world: "It is not-I," and thenceforth living it without any conscious sensing that it is my precious living I am not holding dear.

Thus as a conscious Christian I attack my self as an unconscious Pagan; as a conscious Pagan I attack my self as an unconscious Christian; as a conscious White, I attack my self as an unconscious Black, and the converse; as my conscious Enlightenment, I attack my self as my unconscious Dark Ages; as a conscious Democrat, I attack my self as an unconscious Republican, or the converse; and so on, all and always attacking my self in the name of progress, evolution, learning, history or politics—rather than crediting my self in my right senses and in my own name only. One-times-one equals one. Individuality is the essence of identity. I find it the all-explaining key-word of my life. *I have no doubt that my political scientist's possession of this revivifying key-word is urgently needed to give to his politics the exalted love of individual life it cries out for through his national impoverishment, crime, drugging, warring and every other necessary helpful sign and symptom of his individual-life depreciation.* Were I not fully convinced that individuality is inviolable, that one cannot get at or be gotten at by another, I would surely die of the frustration that I cannot "impart even to my dearest love" any of my finding of all of my helpful truth in my self.

Tracy's devoted compatriot, Mme. de Staël fondly glorified her mind quite as my Tracy or I would,—"the soul is a fire, sending a flame through all the senses—and it is in this fire that existence itself exists."

As far as my imagined external world is concerned I cannot

even affirm (including deny) matter, substance, stimulus, or existence of any kind or degree other than whatever may be the nature of my mind.

My dictionary definition for words is almost entirely unreliable, being specifically untruthful insofar as it conventionally implies that anything or anybody external to me can nevertheless be entering into my mind somehow and *thereby* subjecting me to its meaning (see my *Psychology of Language*). To illustrate, defining freedom as absence of external restraint, or hearing as the sense by which external sound is perceived, or touch as the physiological sense by which external objects or forces are perceived through contact with the body, or objectivity as external or material reality, and so on. Every term thus implying identity other than my own lends itself to seeming to be able to alienate me as self seeker from me as self finder.

Furthermore, "standard generalizations" about a "standardized mass society" signified by such words as normal, average, standard, and the like, violate the irreducible and inextensible reality of all that is individual, in the name of abstractions existing nowhere except in the mind of a specific individual (people, society, mankind, humanity, masses, mob, committee, majority, minority, race, army, civilization, past, future, neighborhood, family, home, school, church, city hall, government, world, or even man when used to name a member of the human race rather than an individual creating his idea named human race). In *Mortal Strife* word-ruler John Cowper Powys records:

> The wisest infants, and the ones destined to be the least slavish in their devotion to the dictionary, are the ones who, for as long as they possibly can, put off learning to talk. And in the same way the wisest men are those who bring their "intellectual prime" to the speediest possible end, and relapse into the absolute uniqueness of their silent sensations.[9]

In 1729, my America's Samuel Johnson, D.D., first president

[9] London: Jonathan Cape, 1942, p. 102.

of King's College, New York, insightfully wrote to George Berkeley, then Dean of Derry:

> We are confounded and perplexed about time. 1) Supposing a succession in God. 2) Conceiving that we have an abstract idea of time. 3) Supposing that the time in one mind is to be measured by the succession of ideas in another. 4) Not considering the true use and end of words, which as often terminate in the will as the understanding, being employed rather to excite, influence, and direct action than to produce clear and distinct ideas.[10]

Of course my mind is capable only of revealing my own living to me, whether or not I develop any competence in acknowledging that vital truth. However, any of my living, pleasing or unpleasing, that I refuse to claim as my own, contributes to my feeling my life is not worth living, quite as any of my living, pleasing or unpleasing, that I claim as my own contributes to my appreciating the wonderfulness of my life.

My self-evident reality, namely, my sensitive living that is consciously growing my feelingful self experience, relegates my every meaning to my self order, recognizing that my only possible reform is self reform, my only possible protest is self protest, my only possible organicity is my own organic individuality, my only possible opposition is my own self helpfulness. Operating my self consciousness I discover that my self development has always been perfect, so that my (including my world's) only possible "progress" has been that of my perfection. Quite as Baruch Spinoza (1632-1677) felt it, the purpose of my life is to feel my self one with all that I name God. My only sensation of divinity is that which I live; my only conscious divinity is that which I make conscious in the spiritual masonry of my soul.

Once I work up my clear self feeling, my vital sensing of my self identity, I may intensify this individuality meaning

[10] E. Edward Beardsley. *Life and Correspondence of Samuel Johnson, D.D.* (New York: Hurd and Haughton, 1874), p. 74.

until I develop the courage to observe that I am absolutely alone (all one), the only possible one. Any feeling of loneliness I may "suffer" merely reports that there must be some of my living I am not acknowledging as mine,—otherwise I could not feel it as if it were missing. My only possible true living is in my individual wholeness that constitutes the soul of me. All that is so-called popular owes its entire possibility to each popular person's underestimation of the immeasurable power of his own individuality. Each worker must find out in and for his own self how to strengthen his mind with self consciousness sufficiently to recognize that his "company spirit" has to be nothing but his freeing of some of his own spirit.

My whole system of advanced industry, based upon so-called division of labor under which I devote my life to creating skill in one trade (profession or vocation) to rely upon exchanging my service for my fellowman's service in another, is dependent solely upon my illusional power I name interpersonal cooperation. The only possible basis for truth is to be found *within* each individual, never in the no man's land "between" one individual and another.

My effort to bring so-called governmental law into economic affairs cannot permit me to avoid or in any way escape my law of laws, namely, the inexorable truth of my inviolable individuality. This life lesson and only this one is the lifesaving truth of all of my organic and inorganic world. I need only look back over the history of my civilization's course, review the developments that have taken place, note the marvelous advance accomplished in my methods of transportation, trade, and organization of industry, to observe how my marvelous technological progress has been achieved upon the principle of orderly development including disregard for the ever-present wholeness, allness, unity, and only abiding reality of my unique human individuality. Nevertheless my experience has demonstrated consistently that I will never yield any already established way of living my self until I have to. I will try everything else possible before being willing to try growing the *additional* self identity that will give me the right view I need.

How to make the most of this individual life that is mine, is naturally my only chief concern. Optimal self fulfillment to realize the wonderful potential that there is in my life itself only, is my choice idea of what to do for my self, with my self and in my self. After I can begin to heed my need for this kind of economy then I can start to sense the truth that my (including my fellowman's) only possible wealth consists of my *living,* that my fundamental economics may best be defined as my science of the business of my living, that biologically adequate production, distribution, and consumption of my vitality is my sane standard of living that pays me most in permitting my conscious economic life-accounting itself.

Hardly ever do I realize that my production of my conscious being must be carried on upon a most specific scale of ideal magnitude in order that I may secure economy in its operation. Rather I tend to regard my ongoing affairs quite as impersonally as I do my every other great industrial corporation. In other words I can and do even set up the unity of my society, industry, government, or any complex organization—any and all of which can amount only to its meaning created by my own mind—as more important than my cultivating my finest appreciation for the unity of my whole individuality. And this stressful condition accurately describes the actual happenings now being taken-for-granted as unalterable in my world.

In my seemingly unselfish eagerness to promote so-called social progress, without ever considering the all of the real consequence, I can emphasize and exalt the authority of each of my own grandiose abstractions to try to make it substitute for my own conscious individual initiative and satisfaction. There can be no creative power in my world except that provided by my own conscious or unconscious individuality. There can be no spontaneous generation in the so-called body of the people.

I can realize no living except that which is mine, but I can either ignore or deny that it really is mine. All of my sensibility is nothing else but existence or being of my own constitutive activity. *The phantom problem of trying to resolve how my very own self's sensibility can appear to report not-self (otherness, plurality rather than unity or oneness) is dispelled by my discovering that whatever mental activity I inhibit from functioning consciously as being my own then proceeds to function unconsciously as if it is not my own.* I tend to inhibit any of my conscious functioning whenever it seems easier to do so, exactly to the extent that my mind has not discovered the lifesaving value in any and all presenting discomfort (unhappiness of any kind or degree). Just as I cannot live long without my ability to feel pain so I cannot preserve my existence long without being able to feel unhappiness warning me of the destructiveness in my unhappiness-creating way of living (see my *Psychology of Emotion*).

The one standard of living that I need to seek is that of being able to spend my own vitality consciously in the interest of my own self-world, by using my feeling of pleasure or its inhibition, pain, to guide me. This *is* the one and only possible subject of my business activity already. My freely acknowledging this fact is the only omission that I (including my every fellowman) must pay for in enormous cost to my healthful prosperity. My study of psychic economics is for the purpose of understanding this desideratum lovingly so that I can heedfully regulate it rather than seem regulated by it. For example, I consider the economy in my being consciously true (faithful) to myself, thus.

My resistance against observing the demonstrable truth that I am always being and doing my very best is traceable to my ignoring the fact that whatever I live is my *perfect* living which can be completely accounted for on the basis of each force of truth present in it. By indulging my comforting illusion that I am not always doing my level best, I need not confront myself with that displeasing realization, and therefore need not face the fact that I must grow further helpfulness so that I shall not have to continue merely my present level of helpfulness. As long as I can delude myself with the wishful notion that I could just as readily have done "better" than I did do, certainly I need feel no necessity to add laboriously to my present self helpfulness. Through my gradual arousal of my conscious self helpfulness I ultimately discover that all of my behavior has always been the expression of my best effort to help myself; that I never did, nor could do, anything wrong despite all of the appearance to the contrary.

I know of no development of my conscious self knowledge that has been more astounding than my discovery that my pain (unhappiness of any kind) is as deserving of my full appreciation as is my pleasure (happiness of any kind); that when I thoroughly understand all that my pain (or unhappiness) can teach me about how to conduct my living (to realize the most out of it), I cannot but be most grateful for it. Only then can I feel the sense in my accounting for my pain as being nothing but my inhibited pleasure. It is solely my lack of this accurate respect for my pain (any displeasure) which can account for my ever complaining about its unapparent goodness. It is by my regularly resorting to such distressfully inaccurate appreciation for any of my tremendous power that I can ever succeed in judging my life as hardly worth living. The merciful lesson in all pain (any unhappiness) is precious self revelation.

In production the only natural unit is the individual worker. Each employee is necessarily his own employer; each employer is necessarily his own employee. The illusional chasm now existing in the life of each employee or employer can be dispelled only by each one cultivating the degree of conscious sanity (acknowledgeable self identity) that will enable him to see his own living experience in his likewise consciously united fellow worker. Either employer or employee can most effectually harmonize prevailing discord in his work-a-day world by developing this right view based upon his honoring his intact wholeness. The expression "individual in his world" for accuracy's sake must be altered to "world in its individual" by every single person, for his world is just exactly what he makes it. Such full self realization rarely if ever enters into my business contract consciously, but the demonstrable proof of it is always present.

The duty of an employer, or an employee, to his self only is his one real obligation but it can rarely be discharged since it is rarely felt consciously by either worker. The consequence is labor trouble for each one. The point to be made here is that so-called labor trouble, including every kind of economic ordeal, is the naturally expectable outcome of my disregard for the truth of my personal identity in any of my living of it.

All such seemingly social complaint of mine is always the trouble of my organic individuality, being accurately localized and interpretable only as my organic health involvement. *My labor trouble, or spouse trouble, or child trouble, or neighbor trouble, is my personal organic difficulty in the same vital sense that is my liver, head, heart or any other visceral disturbance.* This social trouble may seem to me to operate only in my social ideas and feelings so that, possibly apart from insomnia, indigestion, headache, or such obvious mental strain, I do not recognize a sharp pain in my neck, head, back or stomach, or high blood pressure, glandular modification, tumor, or similarly non-psychological appearing sign as an indication of my consciously disowned but nevertheless mind-overburdening political, economic, family or whatever social living.

Despite appearances there can be no unity of interest "between" employer and employee or between any person and another. The most self understanding person makes the best employer or employee, either one, and furthering self understanding is all that can further the employer's or employee's recognizing that his fellowman is and must be only his own living of whatever he names his fellowman. Only my conscious justice to my whole self can determine my fairness for any direction of my attention. Conscious self knowledge embodies the spirit that will provide the motivation for either employer or employee to live and treat his every fellowman as some of his very own sensitive being. My increasing my own conscious living is in no sense a sharing of my self with another. I cannot share my self since I am always also my own fellowman. The nature of my individuality requires that even my so-called giving also amounts only to my getting.

All so-called mental discipline, training, education, or even guidance implies application of external authoritarian influence, however gentle, thereby eliminating itself as safe or sane experience for the developing mind that needs, above all, freedom from any coercion whatsoever except its own will with which its own self love can function. A parent who cannot feel his own identity in his living of his baby is incapable of adequate appreciation for his baby's individuality but rather feels that he possesses him. In Emerson's wise phrase, this parent must disobey his child. What I cannot feel that I am, I can feel that I have. By denying my own conscious self possession I compensate my seemingly impaired wholeness by asserting that I can possess what I feel I am not, in this instance, my baby.

I am is unitive; *I have* is divisive. Hence the desirability in my reducing all of my illusional *having* to my perceptive *being*. As Goethe felt the need: to be everything, to seem nothing. To illustrate, whatever I seem to *have* must also seem foreign to my intrinsic being, which is or has only itself. Thus if I claim to *have* a soul rather than *be* one I find it impossible to describe such a foreign possession. However, my claim that I *am* a soul lends itself to ready description, thus: my soul is my selfness or wholeness in the same sense that the soul of my house is its houseness, of my tree is its treeness, or of my any-subject is its wholeness.

My ideal mental development proceeds whenever I can allow my self to love and do as I please (St. Augustine) without any seemingly outside interference. I find then that I love to live in the way I observe my lovable parent living. Whatever my lovable parent wants to enjoy doing, I also want to enjoy doing, just as soon as I can. All I really need, to be able to grow up desirably, is to be able gradually to continue to feel my self as inviolably my self, and not to have to make my self feel that I am not the only liver of all that I live. My feeling that a foreign control can have power over me is irreconcilable with my feelings of my true wholeness. In unity there can be no separation, only free wholeness.

As a self conscious parent whenever I observe my infant or child apparently endangering his life I can recognize his need to behave in this way even while I am lovingly doing whatever seems to me to be indicated. Thus he can avoid his overemphasizing the said activity by living it as prohibited. If he is interested in running out into the traffic and at the same time lives his lovable parent as naturally appreciating the goodness of his wish, even while introducing other enjoyable experience, then there is no need for him to emphasize that interest by repressing it.

By renouncing my illusion, communication, I could discover the whole truth about my language as its being entirely self activity based upon my growing and naming meaning for my living. By ascribing any of that meaning where I imagined it to be out of my mind I was depriving my self of conscious appreciation for my own life in the name of being able to appreciate living other-than-my-own. A pretty self deception *in status nascendi,* attempting to compensate for my seeming to lose some of my own mind by seeming to appropriate some of the mind of my fellowman.

The consequence of this linguistic delusional system was far too shocking for me to work up at first. Even after I began research upon it, I did not dare confront my self with the full force of its significance for my cultivating my mental strength. Only after discovering the indispensable life importance of this unobtrusive verbal addiction to dangerous self sacrifice could I succeed gradually in bringing it into the open of consciousness (see my *Psychology of Language*).

In this process initially I recognized the helpfulness in my not appearing to be responsible for living of mine that seemed irreconcilable with the current unity of mind I regarded as my personal identity. Merely by nominating such mental experience not-I, I could succeed in maintaining the presence of the amount of conscious mindedness I needed to be able to safeguard my life.

Only later research disclosed the role my clinging to my not-I mentality, as such, played as a kind of umbilical cord sparing (conscious) me the unbearable anxiety of feeling my self to be a whole individual, hence, necessarily discrete from my apparently life-giving parent or surrogate parent. Gradually it became clear to me that this quiet, unconscious motivation accounted perfectly for my resistance to acknowledging my irrefutably solipsistic nature. Careful study continued to reveal my deep conviction called communication as heralding the return of my repressed self consciousness, in its way trying to observe my unity as a whole individual. My self consciousness may dispense entirely with my illusion communication, not needing it for designating my unity; my self unconsciousness however reveals its need to be true to my whole unity and my term communication helps to fill that need.

Self insight is self wholeness sight. I now find peace in renouncing my powerful wish to be helpful to my fellowman (at the cost of my, including his, being consciously self helpful only). At last I found joy in living all of my experience which I formerly must judge unworthy, when my self consciousness only temporarily was not ready (with enough of the truth of that experience) to identify it as lovable living of my wholeness.

I am obedient to my majority rule for it is obvious that I live the majority *of my own* humanity elements in it. Majority rule is the real political power of the individual. It explains Aristotle's description of man as, by nature, a political animal.

The demonstrable fact is that every citizen does live *all* that he calls government. He is the sole subject of his every political meaning, not merely of his direct primary vote. All of the law of his government is his design for safeguarding his living. He is *all* that he lives. The most helpful agency he can cultivate in his being is his self consciousness which alone, but only, can spare him the prolonging of his helpfully distressful living warning him that the all that he names external is truly localized internally in the wholeness of his individuality.

Any study in citizenship that alludes to the individual citizen as one of hundreds of millions of other citizens living in this vast country of the United States, is bound to be woefully inadequate since it is painfully inaccurate. Woodrow Wilson declared that it is not the American citizen's blind worship that honors his Constitution, but rather his open-eyed observation of its need and unhesitating courage of conviction to make self government "of simple method, single, unstinted power, and clear responsibility." *I consider one sure way of honoring my Constitution to be that of modifying its wording so that it unmistakably refers to the American citizen's primary civic duty as being that of steadfastly cultivating his own conscious self sovereignty. Such is the strengthening of my political system that I feel is most urgently needed.*

All leadership is either conscious or unconscious *self* leadership, now mostly the latter it seems to me. Each citizen must be his own leader or follower, whether or not he has awakened to that necessity. His persevering cultivation of his *conscious* self sovereignty is required for his gradually recognizing and honoring this realistic foundation of all law: self obedience is the necessary counterpart of self command (see my *American Government*). In *Politics* Emerson asserts:

> The wise know that foolish legislation is a rope of sand, which perishes in the twisting; that the State must follow, and not lead the character and progress of the citizen; the strongest usurper is quickly got rid of; *and they only who build on Ideas, build for eternity.*[11]

Reference to individual man *en masse* as the electorate is ever at the cost of diluting the meaning of the individual citizen as the only voter, since it supports the illusion that for purpose of democratic government a collective abstraction called the people, not the concrete citizen called the individual, may be the essential base. Andrew Jackson's famous slogan, "Shall the People Rule?" is one historic instance; Abraham Lincoln's "Government of the people, by the people, and for the people," is another. The very Constitution of my country's government reads, "We, the people of the United States, in order to secure the blessings of liberty to ourselves and our posterity, do ordain and establish. . . ." Illustrations too numerous to mention flock to mind: the common people to the rescue, the people have the power, the collective honesty

[11] My italics.

of the people, the people have shown themselves qualified to get honest legislation, many people are wiser than any one for everybody knows more than anybody, and so on.

It is neither accurate nor individuality-respecting to contend that the people consist only of one individual after another. No two same individuals can ever exist, for each one is unique by name and definition. I cannot live the same group or crowd or aggregation of any kind that my neighbor lives. Furthermore I cannot live my self as a member of any such gathering, for all that I experience in my living of any sort exists entirely within me, not I within it.

The reality of every American citizen's United States exists within him (her) as a field of operation where greatest possible production can be created from the most economic expenditure of his (her) labor. All of his (her) natural rights and privileges are secured by the insightful care of his (her) each Founding Father as reflected in the unique principle of free government: conscious or unconscious self sovereignty, the disciplined exercise of the law of *individual* human being.

Such is every American citizen's birthright, a self-world possession never before enjoyed by a citizen of any other here-and-now, a start in conscious self development of such tremendously exciting advantage that the risk is ever present for each one, he (she) may never cultivate the mental strength of conscious self identity to be able to appreciate it. What is always most needed is a man for his life, as St. Paul felt it, "For what man knoweth the things of a man save the spirit of a man which is in him" (1 Cor. ii, 11).

I find my so-called formal education largely unrecognizable as self-education, quite the contrary in fact. Such experience cannot pass for conscious self development of recognizable self knowledge. It is not sufficient to stop with this observation. I must heed what such experience always does counterfeit for being (instead of all of the personal living that it can be), namely impersonal, objective, conventionally scientific knowledge. More to the point of so-called political science, such unconscious self experience passes for the kind of knowledge that decides, through majority rule, just how surplus wealth shall be both accumulated and distributed.

At first it seems too painful to have to try to reconcile in living unity 1) my self as largely individuality unconscious and 2) my corporation as nothing but a conception in my individual mind. A duly passionate but self conscious view of the subject is possible to me only on account of my having grown the stature of my conscious self identity that not only allows but requires such difficult consideration.

I work for the day when my government administrator will no longer be satisfied with blindly attempting production of a consciously self responsible citizen by means of conventional (self neglectful) educational experience. Then may he sense the economy in earnestly devoting his governmental power to gradually explicating for each one of his "constituency" the unique lifesaving in conscious self education as well as the enormous health cost to everyone in unconscious self education.

I face it here and now, *so-called impersonal education is consciously self neglectful experience hardly worthy of the name "free education" or "education for freedom." The only land of liberty is in the living of the individual life.* As a businessman, once I feel large conscious self identity to be more economical and productive than small conscious self identity, my concern for my margin of profit will not allow me to endure any but my most economical methods.

The value of money may be measured by the produce it can buy. Production is a general term for bed, board, health care, education, or whatever lifesaving produce, including its surplus,—all of which constitutes wealth and all of which is reducible to human *individual* energy. *My* exertion (labor) increases in conscious value as my estimation increases for what it can accomplish for my *whole* welfare. Money may be described as stored-up human energy, but *whose* energy? I can store-up only my own energy and must beware of assuming possession of any of my power for which I cannot become trustworthily accountable, self consciously responsible.

Needed most in my "political science" study is the spelled-out discipline acknowledging what must happen in my society as long as I disregard study of the allness and wholeness of my life's individuality. The primary principle of self helpfulness underlying this book is the outgrowth of my strenuous effort to observe feelingly the full measure of my wholeness and allness. It required this specific development, increasing whole self appreciation, to enable me to attribute the full measure of *individuality* to every person and thing of my world.

The above paragraph records the growth of the conscious self knowledge that led to my conviction that it is impossible for one individual to teach or learn from another individual; that all education must be either consciously or unconsciously *self* education; that *conscious* self education is necessary for health; that *unconscious* self education produces danger signals of health called "illness"; that every so-called disease process applies to condition of the microscopic germ rather than the inviolable person; that my growing *conscious* self wholeness redeems all of my cancerigenic hyperplasia and hypoplasia.

As my realization of the powerful truth of oneness grew, I began gradually to see through every kind of so-called duality or plurality as being my unready mind's effort to dispose of its single experience when it was not consciously individualized enough to attribute its due individuality to it. With my mind's eye open to this reality of realities, I was amazed to notice for the first time the enormous extent to which I practiced unconsciously the divide-and-conquer technique in my psychology, e.g., self and society,—not my self including my self's society; individual and state,—not my individuality including my state; labor and management,—not my labor including my management and the converse; wealth and poverty,—not my wealth including my poverty and the converse; God and man,—not my divinity including my humanity; health and sickness,—not my health including my health ordeal; love and hate,—not my love including my hurt love; conscious and unconscious,—not my recognized consciousness including my unacknowledged consciousness.

Contrary to nearly all of the theory of political economy, my society does not consist of two classes, the independent and the dependent, for such a division of human nature is absolutely impossible. All that can be meant by such an attempted schism of *human individual being* is man's having to help himself survive now by denying that he *is* all that he can ever mean by his fellowman of any and every economic condition. I am all of my own independence or dependence. In fact all of my independence consists of my conscious dependence upon my self. However as long as I can seem to be able to dispose safely of either my poverty or wealth stricken fellowman merely by saying, "It is not I," I can have no course available to me other than that of pursuing my time-tested rather than my self-reality tested theory after theory of Political Science. "The" poor can never be "with" me, for I *am* always my poor. Whether I ever feel my self as my only rich or poor man depends solely upon my individual merit as witnessed in my conscious struggle to appreciate the unity of my wholeness.

My labor union or my management incorporation may help me to feel my self in either one, provided my motive for extending my sense of self identity that far *within* is quite evident. However to recognize, with my Emerson, that "all union must be ideal in actual individualism," I must create this self conscious conception through the hard work of giving birth to it at the fearful risk of feeling that my currently conscious self identity is endangered. Once I can feel my wholeness and allness to this extent I need never again feel helplessly subject to the fear of a labor-saving device or organization of any kind. Rather I can then hail every discovery or invention as that much precious self discovery. *The real law of progress must be in line with the continuity of individual human life.*

I cannot but acknowledge that I am always living the best of all possible worlds, once I can fully appreciate the fact of the force of truth. Certainly my reported world events regularly *seem* to leave much to be desired,—cessation of war; relief of poverty; prevention of illness, accident, ignorance, crime, violence, and every other kind of threat to life. However, my study of the sufficient truth entering into all such distressful living constantly reveals it to be so many preciously indispensable signs and symptoms of my existing world-wide disregard for the indescribable value of individual life, my one and only possible expenditure.

Once I do discover that truth is all that ever exists, that nothing but truth can ever be revealed, despite deceptive appearances, then I must work hard at fully respecting such a profound finding. To ease my mind I had been indulging the habit of overlooking that open secret: whatever is, truly is. As I realize that my truth is my mind's only possible reality I first begin to acknowledge the benefit in making my peace with it, and then gradually develop the honesty to extol it as incontrovertible evidence of my own (including my fellowman's) divinity, no less.

However my industriously functioning fellowman is rarely aware that he is divine. It is his habit to ascribe his true greatness to an impersonal god or to one of his own abstractions such as luck or civilization or society. Society is merely a word concealing my inability to acknowledge my fellowman as my own, but it is credited by my self ignoring fellowman as increasing the supply of products for consumption, developing new tastes and faculties, awakening new interests, broadening the field of effort and opportunity, creating new occupations, raising the standard of living, reducing the hours of labor, providing leisure for rest and recreation, enabling division of labor to cultivate special competence, and so on. *All credit for any advancement of any kind or degree is always and only deserved by an individual in the form of his crediting his self with his achievement.*

My peculiarly distinct office as a scientific economist is insistence upon learning to love (difficultly) my one truth of my inviolable and growing self. Why? So that I can then observe exactly where to look for whatever new development I deem desirable, namely to my augmenting of my *conscious* self identity so that I can then control my self with regard to my desire rather than merely feel subject to it. My competence in volitionally regulating my wishes and fears is most helpful of all in my efforts to relieve my aches and pains that I attribute to my Industry. This statement satisfactorily defines the purpose underlying my writing for it has most vital bearing on the clearing up of my problems that I may presume exist external to me (nowhere): my economic law enforces the truth that all solidarity, all union, is ideal, and exists only in my living of it. Only my disciplining my mind with self consciousness can awaken me to my legal responsibility for being all of its (my mind's) worldfulness. *The conditions of my living are always potentially difficult on account of its greatness. These good conditions only grow harder by my refusal to consider them mine.*

Renowned educator Horace Mann remarked how much more can be accomplished by a "right view" of any subject than by great reasoning about it. It is my self consciousness that enables my viewing my (any) subject rightly, as being all and only mine. I need this sanity check when my reading mostly includes the product of a highly educated, hard working individual seemingly unaware that his individuality alone is responsible for his literary production. My B. F. Skinner writes of his book, *Beyond Freedom and Dignity*:

> My book is an effort to demonstrate how things go bad when you make a fetish out of individual freedom and dignity. If you insist that individual rights are the *summum bonum*, then the whole structure of society falls down.[12]

Skinner thus seems to declare his individual autonomy is a myth, that his belief in the responsible internality of man is a superstition.

I find it helpful to acknowledge that my psychological ideal, *solipsism*, is the true condition of being or existence of any kind. It does often *seem* unpractical and impracticable but I waste no argument on the matter, for no amount or kind of reasoning can reveal the illusional nature of that seeming. *Only an increment of self consciousness can ever account for a decrement of self consciousness.* Born with no self con-

[12] *Time*, September 20, 1971, p. 47.

sciousness whatsoever that amounts to *conscious* self consciousness I can grow up from infant to boy and from boy to man increasing my pride in my judgment, logic and reasoning, while increasing my shame for what little self consciousness I have been unable to escape. I shudder when I imagine I could be unable to author consciously my Walt Whitman's self appreciation,

> To breathe the air, how delicious!
> To speak, to walk, to seize something by the hand! . . .
> To be this incredible God I am! . . .
> O amazement of things, even the least particle!
> O spirituality of things!

Plato stated the issue plainly by declaring he "will prize those studies which result in his soul getting soberness, righteousness, and wisdom, and will less value the others." And in the one basic respect my Plato's world was the same as mine, in that he consciously claimed it as his own. Whether I renounce my study of science for my study of literature, or vice versa, the consequence of weak mindedness is the same if I claim to be able to recognize aught but my own living being in either self discipline. "To know the best which has been thought and said in the world," my Matthew Arnold's wording, I must know not only what it is but also that I am the thinker and the sayer of it all.

I call only that teaching best that is consciously laid out systematically as my own mind's willingly generating its own self's meaning, namely, conscious development of my own mental power. No experience can become consciously mind worthy, much less consciously interesting, other than conscious self experience. As usual in my recording my life orientation the operative word is consciousness. Nothing but good can ever come from any of my living, for it, itself, is the source of all and only my good. To make that good my conscious good is my mind's life worthy aim,—my everyday being consciously the first day of the rest of my life. My Baruch Spinoza said, "Man's happiness consists in his being able to preserve his own essence." George W. Norris (1865-1944) noticed, as do I, the truth is that my religion and my politics are one.

I find it good to acknowledge that my study of the truth regarding my every fellowman, whether ghetto, gutter or gold-coast found, provides the same proper source for my revealing his (her) godliness. *Every* human being is divine, but not every human being is able to be conscious for his divinity. The almighty word here is "conscious." Whoever has discovered how to reveal to his own mind the truth of enough of his greatness (by arduously enlarging his conscious self identity to include his all), acts according to his divine self estimate. Whenever I cannot recognize enough of the wholly full wonderfulness of my being I must act accordingly, even holding my life (including any life) not worth living, entirely due to my inhibited consciousness for its *inviolable* wholeness, allness, oneness. *Naming my self God necessitates my attributing my same godliness to whatever and whomever I live, the most difficult conscious self identity.*

However, the divine worth I place upon *consciously* absolute individuality—its inaccessible unrelatedness, its own substantive authority and responsibility, its untouchable independence, its self-existing self sufficiency, its incommunicable resourcefulness, its perfect freedom, its adorably infallible indefectibility—can become thoroughly obvious as self-evident also from the motivation in my realizing the hidden suicidal tendency in my every unrelieved opposite conviction suggesting that I am not my own uncomeatable *all.*

The life of conscious self fulfillment is *most* difficult, quite as my Plato's Socrates declared. It is human nature not only to tend to reject whatever I cannot understand but also to feel fearfully threatened by it, to wish to destroy it before it destroys me, if I cannot seem to safely ignore it. While I excite my instinct of self preservation by observing carefully that I alone am the solipsistic soul of whatever and whomever *I* live, and thereby honor to the utmost that living of mine, my fellowman who has not worked up this comprehensive self identity for his own good must feel his Dorsey as actually rejecting him, rather than really expending his living in his fellowman. Furthermore, while I consciously live all of what I call society, organization, others, and the like, *as extension of my own life,* my fellowman who has not cultivated such enlarged self identity must feel his Dorsey as antisocial, an anarchist, or narrowly rather than broadly selfish. Hence it is, I observe helpfully that I can live my mind as if it is not mine, I can feel completely at home living as my mind-blind fellowman does.

Freedom from my insightless living does not and cannot mean riddance of it, for that would entail my inability to sense my self identity in any fellowman of mine who is fearful of his self consciousness, devoted to his (unrecognized) illusions of externality, dependent upon reasoning rather than self consciousness for his supreme help, and so on.

Therefore, I feel the courageous love for humanity in my every historic figure who has consciously lived his identity in his every fellowman in his every society or class of man. It is thus I account clearly and fully to my self for the consciously unique self significance I have grown also through my study of my own Tracy.

The soul of (my) Tracy's life (including his world) orientation is summed up in his science: Ideology. This science is based in his feeling of conviction that his sensibility (including his every sensation, perception, feeling or sentiment) is all that can be a source of his (self) knowledge. For him to think straight is to not see in any of his experience anything but that which is all and only the possession of his sentient being. Obviously this consciously life-revering self affirmation must free self respecting man with regard to all of his illusional popularity, fame, or similar unconscious dependence, thereby revealing as not merely futile but also fatal his blind reliance upon alien influence for his welfare.

Again, despite every appearance to the contrary, I persevere in observing that my own organized living is the only organization I can ever experience. As already noted, by personifying my term "organization" without realizing that it is entirely a creation of my own mind I can seem to absolve my self from any responsibility for it, assume it can do something on its own, praise or blame it as I please, and so on. Then my conscious irresponsibility for my own living can take the form of my consciously claiming some impersonal organization (of mine) to be responsible. I consistently find this semantic psychosis at the core of all of my mental trouble, beginning with my personification of my family, church, school, neighborhood, national or international organization.

Thus *my* consciously depersonalized "organization" becomes a specific self screen that I preserve for either blaming or praising my self without realizing it. In my mind's eye, as in my writing, I may tend to capitalize such consciously depersonalized terms, e.g., Science, Literature, Communication, Policy, Generation, Property, Humanity, Divinity, Evil, Environment, Heredity, Management, Labor, Credit, Free Trade, Business, Enterprise, Stock Market, Depression, Bargaining Table, Relationships, Team Work, Membership, Collaboration, Wild Cat Strike, Regimentation, Externality, Objectivity, Death, Life, Evolution, Communism, Nationalism, Mysticism, and every other Ism except my conscious psychologism.

My establishment, institution, union, or other abstraction of any kind lends itself to such illusional and delusional systematization, so that I find it necessary to complain bitterly about (my own personified) Education, Government, State of Michigan, United States, United Nations, White or Black Race, Weather, Twentieth Century, Military, Industry, Inflation, Devaluated Dollar, Marriage. Meanwhile my bitterness about my own fellowman is exacting its necessary toll in my visceral tension and glandular secretion which at first I cannot recognize and later cannot identify as the issue of my short self sightedness. *My emancipating my mind from its bondage in its own habit of self depersonalization, is my chief civic obligation to my self government for self freedom.*

In other words, my unenlightened egoism is responsible for the narrow selfishness that does not permit me to feel selfish responsibility for all of my individual world. Unless I define my individuality, in the fullest sense of the word, i.e., to mean my undivided self alone, I cannot begin to understand these lifesaving truths: that all I can live is my own self activity; that all of my self activity is the product of my growing my self; that my inhibiting my self activity involves my inhibiting my growth; that my interfering with my self activity is my only localization of my pain (any unhappiness).

Little wonder the Taoist foregoes the tempting practice of regulation, defining it as interference, recognizing that the riches of contentment derive where ruling begins in conscious self government, heeding that any other law-regulated behavior (most of all, education that is not recognizable as self education) is the specific source of disesteem for the individual's own individuality.

My greatest charity or workable philanthropy (especially educational and political enlightenment) that I need to bestow upon my self I am often sorely tempted, from habit, to try to displace upon a so-called external American Government, namely: keen consciousness for my necessity to mind my own affairs and heed that all education is self education quite as all help must be self help. Whenever I lean upon anything but my own helpfulness, I am behaving as if I can be literally out of my mind. *The principle enunciated in this book, namely, I am all of my own living, is as incommunicable as any other visceral process of mine* (see my *Psychology of Language*).

However, in recognizing my beautiful delusion of communication I succeed in feeling fuller responsibility for my mind as being all my own. Furthermore, I then discover that I have further real power of helping my self that was formerly obscured by my wish to be helped otherwise. What I was allowing to pass for communication all the while was nothing but my mind's own operation, entirely, but I was unable to credit my mind with all of this greatness that had all the appearance of going on outside of me. I then realized that I had been conducting my mind as if I could be subject to my communication instead of its being merely my illusion, hence, subject to me.

As Bastiat keenly felt his sanity: all that can be expected

of law is *justice.*[13] However, it is only natural for my desperate legislator to try to legislate brotherly love or whatever else seems to his own troubled mind to further "ideal legislation," in addition to protecting strict interpretation of the due function of law, namely, *individual* justice. It is precisely at this juncture the fact needs heeding: Only self love can subsume all love. Brotherly love that is not based entirely upon self love is a helpful illusion that exists in the individual mind, however. My faith in "the law" may seem to defraud my mind of that much conscious responsibility, but it cannot and will not do for faith in my self to develop *my* love to extend to *my* fellowman.

Quite as Rudyard Kipling versed it,

> Now these are the Laws of the Jungle,
>   And many and mighty are they;
> But the head and the hoof of the Law and
>   The haunch and the hump is—Obey![14]

I begin to learn to obey my inclinations long before I begin to realize that all obedience is self obedience for it did seem to me that I was required to obey another, usually my parent or my older sibling.

Only after learning that I *am my parent* doing the commanding can I discover that to grow the precious ability to command (my self) I must simultaneously grow the ability to obey (my self). Then I can begin to understand all about inner, or so-called outer, controls. My sane occupation is to try to occupy my self consciously. I observe my living ideally when I can feel me in it. The convexity, concavity or level of my body ego

[13] In his *Theory of Political Economy* (London, 1888) p. xlix, Stanley Jevons wrote, "The true doctrine may be more or less clearly traced through the writings of a succession of great French economists, from Condillac, Baudeau, and le Trosne, through J. B. Say, Destutt de Tracy, Storth and others, down to Bastiat and Courcelle-Senevil."
[14] *Jungle Book.*

is the primary basis for my appreciating my all that passes for geology, astronomy, or theology.

To illustrate positive affirmation, the unity that I call my body merely *seems* to be made up of separate or different parts, for it is really just a single organic whole with one interest only, namely its wholeness. One identity constitutes all of its own nature, embracing head, trunk and extremity absolutely alike. Organ does not cooperate with organ, despite all appearance to the contrary,—rather each so-called organ is really nothing but *integral organic wholeness* itself in operation (instead of cooperation or collaboration in any form). The law of the wholeness of my being is immutable, and innumerable seeming exceptions cannot in the least invalidate its working principle: *the production of the good of the whole of which I am sole creator and proprietor.*

Once felt in my self, then my observation of my every fellow creature proves to me this solipsistic life orientation is a universal one affirmed by being nearly always negated (i.e., unconsciously affirmed only). Probably the official term most used by the citizen for his unconscious self is "the State" or "the Government,"—either being his name for an imagined governmental entity existing in its own right, functioning autonomously and so on, "out there somewhere," rather than a name for a complex of his own self control existing only in his own mind. Bastiat defines the state as "the great fictitious entity by which everyone seeks to live at the expense of everyone else."[15]

I cannot but trace every so-called social, economic, political, scientific, or other seemingly objective or impersonal consideration first to the truth that it is mine and then to the truth that it is strictly my individual *subjective concern* with nothing possibly objective or impersonal about it at all. My science of my world first of all is only mine and second may become my *conscious* mental science. I am *naturally* whatever I am, only and entirely. Whether or not I am able to be consciously sure of it, whatever I experience is my self growth of my

[15] *The State.*

native self property. Contrary to popular belief, I do not and cannot "appropriate" it from someone else.

My living of my own unlimited freedom subsumes my living of my fellowman with his indisputable right to his own unlimited freedom. My natural right includes my social right, quite as my altruism is my grown-up egoism. Of such selffulness is my personal code of honor. On account of its seeming immensity I may choose to judge some of my experience as not mine, but then again my judgment about any of my mental content is all and only my own and, rather than ever serve as evidence of not-self, must always attest my own being. Frederic Bastiat's essay *What Is Seen and What Is Not Seen* is an admirable application of the consequence of self consciousness and self unconsciousness to individual man's political economy.[16]

Everyone of my world who devotes any of his mind's attention to what he may call political science, government, economics, or what not, must really be making some certain living of his own wholly individual mind a subject of his personal concern. And here I mention again a profound truth: Nevertheless *his unconsciousness for his being the only possible subject for his consideration, is helpful to him whenever it occurs.* Indeed each of my *present* methods for conducting politics or business or economic legislation, however appearing to lend itself to immeasurable so-called abuse, is actually now my own institutional form for helping my self. It is my very own personal growth in production, which it benefits me to honor for being as good as it is in any way able to be right now. It constitutes the vital force with which I may then proceed to develop and cultivate political science in recognizable keeping with the existing nature and needs of my forceful individual constitution. My only alternative to working with this reality of my realities is to try to cut my self out from under the ground of my own being and then proceed to try to be able to make something new *out of nothing!*

[16] Bastiat, "friendly and quick to act . . . adopted the liberal ideas of Smith, Say and Destutt de Tracy." Dean Russel, *Frederic Bastiat: Ideas and Influence* (Irvington-On-Hudson, New York: Foundation for Economic Education, Inc., 1969), p. 22.

Whatever is, has its necessary meaning for what is to become of it. To deny the value of its existence is to deny the value of that much of my own living. By not starting from where I am I cannot begin at the beginning, cannot build even upon shifting sand. Naturally (i.e., in the interest of my own welfare) I want everyone of my world to be able to create this powerful self appreciation in his own living, as this book bears witness, even though *my daily experience demonstrates my fellowman's necessarily helping his self by feeling almost totally irresponsible for the way he completely regulates his living of his world.*

The consequent frustration of my innate wish for my neighbor's conscious self fulfilment would be unbearable were it not for my ability not only to recognize that he must help his self as best he can and does right now, but also to use *my mind's lifesaving free imagination* to enjoy my neighbor's living in any and every way I please, such as his calling his political science a consciously minding his own business, calling his ballot-dependent government his own conscious self control, calling his economics his own conscious self accounting, or whatever. Exercising freely this precious use of my mind (to be able to live as I consciously please) is of indescribably practical help for my avoidance of placing undue emphasis upon my frustrating my self (whenever I cannot use my imagination to relieve my self of such distress).

Considering how my self esteem has grown with my working up my world meaning as my own I am mindful of my Hesiod's happy economy, "If thou shouldst lay up even a little upon a little, and shouldst do this often, soon would even this become great." My own power is all that I can ever trust, and I am the responsible trustee wholly accountable to my self for the way I use it. My conscious self confidence must be a plant of seemingly slow or speedy growth depending entirely upon how soon I can make my unconscious self trust (i.e., conscious self distrust) grow into *conscious* self trust (see my *Psychology of Emotion*). Acknowledgeable self credit is my only possible source of development of my appreciation for my full and united human estate. My whole boundless world *is* ever mine. Disraeli soliloquized sanity, "Man is not the creature of circumstances. Circumstances are the creatures of men."

To illustrate further, *I firmly believe that it would be well indeed for the future of my world if every student's responsible individuality orientation could become his sole educational concern, as manifest in his teacher, his textbook, his school living.* However, I realize that it is best that my student not realize that his very own mind is all that there *can* be to whatever he calls labor, land, capital, business, money, trade, bank, exchange, stock, supply, demand, and so on, just as long as he must only overwhelm his mind with such enormous truth thereby forfeiting whatever other presence of his mind he had theretofore arduously succeeded in promoting as recognizably his own.

However as long as I must treat any subject only as not my own, I must seem to take all of the life out of it, for the only life in any of my consideration is the life I give to it. I *am* my only rich or poor. As Andrew Carnegie nearly clarified it, individualism is all that can continue, each millionaire is the trustee for his poor ones either consciously in which case he feels the good of it, or unconsciously in which case he misses feeling the good of it. Thus each poor one *is* clearly the benefactor of his rich fellowman, who is learning "the luxury of doing good" (Oliver Goldsmith). Each shall be of my living as long as its other can be. My mind can neither afford nor grow any separate class interest.

Inequality is and must be non-existent in the unified identity I name my Individual Being. Personally acknowledging this omnific truth I can do no wrong without consciously or unconsciously suffering my lifesaving feeling of wrong (pain or unhappiness or loss of interest in life of any kind or degree). Cervantes said it, "The brave man carves out his own fortune, and every man is the son of his own works." Not seeing my own immutable and inviolable unity, it seems my "head is as full of quarrels, as an egg is full of meat" (Shakespeare).

Conscious self-unconsciousness (named otherness, impersonal or not-I) taxes my human economy more heavily than can my consciously self-alienated government of any kind, obscuring my natural resource, sidetracking my abundance of innate power so that it becomes inaccessible for my volitional use. The extent to which my fellowman completely self-reliantly works up for his own life satisfaction this truth of his individuality is the *only* index of *his* so-called civilization of his world of his self. All truth is indomitable and must ultimately obtain. Meanwhile it is a marvelous creature comfort to be able to realize that there is no easy or difficult way, such as "mass communication of the wise to the unknowing," to influence or be influenced by this real individual man.

Fritz Kunkel, M.D., describes "negative freedom," e.g., how it is possible to develop a theme or positive subject by the use of negative particulars, by treating it negatively while "presupposing the positive." Irony or satire can accomplish similar result. Kunkel calls this method nonic "from the Latin expression *ars nonica,* an art which describes its object by stating what it is not, *quod non est.*[17]

My saying "no" to anything cannot rid me of it by its being consigned "elsewhere," that is, to somewhere other than my own existence. But I can and do deceive myself that such an impossibility is really possible, *whenever I am unable to see my own identity, only and entirely, in whatever experience I live.* Furthermore, only rarely may I take the trouble to consciously heed my experience as all and only *self* experience.

The question arises: How then can I ever succeed in consciously getting my mind, so to speak, back together again? The question: How did I ever succeed in seeming to get it out of my life in the first place? may be nearer its answer.

My scientific evidence has accumulated to indicate that, in its beginning, my mind experienced all of itself, including its every sensation, without resorting to distinctifying any of itself either as being its own or as not being its own. To illustrate, its vision was not either disowned as picturing so-called externality, or owned up to as localized mind sight;

[17] *In Search of Maturity* (New York: Charles Scribner's Sons, 1949), p. 47.

and its hearing likewise was neither disowned as a reporting of localized not-self, nor claimed as its own endogenous auditory experience. Only later did my mind's capacity develop for using each sense either as its contributing to my conscious self identity or *as if* it could somehow get out of my own mind to report upon distant events.

When at last I could use my mind to create some feeling of its own identity, I found this most worthy task to be complicated by my not wishing to live conscious pain or unhappiness of any kind or degree. Nevertheless much of my living was most difficult and distressing. My inability to own up to such as being life worthy, although understandable in terms of my unpreparedness for such hardiness, led to my beginning to dissociate my mind of very early childhood into 1) whatever I could live with satisfaction and nominate mine or I, and 2) whatever I could live only with dissatisfaction motivating my naming it not-mine or not-I. And an enormously expensive development that was, namely, conscious elimination of all of my own living that I was unable to live with sufficient love to even want to recognize it as all and only my own.

Much uninhibited healthfulness depends upon the way I construct all that I can mean by my external world. If I assume that my evidence of my senses is sufficient to attest existence other than my own I commit my self to a life of self sacrifice, discrediting my own nature consistently in the name of a not-self world. Thus I name not-mine all that I cannot claim as my own living, and then construct my external world out of that living of mine that I have repudiated. This method of external world building involves me in my delusion that I can make something out of nothing, especially since I seem to be able to make nothing out of something (my own living).

However, here is a way for me to construct my self world exactly as I have constructed what I call my body image, namely, entirely out of my own acknowledgeable life elements. Thus, I do not hesitate to nominate my own so-called body as my own. I do not have to regard it as foreign to me in order to prevent my self from hurting my self with it.

I can learn to use my sensation, perception, motion, and so on, without injury to my self. Similarly I can learn to use my sensation, perception, motion, and so on that I can attribute to my own self's world without hurting my self with it. I can avoid the danger of traffic, or height, or whatever potential danger in my external world,—all without having to deny that any of it is mine.

In my fictive method of self sacrifice is inherent adequate sign and symptom helpfully indicating that it involves my using my imagination to deny that my soul is my own and that my all is my soul. Out of its life orientation issues nearly all of my human woes, including so-called sickness, crime, political illusion and delusion.

My factive method of self devotion results in my using my imagination to create my self world in my own image, loving all in it as my self, calling all of it what it really is, namely my own soulful creation.

Whenever I say No to any living of mine, I am emotionally controlled, not self conscious. Afresh, "No" is a word denoting that whatever I am negating is not being lived with sufficient conscious self love and therefore must be disposed of as different from the rest of me. To use extreme illustrations: "Black is absolutely white" or "The moon is surely made of green cheese." Each statement *is* merely an assertion, but it is constituted of my actual living (me). Therefore it is only life-affirming for me to recognize the right of such an obviously illogical assertion to exist. My denying that right is tantamount to my denying the right to exist of that much of my own living.

Whatever self consciousness I can command is feeling of utmost importance in that it safeguards whatever sensing of my whole sameness I have thus far worked up by 1) providing awareness for my already acknowledgeable self identity while thus 2) withholding awareness for my, as yet, unacknowledgeable self identity. *It is only my sensing my wholeness identity that enables me to attribute individuality anywhere in my world.*

When Gottfried Wilhelm Leibnitz (1646–1716) grew up his

marvelous truth that no two blades of grass were alike, he proceeded to observe, but also somewhat conceal, his discerning discovery by naming it: the law of the identity of indiscernibles. In his bachelor's dissertation *De principio individui* (1663) he asserted that individuality is constituted by the whole entity or essence of a thing. In my book too much cannot be made over explicating this truth of absolute individuality. Protected as it is from ever becoming a statistic by its inviolable subjectivity, individuality cannot lend itself ever to any kind of so-called classification, for such can be based only upon unwarranted assumption derived entirely from fanciful criteria implying plurality (e.g., arbitrarily *presumed* resemblance or difference).

"Negation" is certainly not riddance. Quite the contrary, it merely augments my involuntary (unconscious) psychic motivation. My negativistic functioning reveals my lack of insight that all of my disobedience must be my self disobedience. Negativism is merely inhibited positivism!

One truth, as certain as any truth can be, reveals: Whatever happens in anybody (or anything) should happen exactly as it is happening. Nothing can occur (or be prevented from occurring) unless the full force required for its occurring (or not occurring) is present. Furthermore, this all-important truth can be scientifically demonstrated and validated.

Now my conscious mindfulness for this truth along with the truth of all of my faultfinding and complaining accompanying innumerable unpleasant events in my living, is necessary if I would account fully for all that passes for my so-called civilization and its discontents. The wishful transition from "I do not like it" to "It is not true, certainly not my truth," occurs with the incalculable speed of thought. However, grievous, symptom-bearing consequence results from it. It is my life's work to redeem with my self consciousness all of my living that I have disowned as too painful to recognize as mine. *My sanity results from all of my living in which I can see my self identity. My insanity results from all of my living in which I cannot see my self identity.* All I can ever do is wholly accomplished through being my self alone. Hence all of my thinking or doing is as organic as my respiration, or my building of my bone.

Most meaningful self observation in this chapter is:

1) By means of my augmenting conscious self identity I can renounce my enormous dependence upon my emotionality with which I do seem to be able to divide my living into good or bad, mine or not mine, depending entirely upon whether I can live it with conscious love or not.

2) With self consciousness derived from my discipline of *living difficultly* the living of mine that has been associated with pain or unhappiness, I have been able to discover that the force of truth (factuality) *always* accounts for whatever happens (or does not happen) politically or otherwise.

3) The truth of my living is always on the side of whatever happens in all of my experience. I am always helping my self with it only.

4) Whatever is, truly is; whatever is, is just; whatever is, is lifesaving; whatever is, wholly is, is all and only about itself. Negation can be only inhibited (unconscious) affirmation.

5) Fully apprised of all of the truth about any of my living, I become capable of seeing the beauty of it, the benefit in it, the glory of it!

6) The best of all possible worlds exists in me, not merely I in it. However I can and do imagine myself as living in a world totally unknowable by me with the sole exception of my own existence.

7) Mine is the best of all possible worlds, unquestionably divinely ordained, for it is absolutely perfect, self-evidently truthful, entirely just, thoroughly good, wholly beautiful, completely desirable and adorably trustworthy.

8) Although in the beginning of my life I was an individual without realizing it, in order to preserve my life and develop its potentiality it has become my life work to recognize that I am all and only individual.

9) Fortunately for the law of my nature's constitution, I can ignore the allness and wholeness of my individuality only

by signs and symptoms indicating that I am risking my health to hasten my dissolution.

10) Therefore in all of my political, societal, religious, or educational existence of any kind it behooves me to observe that my individuality subsumes the all and whole of it.

11) It is my self consciousness only that insures my continuing *peaceful* living of my fellowman as my self; it is my self unconsciousness only that can induce me to live my fellowman unpeacefully (violently) as if not my self.

12) Justification of violence (e.g., war) *after* it has occurred is understandable reliance upon truth, not to be confused with recklessly attempted justification of any making certain that violence (e.g., war) will occur again.

13) My confrontation with the truth of how to insure resort to violence through self unconsciousness also reveals the truth of how to insure resort to peace through self consciousness.

SUMMARY

All that is not One must ever
Suffer with the wound of Absence.

Jelalu'd Din

Since starting to write this treatise my plan has been to try to subsume my Tracy's conscious self responsibility syntonically in mine. His uniquely synoptic comprehension of the single identity underlying natural law, constitutional government and self sovereignty necessitated his inventing a political economy honoring the wholeness of this all-embracing identity. What impels me to complete this book describing my political panacea, *conscious self sovereignty,* is my ever increasing recognition of the urgent need for it, however largely unfelt, in the conscious living of my fellow American citizen, especially in each one required by his office to represent his American government as, more than any other, revering the unique viability in *conscious* human individuality.[1]

With depreciation for my individual life *must* go my dreary depreciation for all that is human, e.g., my meaning of divinity, my meaning of money, my meaning of science or of any other subject of my negating mind. Only paramount appreciation for human life can ever be profitable, enabling the greatest of blessings, namely, self security. Every mind is self-evidently solipsistic, there being no other possibility than for it to be all about itself. With this insight only can my soul feel its worth. However *consciously* solipsistic mindfulness, the touchstone of all sanity, is rarest of all mental conditions merely on account of the individual's spending his life in self-sacrifice (self unconsciousness) instead of in self devotion (self consciousness). The most important truth, rarely even suspected, is the enormous extent to which I (including *my* everyman)

[1] See author's *American Government,* a book describing his ideal American citizenship and exactly how he works toward it.

lack biologically adequate appreciation for my own amazingly wonderful nature. I can revere life in my fellowman just exactly and only as I revere *all of it* in my personal identity.

Furthermore, it is wholly just that I fully acknowledge my present government (world or local) as being the *only possible one for serving me (including my each fellow being) in my present stage of development. Whatever kind of government I might claim I prefer, can grow only out of that which already exists in me, as a natural outgrowth rather than as an "externally imposed order."* This precious understanding of how my mind's growth occurs is born of love of truth (fact) about its real constitution. Without such understanding I can only meddle frantically with external (unconsciously *internal*) force in my worthy effort to order my internal muddle. Proceeding from the principle that somebody else can do something for me, I can unwittingly, and seemingly irresponsibly, expect "them" somehow to make me over, change my nature (as a pill might seem to be able to do) for the better.

All of my desire emerges as a refinement of the natural needs (thirst, hunger, rest, etc.) of the body dimension of my mind. My hunger for food or thirst for drink is a manifestation of my self love only. Indeed my every want must be entirely of and about itself *in my self*, either consciously or unconsciously. How I helped my self by discovering that my every desire, itself, is all and only about *its* self! My assertion that I can love you implics that I can do some of your self-loving for you,—a clearly irrefutable impossibility.

While growing my political self consciously in the specific direction of disciplined self-realization I find it helpful to present a thorough survey of the political science of this daring explorer of the realm of the spirit, Tracy. He *sensed* his spiritual power as the real material of his living, unhesitatingly treating the unity of his subjectivity as his true substance. Intensive force of habitually idiomatic writing is lovingly renounced in favor of my consciously original wordage, to the best of my present ability, but I have far to go in this direction of calling my all my soul. My motivation to see my identity only in *all* of my living comes from my realizing that my conscious (self) hatred becomes intensified and exaggerated when associated with my living that I cannot acknowledge *is* mine. To give a class-name such as singularism[2] or even solipsism to this truth of truths of mine (namely: I am all of my own living) is not at all to my sufficient liking for its allness-and-wholeness cannot be encompassed by any such sophisticated term denying the allness of individuality even as it appears to affirm it.

It is tempting to try to uphold the uniquely vital power of my responsible self consciousness without appearing to appreciate fully the precious providence of my reasoning out of which it has emerged. Heeding that *all* of my living is of magnificent sameness, oneness and wholeness has proved my safest governing aid for securing peace in my world of my own creating. The consciously individualistic way of life takes in every other possible way, however, and my responsible awareness for this truth has spared me immeasurable discomfort associated with any illusion of mine of ever being isolated from the rest of my mankind. Self identity, *ipse,* is all that is possible for me. However, *conscious* self identity, my quality of qualities, is entirely a matter of degree.

For the purpose of rescuing clear understanding about the all-and-only importance of my human individuality (instead of ignoring my diluting its lifegiving nature with pluralistic terminology) I find it necessary to work up a scientific study of what I must mean by any and every "organization" of my world, above all determining whether I seem to belong to it or it to me.

For living my fellow creature *without appearing to lose some of my own living in his name* I need to construct a true psychology of organization based upon my recognizing that my organization is 1) all really mine deriving the whole of its meaning from my mind, and 2) all seeming to be not mine whenever I personify it, by attributing to it power of

[2]See Pitirim A. Sorokin, *Social and Cultural Dynamics,* Vol. 2 (New York: American Book Company, 1937), pp. 261–304.

functioning I do not recognize as my own.

The symptom-forming consequence of my appearing to lose my self identity in what I name my large organized whole (Labor, Management, Society, State, or World) can be avoided only by my developing my mental power to be able to recognize all mine, as really being all and only mine. My conception of my human constitution in its every possible condition is the source of my ideal illustration of the working of absolute unity, provided that my meaning that I name wholeness derives from my arduously cultivated conception of my own absolutely inviolable wholeness. Otherwise it may seem to lend itself to my indulging illusions of all kinds of so-called pluralities instead.[3]

I have helped my self uniquely by willingly working with what seems difficult, in discovering that *I use the term "difficult" mostly to describe whatever effort I cannot exert without protest about having to extend my self consciousness in order to do the work.* Ever since this discovery, so-called difficult work has developed the meaning of my earning my conscious self development and thus proved essential for my realizing recognizable self fulfillment.

Nowhere is it more essential that I observe my solipsistic life orientation than in my applying my appreciation for my own body to my appreciation for the whole body of my world. I can ascribe accurately what belongs to my fellow creature only insofar as I can ascribe accurately my all to my self. Hence it is that my laborer or manager can rarely be recognizable as his own idler any more than my idler can be recognizable as his own laborer or manager. Yet each is and must be my own all, as my nature is constituted. Again, my freedom to be my self alone is most cherished of all, and the foundation of all of my freedom. Without it I could not attribute such freedom to anyone of my world.

[3]For such an application, see Henry Wood, *The Political Economy of Natural Law*, 1894,—a life worthy study.

His experience taught Tracy that the greater his consciousness for all of his self the less the waste, "red tape," extravagance or "spoils" in the economy of his life's energy. In prospecting for his true worth he discovered it by and in his being able to sense it in and as his own marvelous living. Most of all he appreciated this self understanding for it demonstrated itself to him as not only the way of life everyone of his world must live anyway, but also the truth that everyone can discipline himself to live it *consciously*, i.e., freely or willingly.

Tracy sensed also the helpfulness of everyone's resistance to increasing the extent of his conscious living pending his own consciously choosing it as best for him.

Prior to his imperialistic craving Napoleon was friendly with Tracy, but the latter's notion of the ideal empire of the conscious soul could arouse only Napoleon's unconscious love (hatred). The emperor recognized the certain danger to his so-called popularity in anything like appreciation for the complete individuality of man. With adequate respect for all of his fellowman what would become of his method of regimentation! How could he create or justify an army of man! He worded his rejection: "If an empire were made of adamant the economist would grind it to powder."

My research discovers my mind's heroic Tracy a welcome subject for my helping my self to willingly discipline my self to realize:

1) the benefit to me in my cultivating my love around my *present* living so that I can excite my self consciousness in it, thereby augmenting my appreciation for my evident life itself;

2) the life endangering consequence to me in my withholding my conscious love around any of my *present* living, thus necessitating my self unconsciousness in it, thereby augmenting my depreciation for my secret life itself;

3) the life affirming result of extending my sense of self identity to include all of my living;

4) the value in recognizing all of my unhappiness as lifesaving pain warning me of my self neglect, or even self rejection, whenever I help my self temporarily by confounding pain

or unhappiness of any kind with unworthy living (whatever I find it necessary to live, always being life worthy);

5) the helpfulness to my life appreciation in lovingly renouncing every kind of education but conscious self education;

6) the warning pain and suffering consequent upon my indulging my illusion that I can teach or learn from another individual (divinely self continent world).

My heroically persevering effort to impose what I call "unselfishness" upon my living must lead me into disregard for what I cannot call my self, thus necessitating my creating illusional not-self and thereby committing my conscious will to upholding my illusion of manyness in the name of practicality. Only my clearly recognizing that my unselfishness is merely unconscious selfness can dispel this illusion. Rarest of all political insight!

But again I come to most sensible realization. Whatever my system of any kind I now depend upon for helping my self, it is the *only* one that can now serve my purpose in my present stage of my political, social, or whatever mental development. To try to bypass it, or cast it aside, would be a critical instance of the builder's rejecting the very stone he needs most for his desired construction. *All I can ever do is grow my self and my each new growth has its only roots in whatever of my self growth that preceded it.*

Whatever way I have lived my self is all that can account for my further living and only it can be fully relied upon as desirable foundation of conscious truth for my continuing my cultivating my conscious self identity. I have helped my self beyond my most exacting dreaming by awakening to the adorable identity of love-hate, pride-shame, courage-fear, desire-jealousy, innocence-guilt, trust-suspicion, one-many, ego-alter, yes-no, justice-injustice, great-small, whole-part, absolute-relative, conscious-unconscious, on and on.

Law is but another name for the nature of my biological process. Once I recognize *that* identity, of my-law-and-my-human-nature, I cannot but strive to found all of my enactment for *my* world upon it. *My* law is manifest in my every wish (will). There is steady lawfulness in my governing my self in proportion to my understanding my nature.

Conscious self experience alone can teach me this truth, that I grow me only. I embody, ensoul, or entify my self in the name of life experience. My world is full of only positive possibilities for I can really be only positively I. I reduce *all* of my mental trouble to my originally negating, rather than affirming, that whatever I am living *is* mine. Such "mental trouble" is always my only accessible form of self help whenever it occurs, but it is most expensive self helpfulness.

From beginning to end I gladly reiterate my realization that, until *conscious* self education for competent citizenship becomes the established official goal of my public school educator, I expect only his rare and scattered devotion to painstakingly augmenting his own whole life appreciation. I readily find my own identity in the letter of John Adams to Thomas Jefferson, dated March 2, 1819:

> Dear Sir
>
> I have taxed my eyes with a very heavy impost to read the senator Tracy's Political Economy, and been amply rewarded for the expense. When I first saw the volume I thought it was impossible I should get through it, but when I had once made a beginning I found myself led on in so easy a train from proposition to proposition, every one of which appeared to me self evident, that I could not leave the book till I had finished it. . . .
>
> I have endeavored and shall endeavor to draw the attention of all my acquaintances to this work. I would endeavor to get it reviewed but I should despair of success, for there is no man in this quarter who would dare to avow such sentiments; and no printer who would not think himself ruined by the publication of it for it is a magazine of gunpowder placed under the foundation of all our mercantile institutions. Yet every sensible man in the nation knows it to be founded in immutable truth though not one in a hundred would acknowledge it, and they only sub-rosa. I have never been so prudent. I have preached

this doctrine thirty years in season and out of season and this heresy has been one of the principle causes of the immense unpopularity of your old friend and humble servant

John Adams[4]

The crucial self understanding most difficultly attained, and most easily excluded from my daily living, is: My mind's complete unity, wholeness and allness always exist. Only I can be any of my living. Whatever I can mean by INTEGRATION *of racial, religious, international, or any other distinctions is ever an already accomplished fact by virtue of the natural integrity of my own mind. It is only my unconsciousness for this vitalizing truth, the sanifying nature of my fully developed personal identity, that can occur and, if so, helpfully necessitates my suffering painful indication of such life endangering self disregard, namely, my contending with innumerable phantom problems such as family or neighbor trouble, racial prejudice, religious bigotry, or world war.*

[4]Lester J. Cappon, *The Adams-Jefferson Letters,* in two volumes, (Chapel Hill: University of North Carolina Press, 1959), Vol. II, pp. 535-536.

MY AMERICAN POLITICAL INDIVIDUALITY DIAGRAMMED

For cultivating my political wisdom I find but one absolute requirement, namely, my awareness for the truth that all of my living is entirely my own. My devotion to seeing nothing but my own personal identity in all that I live is my number one HEALTH obligation. This self understanding might be diagrammed in innumerable ways, for example, in the form of a man recognizing nothing but his own personal identity in his living of his opposite sex, or the converse. However, the following propitious political illustration is that of my white fellow American seeing naught but his own living in his black fellow citizen, and the converse. Self identity subsumes equality. All equality, as unity, is within, in actual individuality.

I AM THE SOUL OF ALL THAT I CAN SENSE I AM MY ONLY BLACK	I AM THE SOUL OF ALL THAT I CAN SENSE I AM MY ONLY WHITE

APPENDIX

My selection of writings culled from historical and contemporary references to Tracy family background, personal development and works.

Tome 4e.

Premier titre

Elements d'idéologie par le Comte Destutt-Tracy membre du Sénat et de l'Institut de France et de la Société philosophique américaine.

Tome 4e.

Second titre

Elements d'idéologie Second Section Traité de la volonté

Titre Sommaire

Destutt-Tracy.

Élémens d'Idéologie

Tome 4ème

Second titre

Élémens d'Idéologie

Deuxième Section

ou

Application de l'étude de nos moyens de connaître à celle de notre Volonté et de ses effets.

En trois parties qui traitent de nos actions, de nos sentimens, et de la manière de diriger les uns et les autres.

Première partie de la deuxième Section

De nos actions

Avertissement.

A la fin de ma Logique, j'ai tracé le plan d'Élémens d'Idéologie tels que je conçois qu'ils devraient être pour donner une connaissance entière de nos facultés intellectuelles, et pour faire sortir de cette connaissance les premiers principes de toutes les autres branches de nos connaissances qui ne sauraient jamais avoir d'autre base vraiment solide. On a vu que je partage ces élémens en trois sections. La première est proprement l'histoire de nos moyens de connaître ou de ce qu'on appelle communément notre entendement. La seconde est l'application de cette étude à celle de notre Volonté et de ses effets, et elle complète l'histoire de nos facultés. La troisième est l'application de cette connaissance de nos facultés à l'étude des êtres qui ne sont pas

Facsimile pages of original manuscript of Tracy's *Treatise on Political Economy*, translated by Thomas Jefferson, included in this volume. Furnished by William H. Runge, Curator of Rare Books in the Alderman Library at the University of Virginia.

Tome 4e

Extrait raisonné

17

Première partie du Traité de la volonté et de ses effets.

De nos actions.

Chapitre premier.

De la Société.

Dans l'introduction d'un traité de la <u>volonté</u>, nous avons dû indiquer la génération de quelques idées générales qui sont des conséquences nécessaires de cette faculté.

Nous avons même dû examiner sommairement.

1° Ce que sont des êtres inanimés, c'est-à-dire <u>ni sentants ni voulants</u>,

2° Ce que seraient des êtres <u>sentants</u> avec indifférence, <u>sans volonté</u>.

3° Ce que sont des êtres <u>sentants et voulants</u>, mais <u>isolés</u>.

4° Enfin ce que sont des êtres <u>sentants et voulants</u> comme nous, mais <u>mis en contact avec leurs semblables</u>.

Ce sont ces derniers dont nous devons actuellement nous occuper uniquement; car l'homme ne peut exister qu'en <u>société</u>.

Le besoin de la reproduction et le penchant à la sympathie l'amènent nécessairement à cet état; et son jugement lui en fait sentir les avantages.

Je vais donc parler de la <u>Société</u>.

Je ne la considérerai que sous le rapport <u>économique</u>, parce qu'il n'est question dans cette première partie que de nos <u>actions</u> et pas encore de nos <u>sentiments</u>.

Sous ce rapport la Société ne consiste que dans une suite continuelle d'<u>échanges</u>. et l'échange est une transaction telle que les deux contractants y gagnent toujours tous deux. (cet aperçu jettera par la suite un grand jour sur la nature et les effets du commerce.)

On ne peut jetter les yeux sur un pays civilisé sans

voir

Tracy searched out the origin of his noble family of Scotch descent to Walter Stutt, who in 1420 accompanied the earls of Buchan and Douglas to the court of France where his ancestors rose to be counts of Tracy. In 1640 Esmée de la Platière married Francois Destutt de Tracy. She received the chateau Paray-le-Frésil as a wedding gift which, from then on, never left the family.

Paray-le-Frésil

Photographs of Chateau Paray-le-Frésil, published in *La Montagne*, November 15, 1968, taken at the time this beautiful Fifteenth Century chateau was being completely destroyed by fire.

Paray-le-Frésil afire

Excerpts from *The Writings of Thomas Jefferson: Being His Autobiography, Correspondence, Reports, Messages, Addresses, and Other Writings, Official and Private.* Edited by H. A. Washington. Vol. VI and VII. New York: Riker, Thorne & Co., 1855, 1856.

To Colonel Duane.

Monticello, April 4, 1813.

Dear Sir,—Your favor of February 14th has been duly received, and the MS. of the commentary on Montesquieu is also safe at hand. I now forward to you the work of Tracy, which you will find a valuable supplement and corrective to those we already possess on political economy. It is a little unlucky that its outset is of a metaphysical character, which may damp the ardor of perusal in some readers. He has been led to this by a desire to embody this work, as well as a future one he is preparing on morals, with his former treatise on Ideology. By-the-bye, it is merely to this work that Bonaparte alludes in his answer to his Council of State, published not long since, in which he scouts "the dark and metaphysical doctrine of Ideology, which, diving into first causes, founds on this basis a legislation of the people, &c." If, indeed, this answer be not a forgery, for everything is now forged, even to the fat of our beef and mutton: yet the speech is not unlike him, and affords scope for an excellent parody. . . . But the book will make its way, and will become a standard work.

[109]

(Letter to John Adams, October 14, 1816.)

Destutt Tracy is, in my judgment, the ablest writer living on intellectual subjects, or the operations of the understanding. His three octavo volumes on Ideology, which constitute the foundation of what he has since written, I have not entirely read; because I am not fond of reading what is merely abstract, and unapplied immediately to some useful science. Bonaparte, with his repeated derisions of Ideologists (squinting at this author), has by this time felt that true wisdom does not lie in mere practice without principle. The next work Tracy wrote was the Commentary on Montesquieu, never published in the original, because not safe; but translated and published in Philadelphia, yet without the author's name. He has since permitted his name to be mentioned. Although called a Commentary, it is, in truth, an elementary work on the principles of government, comprised in about three hundred pages octavo. He has lately published a third work, on Political Economy, comprising the whole subject within about the same compass; in which all its principles are demonstrated with the severity of Euclid, and, like him, without ever using a superfluous word. I have procured this to be translated, and have been four years endeavoring to get it printed; but as yet, without success. In the meantime, the author has published the original in France, which he thought unsafe while Bonaparte was in power. No printed copy, I believe, has yet reached this country. He has his fourth and last work now in the press at Paris, closing, as he conceives, the circle of metaphysical sciences. This work, which is on Ethics, I have not seen, but suspect I shall differ from it in its foundation, although not in its deductions. I gather from his other works that he adopts the principle of Hobbes, that justice is founded in contract solely, and does not result from the construction of man. I believe, on the contrary, that it is instinct and innate, that the moral sense is as much a part of our constitution as that feeling, seeing, or hearing; as a wise creator must have seen to be necessary in an animal destined to live in society; that every human mind feels pleasure in doing good to another; that the non-existence of justice is not to be inferred from the fact that the same act is deemed virtuous and right in one society which is held vicious and wrong in another; because, as the circumstances and opinions of different societies vary, so the acts which may do them right or wrong must vary also; for virtue does not consist in the act we do, but in the end it is to effect. If it is to effect the happiness of him to whom it is directed, it is virtuous, while in a society under different circumstances and opinions, the same act might produce pain, and would be vicious. The essence of virtue is in doing good to others, while what is good may be one thing in one society, and its contrary in another. Yet, however we may differ as to the foundation of morals, (and as many foundations have been assumed as there are writers on the subject nearly,) so correct a thinker as Tracy will give us a sound system of morals. And, indeed, it is remarkable, that so many writers, setting out from so many different premises, yet meet all in the same conclusions. This looks as if they were guided, unconsciously, by the unerring hand of instinct.

[38, 39, 40]

(Letter to John Adams, January 11, 1817)

Tracy's Commentaries on Montesquieu have never been published in the original. Duane printed a translation from the original manuscript a few years ago. It sold, I believe, readily, and whether a copy can now be had, I doubt. If it can, you will receive it from my bookseller in Philadelphia, to whom I now write for that purpose. Tracy comprehends, under the word "Ideology," all the subjects which the French term *Morale,* as the correlative to *Physique.* His works on Logic, Government, Political Economy and Morality, he considers as making up the circle of ideological subjects, or of those which are within the scope of the understanding, and not of the senses. His Logic occupies exactly the ground of Locke's work on the Understanding. The translation of that on Political Economy is now printing; but it is no translation of mine. I have only had the correction of it, which was, indeed, very laborious. *Le premier jet* having been by some one who understood neither French or English, it was impossible to make it more than faithful. But it is a valuable work.

[55]

Excerpts from *A Commentary and Review of Montesquieu's Spirit of Laws* by Destutt de Tracy, printed by William Duane, Philadelphia, 1811, with translation by Thomas Jefferson.

> Under the name of the nation, there exist only corporations of individuals, and not citizens who merit that title.
>
> Helvetius to A. M. Saurin

In *A Commentary and Review of Montesquieu's Spirit Of Laws*[1] Tracy defines law of nature on the ground

> . . . that an animated being must be either in a state of *enjoying* or *suffering* . . . love or the other sensation takes place in the individual, through the medium of his perceptions, upon which he forms a judgment, which is only the consciousness of the individual to the feeling of pleasure or pain; that in consequence of this judgment, a will and desire are produced to obtain or to avoid the operation of those perceptions. . . .
>
> Here we behold what is meant by the *laws of nature*. . . . So if we do not make provision for the accomplishment of our wishes, or what will amount to the same, if we cherish desires that are unattainable, we become unhappy; this is beyond doubt, the supreme power . . . that follows, in which every consequence arises as if it had been so predetermined. It is sufficient that the laws of nature exist anterior and superior to human laws; that fundamental justice is that only which is conformable to the laws of nature; and that radical injustice is that which is contrary to the laws of nature; and consequently that our posterior and consequent laws should be in unison with those more ancient and inevitable laws. This is the true spirit, or genuine sense, in which all positive laws ought to be established. But this foundation of the laws is not very easily explained or understood: the space between the first principles and the ultimate result is immense. The progressive series of consequences flowing out of the first principles are the proper subject of a treatise on the spirit of laws. . . .

[1] Translated and published by William Duane upon the request of Thomas Jefferson (1811: Philadelphia) who corrected the translation and wrote the author's preface, now as ever it is a contribution to freedom worthy of most careful study. This great study was written fifty years after the publication of Montesquieu's work.

Tracy then proceeds to develop his excellent commentary with great care for signification of his words, indicating that a perfect method of education must depend upon perfect understanding of words. He reduces all government to that which either does or does not have all of its rights and powers belonging to and emanating from *all* of the people (i.e., *every* individual) constituting the organized sovereignty. With profound understanding he then elaborates upon the kind of character a citizen tends to build "under" 1) authoritarian government or raised by 2) acknowledgeable self sovereignty. "The pure representative democracy can in no respect fear truth, its best interest is to protect it; founded solely on reason and nature, its only enemies are error and prejudice; . . . all that is good and true is in its favor. . . ."[2] Throughout his writing, unlike Montesquieu, Tracy upholds as his own ideal his principle of conscious self government. He observes with uniquely conscious identity for his world:

> The more improved society becomes, the more the means and enjoyment of power increases among men, but the chances of inequality are also more multiplied among them; and in all degrees of civilization the laws should tend to diminish inequality as much as possible; for it is fatal to liberty, and is the source of all our evils and vices; every evidence of experience and reasoning proves this great principle, and everything has that tendency.

In the course of his commentary Tracy demonstrates his appreciation for the nature of the mind, *his* mind. To illustrate, his description of will, of freedom of will, is that of a consciously self insightful student of his mental experience.[3] Thus he calls attention to

> one property common to all descriptions of liberty . . . it procures for the individual enjoying it, the exercise of his will in a greater extent than if deprived of that enjoyment . . . and in general, to be free is to be able to do what we please

[2] Ibid., p. 33.
[3] Ibid., pp. 94–109.

> . . . liberty is applicable only to beings endowed with will . . . liberty only relates to the will when formed, and not before the will exists . . . however weak a motive may be, it necessarily determines our will, unless it be balanced by a more powerful motive, and then this is as necessarily determined as the other would have been, if alone; we will or we do not will, but we cannot will to will; and if we could, there would yet be an antecedent cause of this will, and this cause would be beyond the range of the will, as are all those which cause it . . . liberty is no more than the power of executing the will . . . the nature of every being endowed with will, is such that this faculty of willing causes his happiness or unhappiness; he is happy when his desires are accomplished, and unhappy when they are not. . . . It follows that his liberty and happiness are the same thing. He would always be completely happy if he had always the power of executing his will, and the degree of his happiness is always proportioned to the degree of his power . . . and we cannot be free in any other manner. . . .[4]

Merrill D. Peterson writes on *A Commentary and Review of Montesquieu's Spirit of Laws* by de Tracy:

> Jefferson admired the work, thought it soundly republican and liberal, a useful corrective of Montesquieu's heresies, and, on the whole, the most valuable political work of the present age. He induced Duane to undertake the translation and publication, though he contributed to the former, and the work appeared in 1811 under the title *A Commentary and Review of Montesquieu's Spirit of Laws,* with Jefferson's author's preface in the disguise of an unnamed Frenchman. So true, in fact, were its doctrines to those of the Sage of Monticello that the book was adopted as a text at William and Mary and some Frenchmen ascribed the authorship to him. Even Dupont was fooled and began to translate the book back into French. Jefferson persuaded him to desist. After Napoleon's exile, Tracy appeared publicly as the author of the original French version. So successful was this venture that he asked the same favor of Jefferson for his treatise on political economy. Duane botches the translation. Jefferson had to revise the whole—a daily drudgery of

[4] Ibid., p. 200.

many weeks in the winter of 1815-16—and Milligan finally published it, with Tracy's name, in Washington.[5]

Destutt de Tracy as Seen by a Contemporary

On account of its detailed intimacy regarding Tracy's family living and its *numerous* brightly interesting comments, I include most of Marie-Sarah Newton Comtesse de Tracy's extensive death notice of her father-in-law as well as a short biographical sketch of the Comtesse herself. Although her writing may not indicate her too much readiness to see her identity in Tracy's strict self reliance, nevertheless I am most grateful for her intelligent recording of her description of personal characteristics of her consciously self oriented father-in-law.

Madame Tracy (1789-1850) was the great grand niece of Isaac Newton. Her first husband, General Letort, a brave officer, aide-de-camp of Napoleon, was killed in the battle of Ligny, shortly before the battle of Waterloo. During all the political career of her husband, Victor, her salon was one of the most popular in Paris. She was successful in all of the arts, excelling as a musician, writer and painter. She wrote, "That which makes happiness is the mind, the intelligence, the study and elevation of ideas, it is the will, imagination, memory and understanding; all that is the soul."

The quality of her mind is suggested by the following extract from the "Avertissement de l'Editeur," at the beginning of Volume I of Mme. de Tracy's writings. The translation is Iris Hartman's.

[5] *Thomas Jefferson & the New Nation* (New York: Oxford University Press, 1970), p. 948.

Mme. de Tracy wanted to leave a souvenir for her numerous friends. She knew how to create from inner resources activities to relieve boredom, that scourge of women of the world.

Madame de Tracy was born in the Anglican religion and named Sarah Newton, but, raised in France, she was early attracted by the pomp and grandeur of the Roman Catholic church—she was a Catholic at heart from her earliest childhood. Although she did not want to embrace Catholicism, because of an inner conviction, she gave herself over to the reading and study of sacred writers and it became a veritable passion. She read the Peres de l'Eglise in the original, for which she was obliged to learn Latin, which she did by herself. And she was taken with a strong desire to familiarize the people of the world with these writers. This was a big order. Madame de Tracy consecrated the last years of her life to it with ardor and perseverance. What she wrote about the Peres de l'Eglise would have made several volumes in folio. We recommend to the attention of our readers her etude on Saint Anathase and above all her etude on Tertullian (160-230 A.D.), which seems to us to be an appreciation that one would hardly expect to see come forth from the light pen of a woman of the world. . . .

Death Notice on Destutt de Tracy
written by Mme. Victor de Tracy, published 1852, translated by Iris Hartman

The last thoughts and the first years of a remarkable man, one who had honored his country, are always of interest to those who loved him, as well as inspiring curiosity among those who have not known him.

A few days before dying, M. de Tracy had several passages from his writings read to him and said, "Oh! but it is the more one learns, the more one realizes that one knows nothing''—Had de Tracy, then, arrived at the point of acknowledging himself ignorant, with so much veritable knowledge? And did he regret the time given to those studies which showed him the emptiness of study? Or did he think that ''tout a que finit est trop court?''—perhaps.

M. de Tracy spent his childhood in a drawing room filled with aristocrats, bishops and cardinals, it was the ''salon'' of his mother, a devout Italian, very remarkable for her understanding and her character. She attracted to her home the most distinguished persons of her time and they came there eagerly.

At the age of 8, M. de Tracy was present at the death of his father who had been mortally wounded at the battle of Menden where he commanded the gendarmerie of the king. (Note—His grandfather on his mother's side, the Marquis de Druy was killed in the battle of Marsaille at the same age, also commanding the gendarmerie of the king.)

The officer was found dying by an old aide who carried him from the scene. He regained life but for only a short time. ''You will never be afraid, Antoine, will you?'' Those were the last words of a hero of Corneille. He pronounced these last words while kissing his young son who was terrified at the sight of this glorious but cruel death-agony.

Assuredly, no man ever knew fear less than de Tracy did. He always remembered, he said, this advice of his dying father. His mother continued his early education at home, firm, elevated and serious, which gives distinguished children that generous something with which to face the unexpected which may arise. He had the fortune to be closely connected from childhood with people of the highest mind, and to live with men of value, whose conversation, according to him, was his best schooling.

De Tracy used to tell with great feeling about his voyage to Ferney when he was 16 and how Voltaire put his hand on his head. He used to imagine he still felt that hand, and one could believe that Voltaire had pressed into that magnificent young head, the tenacity, the will, and the worship of good sense that animated them, the two men.

The passionate reading of the works of Voltaire which de Tracy undertook starting in his youth, is probably what decided him on the path he followed without distraction: the study of mathematics, the dead languages, natural history, astronomy and chemistry. It led him also to the study of human thought which uncovers and includes all the great concerns of science.

In his regiment, de Tracy distinguished himself as one of the most studious officers and at the same time one of the most adroit in all kinds of exercises.

He used to tell with wonder of his follies of youth, his barracks tales, stories of loves and mystifications, all told with a charming gaiety and worth recording if the seriousness of his character had permitted.

The political life of de Tracy was a model of lack of self interest of the purest sort (of an unselfishness of the purest sort) and of the most enlightened and firm conduct. An account of this belonged in the history of his time. It is well known how, in the hope of being useful to his country, he would not forsake it at a time when to remain meant putting his life in peril.

He thought like Tertullian (whom he scarcely read). He thought that man should not flee persecution, and, in leaving the command that he had in the army in 1793, he returned to his family who had retired to their home in Auteuil where for a short while he tasted the pleasure of tranquility. But this pleasure was short lived because it was not long until he was arrested and incarcerated in the prison at Carmes where he re-discovered many of his friends.

In the evening he played checkers with them, and in the morning he read Condillac, the only reading matter he had at hand. He soon sensed the need to create for himself a long and serious occupation. He got to work and, at the end of a year, when he was let out of prison, he had acquired, simply by reflection and examination of himself, the understanding of a profound thinker. He had discovered, while kept under lock and key and behind bars, that study and the will to follow an occupation could conquer inquietude and sorrow.

Each morning could have been the morn of his last day, but the fact in no way turned him from his daily reading. The sinister rumors from without, which came to him, never troubled the appreciation of his will to *the kind of study which demands the greatest liberty of mind, the study of the development of human faculties.*[6]

After having published many brochures on diverse questions in politics and on administration, all very practicable and filled with new ideas, he published his volume of his Ideology which was more appreciated abroad than in France where the taste for this type of study is not widespread.

Besides, many people feared to praise l'Ideologie and would have suspected the philosophic or philanthropic expression of a great soldier. Other timid souls, different but equally insincere, found passages in the book dangerous to the religious faith. They had weak faith or none at all, because human reasoning of the most subtle kind serves most often to fortify our faith. No dialectic ancient or modern employed toward such an end could fight against these simple words, "All you who mourn, come to me."

But it was the author, rather than the book that was attacked on all sides, that author whose resolute character bent not before any prejudice of the moment and who, speaking of despotism and hypocrisy, so disturbed those of fearful ambition.

De Tracy wanted to keep from filling the well where it is pretended that the ancients kept all truth. He wanted to enlighten ignorance, but he was too fine to ever have the pretention to correct people of bad faith. . . .

For de Tracy, it was humiliating to *believe,* he wanted to *know. He wrote of himself and recognized only that which he had discovered.*[7]

"The study of true philosophy," he said, "gives those who undertake it many ideas. It also gives them a superior ability in other studies and serves well in the difficulties of life."

De Tracy thought that this study could open to man the

[6] My italics.
[7] My italics.

sources of true happiness, that a genuine felicity could be found in the exercise of the mind and of the regular application of it to that which is. The senses become dull, the heart destroys itself, but the mind, on the contrary, nourishes itself and profits from all the changes that time brings.

One lives longer, perhaps, if one lives among books, and it is the longevity of the savants that caused it to be believed that happiness resides in the brain. That idea, old and forgotten, re-emerged, armed by the new culture of the positive sciences, taught in a most luminous manner by the eminent men with whom M. de Tracy had the glory to be connected. His motive, in writing the Ideology, was to sound the depths of the human spirit or mind by means of reason, to analyse its different functions and by this means to arrive as near as possible to truth.

He could not understand what could be above nature nor how one could expect to arrive there by reason. However, one could say that he did raise himself above nature, since, by means of reflection, he analyzed knowledge and decomposed that which nature presented him as composed.

M. de Tracy thought that those who feigned to misprise Ideology deceived themselves, because they are ideologists without suspecting so, each time they are straight in their conceptions without going astray.

By the order that this science established in ideas, it is the cause of all discoveries that are not due to chance. (As for chance, one cannot explain how one made a discovery; it is something spontaneous, inexplicable, it is divine inspiration, that neither de Tracy nor any other savant in the universe, aided by all the help of logic, has ever succeeded in discovering.)

Monsieur de La Grange said that he had resolved as many problems in mathematics in listening to an Italian opera as in the silence of his office. De Tracy regarded Lavoisier as a great ideologist, who, by the chain of his ideas alone, had perceived the greatest part of his discoveries before confirming them in experience. A drop of water, frozen, melted, reduced to vapor, and capable to again become solid, led to the discovery of calorique and perhaps to the formation of the globe.

Anaximenes was doubtless a profound physiologist, he who regarded air as the principle of all bodies.

The opinion of de Tracy concerning the rapport which unites physiology and ideology caused him to be admired by the great medics who could not believe that he could have been a stranger to physiological knowledge because of the many passages where he gives certain phenomena of the sensibility and movement of ideas more correctly and exactly than had been previously done. "This man," they said, "who so thoroughly knows the human mind, could not have acquired such an exact idea without a long study of the vital organism." De Tracy, for his part, sought out the great medics in the hope that one day or another *they would put their hand on the soul.*

The Ideology is a book that was greatly needed by science, science which has moral man as its object and which considers man from a physical viewpoint also. This volume is short for the matters that it contains.

What is it, to think?

"Nobody knows positively," de Tracy used to say, "few people have ever defined it; it is the root of reasoning, and all science must be a resumee of the idea contained in the question."

The philosophers think that the question will be answered sooner or later. Meantime, they disagree among themselves. De Tracy, who expected new discoveries, said "Will we ever know how men and animals acquire their faculties?"

What de Tracy did know was that Condillac was often mistaken.

But it is said that de Tracy was mistaken on his own score, for, if it is a truth for him that to think is to feel, just as to act is not different from to move, then why, since there are many manners of feeling, are there not many ways of thinking. There thinking should be able to be done in as many manners as the soul has of feeling, just as act can mean as many things to move. If to think and to feel are not synonyms for all people, perception and idea should not be synonymous either. One has perception when one feels, but one has not an idea until feeling has become an image; an idea is the image one gives oneself by reflection on any object whatsoever.

"Divine if you can, and choose if you dare"

The volume containing the Ideology leads to that on general Grammar as the latter leads to that on Logic. De Tracy had a great preference for grammar. He would have wished to have nothing taught to men except their perfecting themselves in languages in order to make them philosophers, thinking that they could learn all in that way.

The chapter in which he examines how it is possible to create a perfect language, the use the sciences could make of it, this chapter where the spirit of research is conducted by the most judicious criticism, merits being cited as a model of writing.

The idea of incorporating grammar into ideology and to have envisaged it as a continuation of the science of ideas is a happy one and novel. Before that, grammar was nothing but a surface, but before knowing if there are signs, it must be known if there are ideas, since, before expressing ideas it is first necessary that they be formed. It was the natural thing to go back to the source in order to give the cause of things from their beginning.

The author unscrambles the parts of speech and their origin. His theory of tenses is clearly developed. But it is above all for the chapter on writing that he is distinguished. The origin which he gives it is as ingenious as it seems. He did not fear to stray from the opinions of others no matter how celebrated,—for him reason was always of more value than authority. What he says of the Chinese and hieroglyphics could furnish a chapter on the question of the influence of signs on ideas. The chapter on the subject of a universal language contains in a short space all that is reasonable that can be said on the subject.

In reading the volume one sees how much the author rejoiced in writing. He freely exercised that analytic spirit which possessed him and which he possessed so well.

On other subjects he had the contrariness to be unable

to bend the facts nor to convince those who were not of his opinion, since, as it is said, each one thinks as he feels or feels as he thinks. But in grammar, he was free to demonstrate, prove and practice.

De Tracy detested pedantry. A pedant, he said, is a disagreeable man who fears novelty and who affirms superficial and false things in a doctoral tone. He equally detested affectation and exaggeration. He foresaw that the French language was menaced in its purity by the great number of eccentric, negligent and innovative writers springing up each day. He insisted he could not understand anything subtle or cloudy. He had no taste for the incomprehensible and wasted no time reading mediocre works.

The volume on Logic follows that on Grammar. Logic is the base of all study. It is the science of the human mind.

De Tracy explains the immobility of the science of philosophy from Aristotle to Bacon, for the reason, he says, that the basis of Aristotle's logic is inexact, and that nothing fecund comes from what is not based on truth.

But the truth in the sciences is not very long the same. It changes with each new discovery because the discoveries make it known that what one called truth at one time ceases to be truth at another.

Said de Tracy—"Chancelor Bacon has the glory to have been the first to sense, and to have published at the age of 19 that up until the time when he lived, all scientific research has been fruitless and falsely based; that it is necessary to reconstitute our knowledge and renew the human mind. However necessary this renewal, Bacon provoked, rather than commenced it. All that he did, reduced itself to showing that in the search for truth, one must not take general principles, but rather facts, as a base; that facts, not maxims are the source of all certitude, and that we must not waste our time in vain arguments, but employ it in making observations, and then experiments. Bacon did not see by what observations it is necessary to start, nor what is the first fact of which we can be sure. The rules that he gives in his *Novum Organum* cannot, therefore, lead us to truth.

"Descartes then took all that he found worthwhile in Bacon to compose his *Method.* He conceived the project to remake, not the human understanding in general, but his own. He started by putting in doubt all that he had thought he knew. He certainly took two great steps on the path of truth; he recognized that, wishing to reconstruct all his knowledge, the first thing he had to study was his own mind, since it is in our intelligence that all means of knowing subsist for each individual, and that before any research, it is necessary to know what are one's means of knowing anything whatsoever. Then, in the midst of the entire doubt into which Descartes had plunged himself, he discovered, with an admirable sagacity, one first fact impossible of incertitude. He said, 'I doubt; I feel that I doubt; I am sure of doubting, or at least of believing that I doubt. But to doubt is to feel, to think something; and to feel and to think is to exist: I am therefore sure of existing, of being a thinking being.' "

"It is to have found the true basis of our knowledge and it is to have rendered an immense service," continued de Tracy.

Descartes lived at a time when the science of words, that is to say, verbiage, reigned in the learned professions. It had been barely 4 years since Galileo had been condemned when Descartes published his *Metaphysical Meditations* which he dedicated to the Sorbonne for the reason that, as he said, the truth needs authority to support it.

De Tracy regards Hobbes as founder of Ideology through the precision of his ideas. De Tracy thinks the men of the Port Royal are to Descartes, what Hobbes is to Bacon,—the continuation (continuers). Port Royal gave birth to Locke who refuted their system of innate ideas. Locke's book on human understanding cleared up many obscure points and was very useful to Condillac, who could be regarded as his successor, and who, thanks to Locke, according to the opinion of de Tracy, was transported to the true sources of understanding, by digging deeper into Locke's work than its author.

De Tracy thought that Leibnitz and Malebranche did not

in any way advance the science of logic because their ideas offer nothing new or superior to what their predecessors had made known.

De Tracy's volume on Logic contains very interesting notes on precipitous judgements. The fifth chapter is remarkable and merits profound attention. In passing in review over all the great geniuses who were partial to absolute power, the author notes that it was themselves, by their works, who most efficaciously attacked and shook that power. His resumé of logic was as follow: "The only way to preserve ourselves from error and to assure ourselves of true comprehension of the ideas that we are judging." His book attracted a crowd of discussions, controversies, and more or less malevolent objections; but the author loved discussion and even did not detest moderate teasing that developed the spirit of repartée that he so highly estimated. De Tracy could repeat after Hobbes that in teaching men the truth about men, you must not count on their gratitude. Before them, Aristotle had said to think was a way to attract hatred.

The volume on Logic follows the two other parts of which we have already spoken. Logic is better thus placed after the grammar than in with the science of ideas. To reason is to decompose ideas by the help of words. De Tracy wished to reduce three subjects to a unity in a way that they could mutually help one another. Ideology is the subject, grammar the means, logic the end. The science of ideas includes that of its expression and that of its induction. De Tracy desired that men should become good enough ideologists to be good grammarians and good enough grammarians to be logicians and good enough logicians to be capable of knowing the truth when it is expressed or to discover it when it is unknown. Then only, he used to say, men will be capable of guiding other men and of educating their children.

The treatise on Will remained incompleted. De Tracy brought under the word Will all the diverse sentiments that could be included to bring peace to the conscience of the individual. He insisted that, by all the power of a dominant will that always chose the good, men would arrive at a calm conscience and avoid evil inclinations that render man guilty and therefore unhappy.

He did not believe the bad is inevitable; he had confidence in human nature which he sought to render perfect by confidence and by reason.

The commentary on Montesquieu was an inspiration. It is a piece of writing full of verve, the work of a prudent and hardy man of State. . . . It is above all in this commentary that one can admire the care de Tracy took not to employ any term whose sense was not explicit, nor any thought that was not perfectly clear. The sentences are short, and there are no useless details. Love of humanity was the distinctive trait of the character of de Tracy. He flattered himself that with excellent laws one could assure the honesty of a nation in the aid of civilization, and that condition he believed possible under the ice of the North as in the most burning climates. His thought always returns to the common well-being. His reasoning is never boring, his morality is never heavy; in reading him, one cannot keep from partaking of his enthusiasm for the happiness of humankind.

De Tracy thought that the spirit of laws should be such as to favor the development of the kinder passions, which are the source of contentment, and to prevent or forbid, as much as possible, the hateful passions which cause the unhappiness of people. This principle merits a full treatise on legislation and morals. He says:—

"The first of our sentiments is that which unites the two sexes, and the first basis of society is marriage.

"The couple transforms itself into a family, and *we must take care lest paternal love degenerate into a feeling of ownership which puts the fantasies of the parents in the place of the interest of the children.*[8] We must limit paternal power to the strictly necessary, so that fear may not replace affection, and that the family may not become a little court, and that interest may not give birth to ruse and jealousy."—What essentials

[8] My italics.

are contained in these two first articles!

"It is manifest that, to banish bad sentiments born of oppression or of insolence, it is necessary that laws be equal for everyone, and even for everyplace.

"We must avoid separating men into classes, and land into foreign provinces so that our laws may not foment either avidity or vanity; for those passions do not nourish themselves except on the abasement of others and even on their sufferings.

"A government should be economic and its administration not spendthrift.

"Criminal laws have no object other than to see that the other laws are respected and executed. Politicians should have as their aim, that the other laws are made in good faith. For that, it is necessary that the largest possible part of the citizenry aid in their making, and that each one be free to give his opinion thereon without breeding disorder.

"Politics and morality are not one and the same thing, and laws cannot be good unless made in this spirit."

De Tracy remains in the first ranks as an economist. However, it seems that this has been forgotten and that others are cited who have only delayed his ideas or profited from his manuscripts and copied them, manuscripts which he lent so freely. As soon as he learned that someone was seriously interested in the questions which he was treating himself, he quickly sent that person his note, so fine, so full of method and of ideas. It has happened more than once that he has afterwards seen these notes metamorphosed into thick brochures and distributed under the name of an imitator. This procedure elicited in him no sentiment other than astonishment.

De Tracy's ideas on work, which he regarded as the foundation of the riches in any country, are very good and very clear. Misery, he says, is not a fatality; it is claimed such by people who will not take the trouble to help their neighbor. Work must replace workless charity and thus remedy the general poverty. Give less and lend more: guide, counsel, encourage. In that way one lifts the one he aids, lifts him in his own eyes, and frees him from humiliation. Charity, it is understood, would put an end to the greatest misery, to that which individual charity could not accomplish. But men should all strive to be useful to their kind, and should unite in the effort to work according to the strength of each.

The maxim of de Tracy for a government was that it should have its finances in good state and prompt execution of repressive laws.

His maxim for individuals was to have the least possible false ideas and to cut off short all evil sentiments, by not allowing growth to a doubtful principle which could lead to committing grave faults. He recommended to the young that they not waste time reading mediocre works of any kind.

He was sincerely afflicted when he saw persons waste their time running after the pleasures that life offers so freely without mixing them with any kind of work or any kind of study.

The soul of de Tracy found perpetual nourishment in reflection and in the interest he took in the movement of ideas, an interest which he enjoyed for over sixty years.

It was with sadness that he contemplated the fate of the ignorant; he would have liked to show the entire universe how to read and to write, because, as he said, the education of the masses was the surest means to general and progressive well-being, and that cultivation of intelligence leads to richness and consideration. It is the best remedy against misery, vice and public disorder. De Tracy was astonished that all enlightened men were not of this opinion, and he did not understand why it should be difficult to execute if well conceived and clearly explained. That is because he was innocent of any of these little calculations, interests and vices, and the little fears which render men timid and make them suspicious of any change that might unsettle them. . . . The study of exact sciences had given him the habit of making everything run logically in the home. Those who knew him know with what an accurate memory he caught any minor contradiction in their narration and how he could catch them in the act of wandering from the point of forgetting. He insisted that the end of what one was telling be in accord with its beginning.

De Tracy very much liked the science of astronomy. Undoubtedly that is why he took Dupuis' book so seriously and even made a resumé of it. . . . He said also that medicine was ridiculous in times of ignorance, that magic was medicine elevated, and theology was magic transcended. For him occult science was nonsense. "Science consists of light" he used to say—"Occult *science*, Bah! that is like saying a nightly day; and so long as one is outside of nature, one is in contradiction with her.". . .

For de Tracy the art of persuasion was simply the art of making yourself understood. "The best things are clear and simple, but there are too many people interested in confusing or disguising them."

He made much of the divine precept "Love one another." The difficulties of life are very often born of the antipathy one has for one's neighbor, of pure prejudice, or of ignorance of true sentiments.

Sympathy with all sin was a favorite axiom of de Tracy, he who was eminently good but who understood all human weaknesses. . . .

"Theology is the science of God, the most admirable of all the sciences, but it must be banished from political discussions or it becomes dangerous. It must be kept separate from questions relative to other sciences for it embroils them. It is even wise to turn the mind away from it because it is above its grasp. However, its importance is so great that one cannot revere it too much and one should make all efforts toward progress in it, keeping it from the errors into which it slips in times of ignorance, because it is necessary to know the creation to understand the Creator!" (noté—"To know God one must know ones self" said Saint Athanasia)

De Tracy wrote that theology should be kept separate from politics but he never said that a priest should not mix in the affairs of life, as some insist he said. . . .

He respected liberty of thought over all. But he never could understand the charm of living far from your kind, off in a desert in order to give yourself over to contemplative and solitary reflection. He said that is to live like a wolf instead of being useful to your kind, and that a hermit committed slow moral suicide and could also be capable of impromptu suicide.

De Tracy had an example of this in his own family, an example which constantly furnished him with material for some new reflection, some new surprise. His uncle, Father Tracy, a Theatin, had been born at the chateau of Paray-le-Frésil in 1720. Weak and of delicate health,, he manifested, from childhood, tastes that were sedentary and studious. All of this displeased his parents who wanted a military career for him.

Paray-le-Frésil is situated some leagues from the Abbey of Septfonds and Father Tracy tied himself intimately to some of the monks and retired there often. He got a real taste for the calm life in uniform, and at the age of 18, being perfectly resolved to devote himself to the religious life, he entered the Convent of the Theatins and delivered, on that occasion, a eulogy to the venerable Mother of Chantal, to whom he was related. He refused all employ offered so as not to be turned in any way from his occupation with pure study, for which he was as impassioned as has been his nephew ever since.

The nephew attributed this idea of his uncle's to his reading of ascetic books and the lives of the saints which he found in the library at Paray-le-Frésil and whose margins were covered with Father Tracy's reflections and observations, some naive and some exaggerated. One of these books was the history of a person related to the de Tracy family, M. de Raynal de Clermout, cavalry brigadier in the army of King Louis XIV. . . . It was this story in the opinion of de Tracy that determined the vocation of his uncle, and which decided him on a solitary and meditative life over the military life. He could well do so; he earned his livelihood there, and he lived long in spite of his frail health, whereas his brother, healthy, handsome and vigorous, died at 33 on the battlefield.

Father Tracy wrote many books, the chief of them is his Treatise on the Duties of the Christian Life. This book, the author says, was written in the interest of the middle classes who do not get enough religious instruction. This idea is one that is shared by all the Tracys who have always, for many generations been courageous, generous of soul, compatible and given to aiding all those they could. . . .

The uncle and the nephew, the man of religion and the philosopher, both expressed the same thought on the need to form a will that chooses well and to withhold bad inclinations. They were in accord on the care we must take for the contentment of others, on the satisfaction that comes from correctness, devotion and charity.

De Tracy was astonished to see men thinking of *eternity*, and at least talking as if they thought of it seriously, while their principal occupation was wasting time, frittering away the day, detesting all that is hard, not liking anything but what goes fast and to be always in a hurry, always agitated, as if they had but an instant to live. "Eternity does not seem to suit us," he used to say.

It was with a humorous accent that de Tracy would say "They assure me that I have an eternal soul; that may well be, but I don't know anything about it."

Here are the questions he used to ask himself about the soul, eternal or material:—

Have the animals a soul?—They produce spontaneous effect, not produced by any visible action.

Have the vegetables a soul?—They have the power of assimilation, of nutrition and of development, a power all their own that is doubtless the effect of their organization.

Have less organized and more inanimate beings a soul?—They continually reach toward one another, what is called universal attraction. In addition, each has tendencies proper to it by virtue of which it unites with certain beings sooner than with others and produces, with these preferred beings, new compositions which, in turn, have new tendencies. These tendencies or faculties certainly have a cause unknown to us.

Is it this cause which is the soul of these beings?—The human soul is known to man by its effects, says de Tracy, and it consists in the faculty of feeling, of remembering, of judging, of wishing, and of acting in consequence.

But, when we say that the human soul *possesses* these qualities we real-ize it, in fact we make of it a separate being have an existence of its own.

The universe, has it a soul?—There is a cause by which it exists, and no person can conceive of an effect without a cause.

This universal soul is a creation of the human mind, says M. de Tracy, because it is unknown in itself, and we name it, soul.[9]

So far, very good; but if one believes he has created a being with a word, one gives that being properties and faculties without motive, and it is there that one slips into metaphysics, that science which the author (M. de Tracy) says concerns itself with beings that do not exist; for man thinks, and there is not, in men, a being that calls itself "thought"; they have in themselves ideas and impressions, without having in them a being that calls itself idea or impression.

De Tracy concluded that we have there, just so many abstractions, which is to say, abstract ideas, though this conclusion perhaps did not altogether satisfy him. He concluded that metaphysics was an abyss with no exit where one turns back on oneself, without being able to get out. . . .

Physics, said de Tracy, is the science of nature. It consists of the knowledge of things which exist, and, as for phenomena, the most beautiful are those which concern human intelligence. Beyond physics, there is metaphysics, which, in placc of studying the effects and consequences of human thinking, as de Tracy did, approaches from the other side and has conducted a research into its nature, its destination and its end. There, we are not in relation with beings which exist for us, that is to say, which appear to our senses; there, contests M. de Tracy, one is in the empire of metaphysics, a study which is a stranger to all that is positive. But there is no phenomenon in all nature that cannot be studied both from the physical and from the metaphysical viewpoint. Physics, de Tracy used to say, is the knowledge of natural things, and the other

[9] My italics.

of supernatural things. The one limits its study to that which exists, the other to that which has not been proven. One should call it instead of metaphysics, anti-physics, because it is the product of suppositions without certainty, fruit of too much use of the imagination.

There are as many tastes as there are individuals, and this variety, which so displeased M. de Tracy is the one which gives so much that is delightful and unforeseen to human society. Some see in metaphysics a thick fog, others find that fog in ideology.

One could say that metaphysics neither confuses nor clarifies questions, but that it gives birth to truly beautiful ideas. It is between truth and fable; it has the nature of dreams. Dreams are the thoughts of a sleeping man. But metaphysics is the dream of a man who is awake.

M. de Tracy, to be assured of the exactness of his ideas, carefully examined all his ideas and even all of his words, in order to be clear in what he wrote. He said of morality that it consisted in the knowledge of what conduct to follow and what habits to contract for our own good. But, said he, it is no more true that all men know morality than it is that they know astronomy. All men have a knowledge not to throw themselves into danger, to seek their well-being, but it is not true that men have in them what can be called morality; and when one says men, one obviously excepts children, who have not yet reached reason, and idiots, who will never have it. This reasoning proved to him that man learns all he knows, which would be useless if his ideas were innate. He thought that morality, like all other knowledge, comes through study and reflection. But, said M. de Tracy, morality is less advanced, for, in spite of the most imperious maternal instinct, there still exist nations where they kill their children or sell them, and savages who kill their fathers.

Truth often is lost, in morality, because of all beings, the most difficult for man to know is himself, and it is easier for him to discover the secrets of all sciences and form an idea of all creation than to discover the mystery of his own nature. The more perfect the organization, the more the mind is capable of combinations, the more varied one's knowledge, the more numerous are thoughts. "Morale" according to de Tracy is a science in theory and an art in practice. It is the science of contentment, and the art of how to reach it.

He considered a person who claimed to know morals naturally, about as ridiculous as someone who would declare he knew chemistry without ever having studied it.

One must regard morals as a science, the author said, a science founded on the observation of man, a science having its source in man's true interests, *but it is not an automatic sentiment.*

Does it depend on us to give ourselves our feelings? he asked, apropos of our merits and our faults. To that question, he answered, no, because it is not ourselves who have given us our senses nor who have caused the existence of those who surround us.

If our ideas come from our sensations we are no more masters of our ideas than we are of our feelings. We cannot form an idea of a being who exists other than as the composite of various qualities drawn from beings who exist, and we cannot attribute to him a property which is not relative to any of our senses, for we cannot imagine a new sense.

Therefore, says de Tracy, it is impossible to deny that we are so constructed that we cannot react to our impressions other than by an operation that we call judging, and we cannot even imagine another way of appreciating them. Man is made in such a way that this impression is agreeable to him and that other, disagreeable. It is not in his power to change that.

If our judgments are inevitable or compulsory, then our desires, which follow our judgments, be they true or false, are so also. It is impossible for us not to desire such or such thing in consequence of our judgments,—at least unless a stronger reason makes us desire the contrary. Then, it is because this stronger reason had caused us to make a judgment contrary to the former one; and in this case it is still true that desire follows our judgments.

But, if our desires do not depend on ourselves, if they

arise in us involuntarily, then what becomes of the merit and demerit in our feelings and actions? If that is the case, that is very sad, says de Tracy.

It is no less true that there is veritable merit in our determinations when they are good and in the actions they produce, than that there is real demerit in the opposite case.

But, says de Tracy, we must not rest on vague ideas, because vague ideas easily become false ideas.

"It remains proven for me" he says "that although men's inclinations are the necessary effects of causes which give them birth and develop them, still we have plenty of reasons for giving them our refusal or our esteem according to whether their actions are good or bad. But if men have not the power to keep themselves from being culpable, for what reason would one punish them?"

Punishment is very different from vengeance, and one does not punish the criminal for the pleasure of seeing him suffer, which would be a cruel and stupid motive.

"One could perhaps say" de Tracy adds, "that I justify human justice and temporal punishments, and that I am not preoccupied with divine justice and the punishments of a future life. But I only speak here according to natural light, and I think that a sincere and reasonable man should not affirm anything about the will of God,—something about which he knows nothing."

"We must believe what is revealed, but we must renounce rendering it to conform to our poor 'reason'."

If the author of the above lines, written a few years before his death, had studied the writings of the holy Fathers, he could have cited many passages from their works to support his assertion.

M. de Tracy said, speaking of honor, that it was the need to be pleased with one's self, to be estimable in one's own eyes. It is like self-consciousness, with the addition, the desire to appear estimable in the eyes of others. A man of honor will not hesitate to do his duty at the risk of being blamed; he waits patiently for the uncertain future of a slow justice, or can even do without it.

Vanity is contrary to honor in the sense that the essential for a man of vanity is not to be but to appear. The vain man, de Tracy said, detests people of merit because he is jealous of their superiority, so he flees from them to seek flatterers. He also detests equality, which is such a great source of good and of pleasure to a sensible man.

With vanity, the alliance of power and liberty is impossible, for vanity hates the truth; and truth, as we well know, was qualified with good sense by M. de Tracy, and good sense was necessary to his happiness. That is why he stood against things impossible to understand by the aid of good sense (common sense). He put them to one side, he passed around or skirted them without wanting to either examine them or interpret them as he did with difficulties of another kind, either philosophic or scientific.

But with M. de Tracy, there reigned such perfect method in his errors and such harmony in his prejudices that one pardons them. He made a passionate analysis against certain works of Kant. When one reads this, one has the desire to criticize the analysis. How is it that M. de Tracy, who dug deeply, who compared everything, could not perceive that Kant, whom he treated so disdainfully, often said the same things as Condillac, who received his wholehearted esteem? The ideologist's aversion for all kinds of reverie took precedence here over his natural impartiality.

According to him, whatever is right and true cannot be simple and clear, and that is why he said that Pure Reason and Pure Knowledge are nothing but pure nonsenses, and that to employ abstract ideas and to make real facts of them, warps the mind, that Pure Reason, which consists of drawing from one's own depths principles which are independent of understanding or sensibility, crumbles at its base, that it is an erorr to believe that general ideas give us the means to judge particular ideas; for it is precisely the contrary that is true.

To say that time and space are not attributes of things in themselves, but are forms with which our cognition clothes phenomena is to speak absurdities.

Locke said "Time is measured continuance (measured duration)" and for de Tracy that says it all.

Does there exist in our intelligence any innate ideas not produced by reasoning? De Tracy says, No.

Kant assures us that the absolute cannot be known by man. Condillac concludes the same. One cannot know the all of anything, say these two; one cannot know anything when one divagates, adds de Tracy.

Condillac and Kant both recognize the impossibility of a rational physiology. They both think the same with regards to the ideality of space and time.

Condillac avows he does not know what duration and space are in themselves. Kant says one cannot speak of duration except from the point of view of man. He also says that it is the mind which forms the materials that the senses furnish to it.

Condillac speaks of a sort of sensation which makes us come out of ourselves, but he never looked for its origin as Kant did.

As for space, is it empty on our planet? Here is the opinion of de Tracy on space. It has been proven in physics that even in the most dense bodies, there is more so-called empty space than space filled by solid particles. But this space, considered empty, may possibly be filled with a matter that is more unbounded and less perceptible to our senses.

. . . Newton himself declares that he does not know if light is of matter or not. De Tracy thinks that beyond our atmosphere there is empty space.

All that we know, says de Tracy, we know because we have the faculty of moving, and our existence consists in feeling. We do not know anything else. In so far as we do not come up against anything we can move, and when we come up against something, we are stopped in our will to move. This empty space that we cross freely, is it extended? Yes, since we must make some movement in order to cross it. But does it follow that it is something? No, we can cross it because it is nothing. That reduces it to saying that nothing is something for us because we can cross it. This, like many others, is a bizarre way of expressing ourselves.

When space is not empty, it is no longer space, says de Tracy; and if Voltaire had noticed that, he would not have been so astonished that Newton could believe that creation could be explained by saying that God, by an act of his will and his power had rendered space impenetrable.

If Newton believed these words, he certainly deceived himself, said de Tracy; but he thought he (Newton) had expressed quite well what constitutes creation; it is to make bodies come out of nothing and to put something where there was nothing.

Newton well proved, contrary to Descartes, by examining the laws of movement and of celestial revolutions, that there must be emptiness in nature and the essential quality of a body is not to be extended but to be resistant.

De Tracy thought he could have proven the same thing by examining the intellectual facilities very attentively and of observing the manner in which these intellectual faculties teach men the existence of that which puts them into play. Says de Tracy, if this great man had arrived at his truths by this latter method, he, who had seen and shown that space is empty and that it is nothing, would not have imagined this space to be the sanctuary of God. That emptiness, nothingness could be the exterior organ of God, de Tracy found inconceivable and insisted that Newton had been led to this conclusion by a mania for imagining that which one cannot know and for explaining what is hidden.

In sum, in spite of this idea of Newton's, de Tracy was grateful to him for having said that space is empty when the facts prove that it is. He blamed Descartes and Leibnitz for their pronouncement that emptiness is impossible.

What is there about the idea of emptiness or nothingness that is contrary to reason?, de Tracy asked. He avowed that it was not nothingness that surprised him, but the fact that there are beings.

He was also astonished that Voltaire, while admitting the existence of emptiness, had an air of being frightened of it, for he said "Dare we believe that infinite space exists?"

De Tracy declared that empty space is not a thing; that it is neither finite nor infinite; that it does not exist, that it is the negation of being, and that is all.

One sees, by what one has just read, that M. de Tracy is more advanced than his critics; but they have (in certain kinds of ideas) been outdistanced by the idealist who says "I understand everything" and who often explains that statement in an incomprehensible way. While Condillac avows that such and such a thing exists but that he does not know what it is, de Tracy thinks that things are obscure because men do not know their existence and of all that which exists in relation to them. It is this ignorance, he says, which throws men into deep errors and embroils all their ideas.

De Tracy wrote a treatise on Love which has been translated into Italian and printed in Italy about 35 years ago.

Love, de Tracy, said, absorbs all the power of the individual;[10] it is the most precious of our affections, and the extent of its force has the greatest influence on character and temperament. It is a physical need and it is a passion.

It gives us the consciousness of all our faculties; it exalts us; it lives, by preference, on beauty, but it is not always determined by that. The pleasure of loving and of being loved plays a greater part in it than copulation does; the proof is that easy copulation is savorless because it is denuded of sentiment.

Love is the more profound in proportion as the ideas are more extended and the sentiments more fine and delicate. It is the perfection of friendship, it is the complement of our organization, it is the master work of our being.

Love, says M. de Tracy, is impossible to describe; for one does not think of its power when one feels it, and when one thinks about it, one no longer feels it. It is the extreme good and the extreme bad; it would soon destroy our existence if it could endure in all its first energy. They both strangle, seize our imagination which is enlarged by them.

Love, according to de Tracy, is almost the only business

[10] My italics.

of women and their only interest. Not being strong, to please is their way of being: it is the sentiment of which they have the greatest need, and they know how to love with more delicacy than men do.

Marriage, which ought to have been the most free and gay convention of all, has become a sad slavery.

The men of the north allow the greatest liberty to young girls and are not jealous of their wives; the Orientals assassinate their wives on the slimmest suspicion. There, each house is a prison where there sleeps a useless tyrant, says de Tracy; he makes eunuchs to guard his women the way they make them elsewhere to sing in the churches.

Among the ancient Greeks, marriage was respected, the women lived sequestered; but their virtue became sad and the men found no more pleasure with them. Then the men sought friendship, which they made divine, and they invented platonic love. The society of courtesans, pretty ones, witty ones endowed with talents and of a cultivated mind was sought after because of their gaiety and amiability. But a courtesan can be bought; and it is not there that one finds true love. There is lacking in this sort of an attachment a condition essential to happiness; that is—the interest in the family: for it is this sentiment, drawn from deep in our nature which fortifies and perpetuates all the rest, which forms a more intimate union and which, in youth, renders passion more touching by giving it new subjects on which to be exercised and developed, which ameliorates those it animates, binds them, and makes of old age, destined to be so sad, the evening of a beautiful day, during which one prepares to go to sleep, without regret, in seeing oneself reborn. It does still more: when misfortune, all too common, separates by death two beings who love each other, it permits the survivor to find great consolation in the objects of their mutual affection. It is therefore only in a good household (marriage) that all the good things of love are found.

De Tracy thinks we must not seek love among the Romans, who, always sombre and superstitious, went from the grossest austerity to the most extreme license. Neither must we seek it in the middle ages, for true love cannot exist without refinement and equality. When the light began to break, men familiarized themselves more with women, and both sexes gained.

At present, says de Tracy, women are just about what they ought to be, amiable companions, tender and devoted friends. Now there is more happiness and true virtue.

Nevertheless love is too much a stranger to marriage;—and the theatres give a very false image of society. They think of nothing but love and they talk of nothing but marriage. In comedies they find lovers indecent if they do not marry each other, and in tragedies they find them unworthy if they do not kill each other. That is not the way things go in ordinary life, and the customs of the theatre confuse the mind.

De Tracy was not of the opinion of Buffon who thinks there is nothing but vanity in the mental side of love, and that it is only the physical side of this passion that is good and the rest valueless, and that in this connection, the lot of the animals is better than ours. It is to misunderstand the human heart and to slander the animals and even the insects and birds who have, just as we do, feelings, sentiments, jealousies, preferences, gratitude, memory and other moral affections.

De Tracy was amazed to see philosophers praise friendship excessively and feel obliged to profess a disdain for love, regarding it as a brutal passion.

What real philosophy is, he said, is to recognize that we owe all our happiness, and certainly our existence, to the penchant for love and to our taste for sympathy.

Love is the first seed of our benevolent passions; it develops our virtues.

Love gives birth to the finest ideas in the heads of men in all countries.

Love has been the object of all the most absurd and most barbarous laws.

Love does not demand exterior advantages which often give it birth.

One notices that the less pretty women are loved longer

than the beauties who inspire desires which are soon replaced by boredom, because extreme beauty is often accompanied by egoism.

De Tracy thinks there are more errors in our institutions than in our hearts and that it is because of our established laws that it is complained that love and hymen are two disunited brothers. If they had reflected better, he said, they would have put mercury in the service of hymen and not of love, for the god of the merchants should have been at the service of the hymen which is too often goods for sale. Nature is always on the side of love, just as marriage is always the protege of the legislators.

The author thinks that young girls ready to marry, should enjoy the liberty of choosing for themselves, for they are the owners of their own persons; but then it is necesssary to give care to their reason, give them good taste by a good example, that of the parental home where they will find how to employ their time in varied occupations.

It is the men and women of tender and high sentiments who find the most pleasure in the life of retirement.

We should give our young men the taste for good manners and let them frequent the society of young girls. Said de Tracy, "We should attach less importance to the weaknesses of young men. They would say I teach libertinism and I would respond that they would say the same of me in Turkey if I said a woman could show the tip of her nose without being lost or disgraced; or in China if I spoke against the custom of breaking the feet of the women to keep them from walking. It should be able to be said everywhere that all that harms nobody is indifferent."

If a young girl is seduced by her senses, one can believe that she will often be drawn into other temptations.

If she gives in, to escape from poverty, she is unfortunate and to be pitied.

If she is seduced by money and magnificence, one can believe that she has a vile soul.

If she is betrayed by her heart, by her spirit, by her confidence, there is a tender and generous soul and perhaps a beautiful character. That one will slowly acquire experience.

Says M. de Tracy, why find a young girl who has succumbed so guilty? A scheming person is not lost for doing worse than that;—thus the inequality between men and women is still large.

Why do we who are said to be more or less philosophers find these injustices so simple? One cannot find one single just reason; and justice, in all countries of the world, seems to have the least indulgence for the most irresistible of our inclinations.

The brilliant advantages of women are fragile and passing. The least accident alters them and time quickly destroys them.

In compensation for their weakness, women have received from nature or by necessity, a precocious sagacity, a great talent for observation and a delicate tact which makes them acquire experience quicker then men do, or at least they draw from it greater results. . . .

If one did not know, says M. de Tracy, that legislators have a great desire to render the conjugal bond respectable, one would believe that they had the opposite desire, that is, to make it disagreeable.

Not wanting divorce, they have permitted separation of two parties, always demanded by the wife, for unfaithful husbands separate in fact, and take their liberty without need of a court judgement; or, if, by interest of misfortune, they desire separation, they know very well how to force their poor wives to demand it. . . .

A woman as distinguished by her profound sensibility as for her enlightenment, says M. de Tracy, is endowed with a noble and sincere character (note: La Comtesse de Tesse insisted that if the men of this world renounced useless base actions, and if the women renounced their lovers that they do not even treat well, society would be prodigiously improved, and that divorce had produced many reconciliations and had not caused any rupture that was not prepared in advance.)

Says de Tracy, love is the sweetest of our penchants and marriage is the most important act of life. It is the bond that perpetuates the species and bases society because it is not composed of isolated individuals.

"It is on the state of marriage that the fate of the human race depends. One cannot reflect on that too much."

It is sad to see the treatise de l'Amour finish by necessity with the chapter on divorce.

To the principle argument of de Tracy's in favor of divorce, that: "The necessity to deliver two beings from a slavery which started well but finished badly because time and events brought other ideas and changes in character," one could respond that the same reasons exist for the contrary, that is to say that a marriage which commences badly can end well because of those same changes; and that since the continuation of a marriage is longer than the beginning of it and one is old a longer time than young, it is of the latter part of marriage that one should think. Patience and repentance have brought long days of serenity and joy in marriages that started stormily. If divorce is good for reconciling individuals, patience is worth infinitely more. It is more beautiful and more simple.

M. de Tracy loved the company of women, and knew how to make them love him. The over-use of the intellect had not dried him up, and when it came to women, his heart broke loose. He said that people of intellect know far better how to love than others and that they are always loved. He liked to repeat that their intimacy is the sweetest, the most charming, the most useful thing that exists under the sun. He was interested in their dress and insisted that we see them backwards because of the fashion that hides the bosom and shows the back. He detested the gigantic crackling sleeves of 1830, an invention most contrary to feminine grace. M. de Tracy did not like the current fashion in men's dress which permitted them to wear gloves in the presence of ladies and to wear boots in the evening in their living rooms. To him those things were indecent and only fitting for the valets of the stables.

Nevertheless, one day of a very severe winter, he tried

to put on a pair of trousers that were worn out. When he came into the sitting room where all the family was gathered, wearing this disguise, we found him disfigured, unrecognizable. It was no longer M. de Tracy, the elegant colonel of the regiment of Penthièvre. It was no longer that gentleman of former times, head high, with that distinguished air.

He seemed humiliated and ill at ease all evening and he retired to his apartment much earlier than usual. The next day he put on his usual fine clothes, and one could say that he died in silk stockings.

All the writers of morality novels of all countries and of the two sexes, fanciers of new theories about the lot of women, inventors of new fashionable systems, have written nothing comparable to what de Tracy used to say with such reasonableness, sympathy and enlightenment, on what is due them in society, on the condition of young girls, on the liberty of women inside their own homes, on the respect that one owes to their dependency (which is one of their charms) and on their happiness, most often ruined through the fault of the husbands.

Liberty, to women, is in general the doing of what is not permitted them, for they are always free to practice what is strictly good.

But liberty, according to the heart of M. de Tracy, is an ideal liberty; it should not weigh on anyone, everyone should have it; as general well-being. But it was a dream, for that has never been seen in France nor elsewhere and things will no doubt long remain in their habitual state, some giving while receiving nothing and others receiving but giving nothing. In spite of the apparent injustice toward women, probably not one of them would change places with her husband or her brother, were he the most celebrated man of his time.

People wrote to M. de Tracy, for consultation, from the most far-off countries. They asked him for the plans of the constitution, asked for advice on industry, on poverty, on dueling, on slander, etc. One day he received a very brilliant letter postmarked, Rome, and signed "Stendahl," in which the author asked him to give him his opinion on the cause of laughter and what gives birth to laughter in certain dialogues and certain theatrical characters.

M. de Tracy thought that laughter was caused, in dialogue, by an unexpected response, contrary to what the public had expected, by the ridiculousness of certain characters, certain individuals who were ignorant of their ridiculousness in the eyes of the public.

M. de Tracy made friends with M. de Stendahl, who was no other than the author of Rouge et Noir; but they soon fell out because of the book of that author on the theory of Love demonstrated by "crystallization," which was the ideology of M. de Stendahl. De Tracy tried to read the work, understood nothing in it, and declared to the author that it was absurd.

He employed the proper word on every occasion, never suspecting the violent effect it might produce. He also had a certain way of abruptly pulling out his scent-bottle when an individual for whom he had little esteem spoke to him; and he would sniff at the bottle with a furor that seemed to say to the interlocutor that he was nauseated. His accurate and penetrating mind (esprit) was devoid of exaggeration, except for his horror of lies, a horror which made him seem outraged at those who did not partake of this antipathy. His habitual extreme politeness was, on certain occasions, mixed with a desire to displease, a desire which did not fail to have its effect.

He was nicknamed Tetu de Tracy, Stubborn de Tracy, and he very much enjoyed this little joke; he said that stubbornness was a good fault, and that men were often taken in because they did not know how to say, no.

In proportion as he grew older, he saddened and isolated himself. He had seen all his old friends die; he had lost his wife, his caring and devoted companion whose gaiety rendered her goodness even more lovable. Each day augmented de Tracy's regret that he could not any longer pursue his studies; reading became impossible for him, and his view deteriorated to the point where he had to be operated upon for cataract, but it was not perfectly successful. He bore this operation with extraordinary good will and tranquility, for he made the oculist operate on the two eyes at one time, so that, as he said, he would not be obliged to be awakened at such an early hour and thus change his habits a second time. He preserved his taste for all the little discoveries of a day. If his manners were those of the preceding century, his ideas were certainly of his own time. He disliked agitation, but he was very agitated over the subject of the revolutions in America. He would have liked to be able to rush to the aid of less advanced countries to offer them advice, to make them understand that in giving the exact meaning to words, one saw the birth of more sensible ideas. He would have prevented them from using certain very humble terms for those one had need of, terms, he said, that shock no one, in spite of the fact that they rank a man as a slave, and that are only suitable for children or cattle that you lead to pasture or to shearing.

M. de Tracy kept up a running correspondence with Mr. Rivadavia and he inculcated in him some of his ideas. He would have liked to visit Buenos Aires, Mexico, Chili, Peru and in fact all of that America that he so loved, a country that perhaps God created expressly to show to the men who form the constitutions that nations can go and can fall without government.

We have said that de Tracy sought by preference the conversation of young people who liked study and who had a serious turn of mind.

The best way to know men is to listen to what they have to say and to believe what they express. M. de Tracy listened to them, he believed them,—and he preached to them against obscurity, negligence and laziness. He advised them to dare to speak what they thought, to express it as best they could and to hasten to acquaint others with it, if they thought their work was useful.

He told them what an old English poet said to all the

world, long ago:

> Begin, be bold, and venture to be wise;
> He who defers this work from day to day,
> Does on a river bank expecting stay
> Till the whole stream that stopp'd him shall be gone
> Which runs, and as it runs for ever shall run on.

Not one of those who had him for teacher or friend ever disappointed his hopes. They are pure and elegant in their language, clear in the expression of thoughts they are sure of, as de Tracy was in all that he wrote.

There are two surprising things in his personal life: to have invented a dance (contredanse) that was named after him when he was a beautiful dancer at the queen's balls, and to have built a church, long afterwards, from the debris of a big tower that he had had torn down, he who so seldom frequented churches and who was so attached to the old walls of his manor house of Paray-le-Frésil, which during his last years he preferred over any other place, because one leaves one's heart and one's eternal memory in the place where one has spent one's childhood. He retained a singular mixture of primitive simplicity and of feudal customs. He would call his servants Hola! and he never knew their names. He never permitted the use of a dinner bell in the house, finding this custom full of vanity, and humiliating for the neighbors, although he had no neighbors; and at the same time he loved showing his family portraits decorated with medals *(cordon bleus)* never dreaming that he could thus also humiliate the neighbor he did not have.

De Tracy always went out in silk stockings, but never wanted to adopt the use of an umbrella. It was thus that he would go to see a building that was in process, because he was interested in public constructions and he loved talking to the masons and workmen. When one of them responded in a clear and bright manner, de Tracy went back to see him, for he adored intelligence, that queen of the universe which naturally takes first place wherever it is found, that eclipses all other powers, and that would be alone capable of filling a life without leaving it empty, if the pleasures of intelligence had not in them also the repugnances which trouble them.

The most intimate friends of de Tracy were Count Louis de Narbonne with whom he had been a student, General Lafayette, Doctor Cabanis and Mr. Daunow. He was close friends with many distinguished foreigners for men of a studious spirit understand one another from one end of the earth to the other and their thoughts cross the seas to aid each other.

De Tracy's patriotism did not consist of detesting or disparaging neighbor countries. He desired to conciliate the esteem of other nations toward his country in giving justice to their merits.

De Tracy's hero was Voltaire. He called the century of Louis XV, Voltaire's century. He knew his works by heart. He wanted to publish a new edition of Voltaire, with notes, but he always put it off for later. And later, that was never.

One day he read the article on Voltaire by M. A. in the Biographie de Michaud. This article made him indignant, and he had had the same impression when M. A. had read a piece on the same subject and which was the basis of this article, at the Academie. De Tracy remembered it and wrote in his notes—

"I permitted myself to say to M. A., and right in the Academie, to him who raved to us so about the English, that at least the English have one quality that he seems to have forgotten; that of not belittling their great men, and that if they had had the good fortune to have born among them a man like Voltaire, they would not have permitted the publication of a satire against him such as we have just heard. . . .

Until his last day, de Tracy judged the political events of his country with great sagacity and still he had fixed ideas on politics as on other subjects.

He thought that electricity, better studied, would become the source of a crowd of surprising and unexpected discoveries and that its application would be useful in the most divergent ways.

He thought that the contested ideas of Buffon would be later confirmed by the facts. He regarded Buffon as the purest of writers but he did not think he was an equally good philosopher. De Tracy sought to be useful to all who were occupied with natural history, with which he thought one should commence. He had such a humble manner of giving service that it seemed it was he who was obliging in accepting his offers. He understood all the fine delicacies of charity, and it was thus that the merit of his good works was doubled.

Around the middle of his life, de Tracy had one of those deep friendships of which he speaks in his writings. That friendship, engraved in his memory, remained there without rival unforgotten, for inconstancy is for the weak, and it bespeaks a great moral poverty with those individuals who have need of change in order to have ideas. The sudden loss of this spiritual affection left a great emptiness in the heart of de Tracy, as he was deprived of the mysterious and consoling hope of finding again, in the eternal resting place, those whom he had venerated here on earth. . . .

De Tracy gave himself up, solitarily, to a sentiment of sad abandon where the loss of all that was charming in life leaves us. . . .But de Tracy was a stranger to egotism (egoism). He feared to disturb others, he no longer sought them out, he was content to make observations on his general decline—"I suffer, therefore, I am," he used to say.

He could be seen at his window in contemplation before the clouds that passed and succeeded one another. What did he think of as he thus looked at the sky? Nobody knew.

On the 5th of March, 1836, he had a paralytic attack after lunch while his secretary was reading his paper to him (newspaper). When he recovered from the attack, he wanted the reading continued, and did not want to go to bed, or to interrupt his regular habits. He tried several times that day to walk across the room astonished and impatient at the fact that he could not. He lost the power of speech during the night and died the third day afterward, after a slow and peaceful "agonie" at the age of 82.

De Tracy, in becoming a "savant" never lost his customs

of a man of the world. Voltaire had formed his thinking, Cabanis had developed his taste for the sciences; but his virtues and his pleasantness came to him from his family. He was, as we see in certain chemical substances, the result of the fusion of many ingredients.

His philosophy, which had as its basis the knowledge of human faculties and the amelioration of humanity by the right instruction, had many detractors and many admirers.

The first were those who preferred to cast themselves out of the path of this philosophy which, though reasonable, is without imagination and sees only one half of things. The others were those who believed that that half was enough because reason should be the only basis of all philosophy. . . .

Reason was so natural a sentiment with de Tracy, that he seemed to have forgotten the way to it, for he was astonished at the hatred that was attracted to him by this reason of his constantly employed to combat the errors, prejudices and weaknesses which are hurtful to liberty of thought and which turn it from its true path.

Excerpts from Jean Cruet's *La Philosophie Morale & Sociale de Destutt de Tracy* (1754–1836)[11]

> It is above all to the young people that I am speaking (that I address myself), for they have not yet any fixed opinions, and also because they can tolerate being delayed over details that men of a more advanced age believe they already know, though very often, they haven't examined them sufficiently.
>
> Destutt de Tracy

[11] Translated by Iris Hartman. Jean Cruet's insightful appreciation for his Tracy accounts for my quoting from his translated tribute.

Introductory statement by L. Cruet, Jean's father

It was not the design or the desire of my son Jean Cruet that this work of his youth be published; or it would have appeared earlier and would have been addressed to a more extended public than those relatives and friends for whom I reserve these few volumes today. . . .

In following, thus, from this first and humble volume to his last book "La Vie du Droit" which shines like a ray of young glory and beauty on an unfinished life, but a life already so fecund, his friends will judge that he merited to live, he who promised so much, and that destiny was very cruel to an intelligence which enlarged itself in work and reflection.

But like him who is making the effort to write these lines, they will feel some consolation in the thought that their dear comrade will not have completely disappeared, since in these few books he will have left the fairest part of himself: all his intelligence and all his heart; and they will remember with a sweet emotion their chosen friend whom they will not have entirely lost.

L. C.

Foreword

On the 28th of May, 1842, the secretary of the Académie des Sciences Morales et politique began the reading of a notice on the life and works of Destutt de Tracy with these appreciatory expressions:

> Today I must talk with you of a celebrated philosopher; I must recount for you after what painful vicissitudes a young man who carried the sword, as did his ancestors for 400 years, was led to continue the work of Locke and Condillac; by what unforseen circumstances and by what long hidden vocation, a man of the world, who had shone by the embellishments of his person and the charm of his personality, suddenly became a profound thinker; and how a colonel of the old order, while in prison under the Terreur, by hard and original work, completed

the doctrines of a great philosophical school of which he was the last and the most brilliant exponent.

Such is—according to the historian Mignet—the strange and vivid philosopher whose moral and political ideas we are going to study with some development; and if this study has seemed to present to us a particular interest, it is because *the philosophy of Destutt de Tracy, poorly known and poorly understood, has never been appreciated for its right value.*[12]

In spite of the important place it (his philosophy) has occupied in the history of ideas at the beginning of the Nineteenth Century, in spite of the vivacity of the attacks upon it by enemies of the revolutionary spirit; and lastly, in spite of the singularly engaging biography of the philosopher himself, this philosophy was quickly forgotten by precisely those who continue in the republican tradition of which, in our opinion, it remains the most complete and faithful expression.

Napoleon judged the psychological theories of Destutt de Tracy severely.

"It is to Ideology," he said, "to this shadowy metaphysic, which, in searching with such subtlety for first causes, would found the legislation of the people on these bases; it is to Ideology that you must attribute the misfortune of France. . . . It is this philosophy which brought in the regime of men of blood, which proclaimed insurrection as a duty, which adulated the people in calling them to a sovereignty that they were incapable of exercising, which destroyed the sanctity of and respect for laws in making them depend, not on principles sacred to justice, but only on the will of an assembly of men, strangers to the knowledge of civil, administrative, political and military law."[13] In other terms,—and to translate more simply and more exactly the thought of the emperor,—it is this philosophy which has laid the first foundation for the republican and parliamentary regime.

[12]My italics.
[13]Response to an address of the Senate.

The first generation of the Nineteenth Century, under the vigorous impulse of the spiritualist school and of the theological school, was not slow to separate itself from both the psychological sensualism of Destutt de Tracy and the physiological sensualism of Doctor Cabanis.

The philosophy of Destutt de Tracy, was the living incarnation of the philosophical and political ideas of the end of the Eighteenth Century, as Guizot noted.

Does it not then merit, on this title alone, to occupy a relatively important place in the general history of philosophy? However, it has none whatever. Kuno Fischer completely forgets the author of the Ideologies; Ueberweg makes short mention of Ideology without speaking of the morale and the sociology which de Tracy deduces from it; at last Mr. Fouillée indicates the influence of the philosophy of the ideologists, but passes over the philosopher himself without a word.

In this way Destutt de Tracy, who appears to us in Mignet and in Guizot as a celebrated philosopher, a profound thinker, as the last and most brilliant representative of the sensualist school, would not in reality hold but an insignificant place in whatever concerns psychology, in the general movement of ideas, and no place at all in what concerns morale and sociology.

The violent attacks of Napoleon and of Chateaubriand, and the difficultly explainable silence of historians would perhaps suffice to justify a conscientious and impartial study of the moral and social philosophy of the Count de Tracy. But it is necessary to add two remarks still.

With Destutt de Tracy, and with him alone, can one find an ethic that is veritably sensualist.

Condillac, indeed, always maintained the traditional principles of theology and morality above the experience of free examination. Destutt de Tracy, on the contrary, enamoured of clarity and logic, pushed the sensualist principle to its furthest results, and, from the Treatise on Sensations, reviewed and corrected, he deduced, so to speak, an ethic and a sociology.

As one conceives man, one conceives society; and a society constructed for the economic man of Adam Smith is obviously not identical with a society constructed for the man of Kant or for the man of Lamennais. One can therefore ask oneself if Destutt de Tracy could have been both sensualist and republican without altering the logic of his philosophic system; or, in other terms, if the revolutionary ideal of liberty, equality, fraternity was simply a sensualism, or a utilitarianism, or a social positivism. Is the republican society made for the man of Baron Holbach and of La Mettrie? Serious questions to which we can find the answer in the study of ideologic philosophy which is precisely an essay at a synthesis between republican and political ideas and sensualist and moral ideas, and in psychology a synthesis analogous with that which later tempted the founder of positivism, Auguste Comte.

Between the academic eulogies of Guizot and Mignet and the systematic disdain of Napoleon and Chateaubriand and the tranquil ignorance of posterity is there not a way to sift out the middle truth and to show that the moral and social philosophy of Antoine-Louis-Claude Destutt de Tracy merits neither this excess of honor nor this indignity? We believe so, and an attentive study has proved to us that the ideologic philosophy of Destutt de Tracy—without bringing to the world any profoundly original ideas—is, notwithstanding, one of the most important links in the history of ideas; Destutt de Tracy is the continuer of Condillac, and the precursor of Auguste Comte. He is at once the last of the sensualists and the first of the positivists.

The intellectual development of Destutt de Tracy

Philosophers commence by acquiring knowledge before teaching, and by criticizing before constructing. Aristotle was the disciple and critic of Plato; Leibnitz was the continuer and critic of Descartes; and from this intellectual submission, fecunded by free examination, were born two profoundly original philosophies. This is the habitual progression of human thought; it does not attain unknown summits at one bound, it does not create anything *ex nihilo;* it develops according to a slow or rapid rhythm, but always in a continuing manner, and a philosophic system is always in seed in the often heterogeneous mass of anterior systems. This is why one does not understand Aristotle without Plato, Leibnitz without Descartes; and Destutt de Tracy without Locke, Condillac, Montesquieu and Voltaire. It concerns not only an abstract and logical continuity, but a real historical continuity.

To understand the philosophy of Destutt de Tracy, it is therefore necessary to study the history of his spirit, his origins and his direction, and, so to speak, the biographical circumstances in which he constructed his philosophic system; in fact, the movement of political and economic ideas at the end of the 18th century. . . .

Already devoted to all the social reforms when the revolution blazed up on the 24th January 1789. Destutt de Tracy was elected deputy of the Nobility to the Etats Generaux. It must be noticed that the nobles who had elected him had, under the habitual form of the books, written the most liberal claims; and it is this which explains how Destutt de Tracy could manifest his revolutionary zeal without being false to his commission.

Destutt de Tracy was raised as one raised the young of the French aristocracy of that period. He learned first and above all to ride horseback, to swim and to dance; he even invented a "contredanse" (a quadrille), which was named the Contredanse de Tracy.

Horsemanship, dancing, swimming, tennis, fencing, shooting, however, left the young count de Tracy plenty of time to pursue some excellent study of the classics. He studied Aristotle, and translated the Latin of Cornelius, Nepos and the Greek of Plutarch. He went to the University of Strasbourg before entering the artillery school in that city.

At Strasbourg he took Professor Müller's course and heard him explain and comment on the philosophy of Kant and of Hume. But he seems to have drawn little from these early studies—if one judges from his own description of the public education of his time. He says,

> "One started, then, by teaching the young the ancient languages and the principles of the sciences; then, at the end of all of that, one gave them a supposed course in philosophy, consisting of some false notions, false and feeble, about physics and metaphysics. But this philosophy is so generally recognized as false and useless that no student made even a pretense of studying it."

"It is unbelievable" said de Tracy "to what point conceit can create illusions and induce one to exaggerate his own personal importance. I have seen men obliged by difficulties to leave their Chateaux, who believed in good faith that due to their leaving, all the village would lack work, not perceiving that it was the farmers, and not they themselves, who gave the salaries; and who persuaded themselves sincerely that even when the peasants divided their goods or bought them at a poor price, they would only be more miserable" (Elements l'Ideologie). . . .

The fall of the king and of the royalty, August 10, did not in any way surprise this republican gentleman (de Tracy); he knew better than anyone, the weaknesses of the old regime. The faith of the revolutionists began to turn into fanaticism. Perspicacious minds could easily foresee the tragic days of Terreur.

Lafayette, accused by decree, went to pay a final visit to Destutt de Tracy before crossing the border. De Tracy refused to leave Lafayette and demanded an unlimited leave. Lafayette left for a neutral country with some friends and de Tracy went to Paris, then to Auteuil at the home of Madame Helvetius, of whom a man of wit has said—"she counted the events of her life by the movements of her heart."

At this period, de Tracy started the study of a new science, that of chemistry. He took as his guide, Foucroy, author of *la Philosophie Chimique.* One of his biographers, that is, Mignet, reproaches de Tracy in not having put off the old man, the chemist: in becoming an ideologist, de Tracy, if he always thinks as a philosopher—writes sometimes as the chemist that he was.

In the midst of this peaceful research he seemed to have escaped from the severe judgments of the revolutionary tribunal. But at the end of a year of studious retirement, he was declared suspect of aristocratic and anti-revolutionary incivism. They charged him to pay, within the day, a hundred thousand francs bail-bond for his revolutionary orthodoxy. De Tracy, full of good will, but unable to raise such a sum, offered to turn over all revenue from his properties to the nation. The response was not long in coming. They drew up an arrest order against him and on November 2, 1793, an entire regiment surrounded the little hermitage at Auteuil, took hold of the Count de Tracy, and imprisoned him at l'Abbaye. (L'Abbaye was a prison of the State. On the 2 and 3 of December a troupe of revolutionaries massacred 164 prisoners, among them 18 priests, on the spot).

De Tracy spent six weeks in this unbreathable atmosphere, with 300 other captives. But he found a friend there. One day, a serious and impassive man was seen entering the communal cell. He carried a writing table, paper and pens. This new prisoner sat down without losing a minute, and began writing, peacefully, without seeming in the least moved by the circumstances in which he found himself. It was M. Jollivet, a magistrate judge and juris-consultant.

Encouraged by this cxample, de Tracy started to study the empirical philosophy of Locke and the sensualist philosophy of Condillac, with an increasing interest.

At the age of 20, de Tracy had disdained the philosophies of the schools, and had preferred simply to "study his kind." At 40, desiring to give a solid base to the sciences he had studied, he turned to high philosophic speculations. The tragic events, the approach of old age, the solitude of the prison, all carried his spirit toward serious reflections; and the result of his meditations was a system of philosophy.

An incident came, to interrupt the meditations of the prisoner. He was changed to the prison at Carmes. There, each prisoner awaited the decision of the revolutionary tribunal in anguish.

At last, on the 5th of the Thermidor (eleventh month, July-August on the revolutionary calendar) they commenced to call the 45 prisoners condemmed to the scaffold. The name of Destutt de Tracy figured on the list. All the same, he continued to write, unmoved, the results of his philosophic investigations. He wrote: "Product of the faculty of thinking, knowledge, truth. In the work on which I work, I see that there must be added to this equation, three other members: virtue, happiness, and the sentiment of loving—and in a third work, I shall prove that one should add also these:

Liberty, equality and philanthropy."

When the call of the condemned was terminated, de Tracy added to the above lines, these words: "In the future, I will have this always as my point of departure,—if heaven permits me still some time in which to live and to study."

He held to his promise, and doubtless that is why there reigns in all his philosophical work such a marvelous clarity and such a beautiful unity.

That day, the 5th Thermidor, Destutt de Tracy did not mount the scaffold, but it was in fact only postponed. The revolutionary tribunal set the date of the 11th Thermidor for the definite death of the Comte de Tracy. He waited with courage, reading and working right up to the day before. Happily for our philosopher, his luck changed; The 9th Thermidor, the convention decreed the accusation of Robespierre and his friends, and the next day, Robespierre and 22 of his co-accused mounted the scaffold. The Terreur was finished and the Compte de Tracy left the prison in October, 1794.

He went to Auteuil to the home of Madame Helvetius, and, surrounded by his friends, led the peaceful and laborious life of a scholar and philosopher for many years. In the little house at Auteuil, they continued in the tradition of 1789. There, Destutt de Tracy often encountered the doctor-philosopher Cabanis, author of *Rapports du physique et du moral de l'homme.*

It was during this period that Destutt de Tracy commenced to develop, in seven memoires, the system of philosophy that he had written in a brief resumé on the tragic day of the

5 Thermidor. These memoires created a great stir; reviewed and corrected by their author, they became "Elements d'Ideologie" and it is in this form that we shall study them.

Destutt de Tracy, tired of public life and political combats, desired above all, a rest for body and mind. One can well visualize him the day when the young and ambitious Napoleon, seeking to surround himself with active and intelligent men, offered him the rank of Field Marshall in the army of Egypt. Destutt de Tracy asked for two days of reflection, and refused.

The great crime of the Ideologists was actually to love the Republic. One senses the political character of Napoleon's hatred for the Ideologists in a response he made to an address in the Senate on his return from the Campaign in Russia.

"We had gone to foolishly compromise the French army in Russia; and with the French army, the imperial throne; and what was worse, the greatness of France; we came back conquered, humiliated, and it was the philosophy that was wrong."

It was not wrong for long. On April 3, 1814, Destutt de Tracy voted for the overthrow of the emperor. Louis XVIII returned to Paris "in the wagontrains of the foreigner" and Destutt de Tracy became a member of the Chamber of Peers. He regained the title of Count, which he had abandoned with enthusiasm on April 4, 1789; but he fought for the excesses of the white Terror of 1815 as he had fought the red Terror in 1793.

Since the death of Dr. Cabanis, Destutt had abandoned his philosophical work: "My life is finished," he said. *Traité de la Volunté* was his last work; he had not even the heart to completely edit the final chapter.

He welcomed, almost with indifference, the revolution of 1830. Old, with a green eye-shade on his brow, a cane in his hand, Destutt de Tracy let himself go, in town suit and black stockings, to make a march around the barricades. Indeed he knew how to keep his calm, his perfect calm, on all occasions, as well as the quickness of decision. Seeing himself becoming blind, one day he called for a carriage, got in, and had himself driven to the celebrated oculist Wenzel. Wenzel operated on

De Tracy's cataracts and Destutt de Tracy returned home by foot "with his crystalline lenses in his pocket" as Guizot says.

Destutt de Tracy died at 82, surrounded by the affection of his family and the regrets of his colleagues. Guizot replaced him at the Academie Francaise where he himself had succeeded his friend Cabanis.

Said Michelet—"For the life and the history in which I have lived I see things turned upside down every moment; the spirtualists who go pray to God at Fanchon's, and the materialists who give their life for an idea." Destutt de Tracy is one of those materialists. Those who wish not at all to admit that a materialist can live as an honest man and a good citizen have remarked in astonishment:—"He gave service to that humanity which, if it were not for what he saw in it, would not have been worth such devotion." That was the opinion of Guizot.

Guizot speaks with astonishment of this young officer and of this brilliant man of the world, who suddenly became a profound and original thinker. But why this note of astonishment? One can easily find, in studying the life of Destutt de Tracy, the philosopher in the soldier and the dancer in the philosopher. Destutt de Tracy, musketeer of the king, read Helvetius and the encyclopedists. Destutt de Tracy, member of the Institute, never felt he lowered himself, in extolling, in a long and spirited essay, the usefulness of dancing. At the age of 20 he made a pilgrimage to the Chateau de Ferney; and at 80, he made himself re-read the works of Voltaire, the "hero of reason." The continuity of this admiration is assuredly the best token of his fidelity to one same philosophic and political ideal.

On Pierre Georges Cabanis (1757-1808)

"I pride myself," Tracy wrote to Doctor Cabanis, "that your work was useful to me even before it was completed; that your conversations have been even more (useful to me) and that it is due to you that I have had the courage to undertake the research to which I have set myself with the hope of their having some utility. Thus, the success for which I am the most ambitious is that my work be regarded as a consequence of yours. And that you yourself see in it only a corollary of the principles that you have already exposed " (a letter to Senator Cabanis, 1st floreal an XIII. Idéologie, part 3, I, pp. v-x).

Tracy recognized how much he helped himself by growing appreciation for his extraordinary preceptor, Pierre Jean Georges Cabanis (1757-1808), French physician and philosopher who was professor in the medical school of Paris and a member of the American Philosophical Society of Philadelphia. He was greatly interested in political economy. His choice of medicine was based upon highest ideals of reverence for life and respect for individuality. Graduating as an M.D. in 1784, from then until the French Revolution he was devoted to the practice of his profession. He became intermittently acquainted with Mirabeau, Condorcet and Benjamin Franklin. In 1783 he composed his Oath of Physicians with a free translation of the Hippocratic Oath. In 1791 he wrote his *Essay on the Certainty of Medicine.* In 1802 he published his celebrated work *Rapports du Physique et du Moral de l'homme.* In the spring of 1808 he suffered an attack of apoplexy, dying on the 5th of May. An ardent philanthropist, he was devoted to the science of ideology, preferring it to all else, in that it gave him a wide field for exercising his active imagination. He was widely revered as a medical philosopher, ensouling the ideal of Hipprocrates: *the philosophical physician partakes in some sort of the nature of the Gods.*

Here follow statements of Cabanis demonstrating his medical psychology, excerpted from *An Essay on the Certainty of Medicine* (trans. by R. La Roche, Philadelphia: Robert Desilver, 1823, 97 pp.). The Author's Preface contains the following insights:

> Reflecting minds are moreover perfectly aware of the immense influence which the progress of science, and especially the good philosophical methods have exercised in the development and propagation of the spirit of liberty. It is through the medium of philosophy alone that liberty becomes refined and consolidated, whilst the sciences and the arts, at the same time that they serve to embellish it, convert it into a real system of happiness. [24]

> The physician not only traces to physical sensibility, the origin of ideas and passions, but even discovers, in some sort,

their formation, or at least all that favours or opposes this latter, and it is always in certain organic conditions, that he is led to search for the solution of each problem.

Consequently, we can with propriety regard medicine as furnishing us with foundations, equally solid for that philosophy which ascends to the source of our ideas, and to that which traces the origin of our passions. On the one hand it must serve to direct all good systems of instruction, whilst on the other it discovers in the immutable laws of nature, a basis on which must be erected the rights and duties of man. . . . [25]

Medicine is productive of another very essential service. Together with all other physical sciences, and the arts that are founded on a careful observation of nature, it tends greatly to dissipate all those phantoms by which the imagination is deceived and tormented. By accustoming the mind to see in facts nothing but the facts themselves, or their evident relation, it extinguishes in their very origin, many errors arising from habits of an opposite nature—it destroys more particularly those which are united to physical absurdities, that is to say all superstitious opinions: and in thus promoting an intimate intercourse with nature, causes the mind to assume a spirit of independence, and the soul a degree of strength, which have been remarked at all times, in physicians fully deserving of that name. [26]

The body of the essay continues with further comment indicating the powerful self consciousness of Dr. Cabanis, and I cite some of his medical wisdom.

Singular, and inexplicable appetites, become sometimes the means by which we are aided in discovering the remedies necessary to the restoration of health. In a word, when unsatisfied, all our wants are transformed into sufferings, and in this way nature manifesting her desires in the most positive manner, we may, with an ancient author, apply the name of remedy to all that satisfies a want, and consider instinct, or the cause of automatous movements, as the best of physicians. [28]

Nature is that power which produces those actions peculiar to each body; or else the union of the laws by which this body is governed: in this latter sense it is, that Van Helmont calls it, the *order of God.* [29]

Medical experiments are still more difficult than the study of disease, and of a nature more doubtful and fallacious than the axioms of diagnosis and prognosis, which this study prevents. The effect of a particular remedy may depend upon a multiplicity of causes, entirely unknown to the physician. The silent, yet constant operation of the *vis medicatrix,* always tending to re-establish order in organized bodies; . . . [32]

. . . independently of the agitation caused in the living frame, by the passions, either directly, through the medium of the intimate relation existing between the physical actions, and moral tendencies, or else indirectly, through means of the many derangements introduced by those very passions into all the details of our conduct: finally, independently of those poisonous substances, and of certain contagions, which appear to produce their action in a similar manner, disease and pain are intimately connected with the functions of life. [43]

With respect to chance, it still continues to constitute one of our most fruitful sources of instruction. But by its aid, those only are benefited who observe; and he who searches the most, is always found to make the greatest number of discoveries. [53]

. . . from the experience of mankind, I deduce dietetic rules, similar, for example, to those for which we are indebted to the genius of Hippocrates. [59]

It is confessedly by identifying himself with a patient, and partaking, as it were, of his sufferings, through the medium of the sudden play of a feeling imagination, that a physician is enabled to discover the disease at a single glance, and to seize at once all its various and characteristic features. He thus himself participates to a certain extent in the influence of all these impressions, and this instinct causes him to feel, rather than foresee, the utility of certain remedies with the effects of which he is already acquainted. [66 & 67] [My italics]

Is it not to observation that we are indebted for these first important steps? May not observation then complete what it has commenced? Why should we not be enabled, with its help, to arrange systematically all these different series of facts, which are already regarded as distinct from each other, merely because they have been, at least sometimes, really discriminated? [67]

Objects are continually passing before his [the physician's] eyes, and it is only by their differences or analogies that they strike his senses—by comparing them with each other, and with himself, he becomes acquainted with them, and by comparing himself with them, he finally learns to appreciate himself. [69]

From these circumstances, it naturally follows, that the nosologist and the empirical philosopher, when equally possessed of talents, follow, in the investigation of diseases, paths not so widely different, as might, at first, be imagined. [72]

No two cases of catarrh, or of simple ephemeral fever, are discovered to be alike—there exist between them, as between physiognomies, the most similar in appearance, features or shades by which they are rendered distinguishable. Now, since the slightest modifications in their character occasions analogous changes in their treatment, it naturally follows that we must study each case individually, . . . [73]

The same Hippocrates, in his treatise on primitive medicine, has made on this subject an observation, the most sensible, and which appears to me to reduce the question to its proper value:—"If medicine were not an art like all others, there would be neither good nor bad physicians—they would all be equally good, or rather, all equally bad." [79]

The inventors of medicine, who have opened for themselves new paths, and those philosophical minds who have been careful to arrange their observations systematically, can, in reality, notwithstanding the importance of their labours, only direct the practitioner in his researches, limit, in his eyes, the object which constitutes the subject of them, and strengthen his experience by that of the preceding ages; and perhaps as much talent is required in him, in order that he should be able to appreciate fully and follow their results, as in the former for the purpose of discovering them. [81]

. . . I would beg leave to add, that the intimate connection existing between the physical, and what is denominated the moral system—and likewise the dependence of the ideas or passions, in regard to the condition of the organs, on the nature of the impressions which these latter receive, prevents morals from being established on a solid basis, unless we call to their aid physiological and medical knowledge; and the moralist, before he traces his plans of cure, or his practical precepts, should never neglect to consult the physician. In many cases, a suitable regimen and proper remedies applied to the physical system, will do more towards reclaiming men to the paths of honesty or of virtue, than reasonings, exhortations, or even menaces. And if we examine the subject in a more extensive light, we will readily admit that public education, for the purpose of invigorating the soul, must tend to invigorate the body; that to regulate moral, it must regulate physical habits, and that in order to correct the passions, it must first correct the temperaments. [83 & 84]

Follies and absurdities do not annihilate wisdom or reason, but on the contrary lead us to believe in their existence; for confusion implies order, in a similar manner that falsehood implies truth—*since we cannot conceive of opposites unaccompanied by their opposites.* [87] [My italics]

The practice of all good physicians, let me repeat, is like nature herself, uniformly the same in all ages and in all countries. [92]

Whenever two physicians adopt contradictory views, and recommend the employment of remedies of a nature diametrically opposed, it is concluded, though improperly, that one of them is necessarily in the wrong. Although entertaining different opinions, they nevertheless may both be in the right, and employ very different means to arrive at the same end. Their unanimity could no more serve to substantiate the correctness of their views, than their opposition indicate them to be in the wrong. But this requires some elucidation. [94]

It follows from this, that each physician may have his *materia medica,* and that this latter science should only be studied at the bed-side of the patient. [97]

If therefore we are desirous of knowing in what light medicine should be viewed, let us devest our memories of the opinions entertained by others, and search, examine, and discuss for ourselves. [99]

Absolute certainty in the full acceptation of the term, appertains exclusively to objects of pure speculation: in practice we must content ourselves with approximations more or less exact, and which on this account might be called *practical certainties.* With these we must rest satisifed. . . . [100]

In medicine, every thing or nearly so, depending on *coup d'oeil,* the acuteness of perception, and on an happy instinct—certainties are found to exist, in the sensations of the artist himself, rather than in the principles of the art. [101]

He who despises the art, whatever it be, can never become a great artist. In respect to medicine, more particularly, the studies which it requires are so diversified in their nature, so laborious, and often so disgusting, that it becomes absolutely necessary to inspire a degree of enthusiasm in those who devote themselves to their pursuit. Good practitioners are always found to be men entertaining the greatest confidence in the powers of medicine. This confidence is perhaps in some degree as much the cause as the effect of their success, and has alone been capable of affording them support in the progress of their labours. In this science incredulity can only give rise to idleness, and serve as a shield to ignorance. [103]

In those moments when the equilibrium existing between the functions of the various organs of the body is destroyed, the judgment cannot be supposed to retain its own. [107]

It is perhaps more especially in medicine, that these analytical classifications are found of greater utility, and of easier formation. Nature herself seems to direct us towards them, and in some instances almost without our participation. Instead therefore of resisting her impulses it becomes our duty to follow them with attention—to consult her with confidence and reflection, since she only desires eyes worthy of her, in order to unveil herself. [109]

I dare make bold to predict that together with the true method of observation, the spirit of philosophy which should always predominate in it, will soon revive in medicine, and that the science will assume a different aspect. [110]

In respect to physicians individually, since in abandoning themselves to their mutual injustices, they are always under the influence of their passions, and acting without faith, what are the means best calculated to return them to a sense of reason and justice? An appeal to their conscience, and to the sentiment of their own personal dignity. [113]

Viewed in a certain light, the medical profession may be regarded as a kind of sacerdotal function; under another, as a true magistracy. As the object of a physician's labours is one of no little importance, namely, human life; it naturally follows that his obligations to disclose all useful truths—to pervert none, and to give to his mind, all the perfection of which it is susceptible, becomes of so sacred a nature, that the least violation, forgetfulness, or negligence on either of these points, presents invariably something truly criminal. [114]

Look attentively at those physicians most successful in their practice, and you will discover them in almost every instance to be men skilful in managing and directing in some sort at will, the human soul—in reviving hope—in changing to calmness the various agitations of the mind.

In order to employ with success, the influence of the passions in the treatment of diseases, it is absolutely necessary to possess precise notions of the relation and reciprocal action of these two kinds of affections. [114 & 115]

Apostleship of good sense and virtue, is a sacred duty in all who feel and think, but more particularly in those persons whose opinions can with facility acquire a degree of preponderance. [116]

For such is the charm of a beneficent, and courageous virtue, that in order to afford assistance to one in misfortune, it is not essentially necessary that it should bring succours to him—its voice alone will be sufficient to pour the sweet balm of consolation in the deepest wounds.

But let me repeat it, in proportion as they are deserving of public gratitude, the more they can dispense with it; in doing all that is necessary for obtaining it, they establish the foundation of their happiness on the most solid basis. And, were I permitted, I would even maintain that they should accustom themselves to disregard it, since it often becomes their duty to defy the opinion which grants it. [117]

Physicians love their fellow creatures, and are anxious to serve them, but so far from revolting at their ingratitude, they discover in it sources of pleasure unknown to the vulgar. For a consciousness that it cannot diminish their beneficent intentions, nor extinguish in their hearts the sweetest emotions of humanity, is undoubtedly a pleasure infinitely greater than that procured by the manifestation of gratitude. [117]

It will be perceived that each part of these questions carries, in some sort, along with it its proper answer.

But of this general exposition, as well as of every other of the same kind, no precise idea can be formed, until after having traced up the whole series of particular propositions, which it contains and presents in a summary manner. [119]

True geometricians, however, are those who appreciate the most correctly, the impossibility of applying the science of calculation to the investigation of every subject, and it is likewise a truth that the various applications of it, which to this day, have been made to the healing art, so far from promoting its advancement, have only served to introduce into it, the most erroneous theories and dangerous plans of treatment. [119]

Victor Cousin on Tracy as Philosopher

In his chapter, *Sensualistic School in the Eighteenth Century,*[14] M. Victor Cousin, recording a brief list of famous philosophers beginning with Condillac and Diderot, duly honors Tracy:

> To this list I might, I should perhaps, but I shall not dare to do it, add a man who, by his age, belongs to this generation of celebrated men, rather than to the century and the movement in which we are; the respectable old man who, by the elevation and goodness of his character, by the vigor of his thought and the lucidness of his style, is now among us the most faithful and complete representative of the sensualistic school of the eighteenth century: you are all thinking of our compatriot so justly and so generally esteemed, M. Destutt de Tracy.

Cousin declares, "Locke is the father of the whole sensualistic school of the eighteenth century. He is, incontestably, in time

[14] *Course of the History of Modern Philosophy,* trans. O. W. Wight, vol. II (New York: D. Appleton and Co., 1856), p. 147.

as well as in genius, the first metaphysician of this school."[15] Later Cousin asserts, "Nothing was opposed to the success of Locke except the anger of the enemies of all political and religious liberty."[16] And, "For Locke and his whole school, the study of understanding is the study of ideas: hence the recent and celebrated expression ideology, to designate the science of human understanding. The source of this expression is in 'Essay on the Human Understanding,' and the ideological school is the natural offspring of Locke."[17]

Cousin records Locke's devotion to subjectivity (truth, reality, individuality) as follows:

> Thus, in the last analysis, the object, the original, continually escaping the immediate grasp of the human mind, can never be brought under the eyes of the human mind, nor consequently authorize a comparison with the copy, with the idea. You will therefore never know whether the idea that you have of body is conformed or non-conformed, faithful or unfaithful, true or false. You will have this idea without knowing even whether it has an object or not.[18]

[15] Ibid., p. 159.
[16] Ibid., p. 170.
[17] Ibid., p. 188.
[18] Ibid., p. 333.

Excerpts from *THE PRIVATE DIARIES OF STENDHAL.* Edited and translated by Robert Sage. Doubleday & Company, Inc., Garden City, New York (1954).

Indeed, facts were the fuel of observation-analysis-judgment, that magical truth-detecting triad of Destutt de Tracy's *Ideologie,* which was soon to become his Bible. It was only through the cognizance and analysis of facts that one could reach the WHY of things. [47]

Probably no single day in Beyle's life was more momentous than the one which brought the year 1804 to a close. It started with his meeting Melanie Guilbert, his first mistress and the only woman with whom he ever actually lived, and it ended with him trudging through the snow to buy the *Ideologie* of Destutt de Tracy, his philosophy master and the man whose influence on his thought was the greatest. [88]

He would return from Melanie's [Guilbert] apartment to analyze the day's emotions and, shutting his mind to love's uncertainties, immerse himself in the clean-cut verities of Destutt de Tracy's *Ideologie,* the only work, he afterward said, that brought about a revolution in him. [91]

January 1, 1805.—I read the first hundred and twelve pages of Tracy with the greatest satisfaction and as easily as a novel. [96]

What is a noble character? The notion of asking this question is the first fruit of reading Tracy's *Ideologie.* Only women of a noble character are capable of providing me happiness; I recognize the happy fruits of *Ideologie* by a thousand sprouts of new ideas. [98]

After prescribing daily doses of Tracy's *Ideologie* for Melanie, he decided that the souls of his mistress and his sister Pauline were so much alike that they were "bound to love each other," and accordingly engineered a correspondence between the two. [178]

Henri Beyle (Stendhal) on Tracy

In his *Memoirs Of An Egotist,*[19] Henri Beyle (Stendhal) refers to his Destutt de Tracy with the sincerity of self revelation:

> In 1817, the man I most admired because of his writings, the only one to start a revolution in me, came to see me. I had never been so surprised. For twelve years I had adored the Ideology of this man, who will one day be celebrated. . . . I approached that vast intelligence, I contemplated it, astonished; . . . M. de Tracy has never wished to let anyone paint his portrait. . . . He has perfect manners when he is not overcome by an abominable depression. I only divined his character in 1822. He is an old Don Juan (see the operas of Mozart, Moliere, etc.). Everything annoys him. For instance, in his drawingroom, M. de La Fayette was a slightly greater man than himself (even in 1821). Also, the French have never appreciated Ideology and Logic. . . .
>
> I have just seen, on turning over these pages, that I was busy with M. de Tracy. That old man, so well-built, always dressed in black, with his huge green overcoat, standing in front of his fireplace, now on one foot, now on the other, had a way of speaking that was the opposite of his writing. This conversation was all composed of subtle and elegant points of view; he was as horrified at a vigorous word as at an oath, and he wrote like a village mayor. The energetic simplicity which it seems to me I possessed at that time could hardly have suited him. I had enormous black whiskers, of which Mme. Doligny only made me ashamed a year later. This Italian butcher's head did not appear very agreeable to the former colonel from the reign of Louis XVI.
>
> M. de Tracy, a widow's son, was born about 1765, with an income of three hundred thousand francs. His house was in the Rue de Tracy, near the Rue Saint-Martin.
>
> He played the business man without the knowledge, like a crowd of rich men in 1780. M. de Tracy built his street and lost 200,000 or 300,000 fr. on it, and so continued. In such a way that I well believe that at present this man (so charming when, about 1790, he was the lover of Mme. de Praslin), this

[19] Published, 1824. Trans. and with an introduction by T. W. Earp (New York: Noonday Press, Inc., 1958), pp. 27-198.

profound reasoner, has changed his income of three hundred thousand livres to thirty at the most.

His mother, a woman of rare good sense, was devoted to the court: so, at twenty-two, the son was colonel, and colonel of a regiment where he found among the captains a Tracy, his cousin, apparently as noble as he, and to whom the idea never occurred to be shocked at seeing this little doll of twenty-two coming to command the regiment in which he served.

This little doll, who Mme. de Tracy told me afterwards, had such admirable impulses, yet concealed a fund of good sense. The mother, that rare woman, having heard there was a philosopher at Strasbourg (and note, it was in 1780 perhaps—not a philosopher like Voltaire, Diderot, Raynal), having heard, I say, that there was a philosopher at Strasbourg who analysed man's thoughts, the images and signs of all he has seen and felt, realised that if her son learnt the science of putting those images in motion, it would give him a good head.

Imagine what was the right sort of head in 1785 for a young man who was very good-looking, very noble, devoted to the court, and possessed of an income of three hundred thousand livres.

The Marquise de Tracy got her son posted to the artillery, which, two years running, took him to Strasbourg. If ever I go there, I shall ask who was its famous German philosopher about 1780.

Two years after, I believe, M. de Tracy was at Rethel with his regiment, which, I think was of the dragoons, a matter that can be verified from the Royal Almanach of the period. . . . M. de Tracy had been the intimate friend of the famous Cabanis, the father of materialism, whose book, *The Relation of the Physical and the Moral,* was my Bible when I was sixteen. . . . In the Rue d'Anjou, where, indeed, existed my most respectable society, M. de Tracy, the philosopher, did not pardon my liaison with an actress. . . . in 1822 I did not realise all the weight attached to this question about a man who prints a book that people read, 'What sort of a man is he?'

I was saved from being held in contempt by this answer, 'He goes a great deal to Mme. de Tracy's.' The society of 1829 needs to despise a man to whom, rightly or wrongly, it grants some intelligence in his books. It is afraid; it is no longer an impartial judge.

I agree with Tracy: *nosce te ipsum,* know thyself, is a source of happiness.

The love of glory has again taken the upper hand; it has made me read Tracy.

Brief Observations From Several Sources

Excerpts from *La Tradition Litteraire Des Ideologues* by Emile Cailliet, with an Introduction by Gilbert Chinard. The American Philosophical Society, Independence Square, Philadelphia, 1943.

Professor Cailliet, professor of French literature and civilization at the University of Pennsylvania, has written a very useful study rescuing the memory of the human dignity of Destutt de Tracy. The introduction by Chinard entitled "A Neglected Province of Literary History" contributes substantially to this worthy effort. The ideologues hailed by Napoleon in his early career when he was able to support the concept of the dignity of the individual, later scorned by him, as one might expect, for individuals of rare understanding are just as rarely understandable by their fellowman.

The study of ideology illustrates beautifully the principle that one cannot but exalt what he understands any more than he can help but ignore or depreciate what he cannot understand. For instance, when John Adams first heard from Thomas Jefferson of Destutt de Tracy's three volumes of Ideology his response was as follows:

> Pray explain to me this Neological term! What does it mean? When Bonaparte used it, I was delighted with it, upon the common principle of delight in everything we cannot understand. Does it mean Idiotism? The Science of *Noncomposmentuism?* The Science of Lunacy? The Theory of Delirium? Or does it mean the Science of Self-love, of Amour-propre? Or the elements of Vanity?
>
> [p. 1, to Jefferson, December 16, 1816]

Gilbert Chinard, a valuable source of orientation regarding the Ideologues, points out when Jefferson arrived in Paris, he was more than forty years of age, had already written the Declaration of Independence, and lived vital questions of public living for more than fifteen years. At the time the Spanish colonies revolted, Tracy expected Mr. Jefferson to declare enthusiastically in favor of the South American republic.

On October 24, 1820, Jefferson wrote Destutt de Tracy as follows:

> We go with you all lengths in friendly affections to the independence of S. America, but an immediate acknowledgement of it calls up other considerations. We view Europe as covering at present a smothered fire, which may shortly burst forth and produce general conflagration. From this it is our duty to keep aloof. A formal acknowledgement of the independence of her colonies, would involve us with Spain certainly, and perhaps too with England, if she thinks that a war would divert her internal troubles. Such a war would hurt us more than it would help our brethren of the South; and our right may be doubted of mortgaging posterity for the expenses of a war in which they will have a right to say their interest was not concerned. . . . In the meantime we receive and protect the flag of S. America in it's commercial intercourse with us, on the acknowledged principles of neutrality between two belligerent parties in a civil war; and if we should not be the first, we shall certainly be the second nation in acknowledging the entire independence of our new friends.[20]

Chinard describes the persevering political orientation of his de Tracy, "almost completely blind, dictating his treatise on political economy and appearing in the streets of Paris during the glorious days of 1830; . . . the living embodiment of the political faith of the nineteenth century."[21]

In his fascinating book *Adrienne, The Life of the Marquise de La Fayette*[22] André Maurois states:

> An excellent marriage was being negotiated for George. The young woman was Emilie de Tracy, the daughter of Antoine Claude, Comte Destutt de Tracy, a philosopher and a member of the Institute, who to a large extent shared La Fayette's political views, with this important difference: Tracy had accepted a seat in the Senate from Bonaparte. Destutt de Tracy was a small man, elegant and punctilious, though apt to be gripped

[20] *Thomas Jefferson, The Apostle of Americanism* (Boston: Little, Brown, and Company, 1929), p. 485.

[21] Ibid., p. 514.

[22] Trans. Gerard Hopkins. (New York, Toronto, London: McGraw-Hill Book Company, Inc., 1961).

> by an abominable temper. The idea of this union delighted La Fayette, but as yet neither the young people nor the lawyers of the two families had met. . . .
>
> There are orders of precedence even in misfortune. A more important matter was La Fayette's meeting with Tracy and his daughter Emilie, George's bride presumptive. He found her very charming, and worthy of being his daughter-in-law. . . .
>
> George was at Monza, some twenty miles from Milan, with his hussars. He rode, fenced, sketched, made music, and was delighted with all that his father and sisters wrote to him about Emilie. Being so far away, he was unaware of the immense difficulties his parents were encountering in calming the fear of M. de Tracy, the scruples of Aunt Charlotte, and the untimely zeal of Mme de Tesse. . . .
>
> What mattered to Adrienne, a fond mother for whom money was always a means and never an end, was to reassure her son that his betrothed loved him for himself and not for the towers of Chavaniac. She told him that Destutt de Tracy had realized that the girl's heart was set on George, and that this had put an end to all hesitation and made the decision independent of all monetary considerations. . . . 'Matters are now being settled between Monsieur Beauchet and Monsieur de Tracy's representative. . . . We do not, however, yet know whether Monsieur de Tracy will give his daughter four or six thousand francs a year. I should like it to be six because I know, dear boy, that in spite of your extreme economy unexpected situations are always turning up, especially when traveling, which compel one to spend more than one intended, and that if you have only seven thousand (four plus three) you will never be quite easy in your mind, which does not mean that you will not be happy but only that you will have one pleasure the less. . . .'

Destutt de Tracy did increase the income which he allowed his daughter by the terms of the marriage settlement from 4000 to 6000 francs.

George Boas thus portrays his Tracy's identifying mind as a form of living based upon sensibility:[23]

[23] *The Major Traditions of European Philosophy* (New York: Harper and Brothers, 1929), p. 267.

> Ideology, a term invented by him (Destutt de Tracy) but abused, and ridiculed by Napoleon into a term of reproach, was the analysis of ideas into sensations from which they arise. . . . The zoological aspects of ideology were delineated by Destutt de Tracy's friend Cabanis.

It was Tracy's friend Helvetius who courageously asserted self interest to be the spring of all activity of man:[24]

> Though we may seem to be acting upon altruistic motives, in reality we are selfish and egoistic . . . our laws should therefore be corrected to increase man's interest here below and should recognize that an enlightened egoism is the only possible pattern for man's life.

Tracy's wholeness-unifying conception tracing all of his life experience ultimately to his organic sensibility, of course with its only occurrence in his own existence, thoroughly respects and supports the rare kind of comprehensive self consciousness described by Helvetius.

[24] Ibid., p. 257.

Manuscript Sources and Editions of Tracy's Works

I am grateful for the following entries secured from the American Philosophical Society Library.

Manuscript

Destutt de Tracy, [Antoine Louis Claude, comte de] 1754-1836.

Letter to [American philosophical society]; Paris, Oct. 21, 1811. A.L.S. 2p. and end. 7" x 9 1/4" In French.

Although he has never received notice of his nomination, he has heard from many persons and seen in Vol. 6 of the Transactions of his election to membership in 1804. Expresses appreciation for honor. Presents various works. Mentions Lafayette, Cabanis, and Warden.

[Destutt de] Tracy, [Antoine Louis Claude, comte de] 1754-1836.

Letter to M. [Marie Henri] Beyle, Paris; Sept. 25, 1821. A.L.S. 3 p. and add., end. 7 3/4" x 6 1/4" In French.

Speaks of Beyle's *L'Amour;* mentions M. Compagnoni, the Italian translator.

——Transcription by Dr. Chinard.

[Destutt de] Tracy, [Antoine Louis Claude, comte] 1754-1836.

Letter to [Marie Henri Beyle]; Oct. 10, 1821. A.L.S. 3p. and end. in Beyle's hand. 9 1/2" x 7 1/2" In French.

Beyle's De L'amour. Sends letter to Defendente Sacchi.

——Transcription by Dr. Chinard.

Destutt de Tracy, Antoine Louis Claude, comte de. Commentary . . . Montesquieu's Spirit of laws

Jefferson, Thomas, pres. U.S., 1743-1826

Extract of a letter . . . to Professor Cooper, dated Monticello, Jan. 16, 1814, relative to the Commentary and review of Montesquieu's Spirit of laws . . . (see in *Destutt* de Tracy . . . Commentary . . . Spirit of laws . . . 1811)

Manuscript.

Destutt de Tracy, Antoine Louis Claude, comte de, 1784-1859

Jefferson, Th[omas], pres. U.S., 1743-1826.

Letter to [Robert] Walsh; Monticello, Jan. 9, 1818. Typed

L. 3 p. 11 x 8-1/2. Copy. (see Correa de Serra. Letters . . .)

Concerning philosophical inquiries. Concerning an article by Destutt de Tracy. Refers to Correa.

Destutt de Tracy, A. L. C.

[Marquis de] Lafayette to the President of the A.P.S., La Grange, February 26, 1804.

1 p. and endorsement. 7 1/8″ x 9″. A.L.S.

Presents to the A.P.S. a work by [A. L. C. Destutt de] Tracy, *Analyse raisonnée de l'origine de tous les cultes*, 2 vols.

Destutt de Tracy, Antoine Louis Claude, comte, 1754–1836

Humboldt, [Alexander von], 1769–1859.

Letter to [Henry William] Pickersgill; Saturday.

A. L. in 3rd P. 1p. In French. 8 × 5-1/2 (see Humboldt papers.)

Wishes he could see him. Refers to Tracy and Lafayette.

Destutt de Tracy, Antoine Louis Claude, comte de, 1754–1836

Humboldt, [Alexander, i.e., Friedrich Wilhelm Heinrich Alexander, freiherr von],

Letter to ——; Friday.

Photostat of A.L.S. 1p. In French. (see Humboldt Papers. No. 12.)

Refers to Lafayette and Tracy.

****

Printed

Destutt de Tracy, Antoine Louis Claude comte de.

Analyse raisonnée de l'origine de tous les cultes, ou religion universelle; ouvrage publié en l'an III, par Dupuis, . . . 160 p. 0. Paris, Clurcier, 1804.

Contains autograph inscription by the author.

Authority for authorship—Gilbert Chinard, April, 1935.

Destutt de Tracy, [Antoine Louis Claude]. comte de

Commentaire sur l'Esprit des lois de Montesquieu . . . suivi d'observations inédites de Condorcet sur le vingt-neuvième livre du mème ouvrage, et d'un mémoire . . . écrit . . . par l'auteur du Commentaire . . . xv, 480 p. 0. Paris, Desoer, 1819.

[Destutt de Tracy, Antoine Louis Claude]. comte de
Commentary and review of Montesquieu's Spirit of laws, prepared for press from the original manuscript . . . to which are annexed, Observations on the thirty-first book, by the late M. Condorcet: and two letters of Helvetius . . . viii, 292 p., 0. Phil., Duane, 1811. 2 copies.

Destutt de Tracy, Antoine Louis Claude, comte de. Commentary . . . Spirit of laws . . .
Contains an extract of a letter from Thos. Jefferson to Professor Cooper, dated Monticello, Jan. 16, 1814 in which Jefferson explains that he has the original French ms. of the Commentary, that Gen. Duane translated and edited it, but that the authorship must be anonymous until after the author's death.
Copy 2 was presented by John Vaughan, June 16, 1815.

Destutt de Tracy, Antoine Louis Claude, comte de, 1754-1836.
Elemens d'idéologie . . . 2nd ed. Pt. 1-5 in 4 v. D. Paris, Courcier, 1803-1815.
Vol. 1 contains an autographed inscription by the author.
Vol. 1-3 presented by the author, May 1, 1812.
Vol. 4 presented by the author through Thomas Jefferson, Apr. 4, 1817.
2 copies of Col. 2—c.2 presented by Marquis de Lafayette, Nov. 1, 1805.

Destutt de Tracy, Antoine Louis Claude, comte de, 1754-1836.
Opinion de M. de Tracy, sur les affaires de Saint-Domingue, en septembre, 1791.
23 p. D. Paris, Laillet [1791]
Sabin 96414

Destutt de Tracy, Antoine Louis Claude, comte de, 1754-1836.
Projet d'eléménts d'idéologie . . . Vol. 1, O. Paris, Didot, An IX.
2 copies, both of which appear to have been presented by the author, March 18, 1803.

Destutt de Tracy, Antoine Louis Claude comte de, 1754-1836.
Cabanis, Pierre Jean Georges, 1757-1808.
Rapports du physique et du moral de l'homme et lettre sur les causes premières . . . avec une table analytique

par Destutt de Tracy; huitième èdition augmentée de notes et précèdée d'une notice historique . . . sur la vie, les travaux et les doctrines de Cabanis par L. Peisse. lxviii, 712 p. O. A Paris, J. B. Baillière, 1844.

Destutt de Tracy, Antoine Louis Claude, comte,

Guillois, Antoine, 1855-1913.

. . . Le salon de Madame Helvétius; Cabanis et les idéologues; ouvrage orné de deux portraits d'après des originaux inédits. Paris, Calmann Lévy, 1894.

1p.1., 1v, 350 p. front., port. 18 em.

Contents.—I. Madame Helvétius. La fin de la monarchie. La révolution.—II. Cabanis. Le 18 brumaire. Consulat et commencement de l'empire.—III. Destutt de Tracy. Seconde société d'Auteuil. Fin de l'empire.

1. Helvétius, Mme. Anne Catherine (de Ligniville d'Autricout) 1719-1800. 2. Cabanis, Pierre Jean Georges, 1757-1808. 3. Destutt de Tracy, Antoine Louis Claude, comte, 1754-1836.

Library of Congress DC146.H4G8 15-25273

Destutt de Tracy, Antoine Louis Claude, comte de, 1754-1836.

Principios de economia politica, considerados por las relaciones que tienen con la voluntad humana. Tr. por D. Manuel Maria Gutierrez.

2v. D. Madrid, Cano, 1817.

BIBLIOGRAPHY

Abse, D. Wilfred, and Jessner, Lucie. "The Psychodynamic Aspects of Leadership." *Daedalus*, Journal of the American Academy of Arts and Sciences 90 (Fall 1961): 693–710.

______, and Reckrey, Ruth. "Politics and Personality." *British Journal of Social Psychiatry* 4 (1970).

______. *Speech and Reason.* Language Disorder in Mental Disease, annexing A Translation of *The Life of Speech* by Philipp Wegener. Charlottesville, Va.: University Press of Virginia, 1971.

______. "Charisma, Anomie and the Psychopathic Personality." Mimeographed. Charlottesville, Virginia: University of Virginia.

Adams, Henry. *The Degradation of the Democratic Dogma.* New York: Peter Smith, 1949.

Alden, Joseph. *The Science of Government.* New York: Sheldon & Co., 1870.

Alexander, Franz. "Psychology and the Interpretation of Historical Events." *The Cultural Approach to History.* Ed. Caroline F. Ware. New York: Columbia University Press, 1940.

Angell, Norman. *The Story of Money.* Garden City, New York: Garden City Publishing Co., Inc., 1929.

Arieli, Yehoshua. *Individualism and Nationalism in American Ideology.* Baltimore, Maryland: Penguin Books, 1964.

Aring, Charles D., et al. *Man and Life. A Sesquicentennial Symposium.* Cincinnati: University of Cincinnati, 1969.

______. *The Understanding Physician.* Rev. ed. Detroit: Wayne State University Press, 1971.

Bastiat, Frederic. *The Law.* Trans. Dean Russell. Irvington-On-Hudson, New York: The Foundation for Economic Education, 1950.

______. *Economic Sophisms.* Trans. and ed. Arthur Goddard. Irvington-On-Hudson, New York: The Foundation for Economic Education, 1964.

______. *Selected Essays on Political Economy.* Trans. Seymour Cain and ed. George B. de Huszar. Irvington-On-Hudson, New York: The Foundation for Economic Education, 1964.

Bean, William B. "A Testament of Duty." *J. Laboratory and Clinical Medicine* 39 (January 1952): 4.

Beardsley, E. Edward. *Life and Correspondence of Samuel Johnson, D.D.* New York: Hurd and Haughton, 1874.

Benjamin, A. Cornelius. *An Introduction to the Philosophy of Science.* New York: The Macmillan Company, 1937.

Berenson, Bernard. *Rumor and Reflection.* New York: Simon and Schuster, 1952.

Berlien, Ivan C. Personal observations.

Bernbaum, Ernest. *Guide Through the Romantic Movement.* 2d ed. New York: The Ronald Press Company, 1949.

Beyle, Henri (Stendhal). *Memoirs of an Egotist.* Trans. T. W. Earp. New York: Noonday Press, Inc., 1958.

Boas, George. *The Major Traditions of European Philosophy.* New York: Harper and Brothers, 1929.

Boughey, Arthur S. *Man and the Environment: An Introduction to Human Ecology and Evolution.* New York: MacMillan Company, 1971.

Bowen, Lem W. Personal observations.

Bowne, Borden P. *Introduction to Psychological Theory.* New York: Harper and Brothers, 1886.

Braceland, Francis J. "Hormones and their Influence on the Emotions." *Bull. N.Y. Acad. Med.* (1953): 765-777.

Brandon, Edgar Ewing, ed. *A Pilgrimage of Liberty.* Athens, Ohio: The Lawhead Press, 1944.

Brazier, Mary A. B. "The Growth of Concepts Relating to Brain Mechanisms." *Journal of the History of the Behavioral Sciences* 1 (1965) No. 3.

Bronowski, J. *Science and Human Values.* New York & Evanston: Harper & Row, 1956.

Buckham, John Wright, and Stratton, George Malcolm. *George Holmes Howison, Philosopher and Teacher.* Berkeley: University of California Press, 1934.

Burlingham, Dorothy. "Psychic Problems of the Blind." *American Imago* 2 (1941): 43-85.

Burns, James MacGregor. *The Deadlock of Democracy: Four-Party Politics in America.* Englewood Cliffs, N.J.: Prentice-Hall, Inc., 1963.

Burton, Ralph J. Personal observations.

Butterfield, Herbert. *The Origins of Modern Science.* Rev. ed. New York: The Free Press, Macmillan Co., 1965.

Cabanis, P. J. G. *An Essay on the Certainty of Medicine.* Trans. R. La Roche. Philadelphia: Robert Desilver, 1823.

Cailliet, Emile. *La Tradition Litteraire Des Ideologues.* Philadelphia: American Philosophical Society, 1943.

Camus, Albert. *The Rebel.* New York: Vintage Books, 1960.

Cantril, Hadley. *Human Nature and Political Systems.* New Brunswick, N.J.: Rutgers University Press, 1961.

Cappon, Lester J. *The Adams-Jefferson Letters.* 2 vols. Chapel Hill: University of North Carolina Press, 1959.

Carson, Clarence B. "The American Tradition: The Restoration of the Tradition." *The Freeman* (May 1964): 33-44.

Cassirer, Ernst. *The Individual and the Cosmos in Renaissance Philosophy.*

Trans. Mario Domandi. New York: Harper and Row, 1963.
Childs, Marquis W., and Cater, Douglass. *Ethics in a Business Society.* New York: The New American Library, 1954.
Chinard, Gilbert. *Jefferson Et Les Idéologues.* Baltimore, Maryland: The Johns Hopkins Press, 1925.
______. *The Letters of Lafayette and Jefferson.* Baltimore, Maryland: The Johns Hopkins Press, 1929.
______. *Thomas Jefferson, The Apostle of Americanism.* Boston: Little, Brown, and Company, 1929.
______, ed. *Houdon In America.* Baltimore, Maryland: The Johns Hopkins Press, 1930.
Clapp, Charles L. *The Congressman: His Work as He Sees It.* Washington, D.C.: The Brookings Institution, 1963.
Cleveland, Harlan, and Lasswell, Harold D., eds. *Ethics and Bigness: Scientific, Academic, Religious, Political, and Military.* New York: Conference on Science, Philosophy and Religion in their Relation to the Democratic Way of Life, Inc., 1962.
Clifford, William Kingdon. "Ethics of Belief." *Contemporary Review,* January, 1877.
Cohen, Harry. *The Demonics of Bureaucracy.* Ames, Iowa: The Iowa State University Press, 1965.
Coit, Stanton. *The Soul of America.* New York: The Macmillan Company, 1914.
Conway, Moncure D. *Emerson At Home and Abroad.* Boston: James R. Osgood and Co., 1882.
Cooley, Charles Horton. *Human Nature and the Social Order.* New York: C. Schribner Sons, 1902.
Cordell, William H., and Cordell, Kathryn Coe, eds. *American Points of View.* Garden City, N.Y.: Doubleday, Doran and Co., Inc., 1937.
Coulter, Glenn M. Prismatic address, Notes on Supreme Court.
Cousin, M. Victor. "Sensualistic School in the Eighteenth Century." *Course of the History of Modern Philosophy.* Trans. O. W. Wight, vol. II. New York: D. Appleton and Co., 1856.
Cowin, William T. *In Other Words.* Liverpool, England: Nora Cowin, 1972.
Cram, Ralph Adams. *The End of Democracy.* Boston: Marshall Jones Company, 1937.
Crandall, Robert W., and Eckaus, Richard S. *Contemporary Issues In Economics.* Boston: Little, Brown and Company, 1972.
Curti, Merle. *The Growth of American Thought.* 3rd ed. New York: Harper and Row, 1964.
Cushman, Edward L. Personal observations.
Dahl, Robert A. *Who Governs?* New Haven and London: Yale University Press, 1961.
D'Alembert, Jean Le Rond. *Discours Préliminaire de L'Encyclopédie.*

Paris: Librairie Armand Colin, 1929.
Danhof, John J. Personal observations.
Day, Stacey B. *American Lines.* Montreal, P. Q.: Three Star Printing and Pub. Co., 1967.
De Gourmont, Remy. *The Natural Philosophy of Love.* New York: Rarity Press, 1931.
de Rivera, Joseph H. *The Psychological Dimension of Foreign Policy.* Columbus, Ohio: Charles E. Merrill Pub. Co., 1968.
Deutsch, Karl W. *The Nerves of Government.* London: The Free Press of Glencoe, 1963.
Dewey, John. *Individualism Old and New.* New York: Minton, Balch and Company, 1930.
Dorfman, Joseph. *The Economic Mind in American Civilization.* 5 vols. New York: Viking Press, 1946–1959.
Dorsey, Edward C. "Approach to the Clinic." Presented at a scientific program in honor of John M. Dorsey's seventieth year, sponsored by the Michigan Society of Neurology and Psychiatry and the Wayne State University School of Medicine Alumni Association, September 16, 1971, Detroit, Michigan.
———. His Journal, February, 1971.
Dorsey, George C., Sr. Personal communication.
Dorsey, John M., Jr. Letter to the Editor, *The Detroit Free Press,* December 29, 1970.
———. Personal observations.
Dorsey, John M. *American Government, Conscious Self Sovereignty.* Detroit: Center for Health Education, 1969.
———, ed. *The Growth of Self Insight.* Detroit: Wayne State University Press, 1960.
———. *Illness or Allness.* Detroit: Wayne State University Press, 1965.
———, ed. *The Jefferson-Dunglison Letters.* Charlottesville, Va.: University of Virginia Press, 1960.
———, and Seegers, Walter H. *Living Consciously: The Science of Self.* Detroit: Wayne State University Press, 1959.
———. *Psychology of Emotion: Self Discipline by Conscious Emotional Continence.* Detroit: Center for Health Education, 1971.
———. *Psychology of Language: A Local Habitation and a Name.* Detroit: Center for Health Education, 1971.
Dorsey, Mary Louise Carson. Letters and Notes to John M. Dorsey, unpublished.
———. Personal observations.
Douglas, Paul H. "Three Saints in Politics." *The American Scholar* 40 (Spring, 1971): 223-232.
Dow, Alex. *Some Public Service Papers, 1892–1927.* Detroit, 1927.
Dow, Douglas. "Simplified Economics." Paper delivered to Prismatic Club (Detroit), 1972.

Dowden, Edward. *A History of French Literature.* London: William Heinemann, 1897.
Dror, Yehezkel. "Policy Analysts: A New Professional Role in Government." *Public Administration Review* 27 (September 1967): 197-203.
_____. "Futures in Government." *Futures*, August 1968.
_____. "Alternative Domestic Politics Futures (ADPF): Research Needs and Research Design." Presented at the International Future Research Conference, Kyoto, Japan, April, 1970.
Drucker, Peter F. *The Age of Discontinuity.* New York: Harper and Row, 1969.
_____. *Landmarks of Tomorrow.* New York: Harper and Brothers, 1957.
_____. "Saving the Crusade." *Harper's Magazine* (January 1972): 66–71.
Dunne, Finley Peter. *Observations By Mr. Dooley.* New York: R. H. Russell, 1902.
Eckstein, Gustav. *The Body Has A Head.* New York: Harper and Row, 1970.
Edman, Irwin. "The Autobiography of a Symptom." *Under Whatever Sky.* New York: The Viking Press, 1951.
Edwards, George C. *The Police on the Urban Frontier.* New York: Institute of Human Relations Press, 1968.
Elston, Wilbur. "The Limits to Press Freedom." *The Torch* 45 (January 1972): 9-13.
Fand, David I. "A Monetary Interpretation of the Post-1965 Inflation in the United States." *Banca Nazionale del Lavoro Quarterly Review*, No. 89 (June 1969).
_____. "Some Issues in Monetary Economics." *Review*—Federal Reserve Bank of St. Louis, Reprint Series No. 51 (January 1970).
_____. "Money, Interest and Prices." Savings and Residential Financing 1970 Conference Proceedings. Ed. Donald P. Jacobs. Chicago, Illinois, May 7 & 8, 1970.
_____. "Monetarism and Fiscalism." *Banca Nazionale del Lavoro Quarterly Review* No. 94 (September 1970).
_____. "The Controversy Over Money." *Nebraska Journal of Economics and Business* 9 (Autumn 1970): 66-80.
_____. "Some Observations on Current Stabilization Policy." *Economic Policies in the 1970's.* Ed. Alfred K. Ho. Michigan Business Papers No. 57 (Winter 1971): 31-47.
Farber, Marvin, ed. *Philosophic Thought in France and the United States.* Buffalo, New York: University of Buffalo Publications in Philosophy, 1950.
Fisher, Frederick B. *Personology, The Art of Creative Living.* New York: Abingdon Press, 1930.
Flugel, J. C. *The Psycho-Analytic Study of the Family.* London: Hogarth Press and The Institute of Psycho-Analysis, 1948.

Ford, Henry II, and Portman, John. "Can the New Riverfront Development Revitalize Detroit?" Address before the Economic Club of Detroit, May 22, 1972, Max M. Fisher, Presiding Officer.

Foundation for Economic Education, Inc. *Clichés of Socialism.* Irvington-on-Hudson, New York: The Foundation for Economic Education, Inc., 1970.

Foxe, Arthur N. *Plague: LaEnnec (1782–1826) Inventor of the Stethescope and Father of Modern Medicine.* New York: The Hobson Book Press, 1947.

______. *The Common Sense from Heraclitus to Peirce.* New York: Tunbridge Press, 1962.

______. "Attica and the United Nations." Delivered before the Medical Correctional Association, New York City, October 23, 1971.

Freud, Anna. *The Writings of Anna Freud.* 7 vols. New York: International Universities Press, 1966.

Freud, Ernst L., ed. *Letters of Sigmund Freud.* Trans. Tania and James Stern. New York: Basic Books, Inc., 1960.

Freud, Sigmund. *The Standard Edition of the Complete Psychological Works of Sigmund Freud.* Trans. John Strachey in collaboration with Anna Freud. 24 vols. London: Hogarth Press, 1953.

Friedman, Milton. *Essays in Positive Economics.* Chicago: University of Chicago Press, 1953.

Galbraith, John Kenneth. *American Capitalism.* Boston: Houghton Mifflin Company, 1952.

______. *The Affluent Society.* New York and Toronto: New American Library, 1958.

Golightly, Cornelius L. "The James-Lange Theory: A Logical Post-Mortem." *Philosophy of Science* 20 (October 1953): 286–299.

______. "A Philosopher's View of Values and Ethics." *Personnel and Guidance Journal* 50 (December 1971): 289–294.

Gooch, G. P. *English Democratic Ideas in the 17th Century.* 2nd ed. New York: Harper & Row, 1898.

Goodhart, Arthur L. *English Contributions to the Philosophy of Law.* New York: Oxford University Press, 1949.

Graven, Philip S. *Social Sanity and the Birth of Words.* Parts I and II. Monographs.

Gregory, John M. *A New Political Economy.* New York: American Book Co., 1882.

Grindley, Robert F. Personal observations.

Grundstein, Nathan D. "Bentham's Introduction to the Principles of Morals and Legislation." *Journal of Public Law*, Vol. 2, No. 2 and Vol. 3, No. 1, 1954–55.

______. "Law and the Morality of Administration." Presented at a Panel of the Forty-eighth Annual Meeting of the American Political Science Association, August 26, 1952, Buffalo, New York.

Gullen, George E., Jr. Personal observations.

Hagman, Harlan L. Personal observations.

Hall, G. Stanley. *Life and Confessions of a Psychologist.* New York: D. Appleton & Co., 1923.

Hamachek, Don E., ed. *The SELF in Growth, Teaching and Learning.* Selected readings. Englewood Cliffs, New Jersey: Prentice-Hall, Inc., 1965.

Hancock, M. Donald, and Sjoberg, Gideon, eds. *Politics in the Post-Welfare State: Responses to the New Individualism.* New York and London: Columbia University Press, 1972.

Heilbroner, Robert L. *The Worldly Philosophers.* 3rd ed., rev. New York: Simon and Schuster, 1967.

Hellyer, Paul T. *Agenda, A Plan for Action.* Scarborough, Ontario: Prentice Hall of Canada, Ltd., 1971.

Herriot, Edouard. *The Wellsprings of Liberty.* New York: Funk and Wagnalls Company, 1939.

Hoernle, R. F. Alfred. *Idealism as a Philosophy.* New York: George H. Doran Company, 1927.

Hoffding, Harold. *A History of Modern Philosophy.* 2 vols. Trans. B. E. Meyer. New York: Dover Publications, Inc., 1955.

Holden, W. Sprague. "Two Centuries with the First Amendment." *The Torch* 45 (January 1972): 8, 13–16.

Howe, Reuel L. *Survival Plus.* New York: Seabury Press, 1971.

Hugh-Jones, E. M. *Woodrow Wilson and American Liberalism.* London: Hodder & Stoughton Limited, 1947.

Humboldt, Wilhelm von. *Humanist Without Portfolio.* Trans. Marianne Cowan. Detroit: Wayne State Univ. Press, 1963.

Johnston, Thomas. *Freud and Political Thought.* New York: The Citadel Press, 1965.

Kahn, Mark L. "The National Airlines Strike: A Case Study." *Journal of Air Law and Commerce* 19 (Winter 1952): 11–24.

______. "Contemporary Structural Changes in Organized Labor." *Proceedings of the Tenth Annual Meeting* (September 1957) of the Industrial Relations Research Association.

______. "Airline Flight Crews: Adjustment to Technological Change in a Regulated Growth Industry." *Proceedings of the Eighteenth Annual Meeting* of the Industrial Relations Research Association.

Kallen, Horace. *Individualism: An American Way of Life.* New York: Liveright, 1933.

Kant, Emmanuel. *Critique de La Raison Pratique.* Paris: Presses Universitaires de France, 1943.

Kellenberger, Richard K. Personal correspondence.

Kelly, Alfred H., and Harbison, Winfred A. *The American Constitution.* 4th ed. New York: W. W. Norton and Co., 1970.

King, Lawrence S. Personal observations.

Kipling, Rudyard. *Jungle Book.*

Krystal, Henry, and Raskin, Herbert A. *Drug Dependence.* Detroit: Wayne State University Press, 1970.

Kunkel, Fritz. *In Search of Maturity.* New York: Charles Scribner's Sons, 1949.

Laird, Margaret. *Government Is Self Government.* Portal Press, 1970.

Laski, Harold J. *The American Democracy.* New York: The Viking Press, 1948.

Lee, Otis. *Existence and Inquiry.* Chicago: University of Chicago Press, 1949.

Levy, Leonard W. *Jefferson and Civil Liberties.* Cambridge, Mass.: The Belknap Press of Harvard University Press, 1963.

Lipset, Seymour Martin. *Political Man.* New York: Doubleday and Company, Inc., 1960.

———, and Raab, Earl. *The Politics of Unreason.* New York, Evanston, and London: Harper & Row, Publishers, 1970.

Lovejoy, Arthur O. *Essays in the History of Ideas.* Baltimore: Johns Hopkins Press, 1948.

Mach, Ernst. *Contributions to the Analysis of Sensations.* Trans. C. M. Williams. Chicago: Open Court Pub. Co., 1897.

MacLeish, Archibald. *Freedom is the Right to Choose.* Boston: The Beacon Press, 1951.

———. Guest Editorial, *Saturday Review* (November 13, 1971): 40.

Malone, Dumas. *Jefferson the Virginian.* Boston: Little, Brown and Company, 1948.

———. *Jefferson and the Rights of Man.* Boston: Little, Brown and Company, 1951.

Marique, Pierre J. *The Philosophy of Christian Education.* Westport, Connecticut: Greenwood Press, 1970.

Mark, Max. "The End of Power Politics." *The Virginia Quarterly Review* 44 (Summer 1968): 353-368.

Martin, Kingsley. *The Rise of French Liberal Thought: A Study of Political Ideas From Bayle to Condorcet.* Ed. J. P. Mayer. New York: New York Univ. Pess, 1954.

Martin, Peter A. *Selected Papers of Peter A. Martin, M.D.* 1966.

Mason, Alpheus Thomas. *Brandeis: Lawyer and Judge in the Modern State.* Princeton, N.J.: Princeton University Press, 1933.

Maurois, André. *Adrienne, The Life of the Marquise de La Fayette.* Trans. Gerard Hopkins. New York, Toronto, London: McGraw-Hill Book Co., Inc., 1961.

Mayer, Milton. *On Liberty: Man v. The State.* Santa Barbara, Calif.: The Center for the Study of Democratic Institutions, 1969.

Mayo, Bernard, ed. *Jefferson Himself: The Personal Narrative of a Many-Sided American.* Boston: Houghton Mifflin Company, 1942.

McDonald, Donald. "Is Objectivity Possible?" *The Center Magazine,* Vol. 4, No. 5, ed. John Cagley. Center for the Study of Democratic Institutions, Santa Barbara, Calif., p. 29.

McEachren, John W. Personal observations.

Menninger, Karl. *Man Against Himself.* New York: Harcourt, Brace, 1938.

Menninger, William C. *Psychiatry: Its Evolution and Present Status.* Ithaca, N.Y.: Cornell University Press, 1948.

Meyer, Max F. *The Psychology of The Other One.* Columbia, Missouri: Missouri Book Co. Publishers, 1922.

Mises, Ludwig von. *Planning for Freedom.* South Holland, Illinois: Libertarian Press, 1952.

Montgomery, George S., Jr. *The Return of Adam Smith.* Caldwell, Idaho: The Caxton Printers, Ltd., 1949.

Muller, Herbert J. *Freedom in the Modern World.* New York: Harper & Row, Publishers, 1966.

Munro, William Bennett, and Ozanne, Charles Eugene. *Social Civics.* New York: Macmillan Company, 1922.

Muzumdar, Haridas T. *The United Nations of the World.* 2nd ed. New York: Universal Publishing Co., 1944.

Newman, James R. *Science and Sensibility.* New York: Simon and Schuster, 1961.

Newman, Philip Charles. *The Development of Economic Thought.* New York: Prentice-Hall, Inc., 1952.

Norton, William J. Personal observations.

Novak, Michael. "Politics As Drama." *The Center Magazine* (a publication of the Center for the Study of Democratic Institutions) 5 (May/June 1972): 4–14.

Paarlberg, Don. *Great Myths of Economics.* New York: New American Library, 1968.

Palmer, R. R. *The Age of the Democratic Revolution.* Princeton, N.J.: Princeton University Press, 1964.

Parrington, Vernon Louis. *The Romantic Revolution In America 1800–1860.* New York: Harcourt, Brace and Company, 1927.

Parrish, Charles J. "Bureaucracy, Democracy, and Development: Some Considerations Based on the Chilean Case." *Latin American Development Administration Committee Occasional Papers,* Series 2, No. 1. Austin: Institute of Latin American Studies, Univ. of Texas, 1971.

______; Booth, John A.; and White, Robert. "*La Violencia* In Colombia: A Theoretic Exploration." Unpublished paper.

Pei, Mario A. "The America We Lost." *The Freeman* (May 1964): 7–9.

Perry, Bliss. *The American Spirit In Literature.* New Haven, Conn.: Yale University Press, 1918.

Perry, Ralph Barton. *Puritanism and Democracy*. New York: The Vanguard Press, 1944.
Peter, Julius C. Personal observations.
Peterson, Merrill D. *Thomas Jefferson & the New Nation*. New York: Oxford University Press, 1970.
Philipson, Morris, ed. *Aesthetics Today*. Cleveland and New York: The World Publishing Company, 1961.
Picavet, Francois. *Essais Sur L'Histoire Générale et Comparée des Théologies et des Philosophies*. Paris: Librairie Felix Alcan, 1913.
Powys, John Cowper. *The Philosophy of Solitude*. New York: Simon and Schuster, 1936.
______. *Mortal Strife*. London: Jonathan Cape, 1942.
Pratt, Henry J. "Politics, Status and the Organization of Ethnic Minority Group Interests: The Case of the New York Protestants." *Polity: The Journal of the Northeastern Political Science Association* 3 (Winter 1970): 222-246.
Pratt, James Bissett. *The Religious Consciousness*. New York: Macmillan Company, 1924.
Rangell, L. "The Intrapsychic Process and its Analysis: A Recent Line of Thought and its Current Implications." *Int. J. Psycho-Anal.* 50 (1969a): 55-77.
Read, Sir Herbert. *To Hell With Culture*. New York: Schocken Books, 1967.
Read, Leonard E. *Students of Liberty*. Irvington-On-Hudson, New York: The Foundation for Economic Education, Inc., 1950.
______. *Government—An Ideal Concept*. Irvington-On-Hudson, New York: The Foundation for Economic Education, Inc., 1954.
______. *Anything That's Peaceful*. Irvington-On-Hudson, New York: The Foundation for Economic Education, Inc., 1964.
______. *Deeper Than You Think*. Irvington-On-Hudson, New York: The Foundation for Economic Education, Inc., 1967.
______. *Accent on the Right*. Irvington-On-Hudson, New York: The Foundation for Economic Education, Inc., 1968.
______. *The Coming Aristocracy*. Irvington-On-Hudson, New York: The Foundation for Economic Education, Inc., 1969.
______. *Let Freedom Reign*. Irvington-On-Hudson, New York: The Foundation for Economic Education, Inc., 1969.
______. *Then Truth Will Out*. Irvington-On-Hudson, New York: The Foundation for Economic Education, Inc., 1971.
Reeves, Jesse S. "Perspectives in Political Science 1903-1928." *The American Political Science Review* 23 (February 1929).
Rood, John R. *This Way Out*. Detroit: Detroit Law Book Company, 1935.
______. *Building the Constitution*. Detroit: Detroit Law Book Company, 1948.

Russell, Dean. *Frederic Bastiat: Ideas and Influence.* Irvington-On-Hudson, New York: The Foundation for Economic Education, Inc., 1969.
Sabine, George H. *A History of Political Theory.* New York: Henry Holt and Company, 1937.
Sage, Robert, ed. *The Private Diaries of Stendhal.* Garden City, New York: Doubleday & Company, Inc., 1954.
Santayana, George. *The Realm of Spirit.* New York: Charles Scribner's Sons, 1940.
Schumpeter, Joseph A. *History of Economic Analysis.* New York: Oxford University Press, 1954.
Schweitzer, Albert. *The Philosophy of Civilization.* Trans. C. T. Campion. New York: Macmillan Co., 1950.
Seligman, Ben B. *Main Currents in Modern Economics.* 3 vols. Chicago, Quadrangle Books, 1962.
Selye, H. "Language, Science and Creativity." *Totus Homo* 2 (1970), n. 1.
Shaw, Wilfred B., ed. *A University Between Two Centuries.* Ann Arbor, Michigan: University of Michigan Press, 1937.
Sieyes, Emmanuel Joseph. *What is the Third Estate?* Trans. M. Blondel, ed. S. E. Finer. London: Pall Mall Press, 1963.
Silk, Leonard, et. al. "Does Economics Ignore You." *Saturday Review* (Jan. 22, 1972): 33–57.
Simon, Yves R. *Philosophy of Democratic Government.* Chicago: University of Chicago Press, 1951.
Slattery, Sister Mary Francis. *Hazard, Form, and Value.* Detroit: Wayne State University Press, 1971.
Slichter, Sumner H. *The American Economy: Its Problems and Prospects.* New York: Alfred A. Knopf, 1948.
Slomovitz, Philip. Editorials and comments, *The Detroit Jewish News.*
Smith, Adam. *The Wealth of Nations.* London: Ward, Lock, & Co., 1812.
Smith, Charles. *Sensism: The Philosophy of the West.* New York: The Truth Seeker Co., 1956.
Sorokin, Pitirim A. *Social and Cultural Dynamics.* Vol. 1 and 2. New York: American Book Company, 1937.
Soule, George. *Ideas of the Great Economists.* New York: Viking Press, 1952.
St. John-Stevas, Norman, ed. *Bagehot's Historical Essays.* New York: New York University Press, 1966.
Stagner, Ross. *Psychological Aspects of International Conflict.* Belmont, Cal.: Brooks/Cole Publishing Co., 1967.
Stapleton, William J., Jr. *A History of the Michigan State Medical Society: A Century of Service in Medicine.* East Lansing, Michigan: Michigan State Medical Society, 1965.
Steell, Willis. *Benjamin Franklin of Paris.* New York: Minton, Balch

and Company, 1928.

Stepanowa, Vera. *Destutt de Tracy, eine historisch-psychologische Untersuchung.* Zürich: Druck von Zürcher & Furrer, 1908.

Strong, Augustus Hopkins. *The Great Poets and Their Theology.* Philadelphia: The Griffith and Rowland Press, 1897.

Stulman, Julius. "Climbing to Mankind Solutions." *Fields Within Fields . . . Within Fields.* The World Institute, Vol. 1, No. 3, 1968.

Sullivan, Lawrence. *Bureaucracy Runs Amuck.* New York: The Bobbs-Merrill Company, 1944.

Thornton, Robert M., ed. *Cogitations from Albert Jay Nock.* Irvington-On-Hudson, New York: The Nockian Society, 1970.

Tourney, Garfield, and Gottlieb, Jacques S., eds. *Lafayette Clinic Studies on Schizophrenia.* Detroit: Wayne State University Press, 1971.

Tourtellot, Arthur Bernon. *An Anatomy of American Politics.* Indianapolis and New York: The Bobbs-Merrill Company, Inc., 1950.

Tracy, Destutt de. *Eléméns D'Idéologie.* 2nd ed. Paris: Chez Courcier, Imprimeur. Libraire pour les Mathematiques, Quai des Augustins, No. 71. An XIII, 1804. Volumes 1-4.

______. *A Commentary and Review of Montesquieu's Spirit of Laws.* Philadelphia: William Duane, 1811.

______. *De L'Amour* (with an introduction on Stendhal and Destutt de Tracy by Gilbert Chinard). Paris: Societe D'Edition (Les Belles-Lettres), 1926.

______. *A Treatise on Political Economy.* Trans. Thomas Jefferson. Georgetown, D.C.: Joseph Milligan, 1817.

Travis, Lee Edward. *Handbook of Speech Pathology and Audiology.* New York: Appleton-Century-Crofts, 1971.

Trueblood, Benjamin F. *The Federation of the World.* Boston and New York: Houghton, Mifflin and Company, 1899.

Ulmer, Melville J. *The Welfare State: U.S.A.* Boston: Houghton Mifflin Company, 1969.

van der Hoop, J. H. *Conscious Orientation.* Trans. Laura Hutton. New York: Harcourt, Brace and Co., 1939.

Van Dyke, Vernon. *Political Science: A Philosophical Analysis.* Stanford, Calif.: Stanford University Press, 1960.

Waelder, Robert. *Progress and Revolution: A Study of the Issues of Our Age.* New York: International Univ. Press, 1967.

Ward, A. Dudley, ed. *Goals of Economic Life.* New York: Harper & Brothers, 1953.

Washington, H. A., ed. *The Writings of Thomas Jefferson: Being His Autobiography, Correspondence, Reports, Messages, Addresses, and Other Writings, Official and Private.* Vol. VI. New York: Riker, Thorne & Co., 1855.

______, ed. *The Writings of Thomas Jefferson: Being His Autobiography, Correspondence, Reports, Messages, Addresses, and Other Writings,*

Official and Private. Vol. VII. New York: J. C. Riker, 1856.

Weaver, Richard M. *Life Without Prejudice and Other Essays.* Chicago: Henry Regnery Company, 1965.

Weipert, William J., Jr. Written contribution.

Weissberg, Robert. "Adolescents' Perceptions of Political Authorities: Another Look at Political Virtue and Power." *Midwest Journal of Political Science* 16 (February 1972): 147-168.

Wheeler, Harvey. "The New Balance of Power Politics." *Center Report,* ed. Mary Kersey Harvey, Center for the Study of Democratic Institutions (June 1972): 11-14.

Whitehead, A. N. *An Introduction to Mathematics.* New York: Henry Holt & Co., 1911.

Whittaker, Alfred H. Personal observations.

Wiener, Philip P., ed. *Values in a Universe of Chance.* Selected Writings of Charles S. Peirce (1839-1914). Garden City, N.Y.: Doubleday and Co., Inc., 1958.

Wilhite, Virgle Glenn. *Founders of American Economic Thought and Policy.* New York: Bookman Associates, 1958.

Wilson, Woodrow. *Mere Literature and Other Essays.* Boston and New York: Houghton, Mifflin and Company, 1896.

Windelband, W. *A History of Philosophy.* Trans. James H. Tufts. New York: Macmillan and Co., 1896.

Winn, Ralph B., ed. *American Philosophy.* New York: Philosophical Library, Inc., 1955.

Wood, Henry. *The Political Economy of Natural Law.* Boston: Lee and Shepard, 1894.

SUPPLEMENTARY BIBLIOGRAPHY

Aring, Charles D. "A Sense of Humor." *JAMA* 215 (March 29, 1971): 2099.

Babcock, Winifred. "Light: The Phoenix that Arises from its Own Ashes." *Portal, Journal of Interdisciplinary Thought,* 8: 9-17. Published by the Phoenix Institute.

Bartemeier, Leo H. *A Physician in the General Practice of Psychiatry.* Selected Papers. Ed. Peter A. Martin, A. W. R. Sipe and Gene L. Usdin. New York: Brunner/Mazel, 1970.

Basler, Roy. "A Literary Enthusiasm; or, the User Used." Phi Beta Kappa Address, College of William and Mary, December 5, 1969.

Bean, William B. "President's Address—The Ecology of the Soldier in World War II." *Transactions of the Am. Clinical and Climatological Assoc.* 79 (1967).

Bender, Lauretta, and Schilder, Paul. "Suicidal Preoccupations and Attempts in Children." *Am. J. Orthopsychiat.* 7 (1937): 225-234.

Bibring, Edward. "The Mechanism of Depression." *Affective Disorders,* ed. P. Green.

Bibring, Grete L., and Kahana, Ralph J. *Lectures in Medical Psychology: An Introduction to the Care of Patients.* New York: International Univ. Press, Inc., 1968.

Binger, Carl. *The Doctor's Job.* New York: W. W. Norton & Co., 1946.

Bredvold, Louis I. *The Natural History of Sensibility.* Detroit: Wayne State University Press, 1962.

Brierley, Marjorie. *Trends in Psychoanalysis.* London: Hogarth Press, Ltd., and Institute of Psycho-Analysis, 1951.

Chomsky, Noam. *Aspects of the Theory of Syntax.* Cambridge, Mass.: M. I. T. Press, 1965.

Dubos, Rene. *So Human an Animal.* New York: Charles Scribner's Sons, 1968.

Edman, Irwin, and Schneider, Herbert W. *Fountainheads of Freedom.* New York: Reynal and Hitchcock, 1941.

Eissler, Kurt R. *Goethe: A Psychoanalytic Study.* Detroit: Wayne State University Press, 1963.

George, Henry. *The Law of Human Progress (1879).* New York: Jose Fels, Int. Commiss., 1917.

Ginsberg, Louis. *Morning In Spring.* New York: William Morrow and Co., Inc., 1970.

Glover, Edward. "The Psycho-Analysis of Affects." *Int. J. Psycho-Anal.* 20 (1939): 299-307.

Grinstein, Alexander. *On Sigmund Freud's Dreams*. Detroit: Wayne State University Press, 1968.

Harold, Preston, and Babcock, Winifred. *The Single Reality*. New York: A Harold Institute book. Distributed by Dodd, Mead and Co., 1971.

Hartmann, Heinz. "Psychoanalysis and the Concept of Health." *Int. J. Psycho-Anal.* 20 (1939): 308-321.

Hastings, Donald W. Personal communication.

Heldt, Thomas J. "Positive Psychiatric Diagnosis Versus Psychiatric Diagnosis by Exclusion." *Diseases of the Nervous System* 31 (December 1970) No. 12.

Hitschmann, Edward. *Freud's Theories of the Neuroses*. London: Kegan Paul, 1913.

Hoffer, Wilhelm. "Analyse einer postenzephalitischen Geistesstorung." *Int. Zeitschrift f. Psychoanalyse* 25 (1940): 264-286.

Hutchins, Robert M. *The Learning Society*. New York: Praeger, 1968.

Jacobsen, Edith. "Depression, the Oedipus Complex in the Development of Depressive Mechanism." *Psychoanal. Q.* 12 (1943): 541-560.

Kris, Ernst. *Psychoanalytic Explorations in Art*. New York: International Universities Press, 1952.

Kubie, L. S. "The Central Representation of the Symbolic Process in Relation to Psychosomatic Disorders." In *Recent Developments in Psychosomatic Medicine*. Ed. E. D. Wittkower and R. A. Cleghorn. London: Sir Isaac Pitman and Sons, 1954.

Laird, Margaret. *Christian Science Re-Explored, A Challenge to Original Thinking*. Rev. ed. Los Angeles: The Margaret Laird Foundation, 1971.

Laughlin, Henry P. *The Neuroses*. Washington: Butterworth, 1967.

Lipps, T. *Leitfaden der Psychologie*. 3d ed. Leipzig, 1909.

MacLeish, Archibald. "The Irresponsibles." *Nation*, May 18, 1940, reprinted in *The Intellectuals*. Ed. George de B. Huszar. Glencoe, Ill.: Free Press, 1961.

Mayo, Bernard. "Thomas Jefferson's Faith in Human Integrity." In *The Growth of Self-Insight*. Ed. John M. Dorsey. Detroit: Wayne State University Press, 1962.

Milbright, Don (Pen name, Sylvester). "The Logic in Truth and Love." Mimeographed material.

Moser, Robert H., ed. *Adventures in Medical Writing*. American Lecture Series. Springfield, Ill.: Charles C. Thomas, 1970.

Nunberg, Herrmann. *Allgemeine Neurosenlehre*. Bern, 1932.

Ogden, C. K., and Richards, I. A. *The Meaning of Meaning*. New York: Harcourt, Brace and Co., 1923.

Pareto, Vilfredo. *The Mind and Society*. Ed. Arthur Livingston. New York: Harcourt, Brace and Co., 1935.

Pfister, Oscar. *Love in Children and its Aberrations*. New York: Dodd, Mead, 1924.

Redl, Fritz. "Zum Begriff der Lernstoerung." *Zeits. f. psychoanal. Paedogogik* 8 (1934).

Ross, Helen. "Play Therapy." *Am. J. Orthopsychiat.* 8 (1938): 499-524.

Sachs, Hans. "Das Thema 'Tod'." *Imago* 3 (1914).

Saul, L. J. *Emotional Maturity.* Philadelphia: Lippincott, 1947.

Schilder, P. *Brain and Personality* (1931). New York: International Universities Press, 1951.

Schmideberg, Melitta. "A Contribution to the Psychology of Persecutory Ideas and Delusions." *Int. J. Psycho-Analysis* 12 (1931): 331-367.

Schwartz, Steven H., and Fattaleh, Daniel L. "Mode of Representation and Performance in Deductive Problem Solving." Paper presented at meetings of Midwest Psychological Association, May, 1971, Detroit, Michigan.

Seegers, Walter H. *My Individual Science.* Detroit: Center for Health Education, 1968.

Seltzer, Lawrence H. "The United States and the Common Market." Leo M. Franklin Memorial Lecture in Human Relations, April 30, 1962.

Sherrington, Sir Charles. *The Integrative Action of the Nervous System* (1947). Cambridge: University Press, 1952.

Smith, Robert A. III. "The Psychiatrist and the Psychic Elements of Rebellion." Unpublished paper.

Snow, Wilbert. *The Collected Poems of Wilbert Snow.* Middletown, Conn.: Wesleyan University Press, 1957.

Solley, Charles M., and Murphy, Gardner. *Development of the Perceptive World.* New York: Basic Books, 1960.

Spitz, Rene. "Wiederholung, Rhythmus, Langeweile." *Imago* 23 (1937): 171-196.

Sprague, George S. "Ideas of Contamination as a Defense Against Sexuality." *Am. J. Psy.* 97 (1940): 659-666.

Stagner, Ross. "Psychological Dynamics of Inter-City Problems." In *Seminar on Manpower Policy and Program.* Manpower Administration, U.S. Dept. of Labor, 1968.

——, and Solley, Charles M. *Basic Psychology.* New York: McGraw-Hill, 1970.

Sterba, Editha. "Nacktheit und Scham." *Zeit. F. Psychoanalyse* 3 (1929).

Sterba, Richard. *Introduction to the Psychoanalytic Theory of the Libido.* New York and Washington: Nervous and Mental Disease Publ. Co., 1942.

Sumner, William Graham. *Folkways.* Boston: Ginn and Co., 1906.

Szasz, T. S. "Comments on 'The Definition of Psychosomatic Disorder'." *Br. J. Phil. Sci.* 7 (1956): 231.

Untermeyer, Louis. *A Treasury of Great Poems, English and American.* New York: Simon and Schuster, 1955.

Van Doren, Mark. *Autobiography of Mark Van Doren.* New York:

Harcourt, Brace and Co., 1958.
Waelder, Jenny. "Analyse eines Falles von Pavor Nocturnus." *Zeitschrift f. Psychoanalytische Paedogogic* 9 (1935): 5–70.
Waelder, Robert. "The Problem of Freedom in Psychoanalysis." *Internat. J. Psycho-Analysis* 17 (1936): 89–108.
Walshe, Sir Francis. Observations in medical psychology.
White, W. A. "The Frustration Theory of Consciousness." *Psychoanal. Rev.* 16 (1929): 143–162.
Whitehead, A. N. *Modes of Thought.* Cambridge: University Press, 1938.
Whittaker, Alfred H., and Sloan, Ralph E. "The Roots of Medical Writing." *Journal of the Michigan State Medical Society* 60 (1961): 195.
Wilcox, Herbert G. "Hierarchy, Human Nature, and the Participative Panacea." *Public Administration Review* 29 (January/February 1969): No. 1.
______. "The Demand for Self-Determination: Can It Be Used to Get the Work Done?" Paper delivered at the conference, "Participation in Administration," Louisiana State University in New Orleans, May, 1970.
______. "Goods Consumption for a Better Way of Life: A Closed System for Man's Destruction?" Paper delivered at the Annual meeting of the West Virginia Political Science Association, Concord College, Athens, West Virginia, October, 1970.
______. "The Greening of Reich: How a Yale Law Professor 'Cons' America's Youth and Walks Away Counting Dad's Long Green Folding Money." A Book Review given at The Kanawha County Public Library, Charleston, West Virginia, Feburary 18, 1971.
Wundt, Wilhelm. *Volkerpsychologie.* Vol. 1, Part 1, 1900.
Wylie, Ruth C. *The Self Concept.* Lincoln, Nebraska: University of Nebraska Press, 1961.

INDEX

NAMES

SUBJECTS